Helck

6

Story and Art by
Nanaki Nanao

Contents

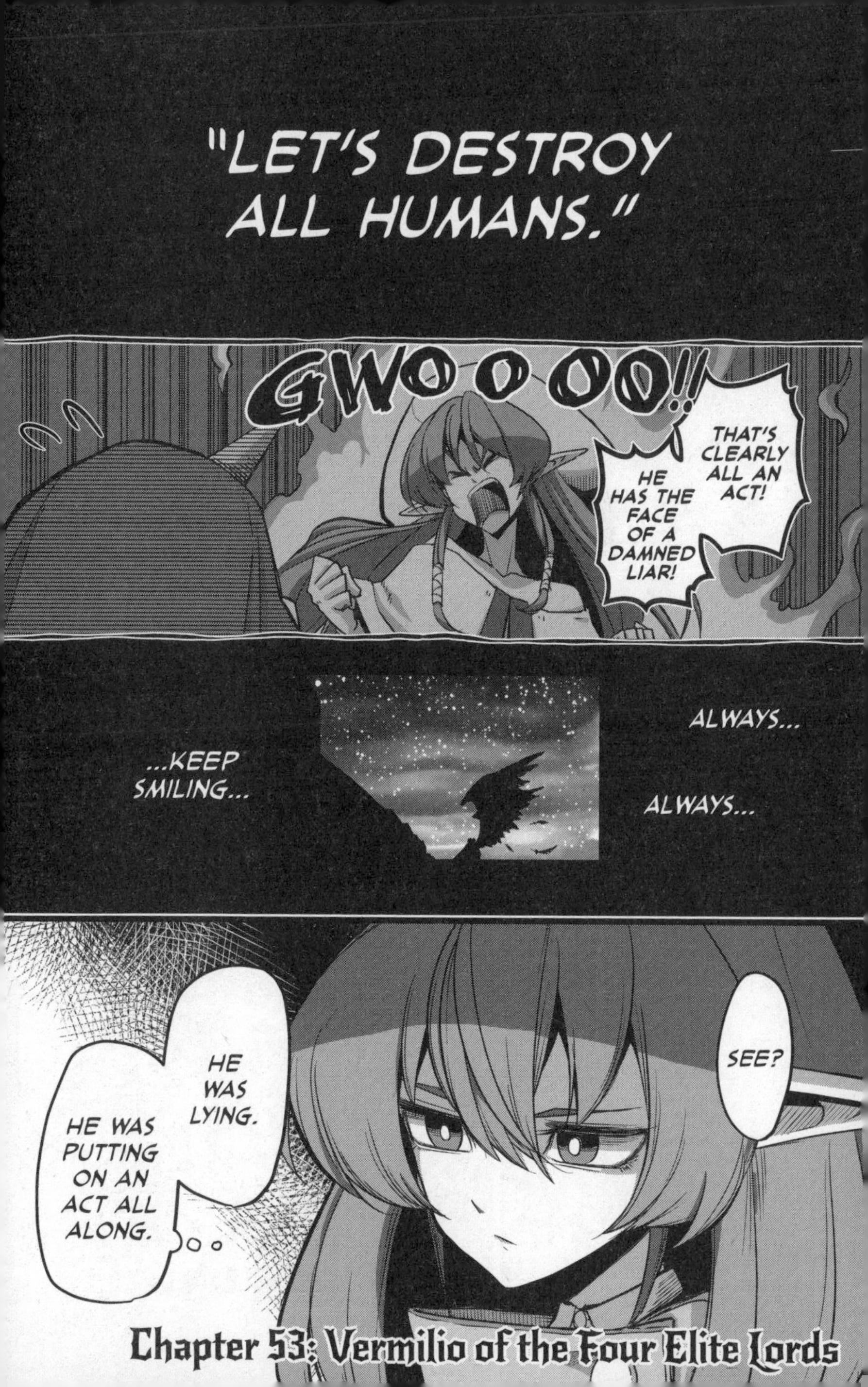
"LET'S DESTROY ALL HUMANS."
GWO O OO!!
THAT'S CLEARLY ALL AN ACT!
HE HAS THE FACE OF A DAMNED LIAR!
ALWAYS...
ALWAYS...
...KEEP SMILING...
SEE?
HE WAS LYING.
HE WAS PUTTING ON AN ACT ALL ALONG.
Chapter 53: Vermilio of the Four Elite Lords

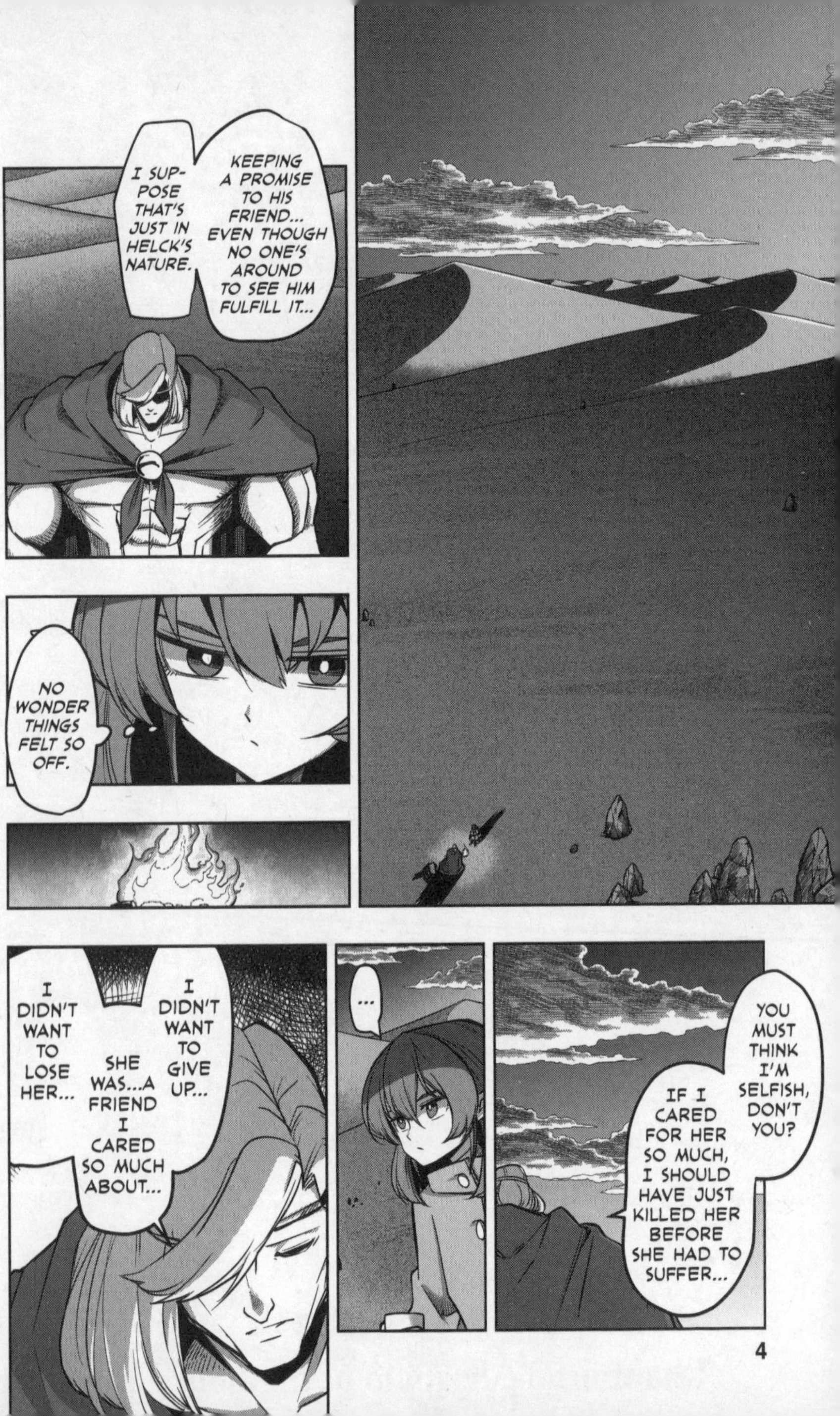
KEEPING A PROMISE TO HIS FRIEND... EVEN THOUGH NO ONE'S AROUND TO SEE HIM FULFILL IT...
I SUP-POSE THAT'S JUST IN HELCK'S NATURE.
NO WONDER THINGS FELT SO OFF.
YOU MUST THINK I'M SELFISH, DON'T YOU?
IF I CARED FOR HER SO MUCH, I SHOULD HAVE JUST KILLED HER BEFORE SHE HAD TO SUFFER...
...
I DIDN'T WANT TO GIVE UP...
SHE WAS...A FRIEND I CARED SO MUCH ABOUT...
I DIDN'T WANT TO LOSE HER...

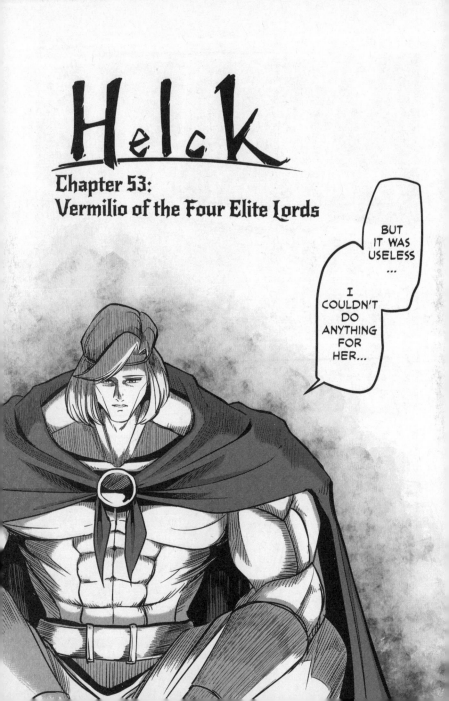

Helck

Chapter 53:
Vermilio of the Four Elite Lords

BUT IT WAS USELESS ...

I COULDN'T DO ANYTHING FOR HER...

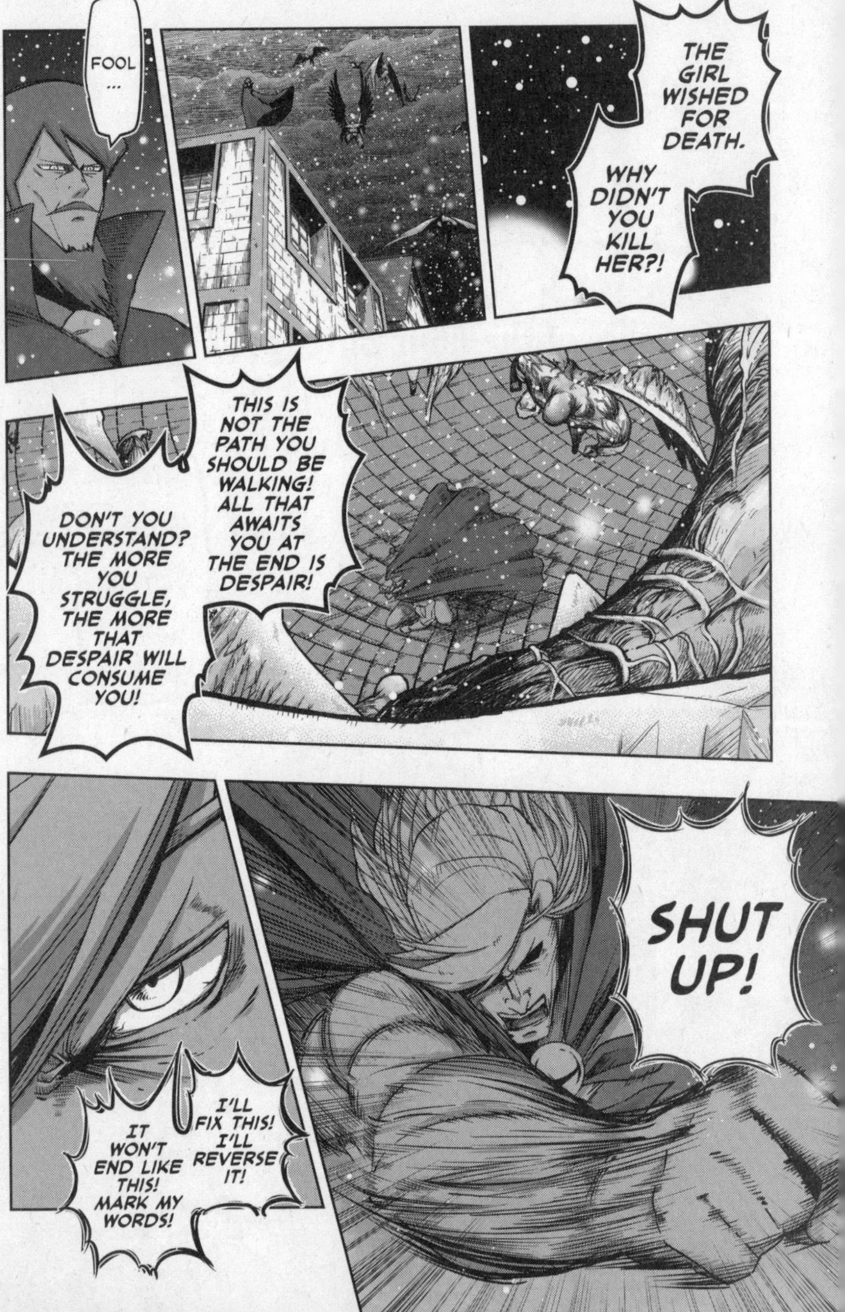
THE GIRL WISHED FOR DEATH.
WHY DIDN'T YOU KILL HER?!
FOOL ...
THIS IS NOT THE PATH YOU SHOULD BE WALKING! ALL THAT AWAITS YOU AT THE END IS DESPAIR!
DON'T YOU UNDERSTAND? THE MORE YOU STRUGGLE, THE MORE THAT DESPAIR WILL CONSUME YOU!
SHUT UP!
I'LL FIX THIS! I'LL REVERSE IT!
IT WON'T END LIKE THIS! MARK MY WORDS!

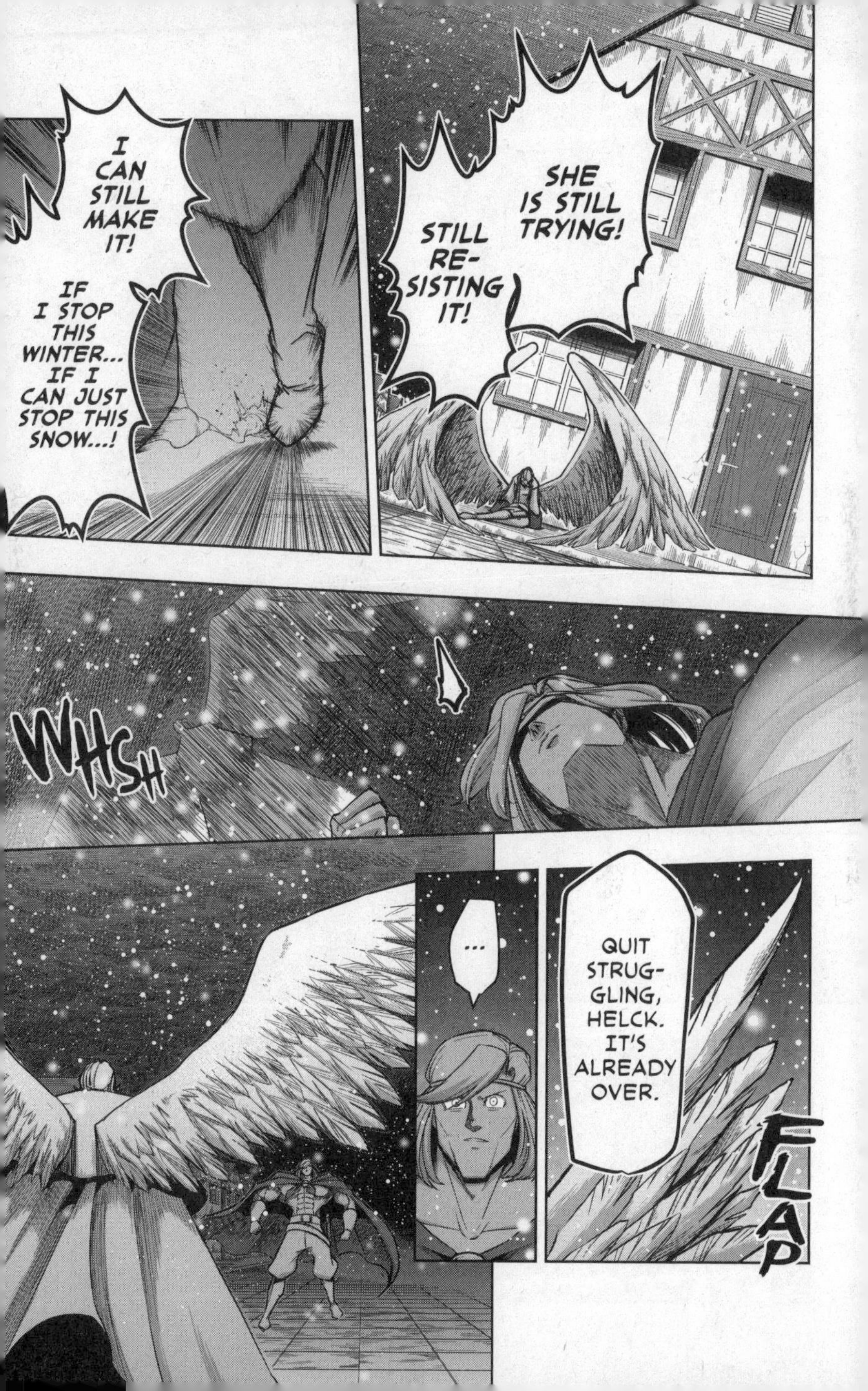
SHE IS STILL TRYING!
STILL RE-SISTING IT!
I CAN STILL MAKE IT!
IF I STOP THIS WINTER... IF I CAN JUST STOP THIS SNOW...!
WHSH
QUIT STRUG-GLING, HELCK. IT'S ALREADY OVER.
FLAP
...

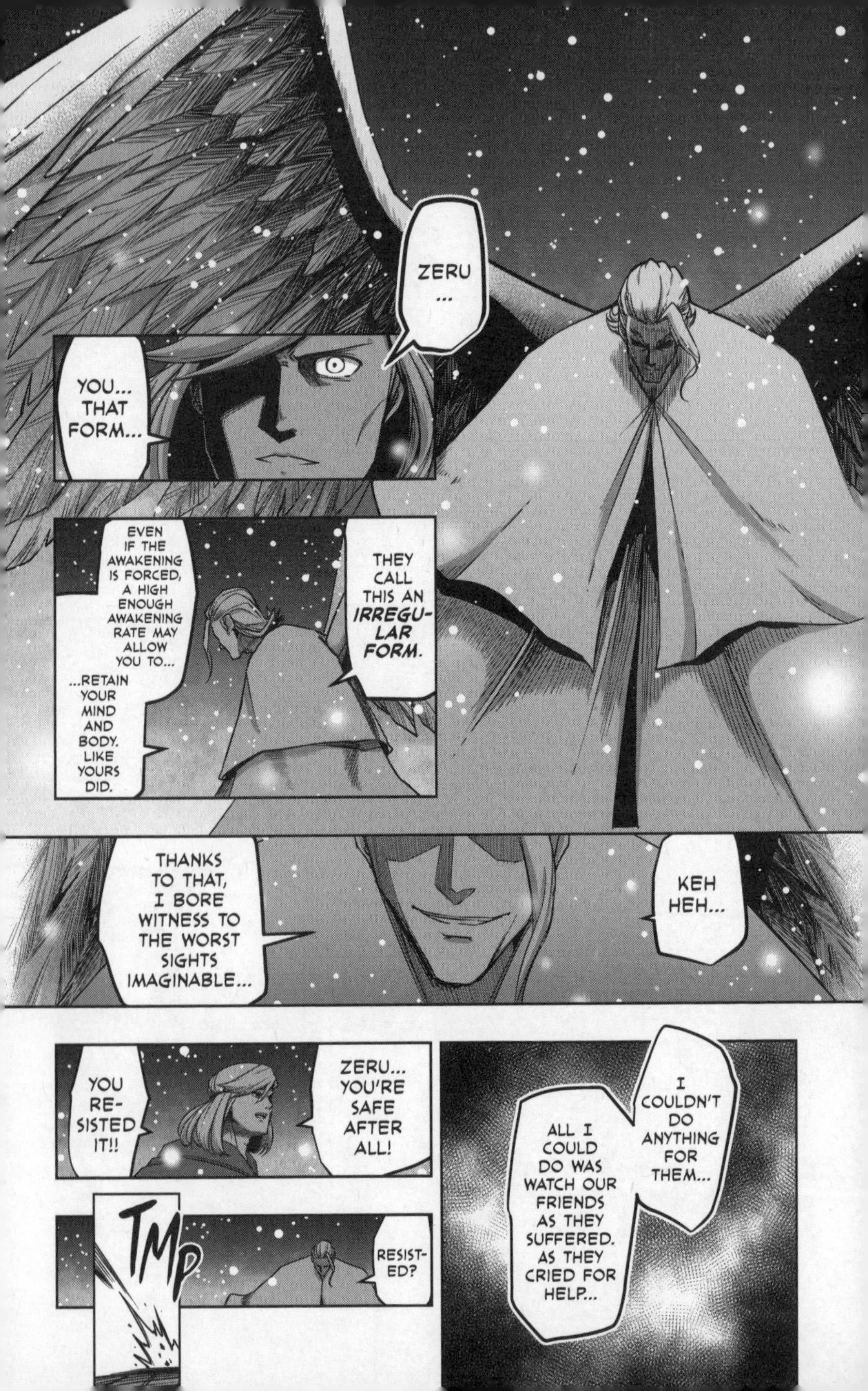
ZERU...
YOU... THAT FORM...
THEY CALL THIS AN *IRREGULAR FORM.*
EVEN IF THE AWAKENING IS FORCED, A HIGH ENOUGH AWAKENING RATE MAY ALLOW YOU TO...
...RETAIN YOUR MIND AND BODY. LIKE YOURS DID.
KEH HEH...
THANKS TO THAT, I BORE WITNESS TO THE WORST SIGHTS IMAGINABLE...
I COULDN'T DO ANYTHING FOR THEM...
ALL I COULD DO WAS WATCH OUR FRIENDS AS THEY SUFFERED. AS THEY CRIED FOR HELP...
ZERU... YOU'RE SAFE AFTER ALL!
YOU RESISTED IT!!
RESISTED?
TMP

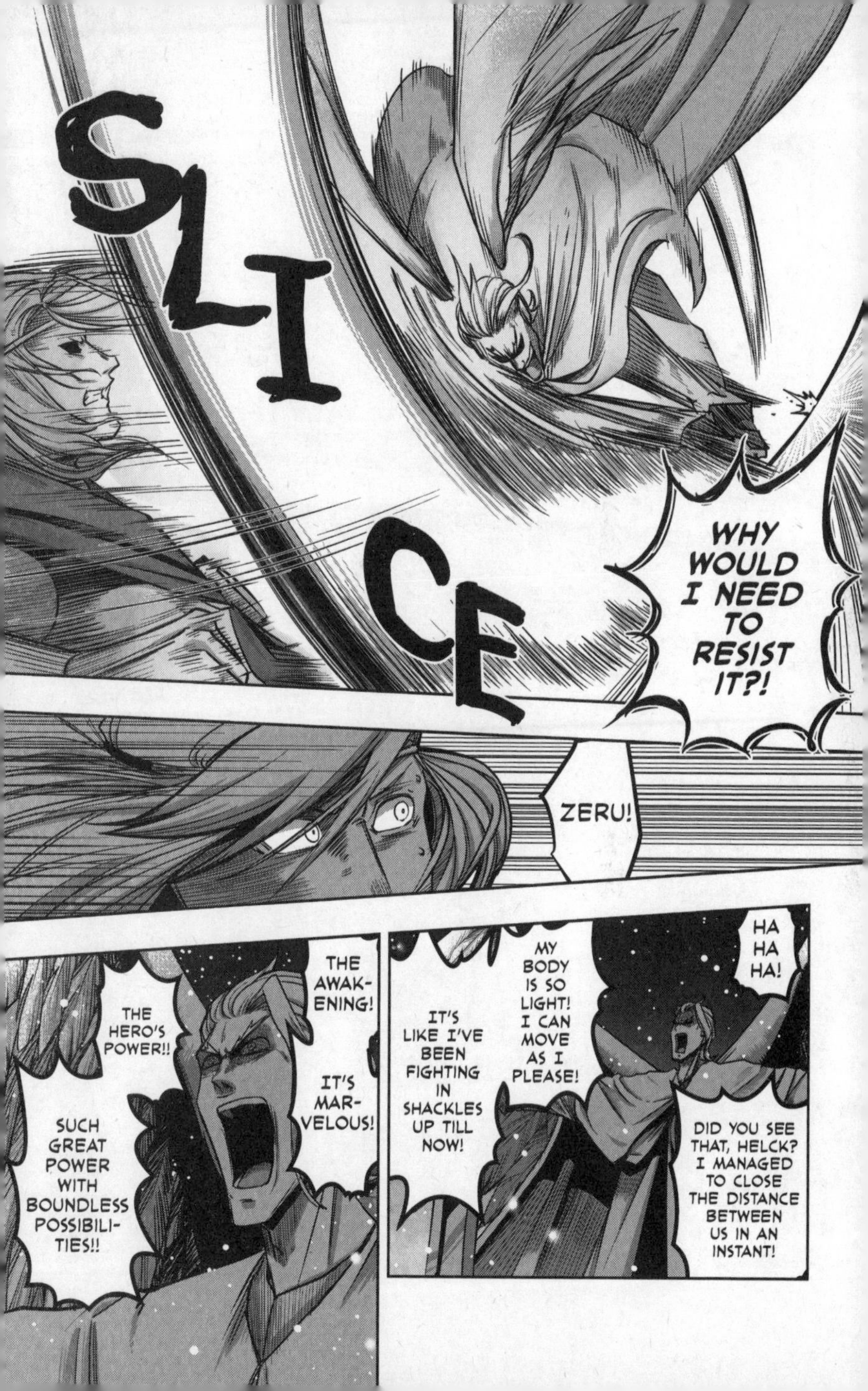
SLICE
WHY WOULD I NEED TO RESIST IT?!
ZERU!
HA HA HA!
MY BODY IS SO LIGHT! I CAN MOVE AS I PLEASE!
IT'S LIKE I'VE BEEN FIGHTING IN SHACKLES UP TILL NOW!
DID YOU SEE THAT, HELCK? I MANAGED TO CLOSE THE DISTANCE BETWEEN US IN AN INSTANT!
THE AWAKENING!
IT'S MARVELOUS!
THE HERO'S POWER!!
SUCH GREAT POWER WITH BOUNDLESS POSSIBILITIES!!

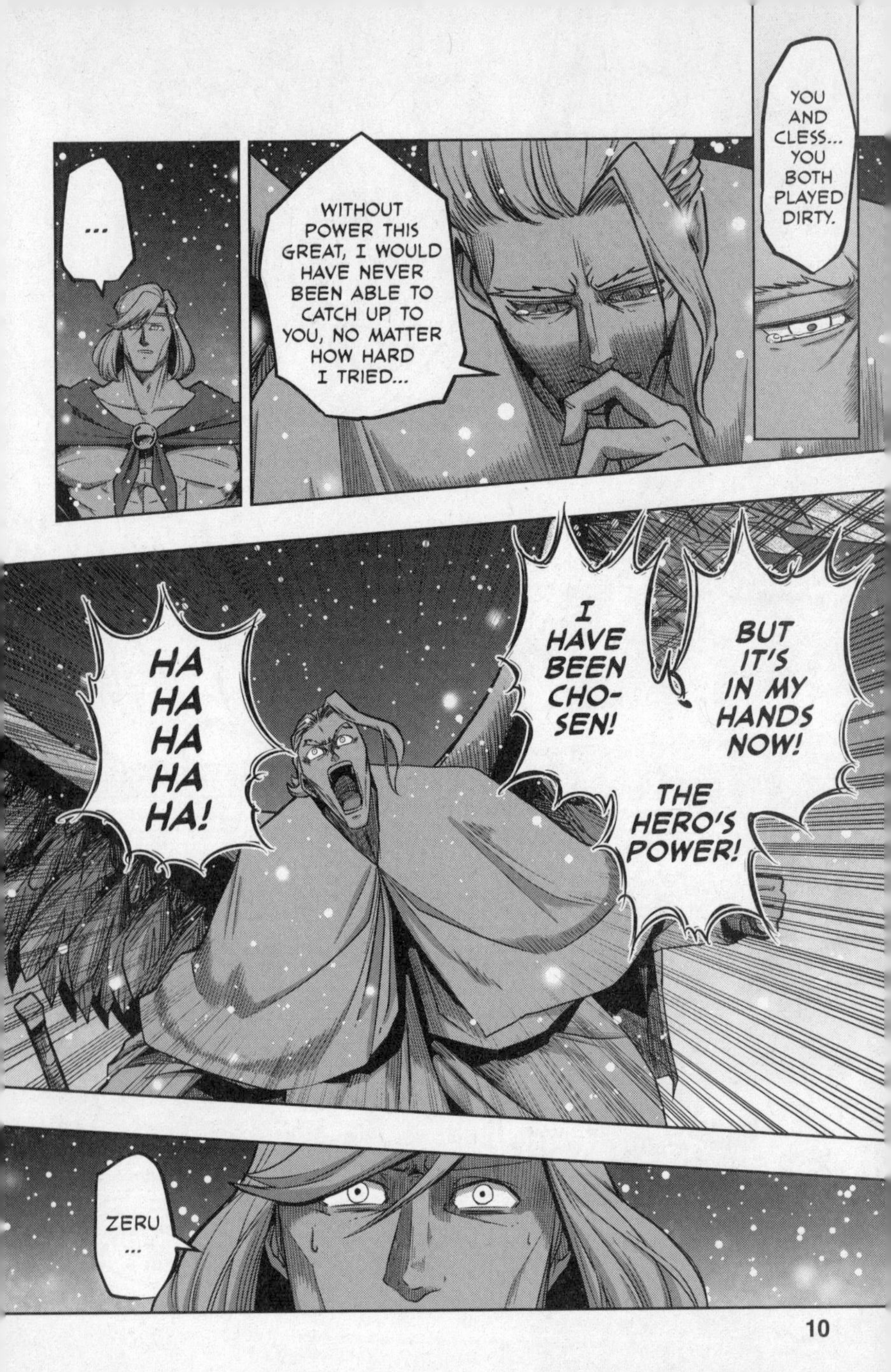
YOU AND CLESS... YOU BOTH PLAYED DIRTY.
WITHOUT POWER THIS GREAT, I WOULD HAVE NEVER BEEN ABLE TO CATCH UP TO YOU, NO MATTER HOW HARD I TRIED...
...
BUT IT'S IN MY HANDS NOW!
I HAVE BEEN CHO-SEN!
THE HERO'S POWER!
HA HA HA HA HA HA!
ZERU ...

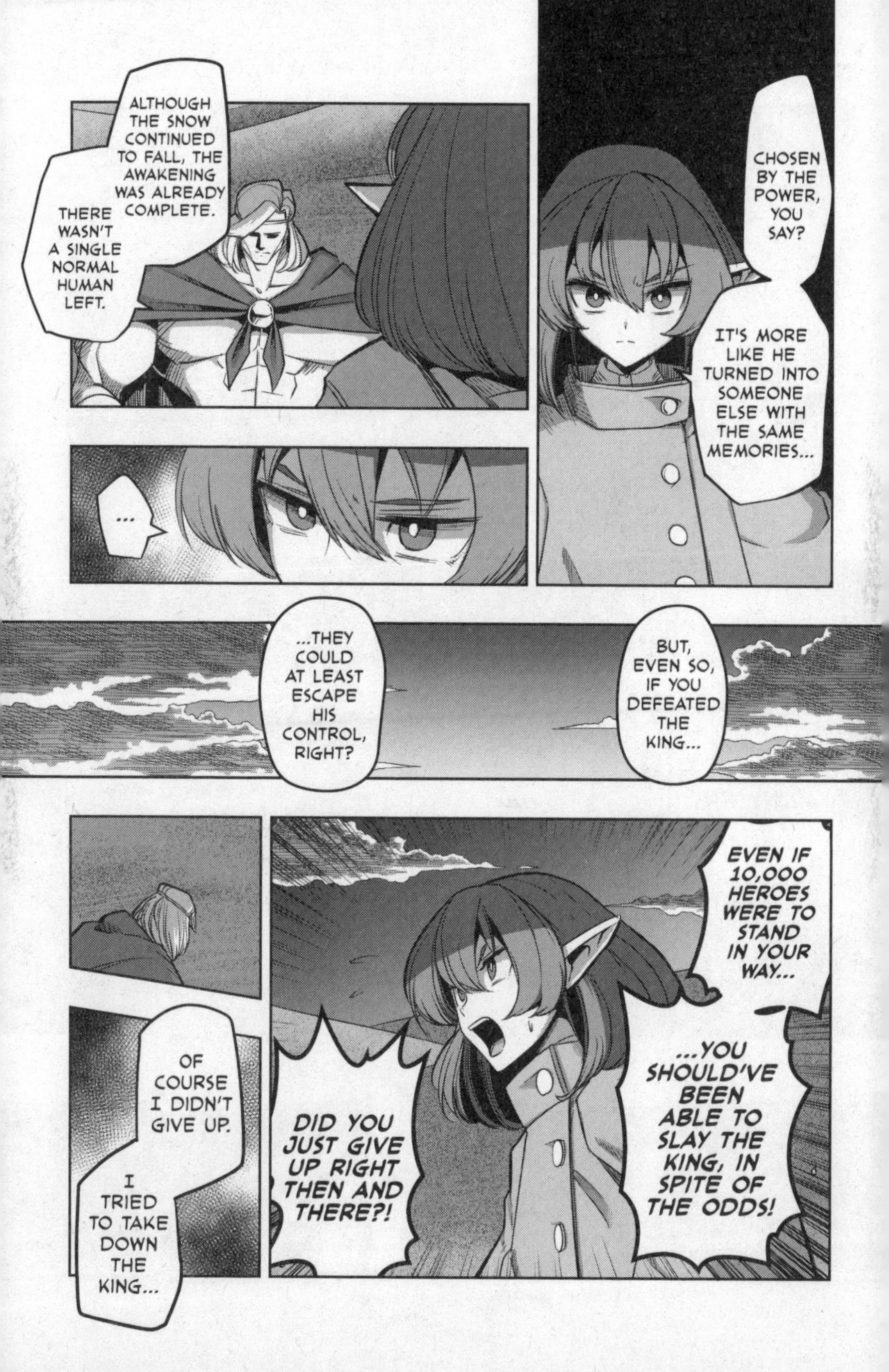
CHOSEN BY THE POWER, YOU SAY?
IT'S MORE LIKE HE TURNED INTO SOMEONE ELSE WITH THE SAME MEMORIES...
ALTHOUGH THE SNOW CONTINUED TO FALL, THE AWAKENING WAS ALREADY COMPLETE.
THERE WASN'T A SINGLE NORMAL HUMAN LEFT.
...
BUT, EVEN SO, IF YOU DEFEATED THE KING...
...THEY COULD AT LEAST ESCAPE HIS CONTROL, RIGHT?
EVEN IF 10,000 HEROES WERE TO STAND IN YOUR WAY...
...YOU SHOULD'VE BEEN ABLE TO SLAY THE KING, IN SPITE OF THE ODDS!
DID YOU JUST GIVE UP RIGHT THEN AND THERE?!
OF COURSE I DIDN'T GIVE UP.
I TRIED TO TAKE DOWN THE KING...

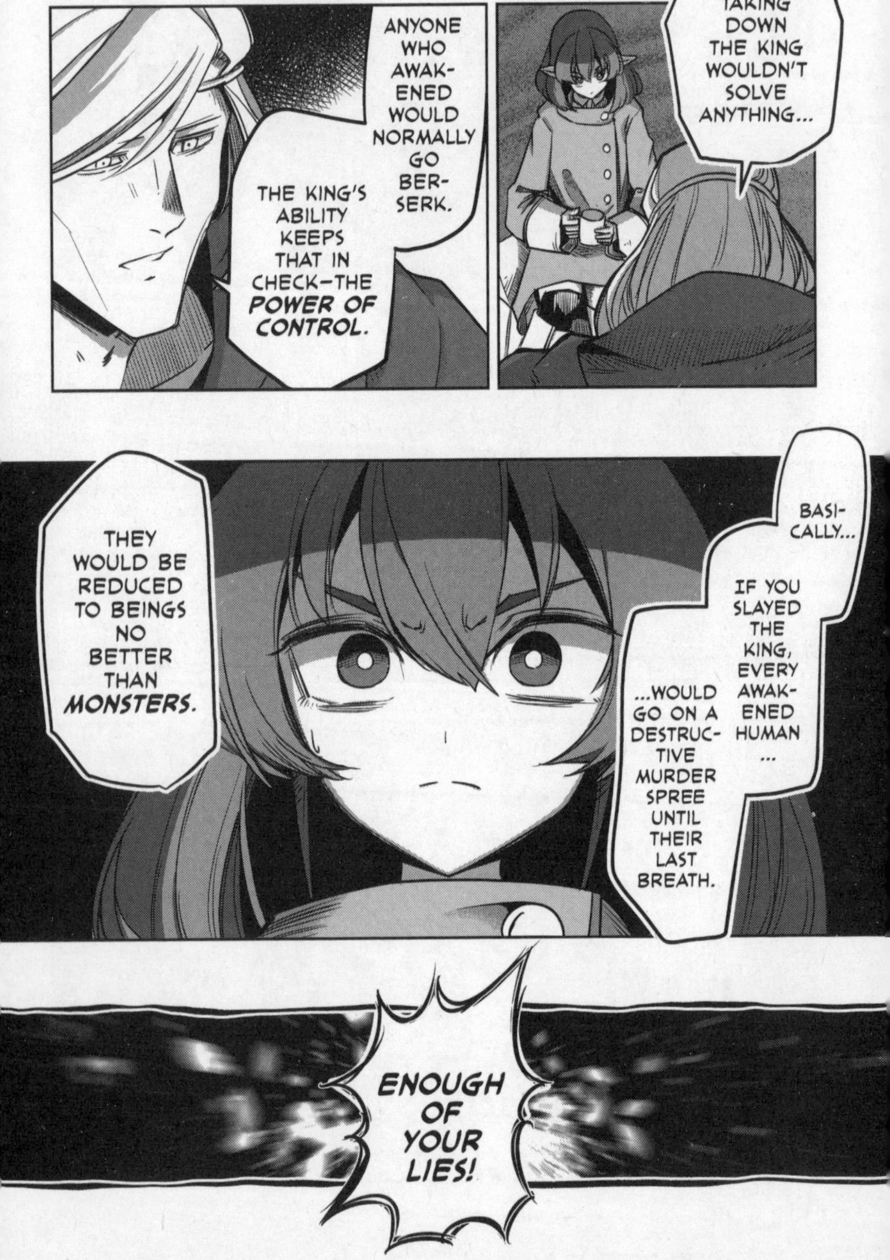

BUT TAKING DOWN THE KING WOULDN'T SOLVE ANYTHING...
ANYONE WHO AWAKENED WOULD NORMALLY GO BERSERK.
THE KING'S ABILITY KEEPS THAT IN CHECK—THE *POWER OF CONTROL.*
BASICALLY...
IF YOU SLAYED THE KING, EVERY AWAKENED HUMAN...
...WOULD GO ON A DESTRUCTIVE MURDER SPREE UNTIL THEIR LAST BREATH.
THEY WOULD BE REDUCED TO BEINGS NO BETTER THAN *MONSTERS.*
ENOUGH OF YOUR LIES!

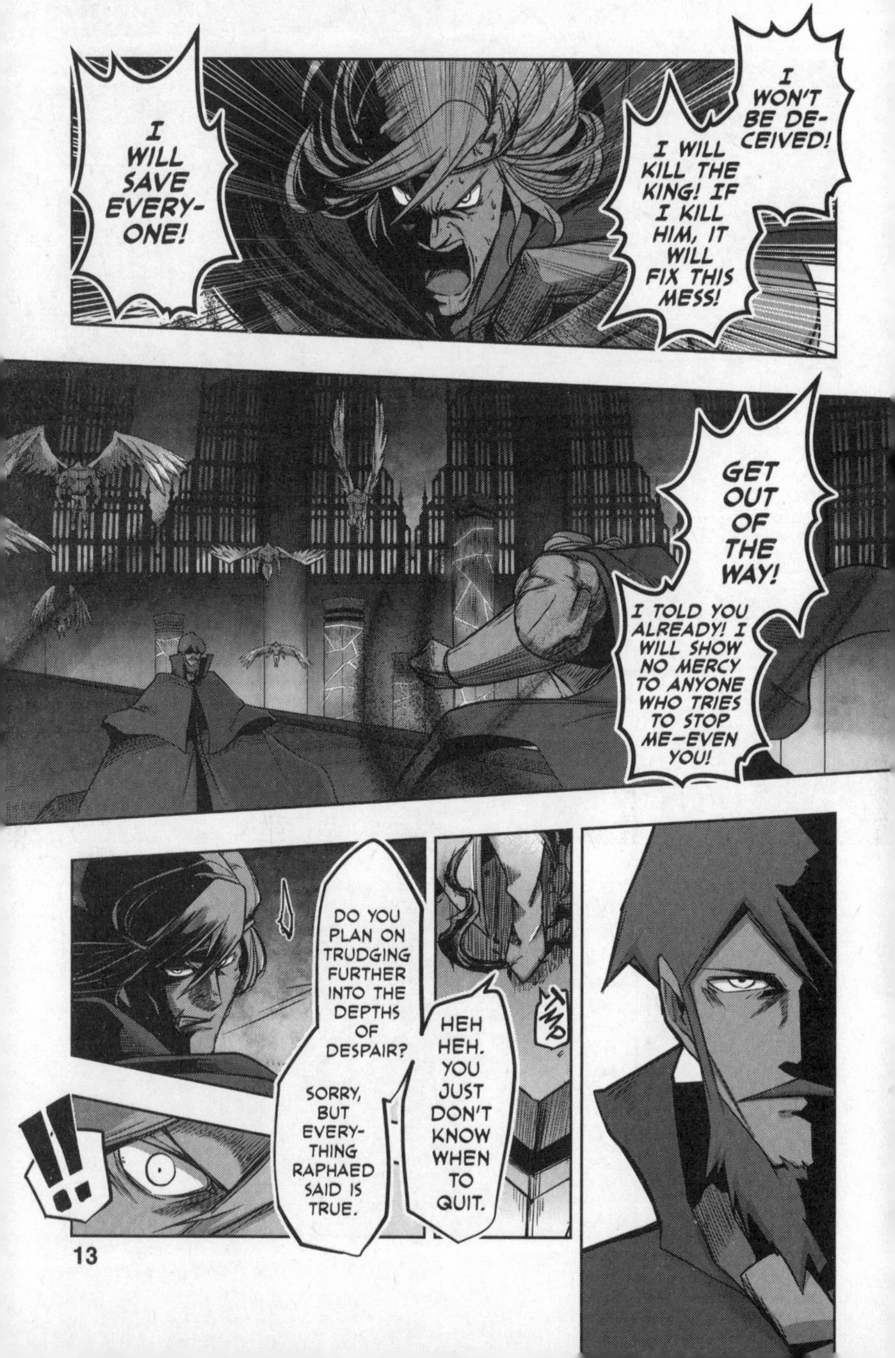
I WON'T BE DE-CEIVED!
I WILL KILL THE KING! IF I KILL HIM, IT WILL FIX THIS MESS!
I WILL SAVE EVERY-ONE!
GET OUT OF THE WAY!
I TOLD YOU ALREADY! I WILL SHOW NO MERCY TO ANYONE WHO TRIES TO STOP ME—EVEN YOU!
TMP
HEH HEH. YOU JUST DON'T KNOW WHEN TO QUIT.
DO YOU PLAN ON TRUDGING FURTHER INTO THE DEPTHS OF DESPAIR?
SORRY, BUT EVERY-THING RAPHAED SAID IS TRUE.
!!

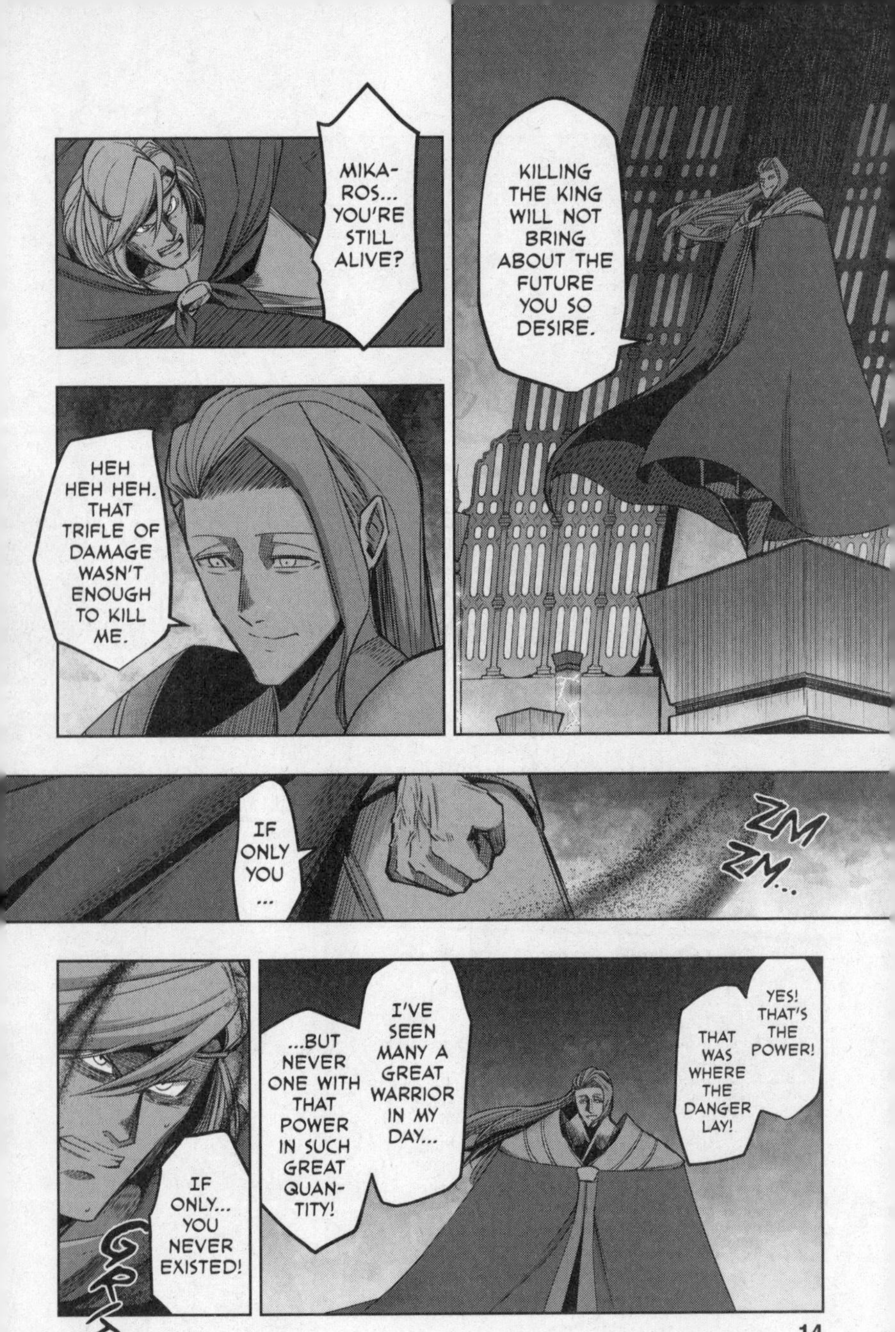
KILLING THE KING WILL NOT BRING ABOUT THE FUTURE YOU SO DESIRE.
MIKA-ROS... YOU'RE STILL ALIVE?
HEH HEH HEH. THAT TRIFLE OF DAMAGE WASN'T ENOUGH TO KILL ME.
ZM ZM...
IF ONLY YOU ...
YES! THAT'S THE POWER!
THAT WAS WHERE THE DANGER LAY!
I'VE SEEN MANY A GREAT WARRIOR IN MY DAY...
...BUT NEVER ONE WITH THAT POWER IN SUCH GREAT QUAN-TITY!
IF ONLY... YOU NEVER EXISTED!

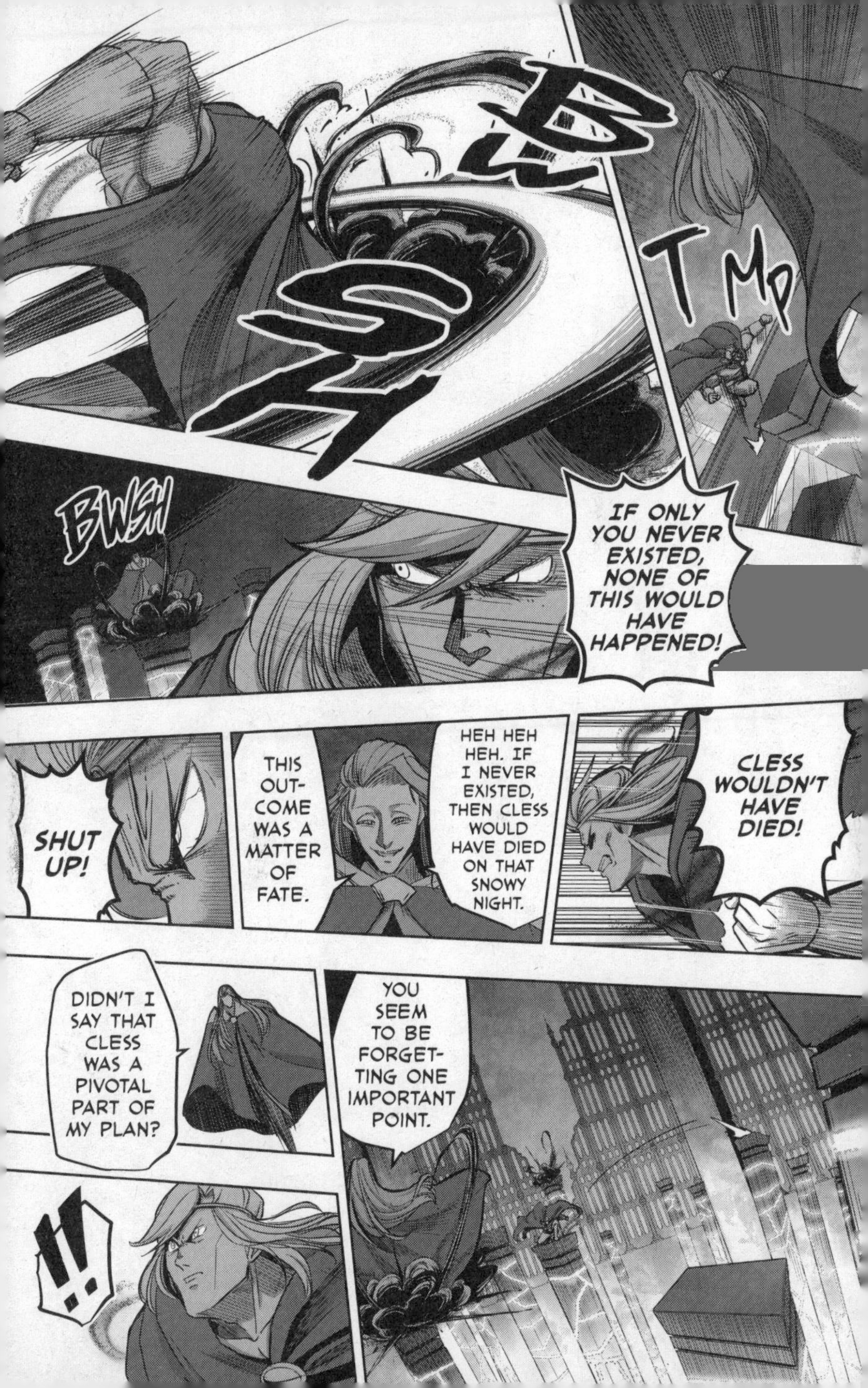
TMP
BWSH
BWSH
IF ONLY YOU NEVER EXISTED, NONE OF THIS WOULD HAVE HAPPENED!
CLESS WOULDN'T HAVE DIED!
HEH HEH HEH. IF I NEVER EXISTED, THEN CLESS WOULD HAVE DIED ON THAT SNOWY NIGHT.
THIS OUT-COME WAS A MATTER OF FATE.
SHUT UP!
YOU SEEM TO BE FORGET-TING ONE IMPORTANT POINT.
DIDN'T I SAY THAT CLESS WAS A PIVOTAL PART OF MY PLAN?
!!

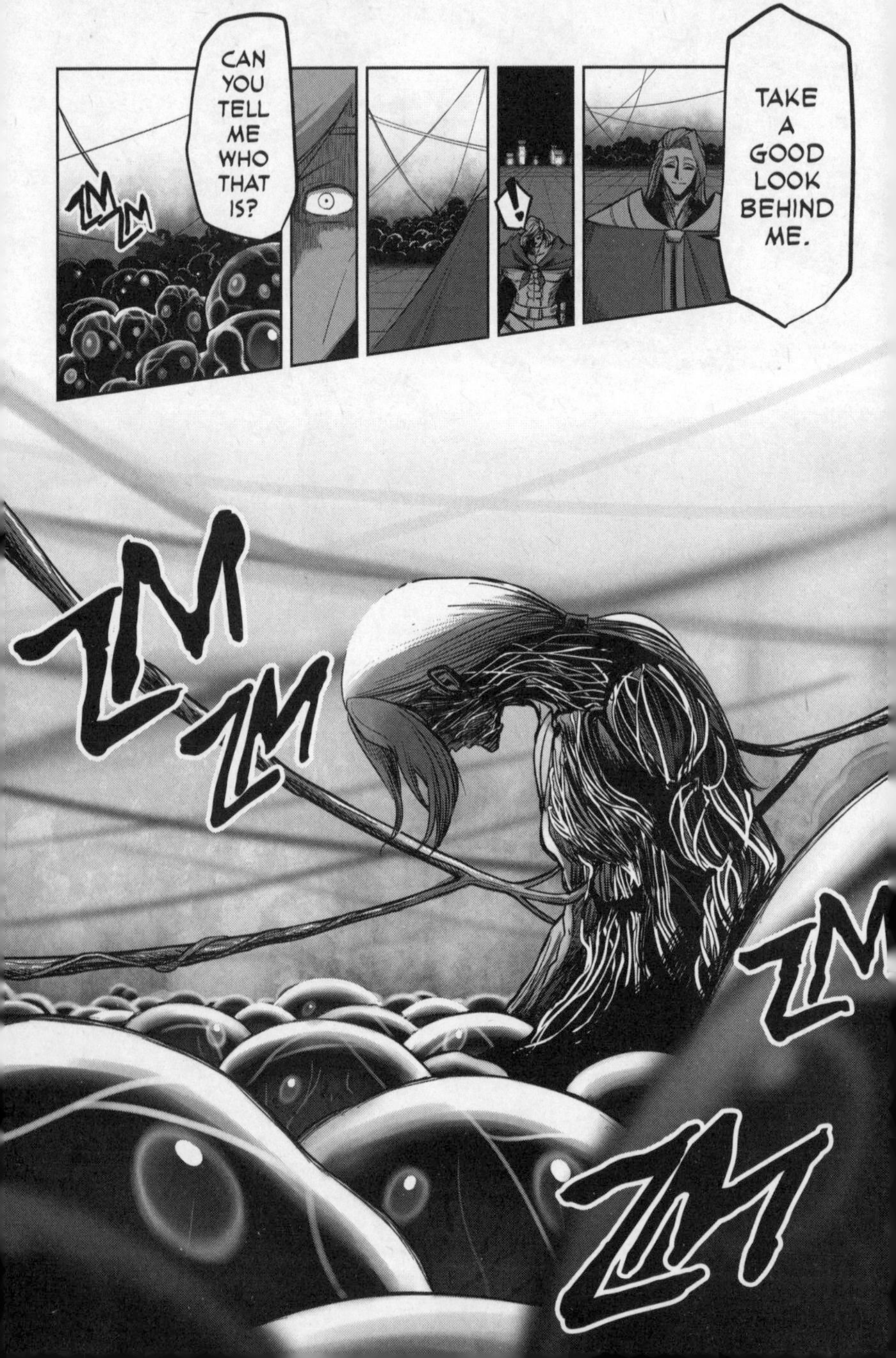
TAKE A GOOD LOOK BEHIND ME.
!
CAN YOU TELL ME WHO THAT IS?
ZM ZM
ZM ZM
ZM
ZM

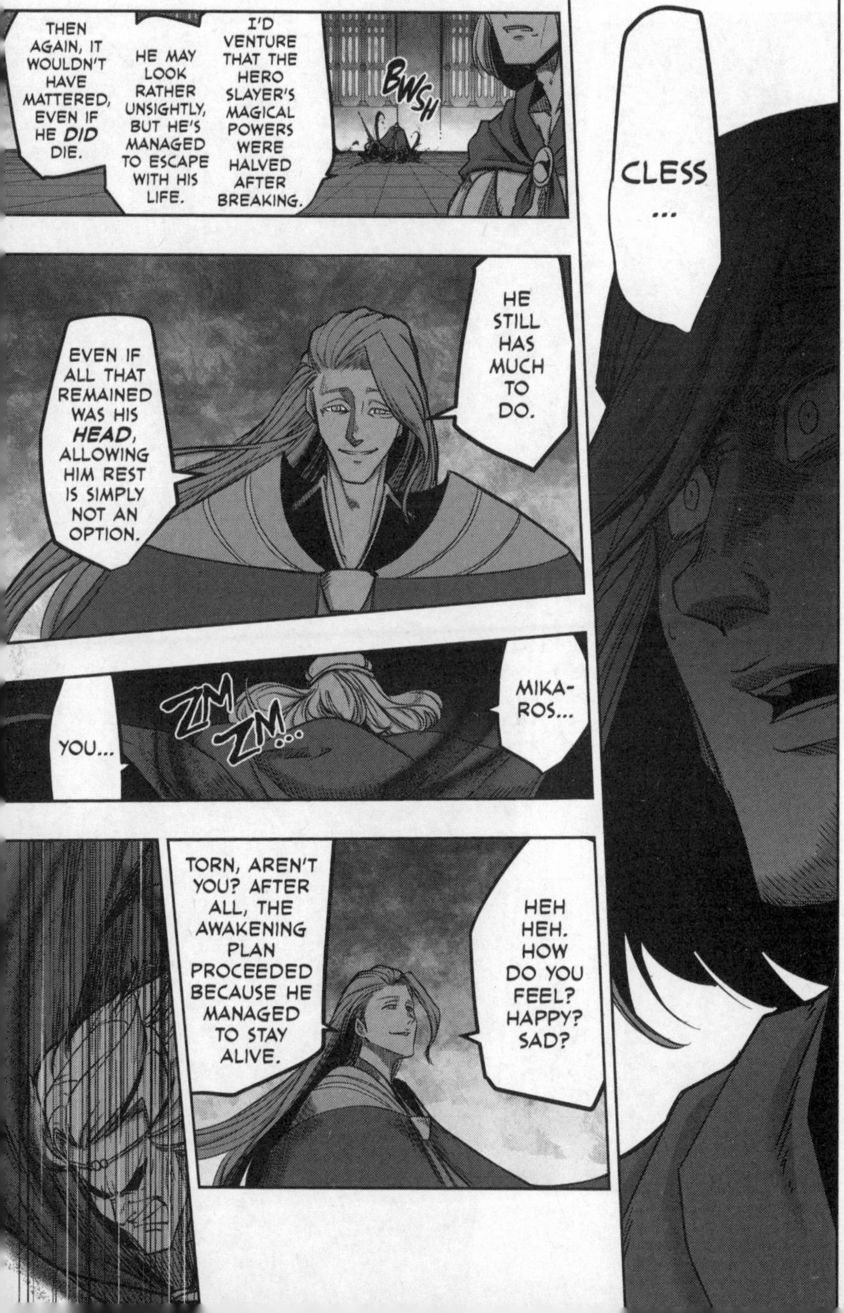
CLESS ...
BWSH
I'D VENTURE THAT THE HERO SLAYER'S MAGICAL POWERS WERE HALVED AFTER BREAKING.
HE MAY LOOK RATHER UNSIGHTLY, BUT HE'S MANAGED TO ESCAPE WITH HIS LIFE.
THEN AGAIN, IT WOULDN'T HAVE MATTERED, EVEN IF HE *DID* DIE.
HE STILL HAS MUCH TO DO.
EVEN IF ALL THAT REMAINED WAS HIS ***HEAD***, ALLOWING HIM REST IS SIMPLY NOT AN OPTION.
MIKA-ROS...
ZM ZM...
YOU...
HEH HEH. HOW DO YOU FEEL? HAPPY? SAD?
TORN, AREN'T YOU? AFTER ALL, THE AWAKENING PLAN PROCEEDED BECAUSE HE MANAGED TO STAY ALIVE.

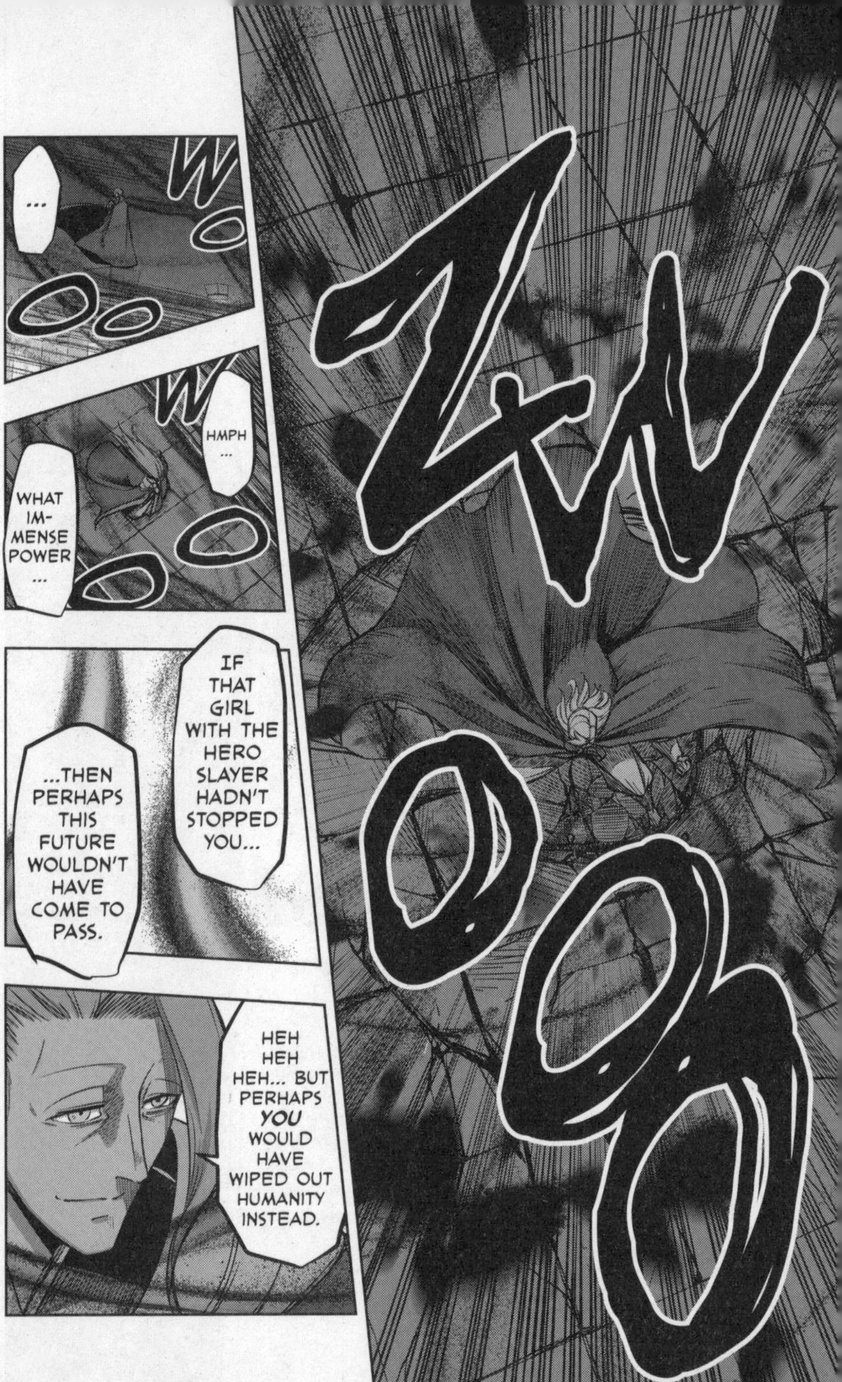
ZWOOO
WOOO
...
WOO
HMPH...
WHAT IMMENSE POWER...
IF THAT GIRL WITH THE HERO SLAYER HADN'T STOPPED YOU...
...THEN PERHAPS THIS FUTURE WOULDN'T HAVE COME TO PASS.
HEH HEH HEH... BUT PERHAPS *YOU* WOULD HAVE WIPED OUT HUMANITY INSTEAD.

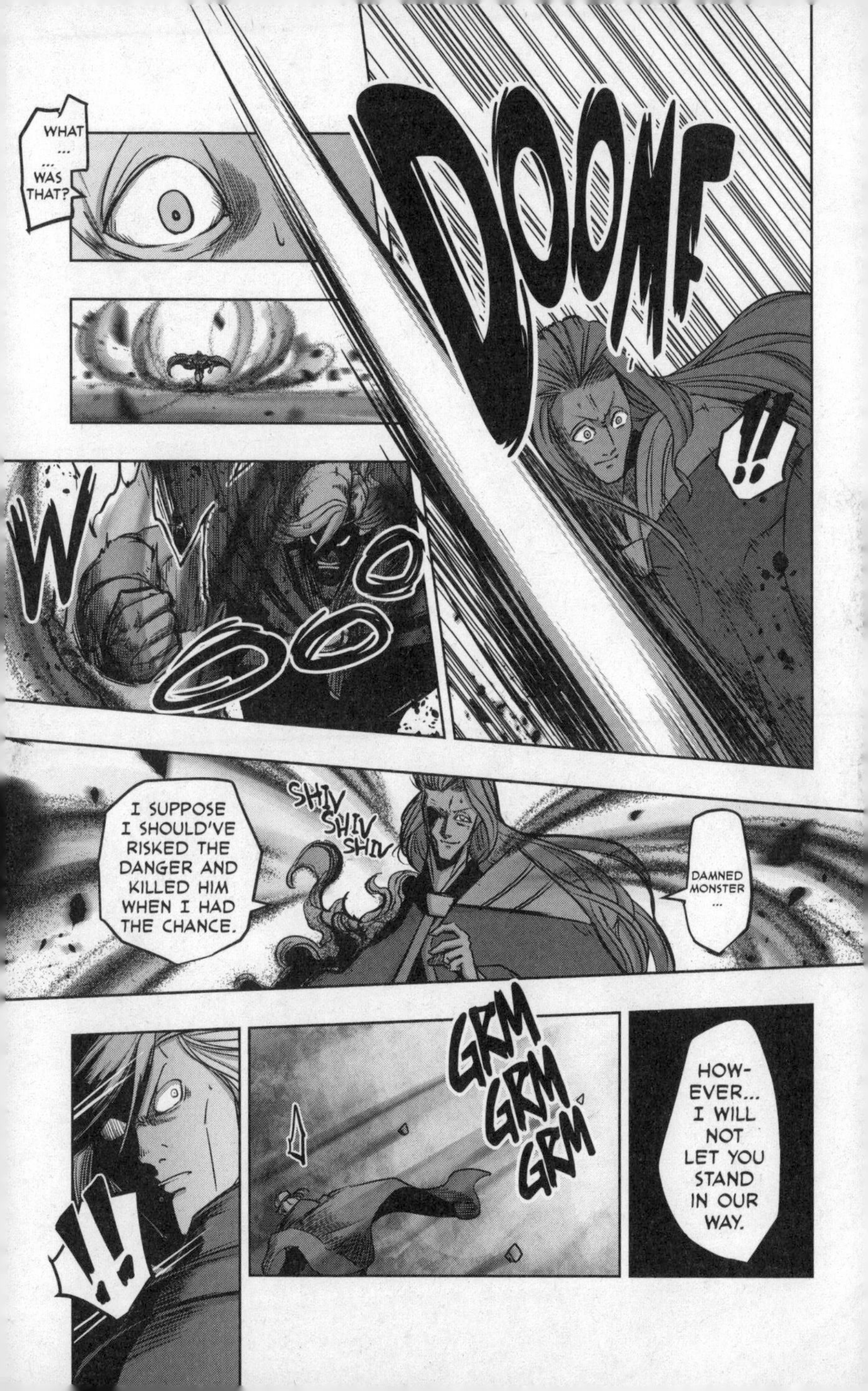
DOOMF
!!
WHAT ... ... WAS THAT?
W M
DAMNED MONSTER ...
SHIV SHIV SHIV
I SUPPOSE I SHOULD'VE RISKED THE DANGER AND KILLED HIM WHEN I HAD THE CHANCE.
HOW-EVER... I WILL NOT LET YOU STAND IN OUR WAY.
GRM GRM GRM
!!

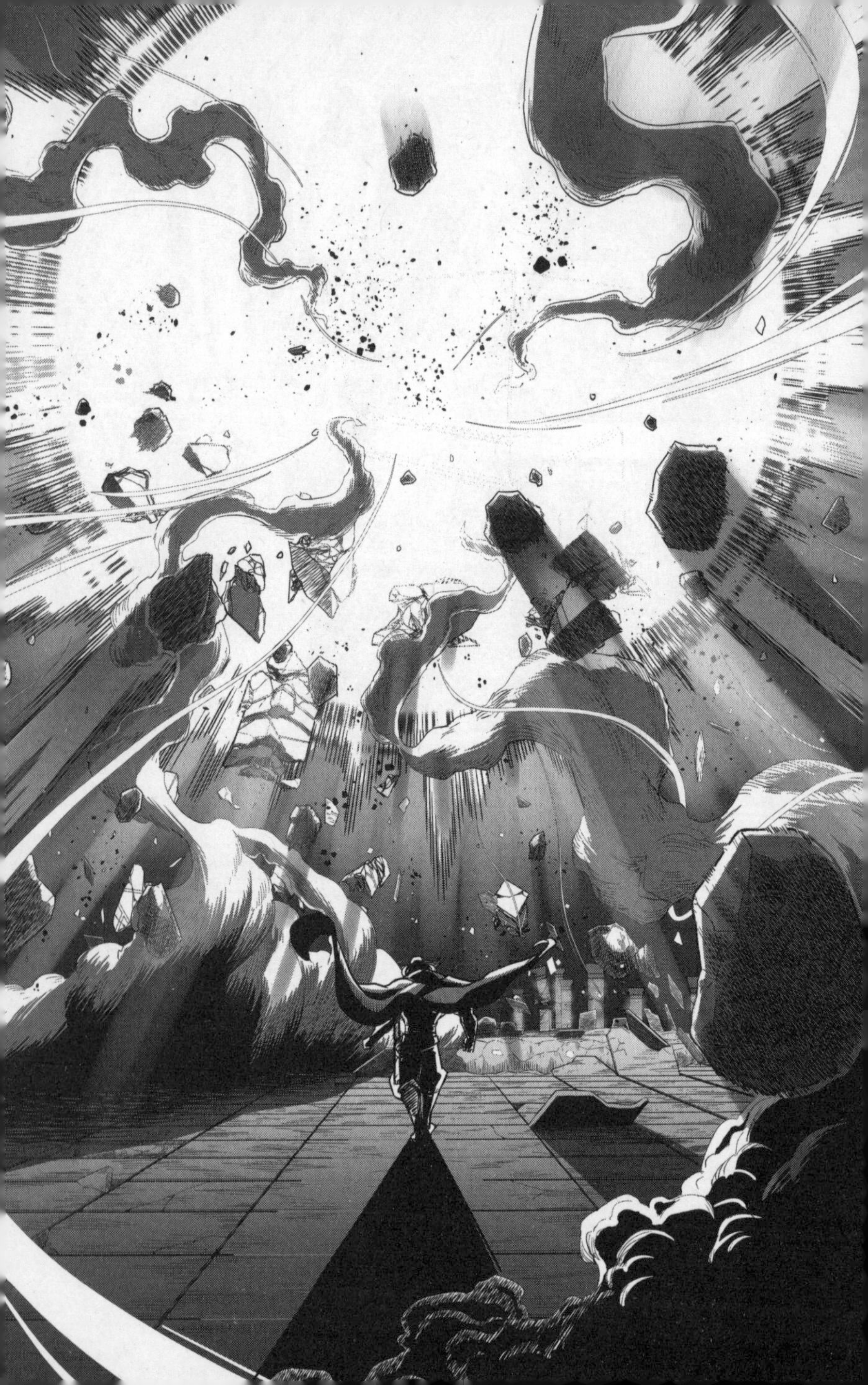

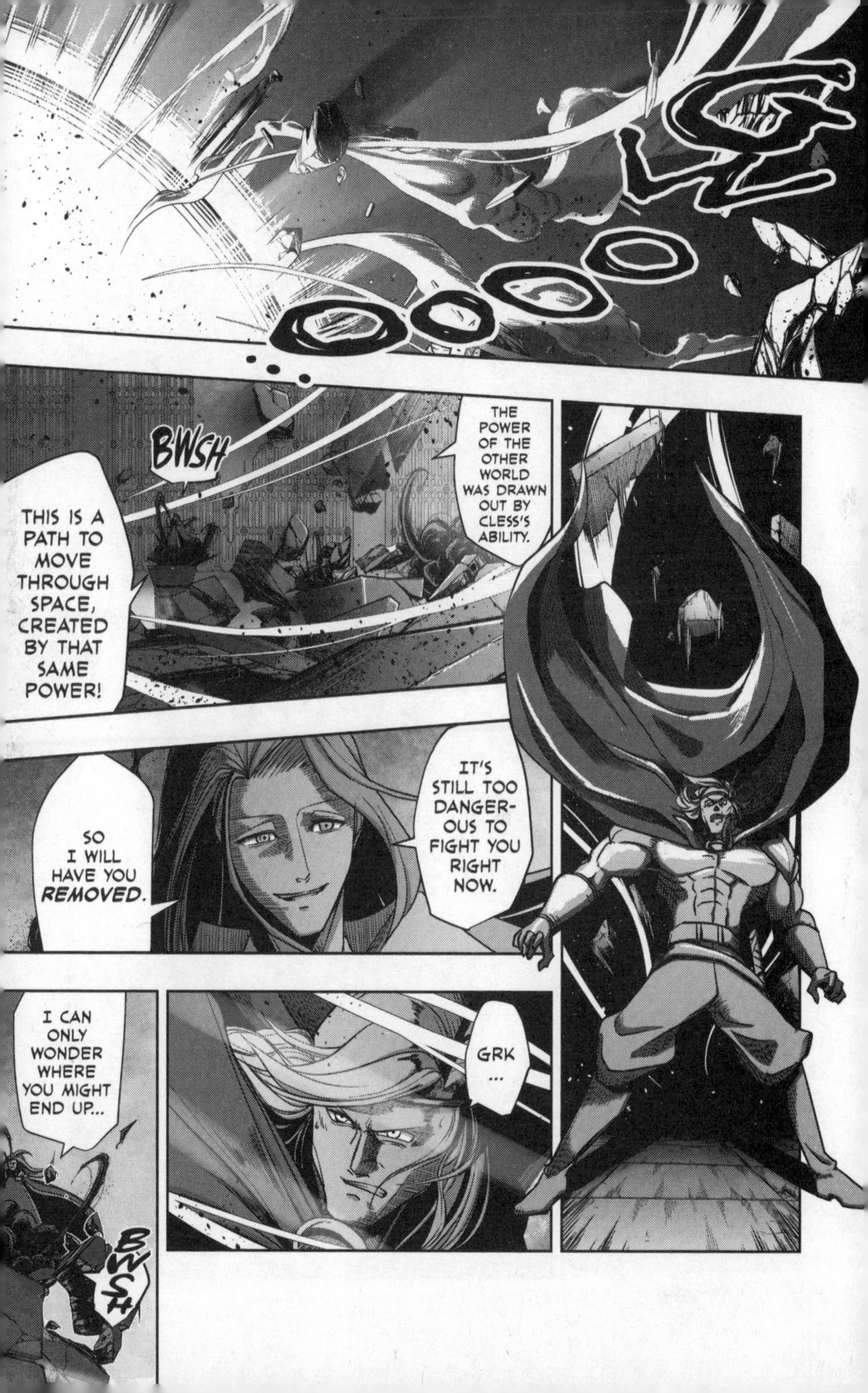
BWSH
THE POWER OF THE OTHER WORLD WAS DRAWN OUT BY CLESS'S ABILITY.
THIS IS A PATH TO MOVE THROUGH SPACE, CREATED BY THAT SAME POWER!
IT'S STILL TOO DANGER-OUS TO FIGHT YOU RIGHT NOW.
SO I WILL HAVE YOU *REMOVED*.
GRK ...
I CAN ONLY WONDER WHERE YOU MIGHT END UP...
BWSH

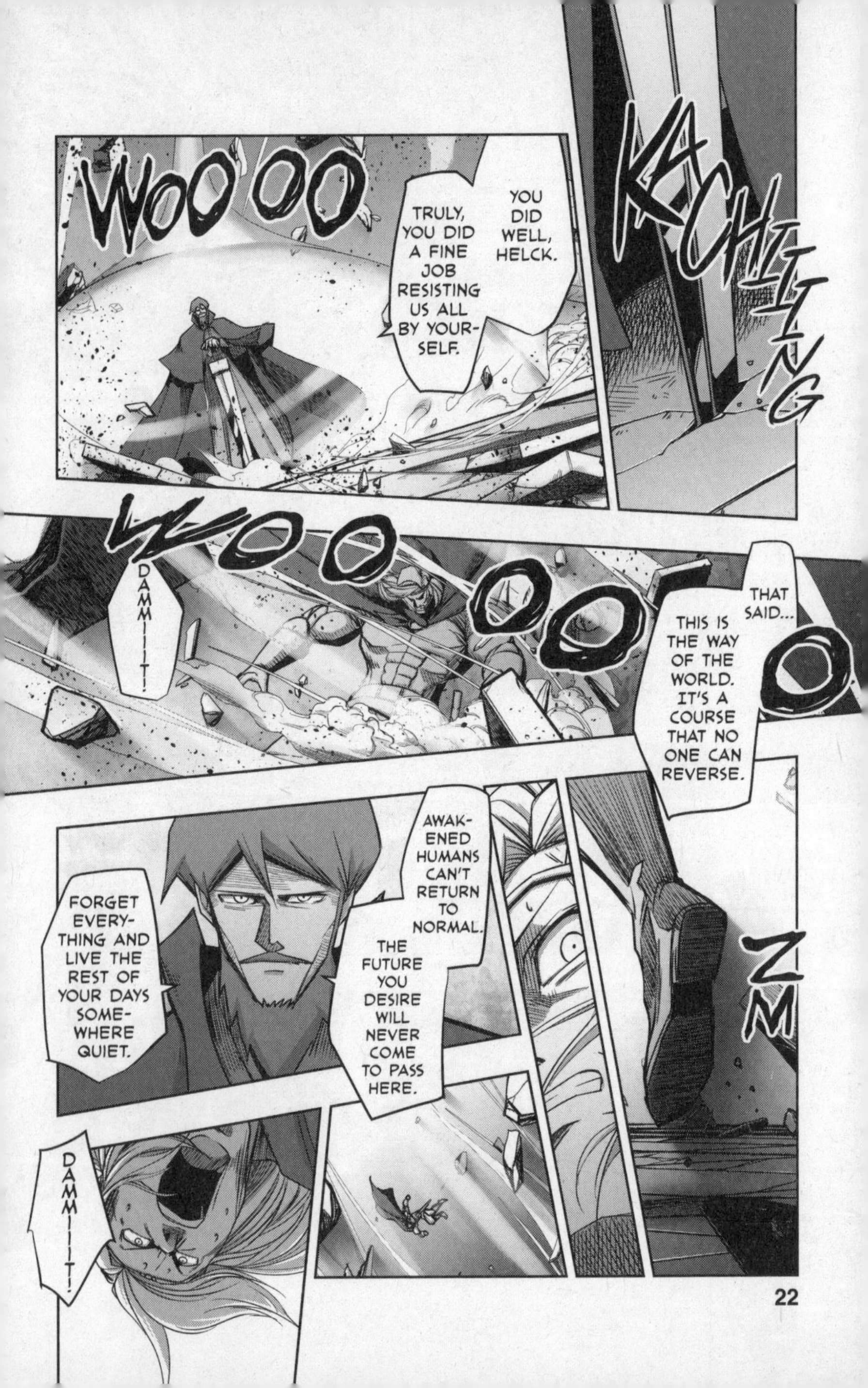
KACHIIING
WOO OO
YOU DID WELL, HELCK.
TRULY, YOU DID A FINE JOB RESISTING US ALL BY YOURSELF.
THAT SAID...
THIS IS THE WAY OF THE WORLD. IT'S A COURSE THAT NO ONE CAN REVERSE.
WOOOOOOO
DAMMIIIT!
ZM
AWAKENED HUMANS CAN'T RETURN TO NORMAL.
THE FUTURE YOU DESIRE WILL NEVER COME TO PASS HERE.
FORGET EVERYTHING AND LIVE THE REST OF YOUR DAYS SOMEWHERE QUIET.
DAMMIIIT!

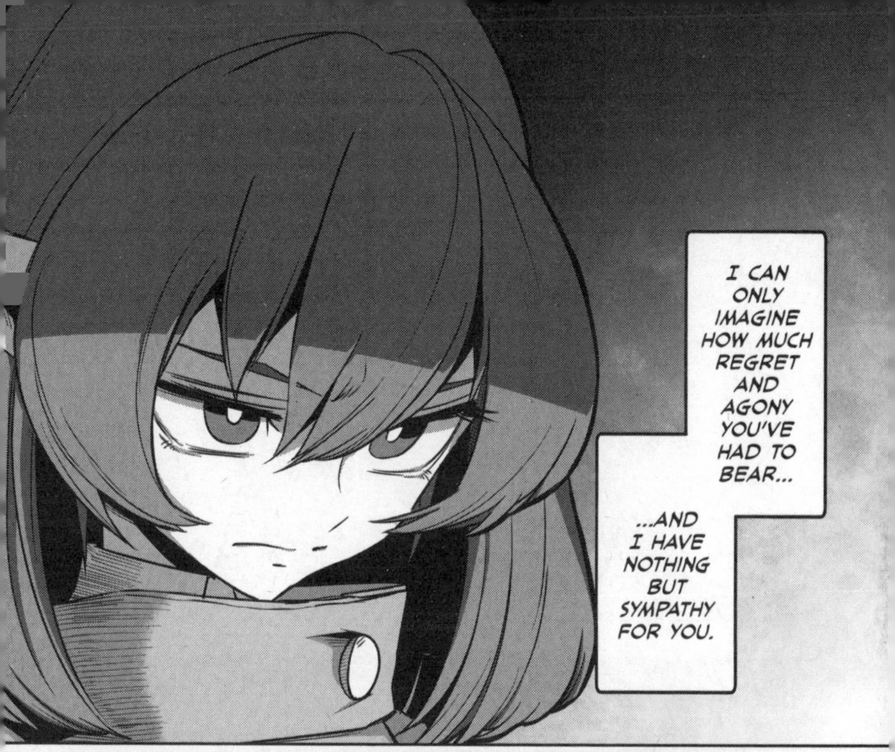
I CAN ONLY IMAGINE HOW MUCH REGRET AND AGONY YOU'VE HAD TO BEAR...
...AND I HAVE NOTHING BUT SYMPATHY FOR YOU.
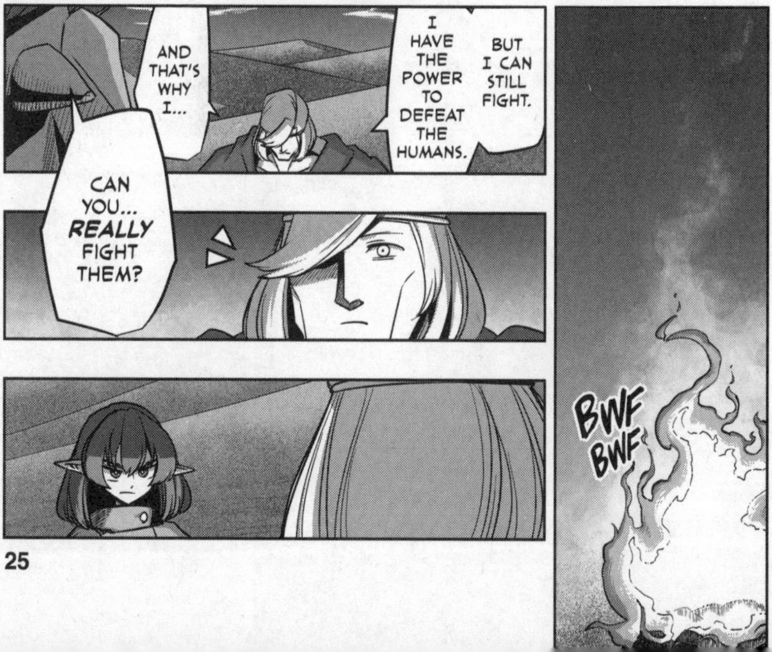
BWF BWF
BUT I CAN STILL FIGHT.
I HAVE THE POWER TO DEFEAT THE HUMANS.
AND THAT'S WHY I...
CAN YOU... *REALLY* FIGHT THEM?

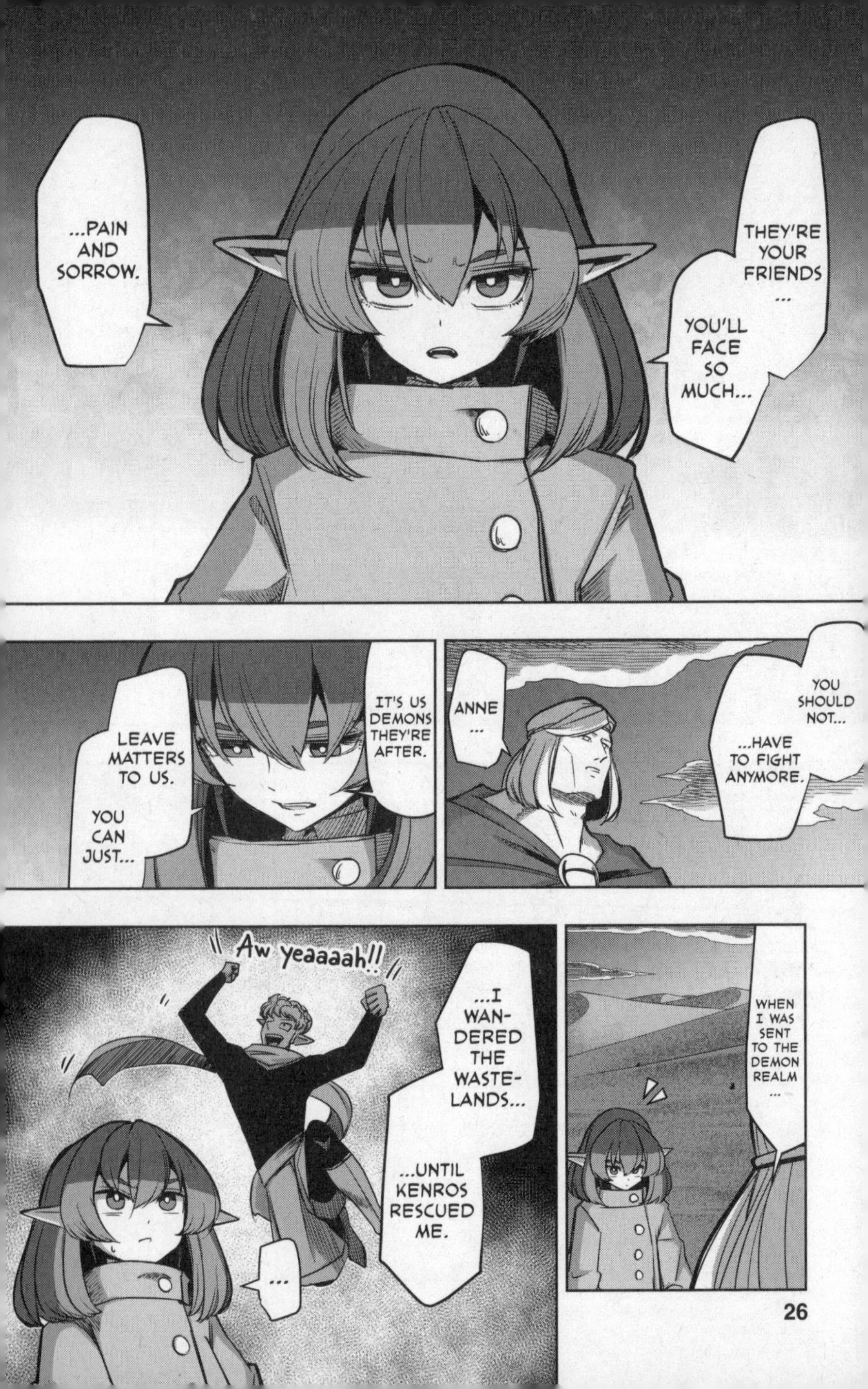
THEY'RE YOUR FRIENDS ...
YOU'LL FACE SO MUCH...
...PAIN AND SORROW.
YOU SHOULD NOT...
...HAVE TO FIGHT ANYMORE.
ANNE ...
IT'S US DEMONS THEY'RE AFTER.
LEAVE MATTERS TO US.
YOU CAN JUST...
WHEN I WAS SENT TO THE DEMON REALM ...
...I WAN-DERED THE WASTE-LANDS...
...UNTIL KENROS RESCUED ME.
Aw yeaaaah!!
...

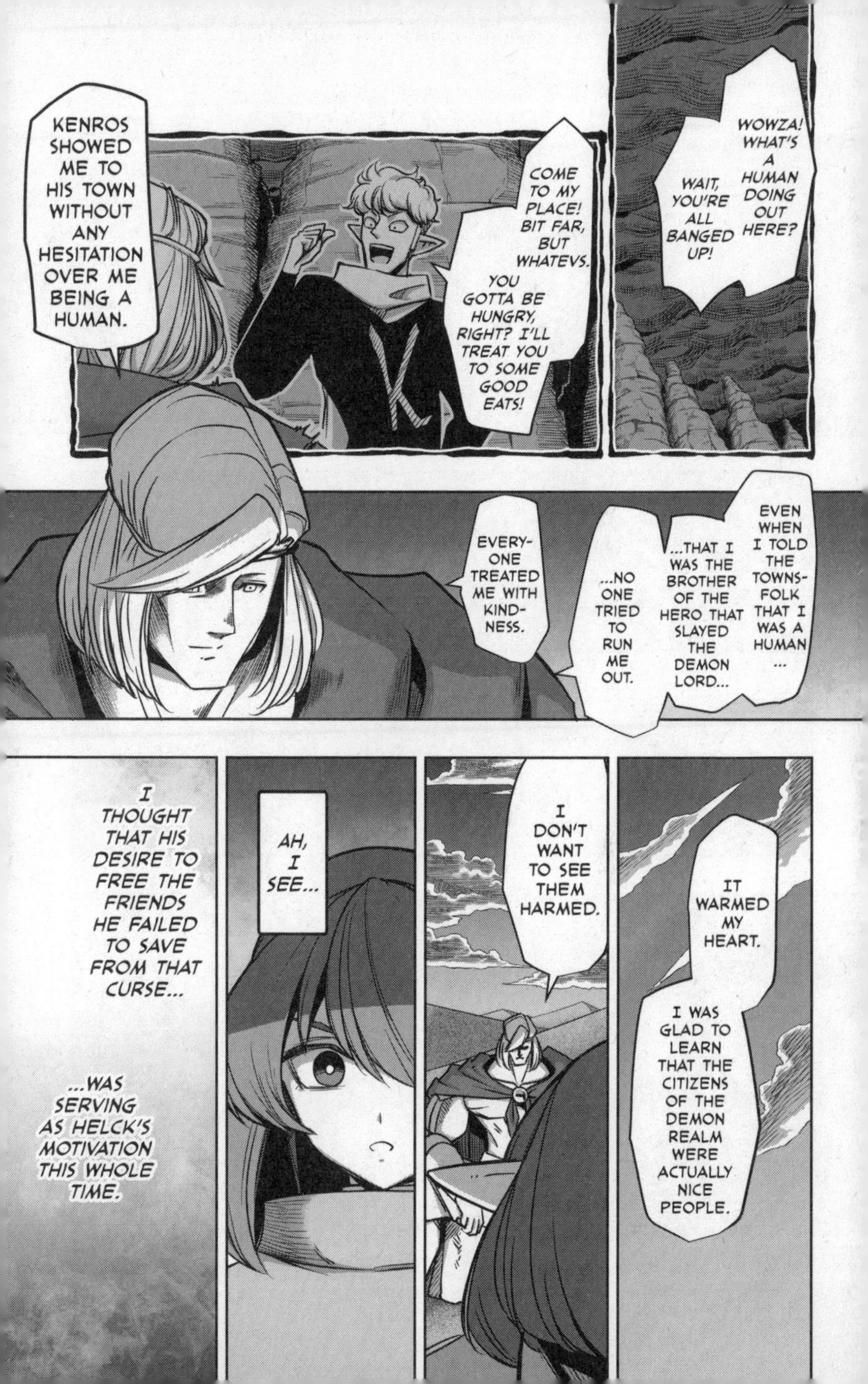
WOWZA! WHAT'S A HUMAN DOING OUT HERE?
WAIT, YOU'RE ALL BANGED UP!
COME TO MY PLACE! BIT FAR, BUT WHATEVS.
YOU GOTTA BE HUNGRY, RIGHT? I'LL TREAT YOU TO SOME GOOD EATS!
KENROS SHOWED ME TO HIS TOWN WITHOUT ANY HESITATION OVER ME BEING A HUMAN.
EVEN WHEN I TOLD THE TOWNS-FOLK THAT I WAS A HUMAN...
...THAT I WAS THE BROTHER OF THE HERO THAT SLAYED THE DEMON LORD...
...NO ONE TRIED TO RUN ME OUT.
EVERY-ONE TREATED ME WITH KIND-NESS.
IT WARMED MY HEART.
I WAS GLAD TO LEARN THAT THE CITIZENS OF THE DEMON REALM WERE ACTUALLY NICE PEOPLE.
I DON'T WANT TO SEE THEM HARMED.
AH, I SEE...
I THOUGHT THAT HIS DESIRE TO FREE THE FRIENDS HE FAILED TO SAVE FROM THAT CURSE...
...WAS SERVING AS HELCK'S MOTIVATION THIS WHOLE TIME.

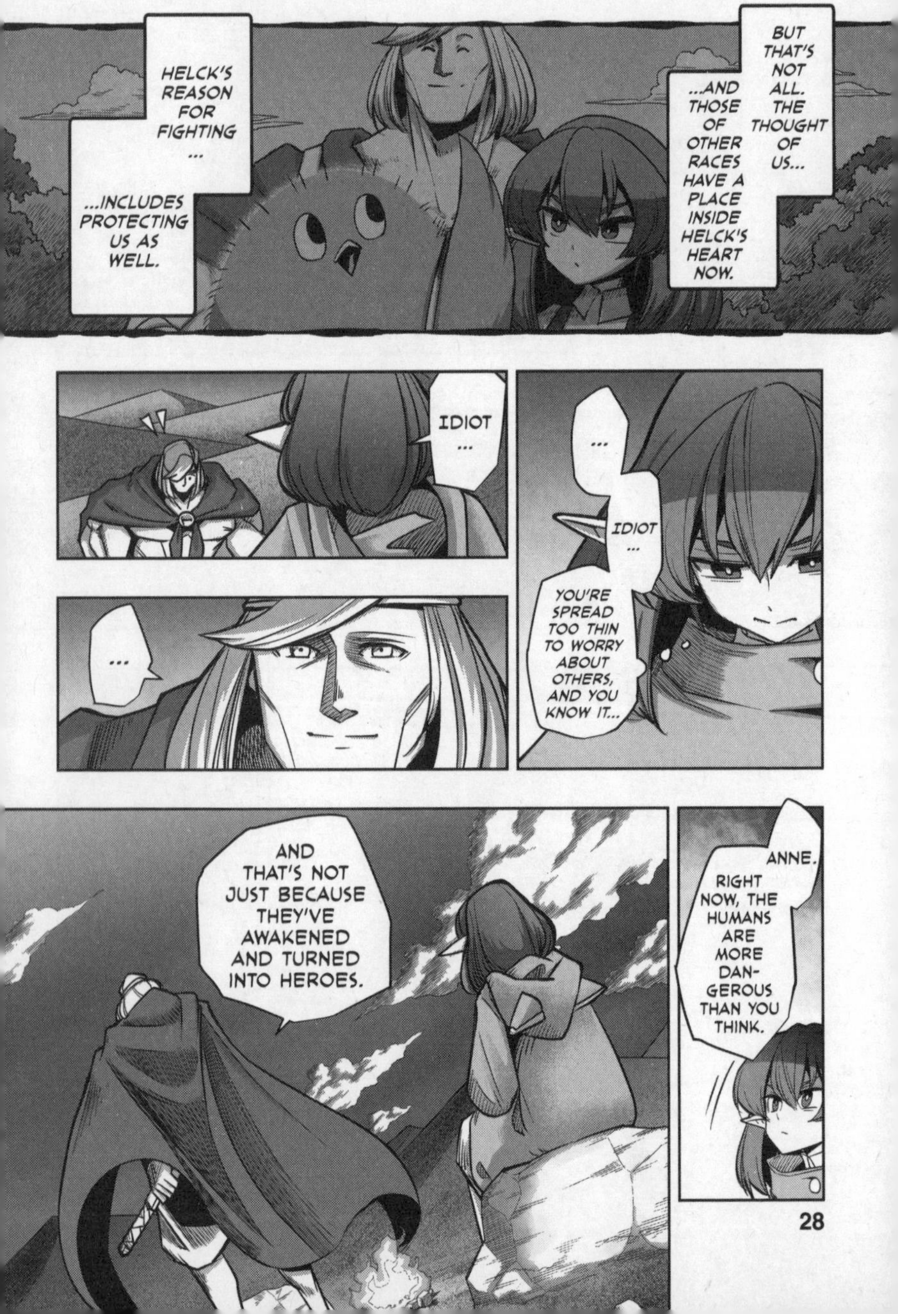
BUT THAT'S NOT ALL. THE THOUGHT OF US...
...AND THOSE OF OTHER RACES HAVE A PLACE INSIDE HELCK'S HEART NOW.
HELCK'S REASON FOR FIGHTING...
...INCLUDES PROTECTING US AS WELL.
...
IDIOT...
YOU'RE SPREAD TOO THIN TO WORRY ABOUT OTHERS, AND YOU KNOW IT...
IDIOT...
...
ANNE.
RIGHT NOW, THE HUMANS ARE MORE DANGEROUS THAN YOU THINK.
AND THAT'S NOT JUST BECAUSE THEY'VE AWAKENED AND TURNED INTO HEROES.

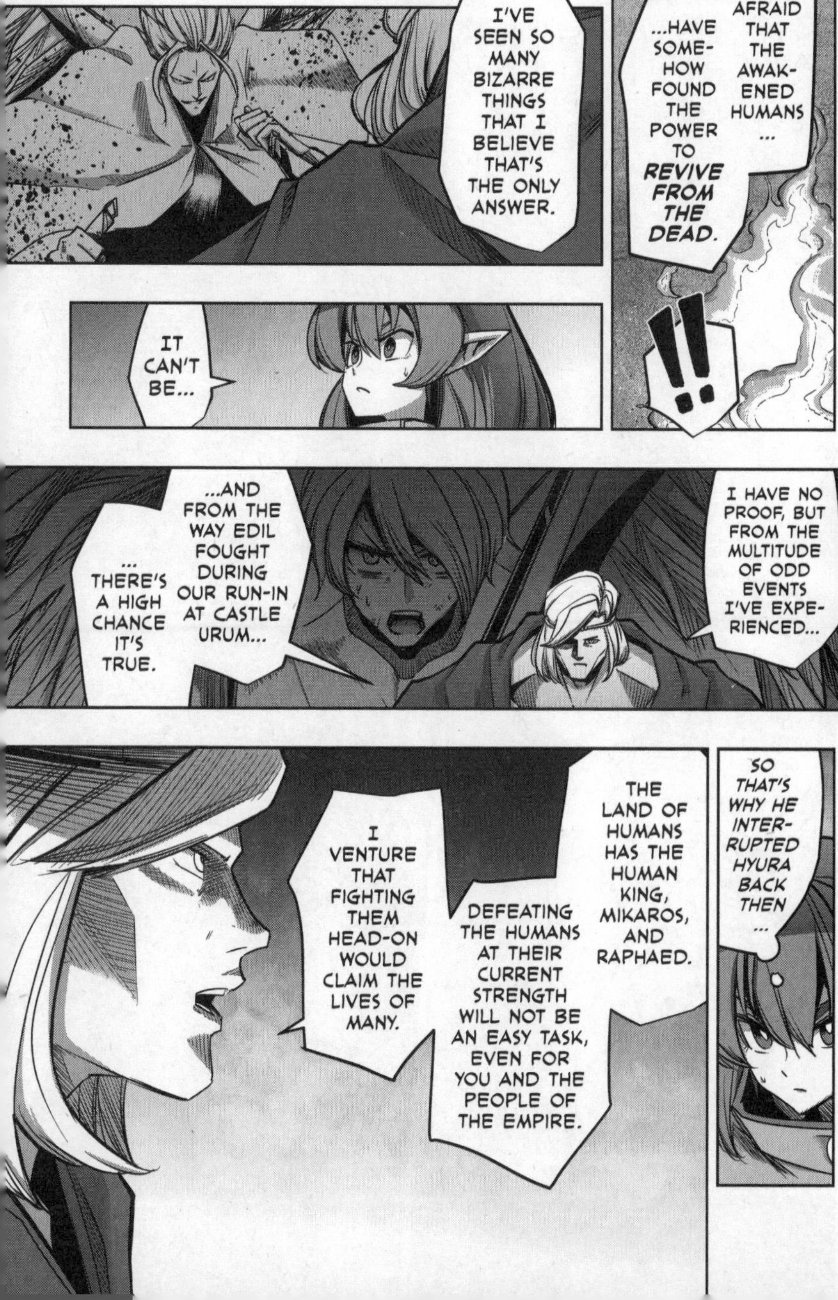
I'M AFRAID THAT THE AWAKENED HUMANS...
...HAVE SOMEHOW FOUND THE POWER TO *REVIVE FROM THE DEAD.*
!!
I'VE SEEN SO MANY BIZARRE THINGS THAT I BELIEVE THAT'S THE ONLY ANSWER.
IT CAN'T BE...
I HAVE NO PROOF, BUT FROM THE MULTITUDE OF ODD EVENTS I'VE EXPERIENCED...
...AND FROM THE WAY EDIL FOUGHT DURING OUR RUN-IN AT CASTLE URUM...
...THERE'S A HIGH CHANCE IT'S TRUE.
SO THAT'S WHY HE INTERRUPTED HYURA BACK THEN...
THE LAND OF HUMANS HAS THE HUMAN KING, MIKAROS, AND RAPHAED.
DEFEATING THE HUMANS AT THEIR CURRENT STRENGTH WILL NOT BE AN EASY TASK, EVEN FOR YOU AND THE PEOPLE OF THE EMPIRE.
I VENTURE THAT FIGHTING THEM HEAD-ON WOULD CLAIM THE LIVES OF MANY.

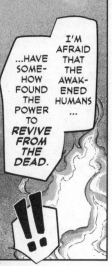

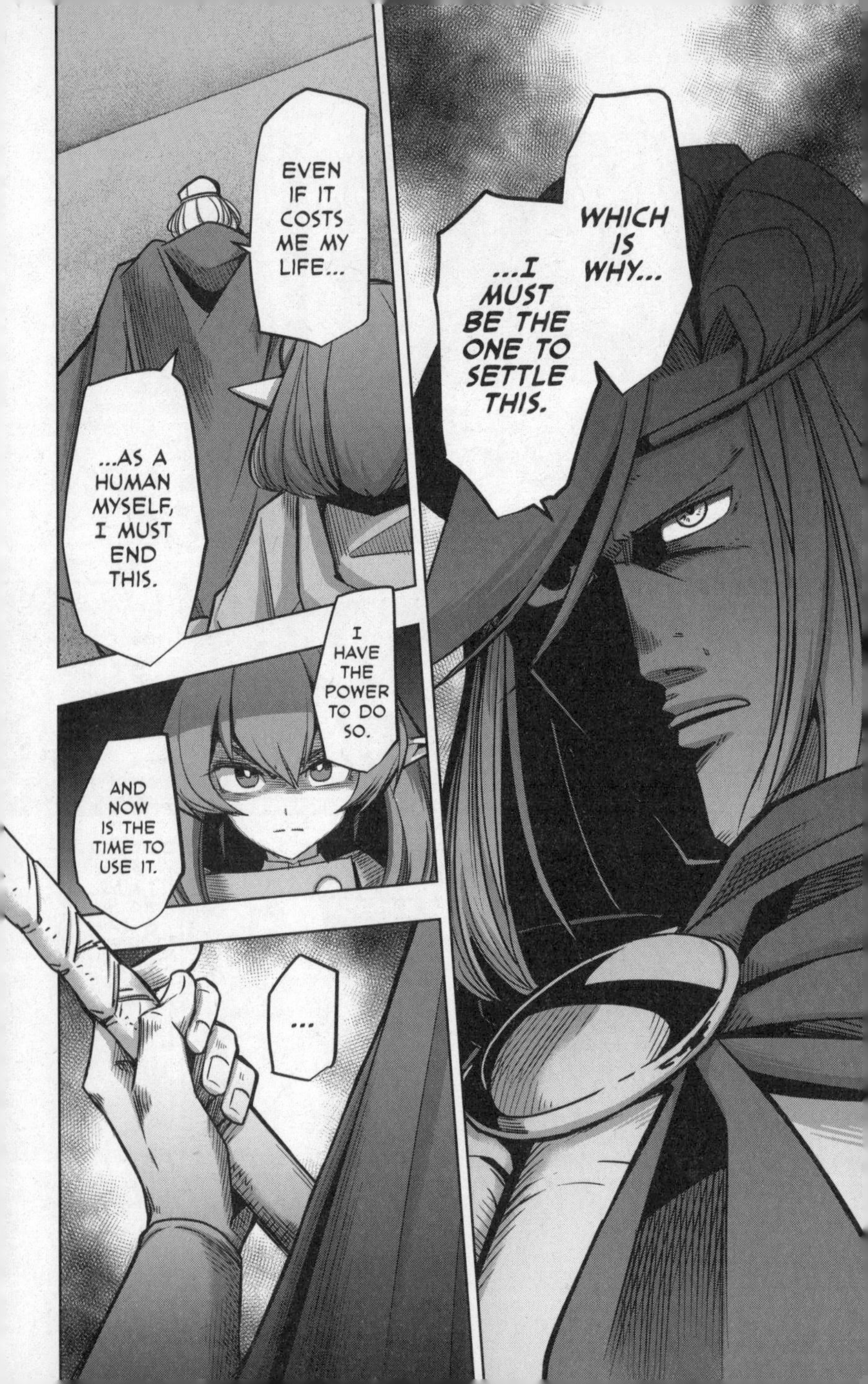
WHICH IS WHY...
...I MUST BE THE ONE TO SETTLE THIS.
EVEN IF IT COSTS ME MY LIFE...
...AS A HUMAN MYSELF, I MUST END THIS.
I HAVE THE POWER TO DO SO.
AND NOW IS THE TIME TO USE IT.
...

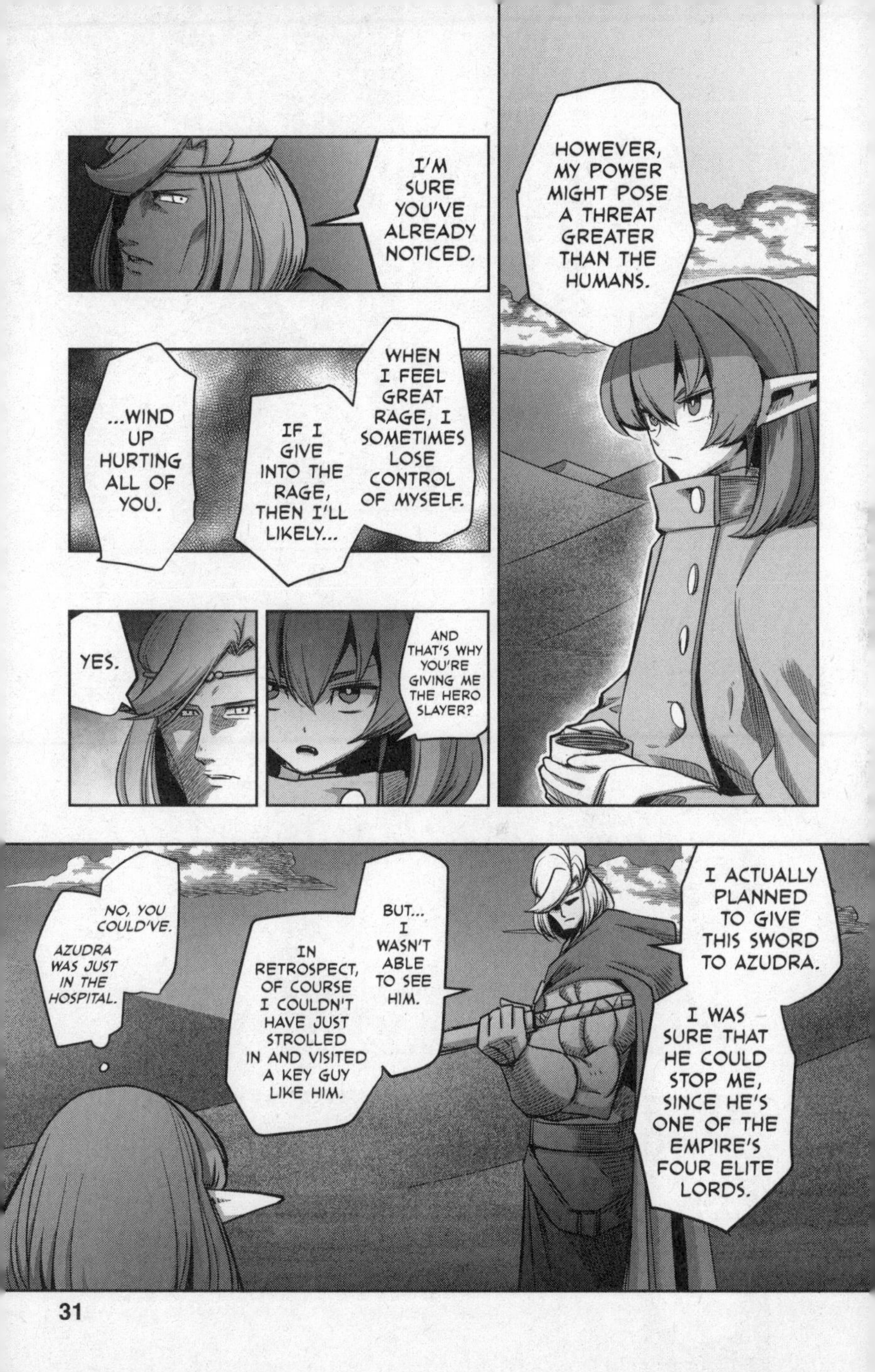
HOWEVER, MY POWER MIGHT POSE A THREAT GREATER THAN THE HUMANS.
I'M SURE YOU'VE ALREADY NOTICED.
WHEN I FEEL GREAT RAGE, I SOMETIMES LOSE CONTROL OF MYSELF.
IF I GIVE INTO THE RAGE, THEN I'LL LIKELY...
...WIND UP HURTING ALL OF YOU.
AND THAT'S WHY YOU'RE GIVING ME THE HERO SLAYER?
YES.
I ACTUALLY PLANNED TO GIVE THIS SWORD TO AZUDRA.
I WAS SURE THAT HE COULD STOP ME, SINCE HE'S ONE OF THE EMPIRE'S FOUR ELITE LORDS.
BUT... I WASN'T ABLE TO SEE HIM.
IN RETROSPECT, OF COURSE I COULDN'T HAVE JUST STROLLED IN AND VISITED A KEY GUY LIKE HIM.
NO, YOU COULD'VE.
AZUDRA WAS JUST IN THE HOSPITAL.

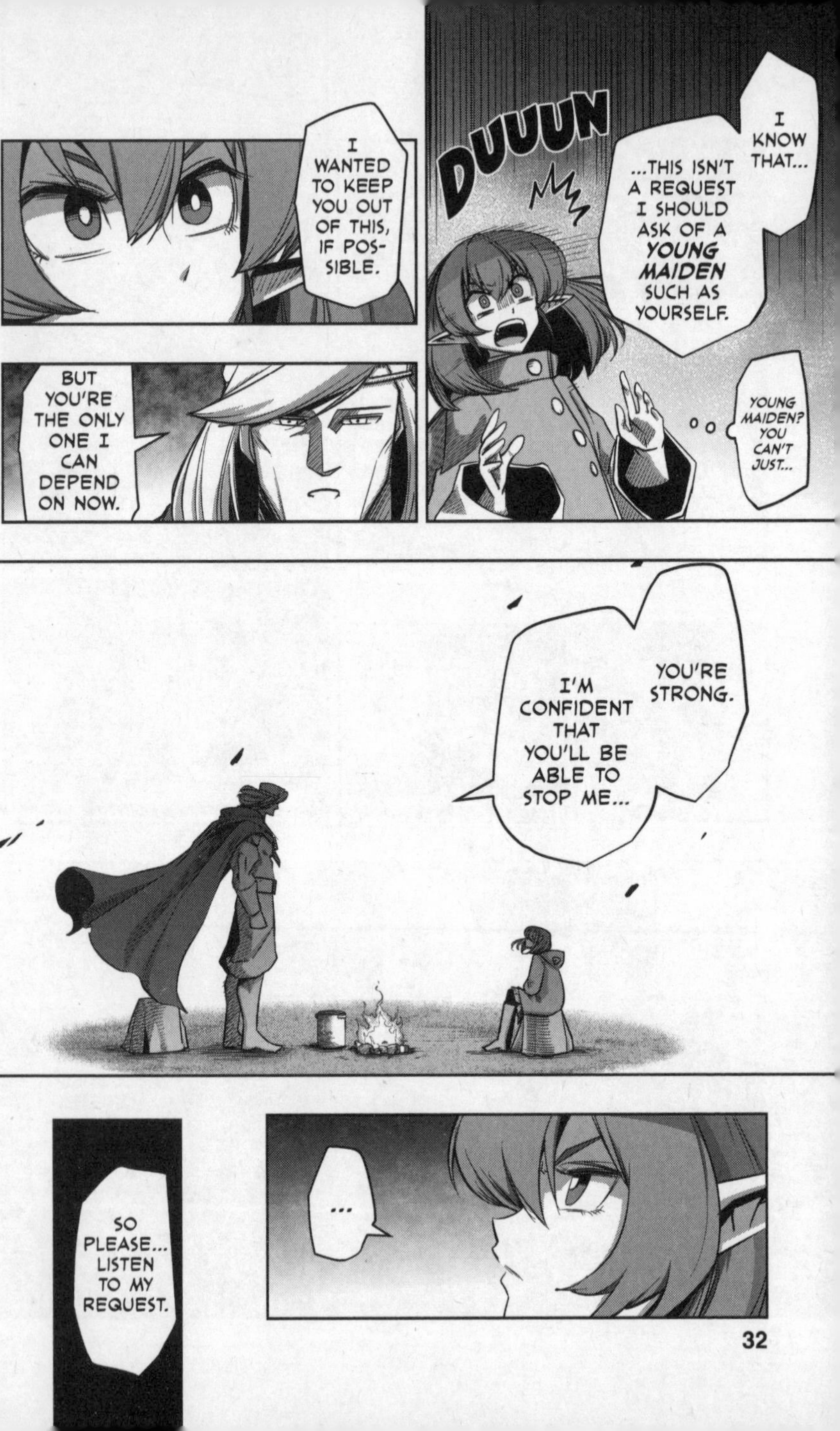
I KNOW THAT...
...THIS ISN'T A REQUEST I SHOULD ASK OF A *YOUNG MAIDEN* SUCH AS YOURSELF.
DUUUN
YOUNG MAIDEN? YOU CAN'T JUST...
I WANTED TO KEEP YOU OUT OF THIS, IF POS-SIBLE.
BUT YOU'RE THE ONLY ONE I CAN DEPEND ON NOW.
YOU'RE STRONG.
I'M CONFIDENT THAT YOU'LL BE ABLE TO STOP ME...
...
SO PLEASE... LISTEN TO MY REQUEST.

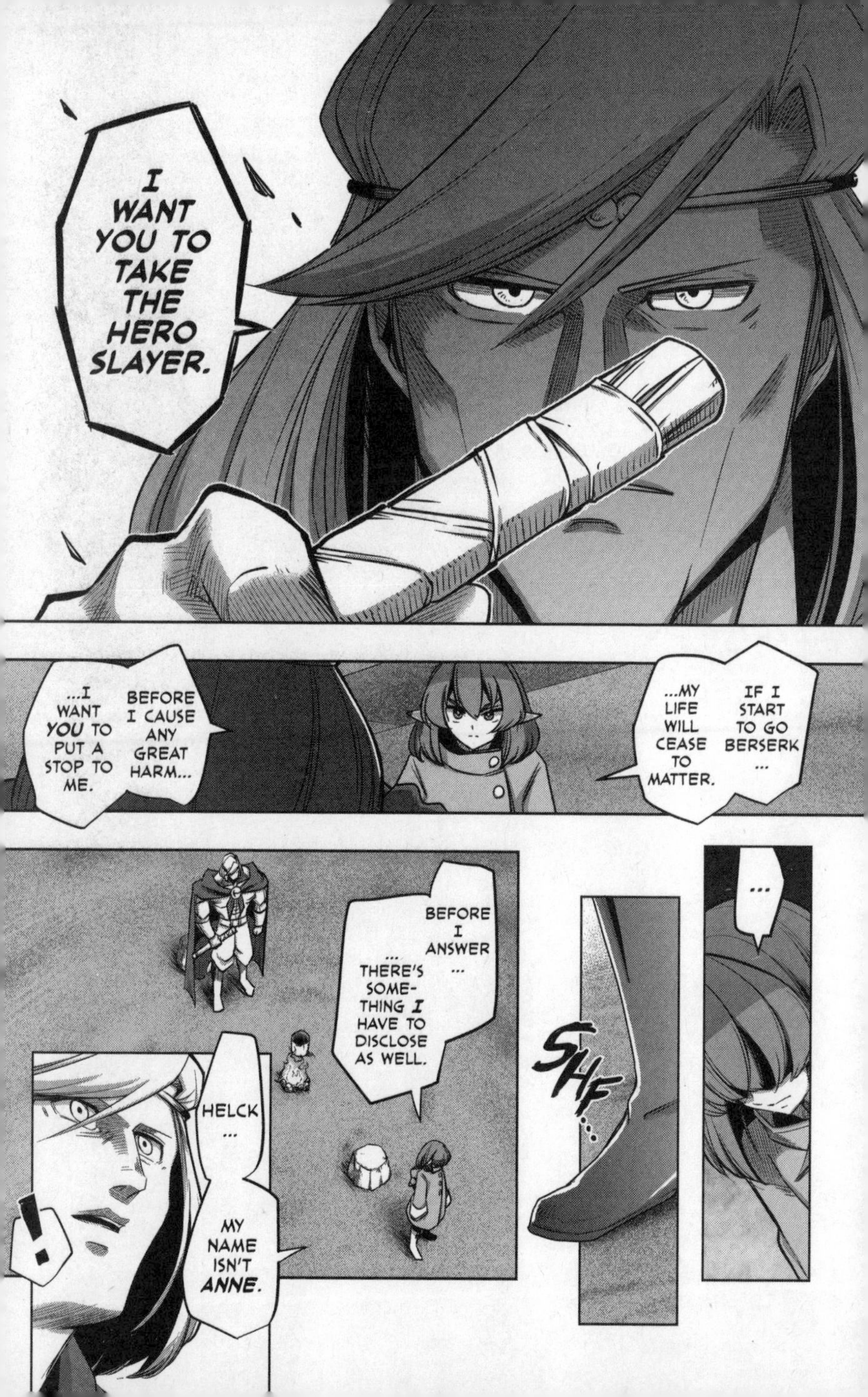
I WANT YOU TO TAKE THE HERO SLAYER.
IF I START TO GO BERSERK ...
...MY LIFE WILL CEASE TO MATTER.
BEFORE I CAUSE ANY GREAT HARM...
...I WANT YOU TO PUT A STOP TO ME.
...
SHF...
BEFORE I ANSWER ...
... THERE'S SOMETHING I HAVE TO DISCLOSE AS WELL.
HELCK ...
MY NAME ISN'T ANNE.
!

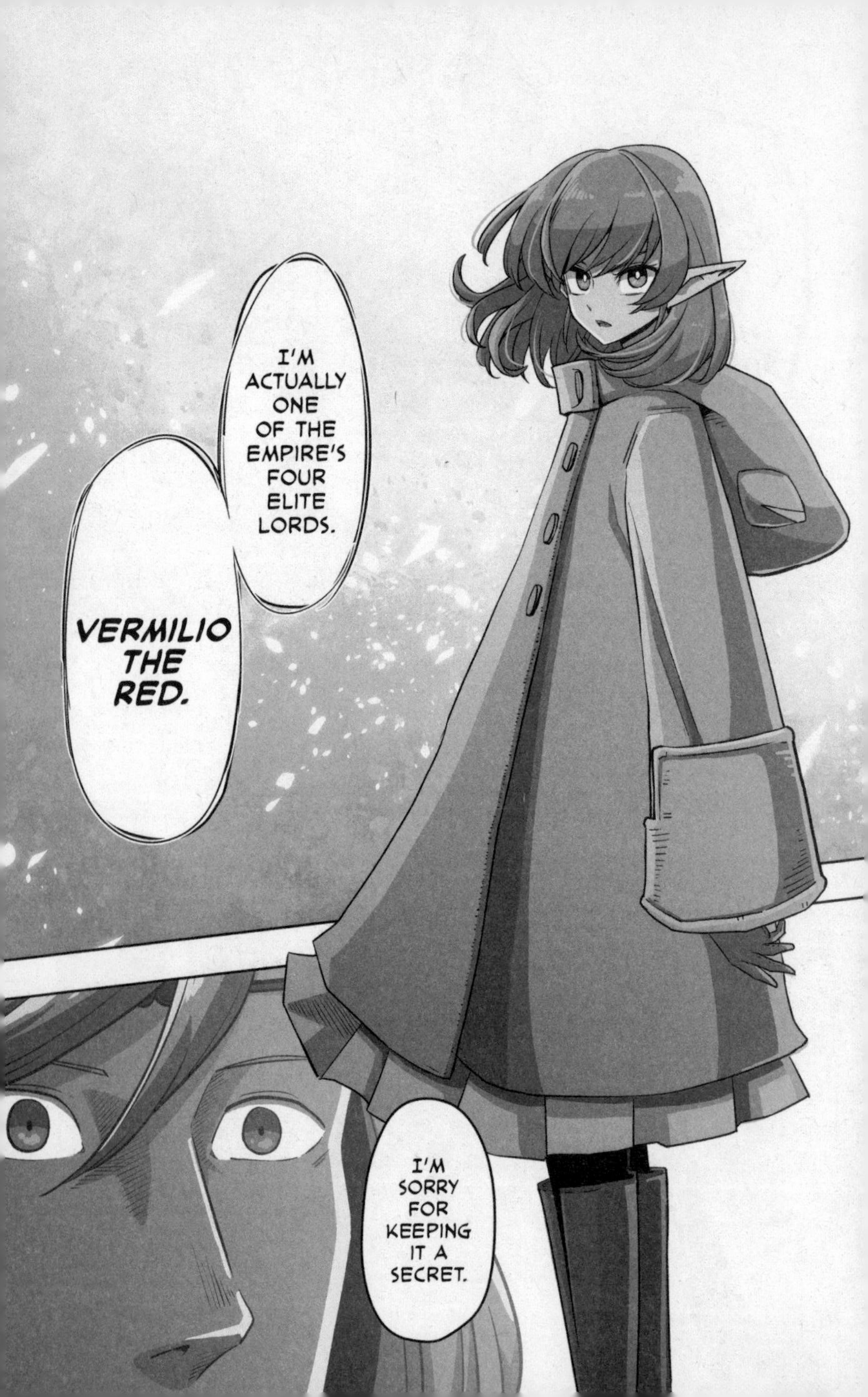
I'M ACTUALLY ONE OF THE EMPIRE'S FOUR ELITE LORDS.
VERMILIO THE RED.
I'M SORRY FOR KEEPING IT A SECRET.

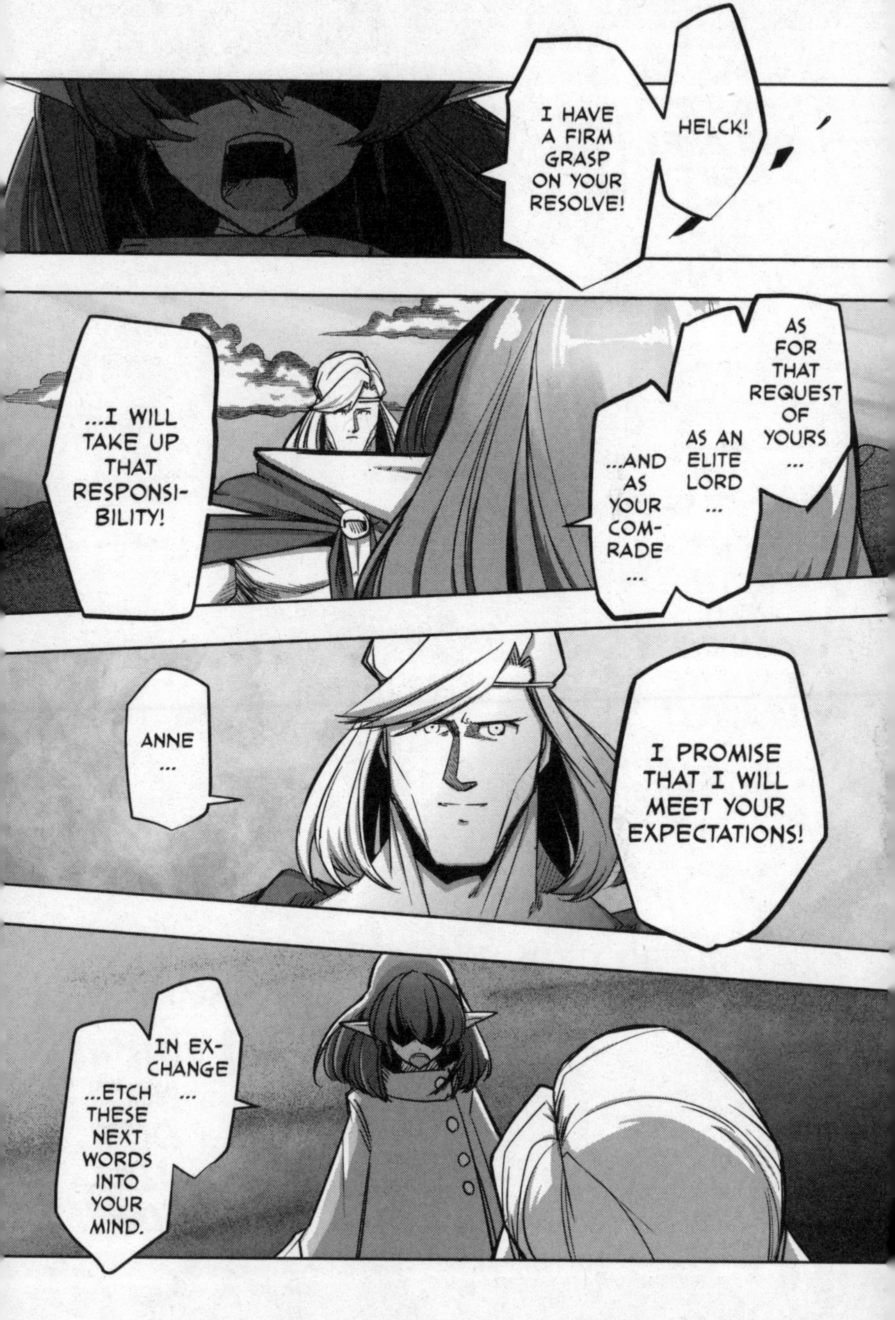
HELCK!
I HAVE A FIRM GRASP ON YOUR RESOLVE!
AS FOR THAT REQUEST OF YOURS...
AS AN ELITE LORD...
...AND AS YOUR COMRADE...
...I WILL TAKE UP THAT RESPONSIBILITY!
I PROMISE THAT I WILL MEET YOUR EXPECTATIONS!
ANNE...
IN EXCHANGE...
...ETCH THESE NEXT WORDS INTO YOUR MIND.

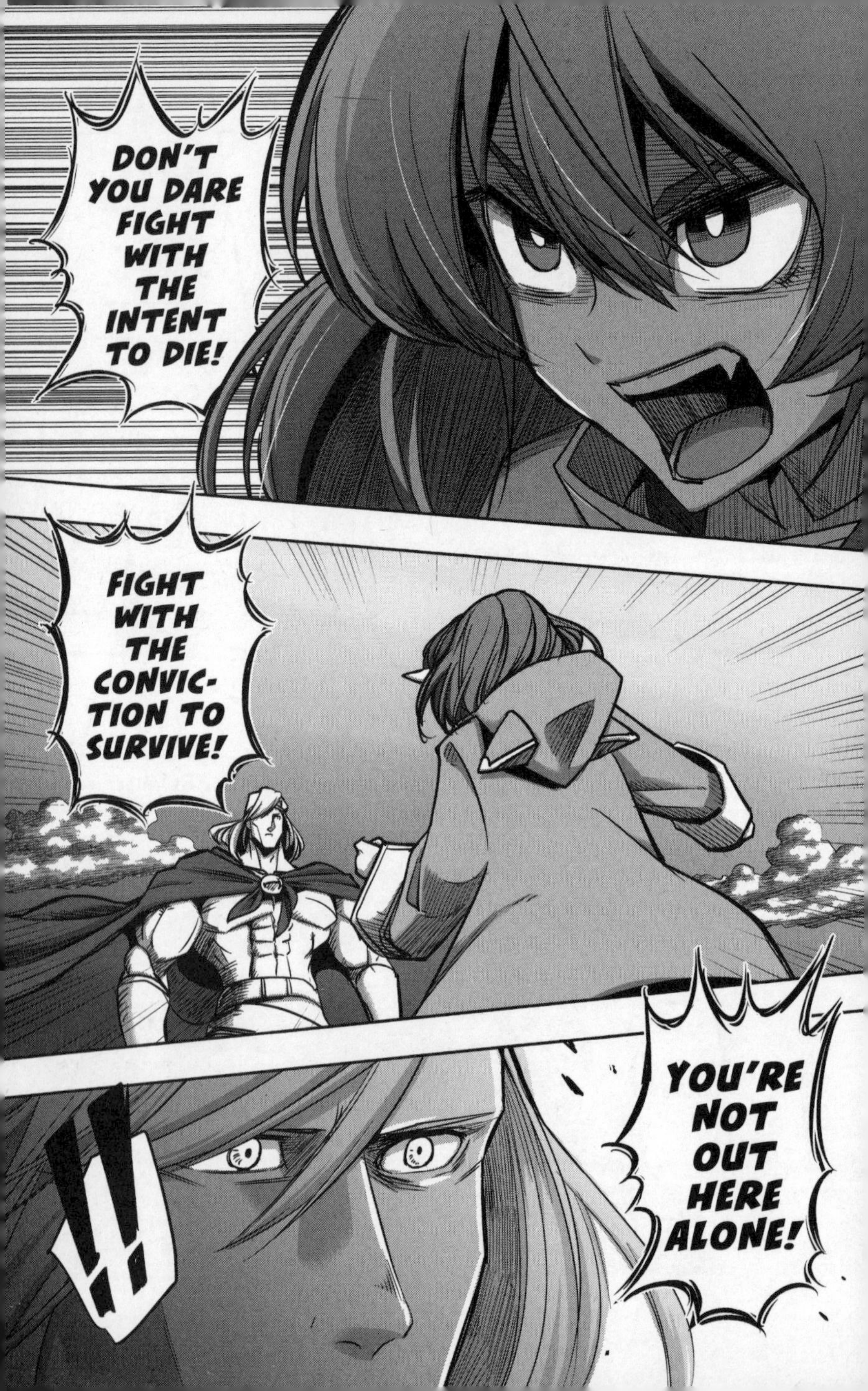
DON'T YOU DARE FIGHT WITH THE INTENT TO DIE!
FIGHT WITH THE CONVIC-TION TO SURVIVE!
YOU'RE NOT OUT HERE ALONE!
!!

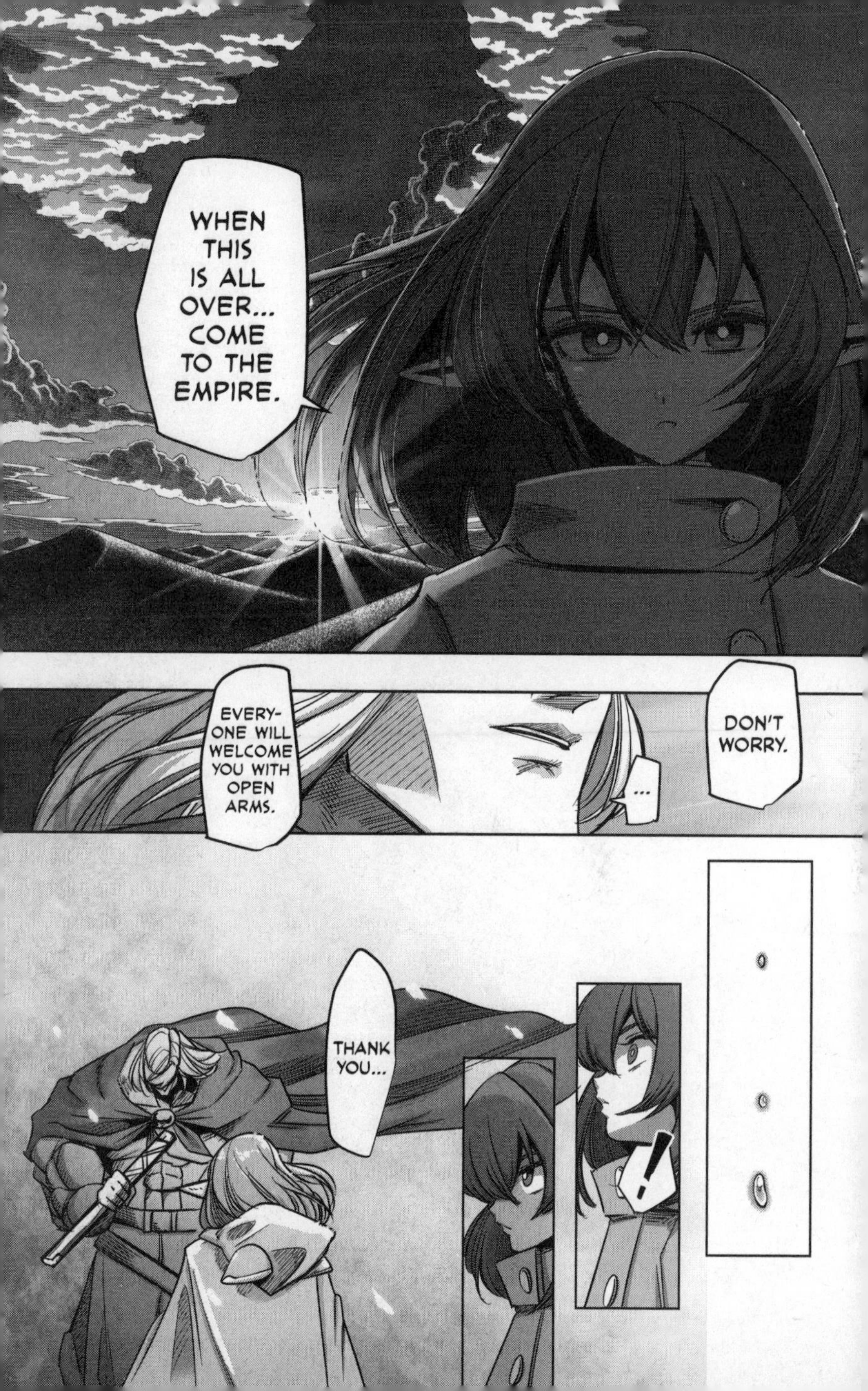
WHEN THIS IS ALL OVER... COME TO THE EMPIRE.
DON'T WORRY.
...
EVERY-ONE WILL WELCOME YOU WITH OPEN ARMS.
!
THANK YOU...

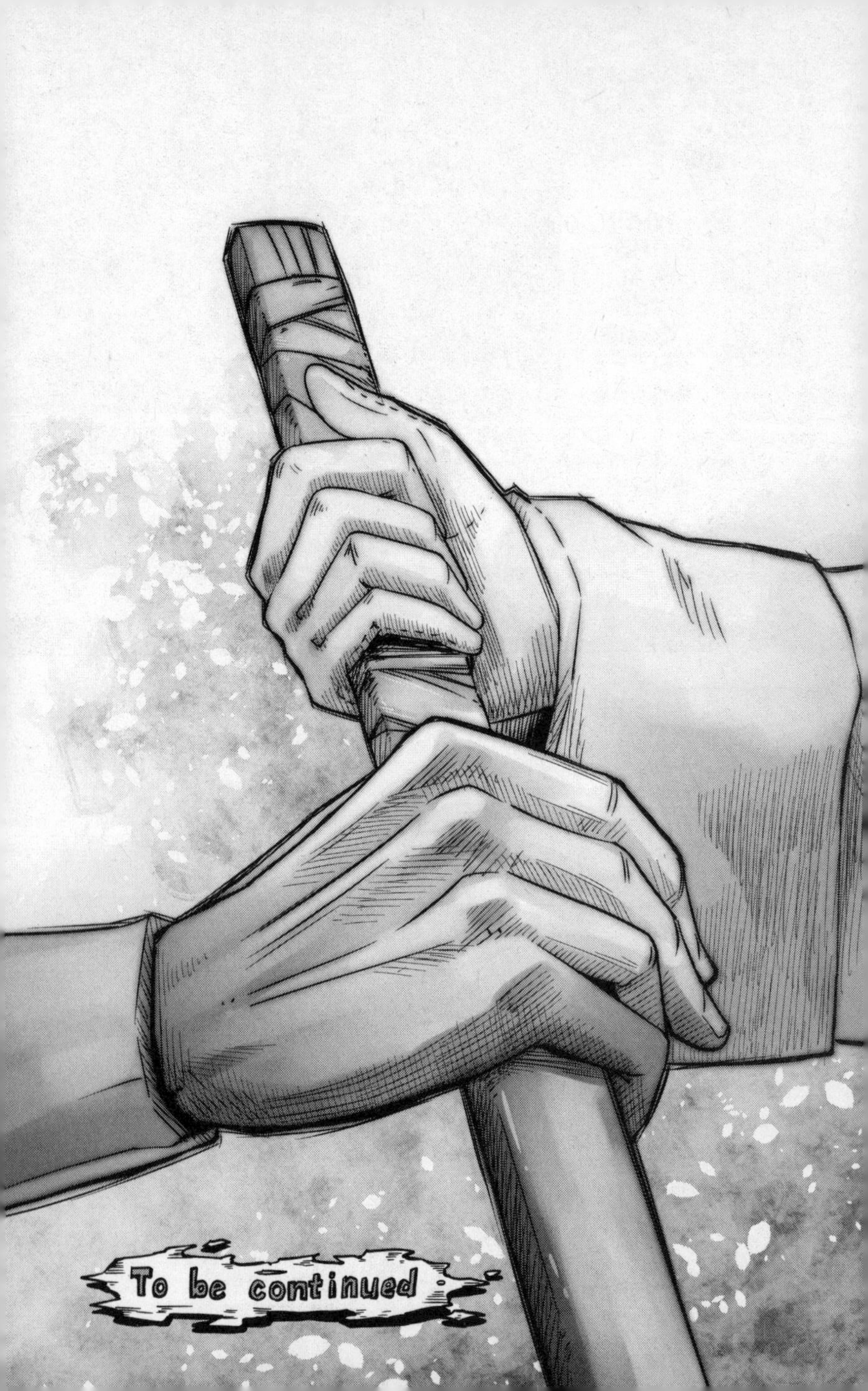
To be continued

Chapter 54: Breather on the Train

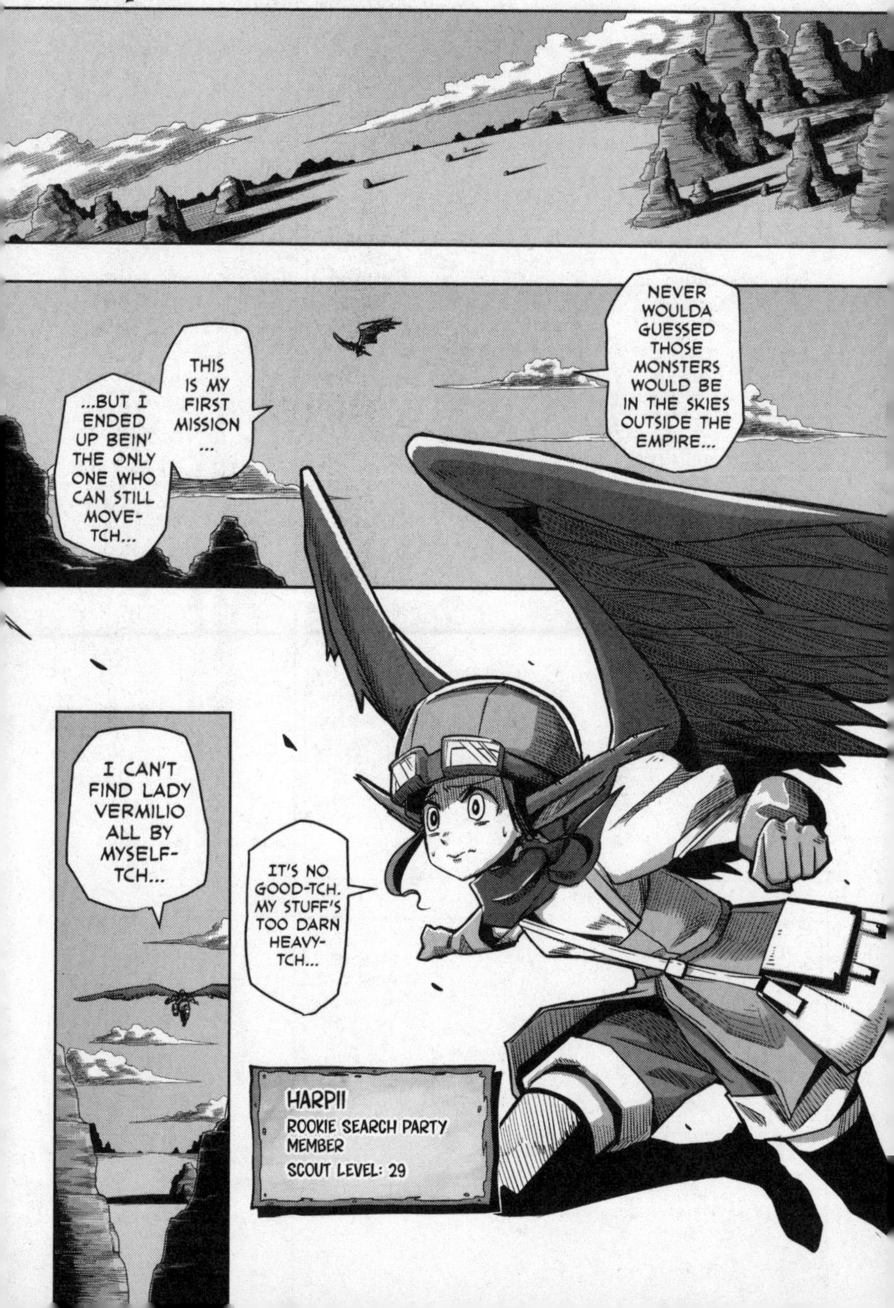
NEVER WOULDA GUESSED THOSE MONSTERS WOULD BE IN THE SKIES OUTSIDE THE EMPIRE...
THIS IS MY FIRST MISSION...
...BUT I ENDED UP BEIN' THE ONLY ONE WHO CAN STILL MOVE-TCH...
IT'S NO GOOD-TCH. MY STUFF'S TOO DARN HEAVY-TCH...
HARPII
ROOKIE SEARCH PARTY MEMBER
SCOUT LEVEL: 29
I CAN'T FIND LADY VERMILIO ALL BY MYSELF-TCH...

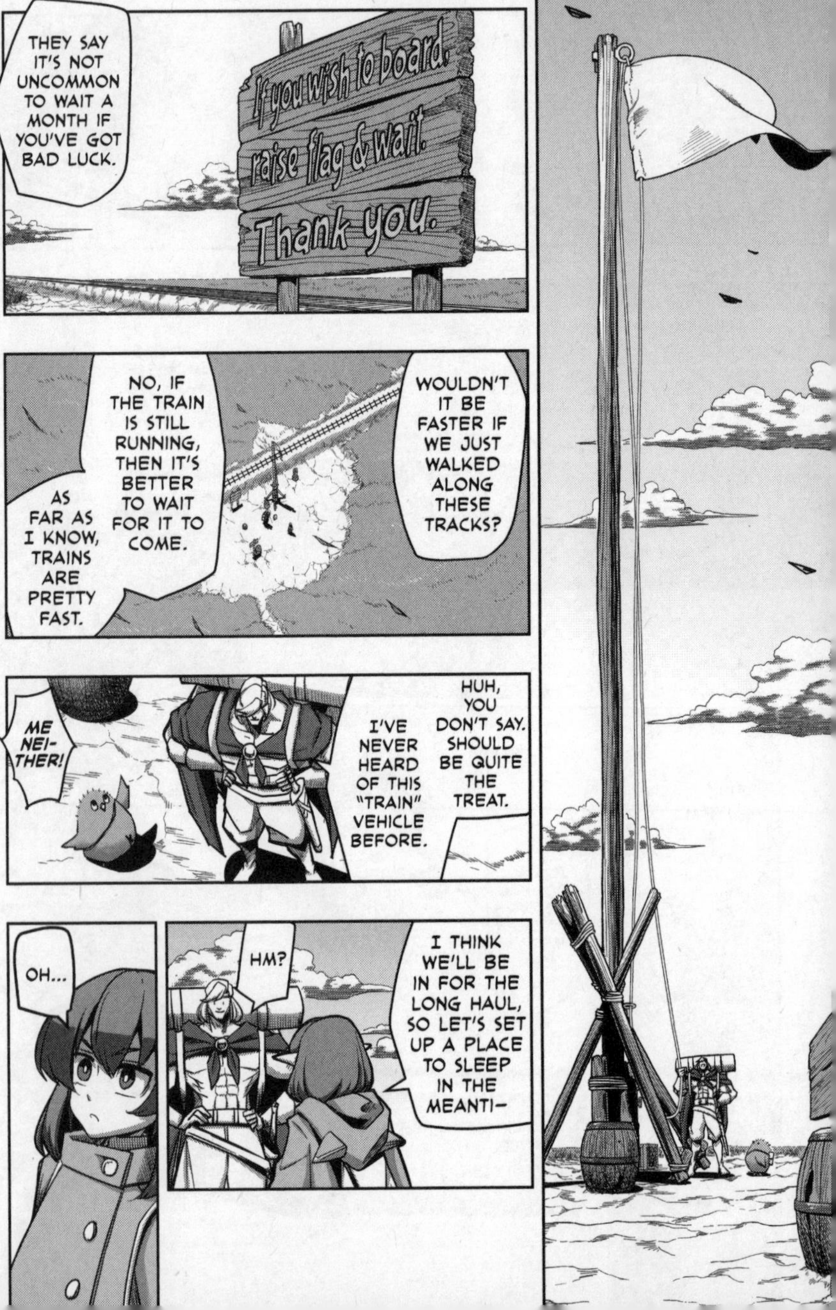
THEY SAY IT'S NOT UNCOMMON TO WAIT A MONTH IF YOU'VE GOT BAD LUCK.
If you wish to board.
raise flag & wait.
Thank you.
WOULDN'T IT BE FASTER IF WE JUST WALKED ALONG THESE TRACKS?
NO, IF THE TRAIN IS STILL RUNNING, THEN IT'S BETTER TO WAIT FOR IT TO COME.
AS FAR AS I KNOW, TRAINS ARE PRETTY FAST.
HUH, YOU DON'T SAY. SHOULD BE QUITE THE TREAT.
I'VE NEVER HEARD OF THIS "TRAIN" VEHICLE BEFORE.
ME NEI-THER!
I THINK WE'LL BE IN FOR THE LONG HAUL, SO LET'S SET UP A PLACE TO SLEEP IN THE MEANTI—
HM?
OH...

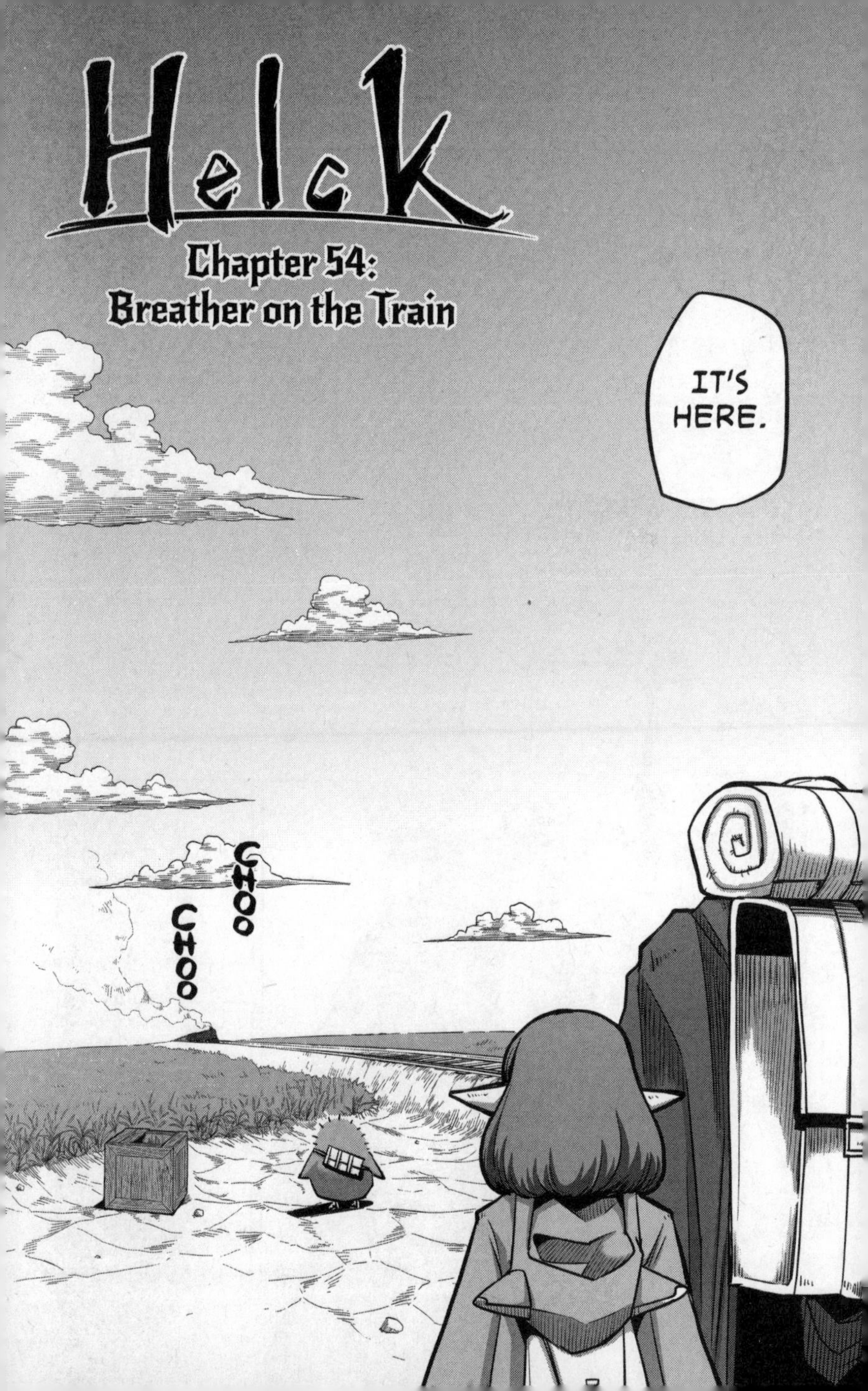
Helck
Chapter 54:
Breather on the Train
IT'S HERE.
CHOO
CHOO

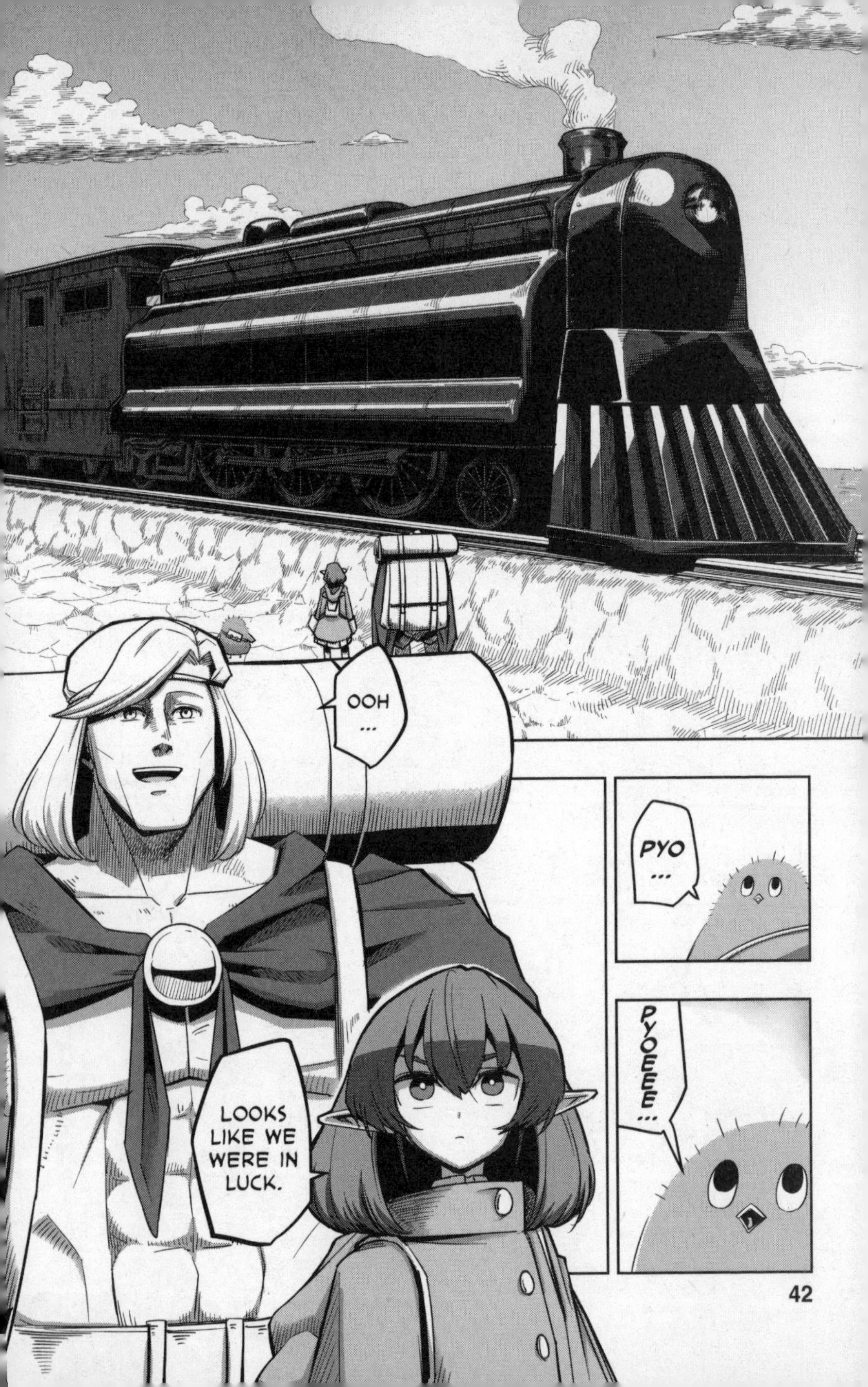
PYO ...
PYOEEE ...
OOH ...
LOOKS LIKE WE WERE IN LUCK.

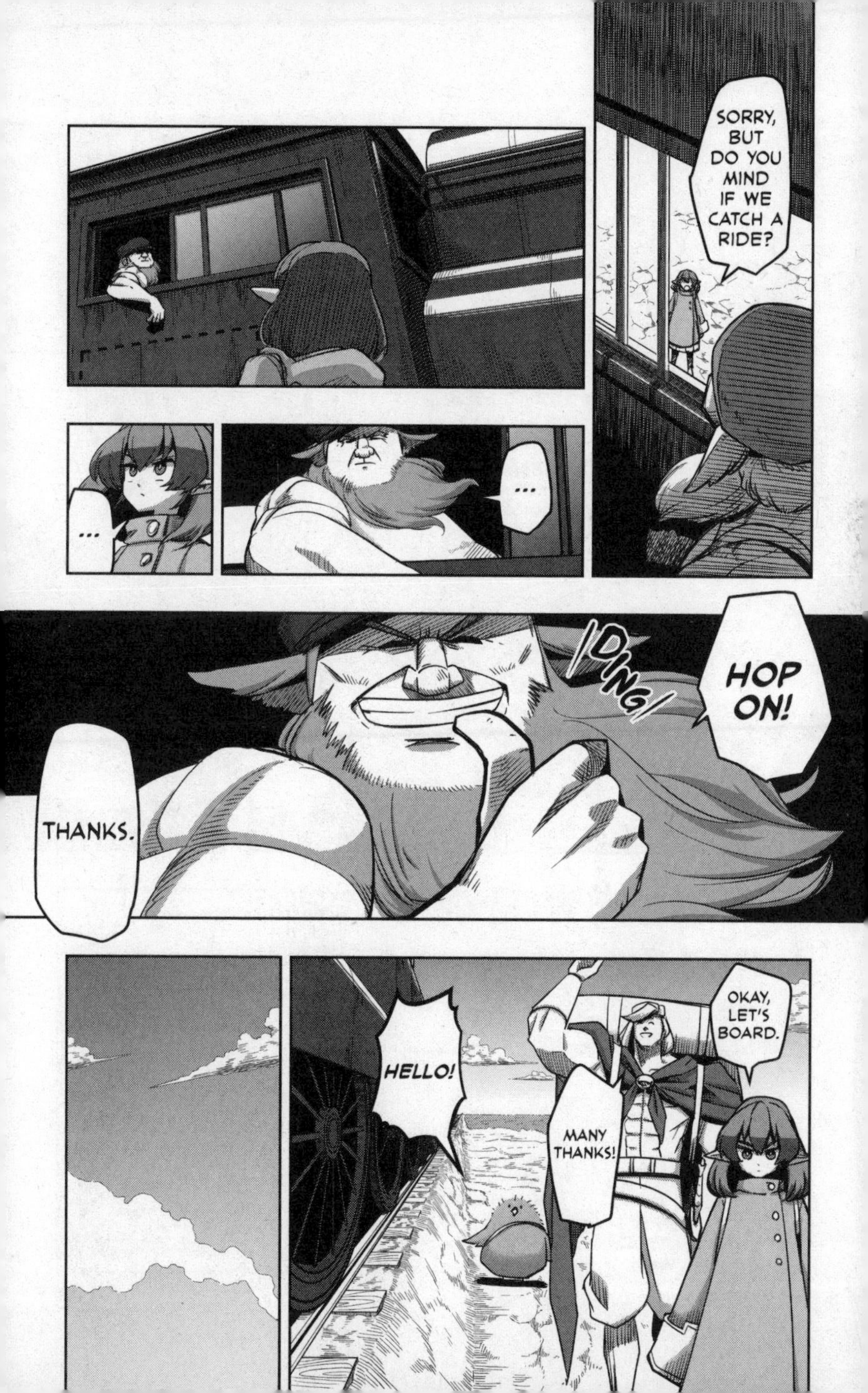
SORRY, BUT DO YOU MIND IF WE CATCH A RIDE?
...
...
DING!
HOP ON!
THANKS.
OKAY, LET'S BOARD.
MANY THANKS!
HELLO!

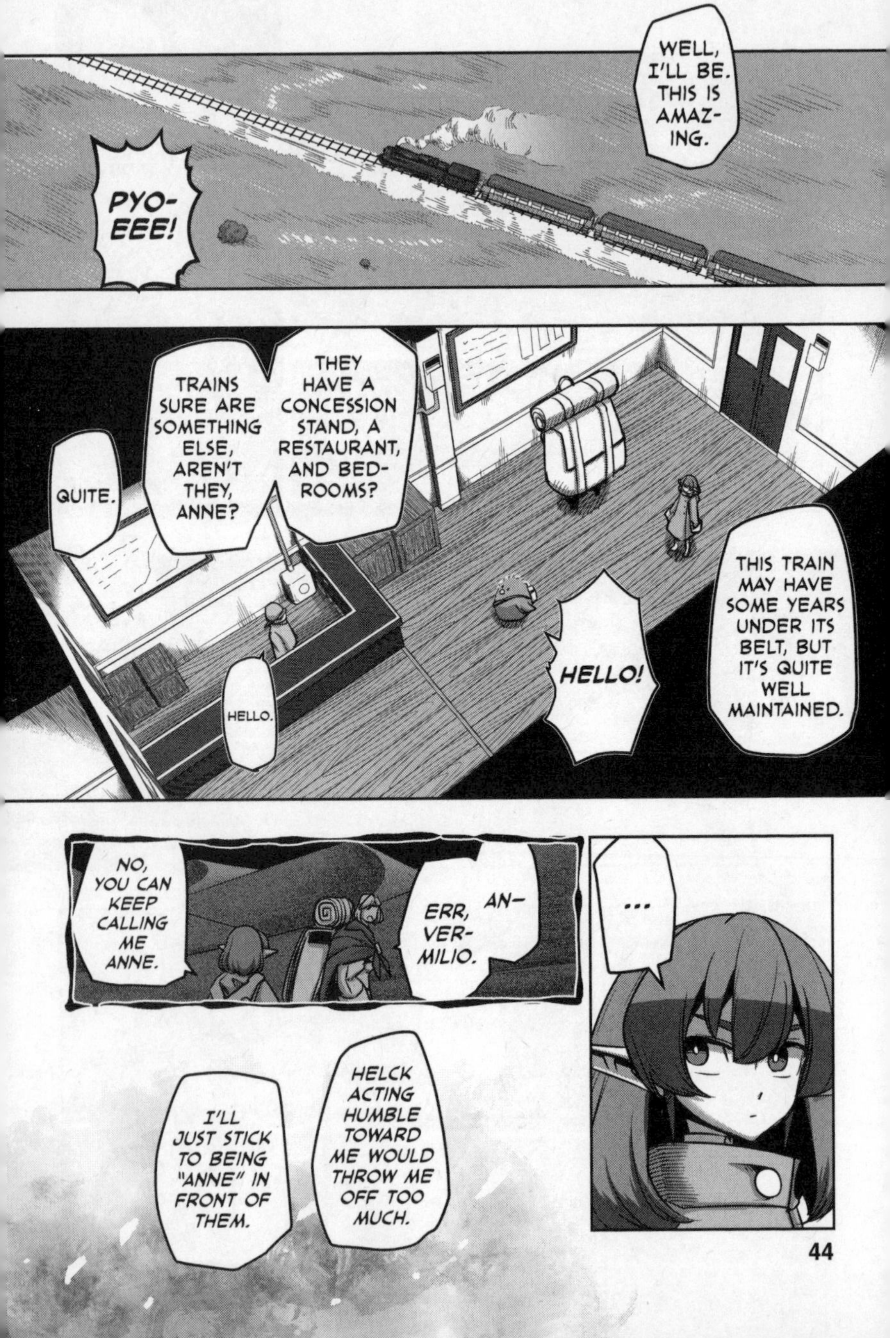

WELL, I'LL BE. THIS IS AMAZ-ING.
PYO-EEE!
THEY HAVE A CONCESSION STAND, A RESTAURANT, AND BED-ROOMS?
TRAINS SURE ARE SOMETHING ELSE, AREN'T THEY, ANNE?
QUITE.
THIS TRAIN MAY HAVE SOME YEARS UNDER ITS BELT, BUT IT'S QUITE WELL MAINTAINED.
HELLO!
HELLO.
...
AN—
ERR, VER-MILIO.
NO, YOU CAN KEEP CALLING ME ANNE.
HELCK ACTING HUMBLE TOWARD ME WOULD THROW ME OFF TOO MUCH.
I'LL JUST STICK TO BEING "ANNE" IN FRONT OF THEM.

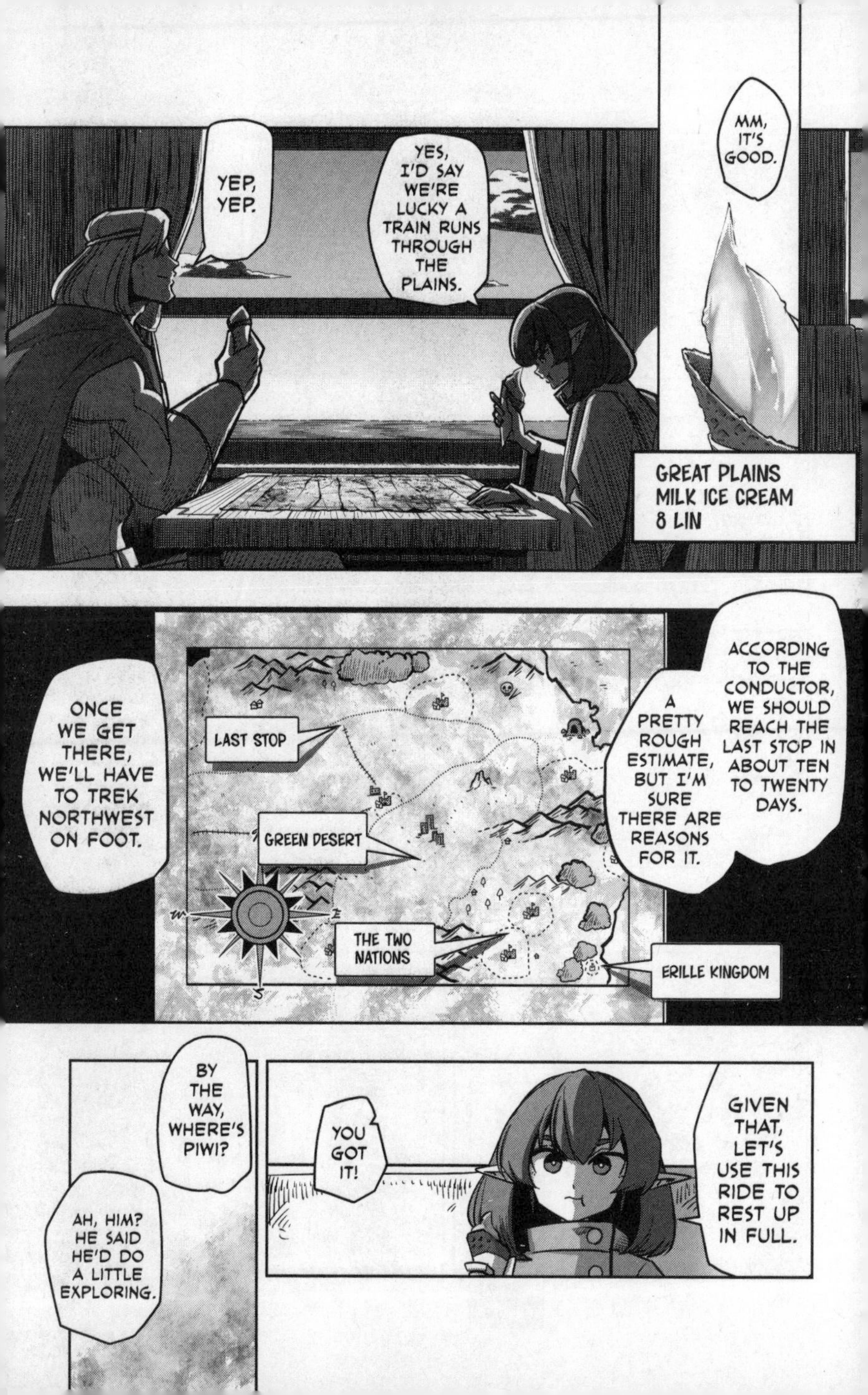
MM, IT'S GOOD.
GREAT PLAINS MILK ICE CREAM 8 LIN
YES, I'D SAY WE'RE LUCKY A TRAIN RUNS THROUGH THE PLAINS.
YEP, YEP.
ACCORDING TO THE CONDUCTOR, WE SHOULD REACH THE LAST STOP IN ABOUT TEN TO TWENTY DAYS.
A PRETTY ROUGH ESTIMATE, BUT I'M SURE THERE ARE REASONS FOR IT.
LAST STOP
ONCE WE GET THERE, WE'LL HAVE TO TREK NORTHWEST ON FOOT.
GREEN DESERT
THE TWO NATIONS
ERILLE KINGDOM
GIVEN THAT, LET'S USE THIS RIDE TO REST UP IN FULL.
YOU GOT IT!
BY THE WAY, WHERE'S PIWI?
AH, HIM? HE SAID HE'D DO A LITTLE EXPLORING.

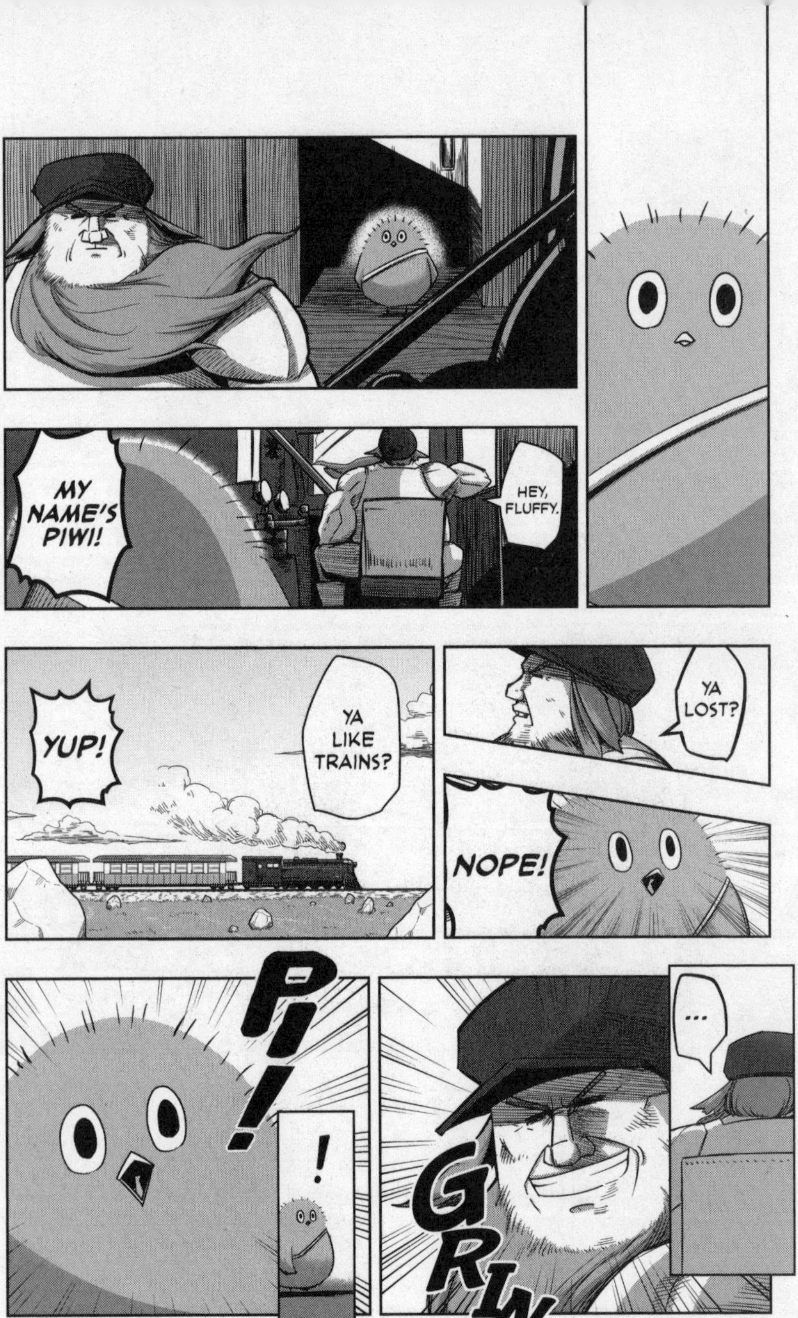
HEY, FLUFFY.
MY NAME'S PIWI!
YA LOST?
NOPE!
YA LIKE TRAINS?
YUP!
...
GRIN
!
PI!

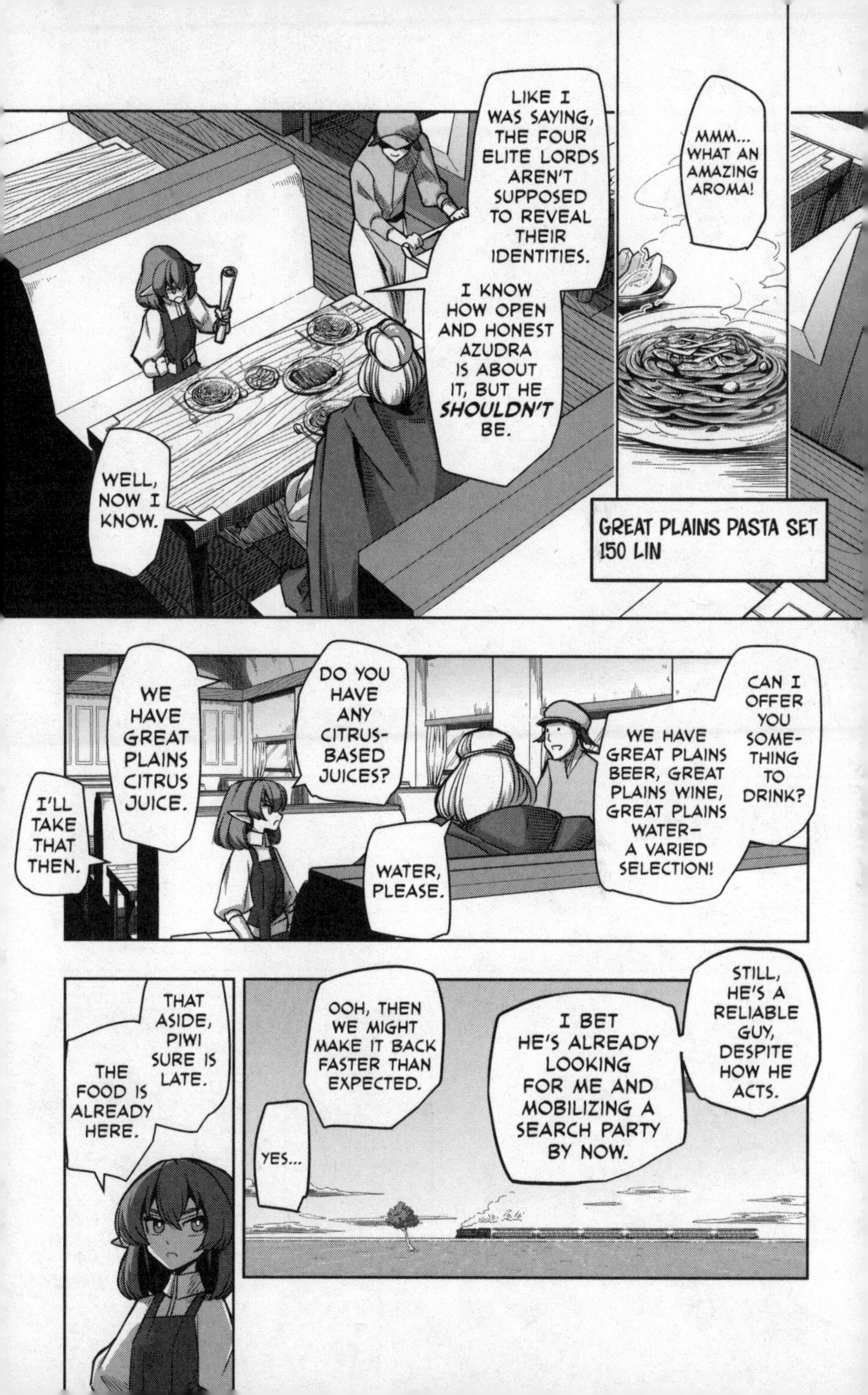
MMM... WHAT AN AMAZING AROMA!
GREAT PLAINS PASTA SET 150 LIN
LIKE I WAS SAYING, THE FOUR ELITE LORDS AREN'T SUPPOSED TO REVEAL THEIR IDENTITIES.
I KNOW HOW OPEN AND HONEST AZUDRA IS ABOUT IT, BUT HE *SHOULDN'T* BE.
WELL, NOW I KNOW.
CAN I OFFER YOU SOME-THING TO DRINK?
WE HAVE GREAT PLAINS BEER, GREAT PLAINS WINE, GREAT PLAINS WATER– A VARIED SELECTION!
WATER, PLEASE.
DO YOU HAVE ANY CITRUS-BASED JUICES?
WE HAVE GREAT PLAINS CITRUS JUICE.
I'LL TAKE THAT THEN.
STILL, HE'S A RELIABLE GUY, DESPITE HOW HE ACTS.
I BET HE'S ALREADY LOOKING FOR ME AND MOBILIZING A SEARCH PARTY BY NOW.
OOH, THEN WE MIGHT MAKE IT BACK FASTER THAN EXPECTED.
YES...
THAT ASIDE, PIWI SURE IS LATE.
THE FOOD IS ALREADY HERE.

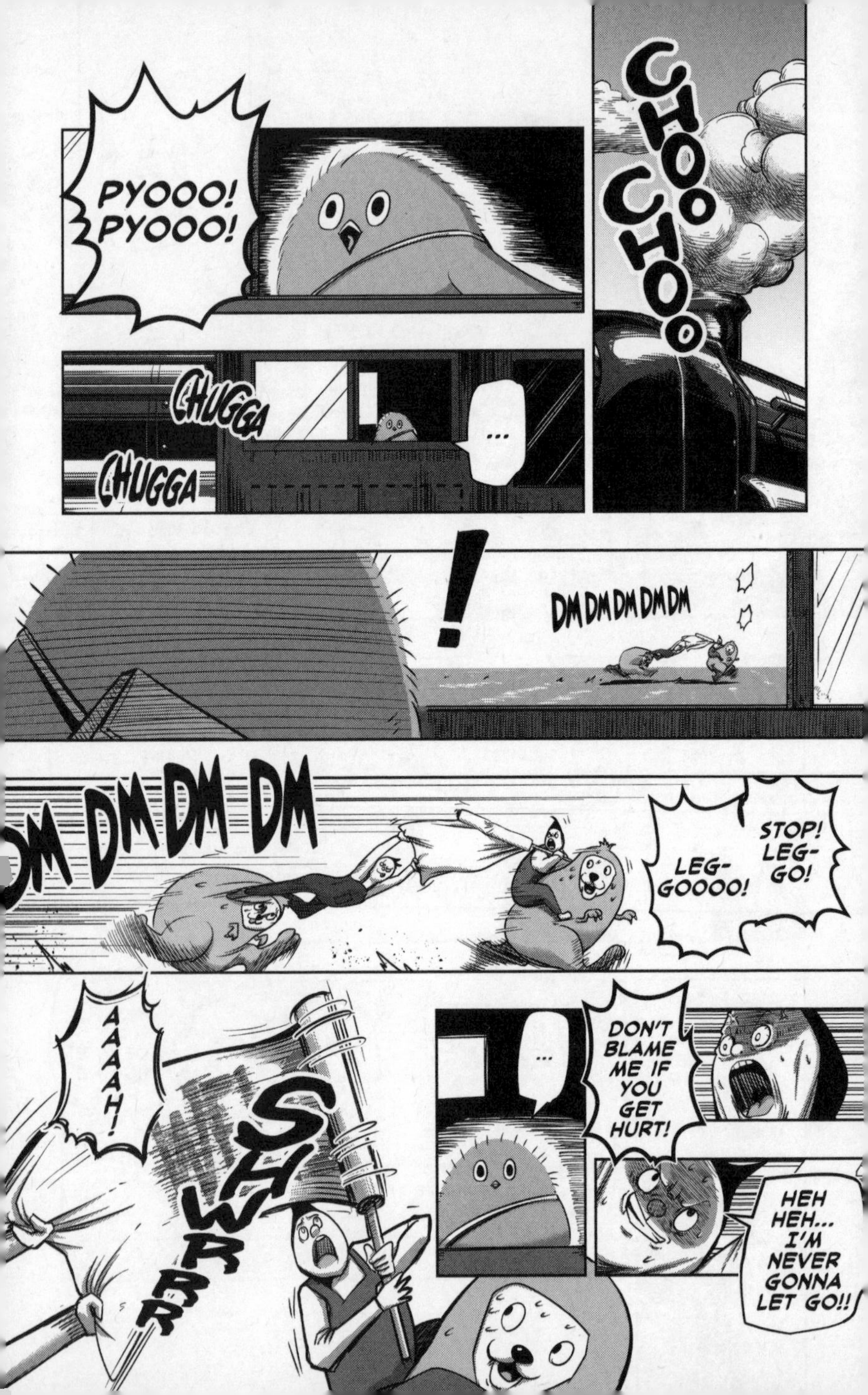
CHOO CHOO
PYOOO! PYOOO!
CHUGGA
CHUGGA
...
!
DMDMDMDMDM
DM DM DM DM
STOP! LEG-GO!
LEG-GOOOO!
DON'T BLAME ME IF YOU GET HURT!
HEH HEH... I'M NEVER GONNA LET GO!!
...
AAAAH!
SHWRRR

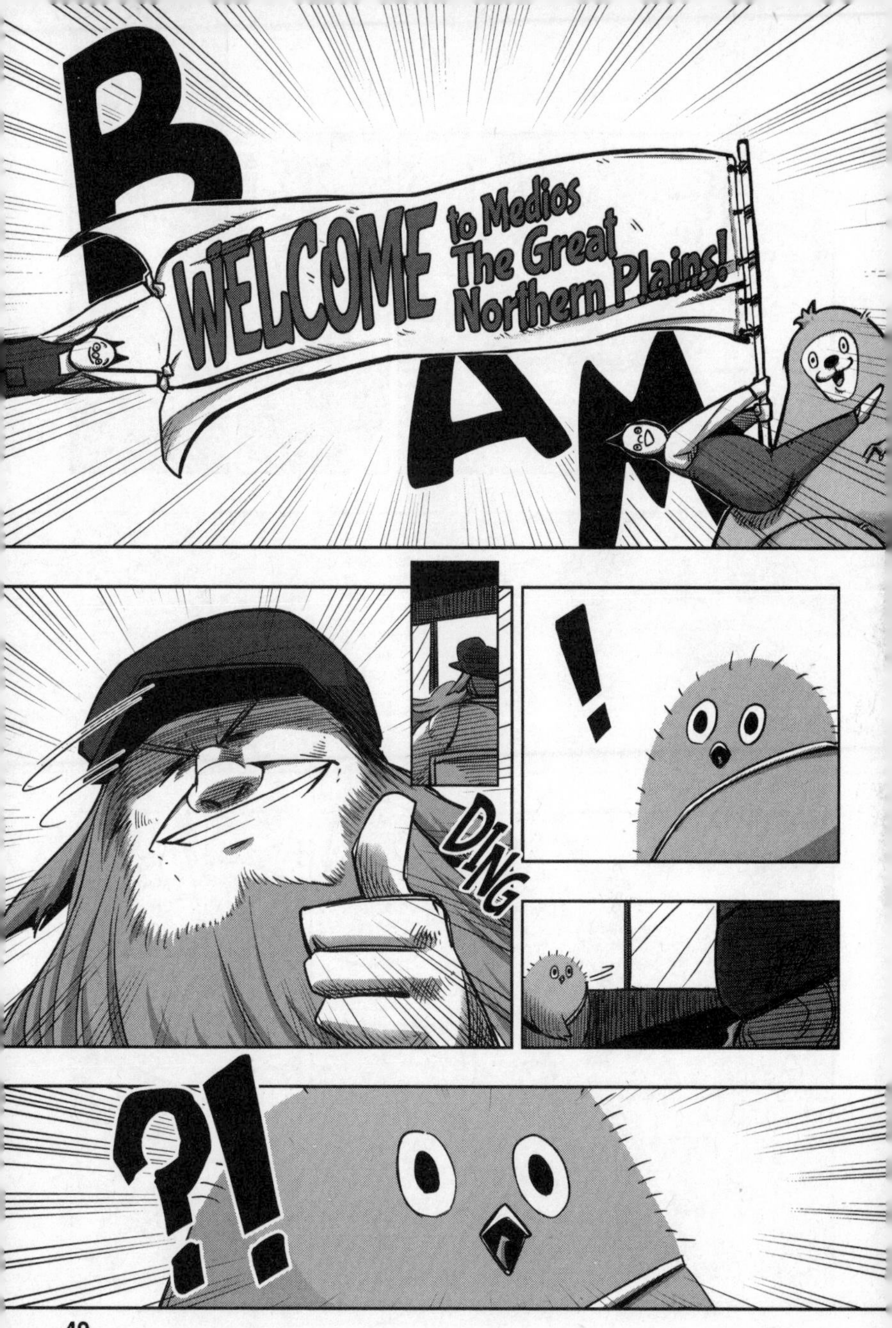
BAM
WELCOME to Medios The Great Northern Plains!
!
DING
?!

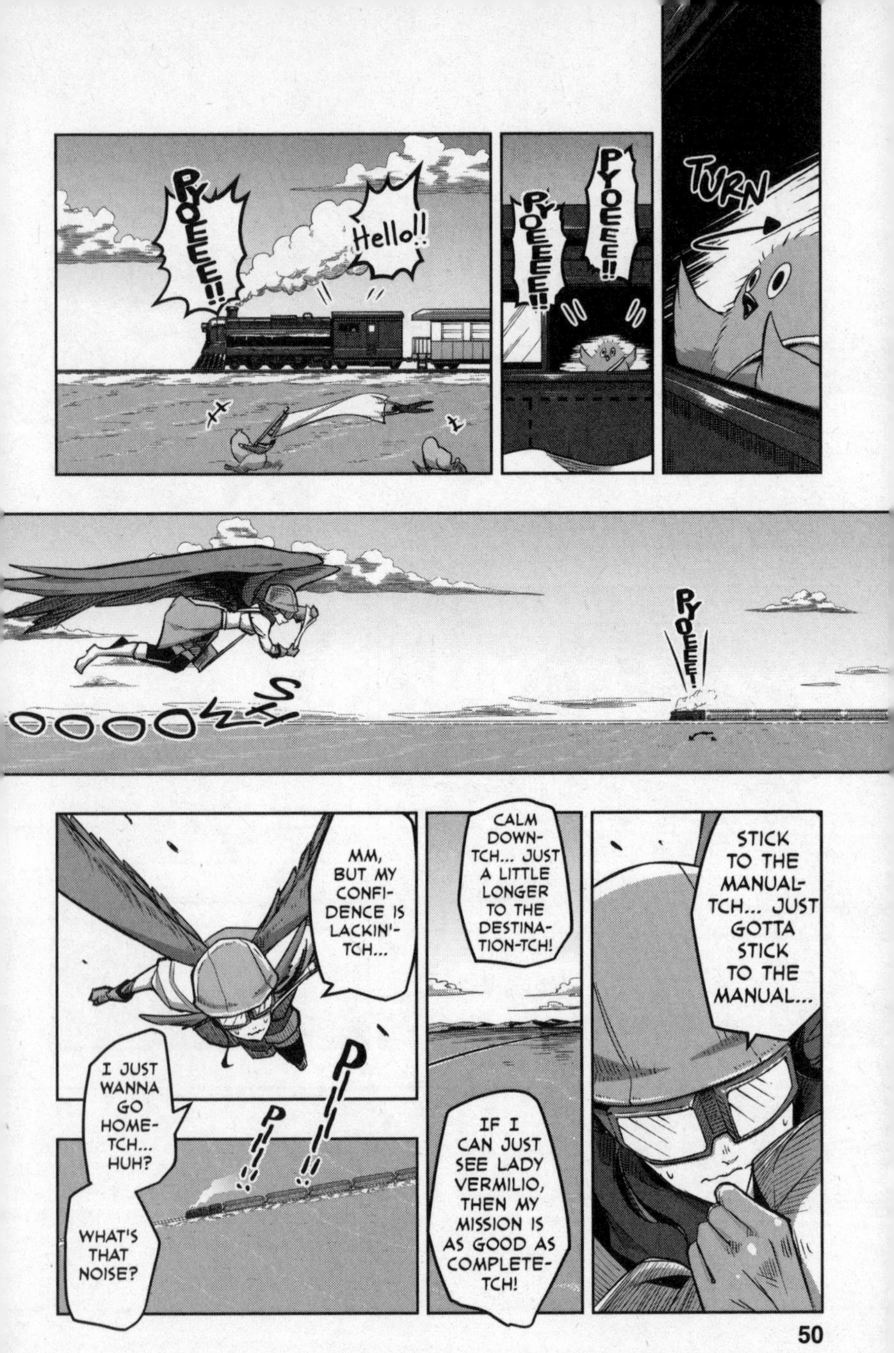
TURN
PYOEEE!!
PYOEEEE!!
Hello!!
PYOEEE!!
PYOEEE!
STICK TO THE MANUAL-TCH... JUST GOTTA STICK TO THE MANUAL...
CALM DOWN-TCH... JUST A LITTLE LONGER TO THE DESTINATION-TCH!
IF I CAN JUST SEE LADY VERMILIO, THEN MY MISSION IS AS GOOD AS COMPLETE-TCH!
MM, BUT MY CONFIDENCE IS LACKIN'-TCH...
I JUST WANNA GO HOME-TCH... HUH?
PI!!
PI!!
WHAT'S THAT NOISE?

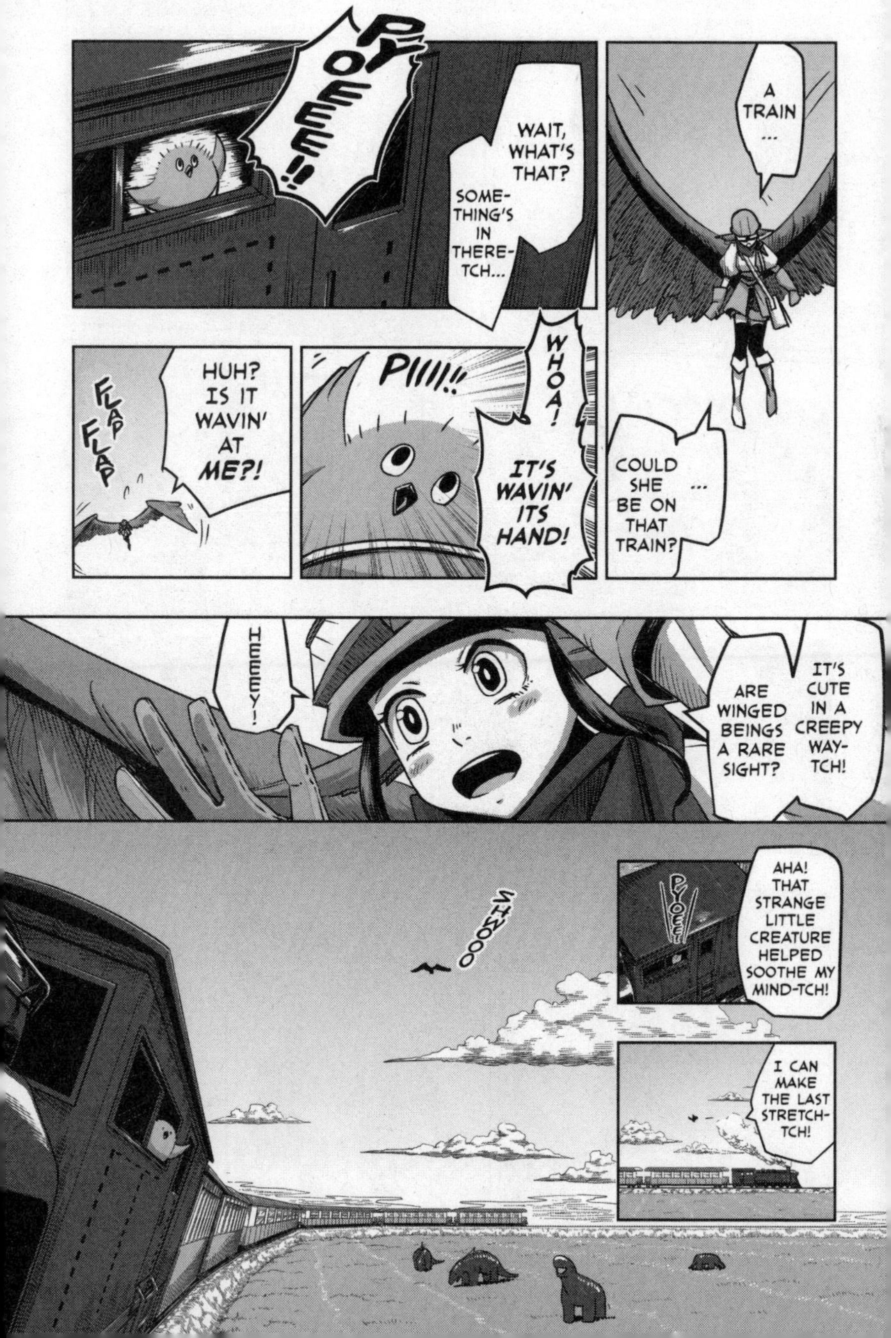
A TRAIN ...
PYOEEE!!
WAIT, WHAT'S THAT?
SOMETHING'S IN THERE-TCH...
COULD SHE BE ON THAT TRAIN? ...
WHOA!
IT'S WAVIN' ITS HAND!
PI!!!!!
HUH? IS IT WAVIN' AT ME?!
FLAP FLAP
IT'S CUTE IN A CREEPY WAY-TCH!
ARE WINGED BEINGS A RARE SIGHT?
HEEEEY!
AHA! THAT STRANGE LITTLE CREATURE HELPED SOOTHE MY MIND-TCH!
PYOEE!!
I CAN MAKE THE LAST STRETCH-TCH!
SHWOOO

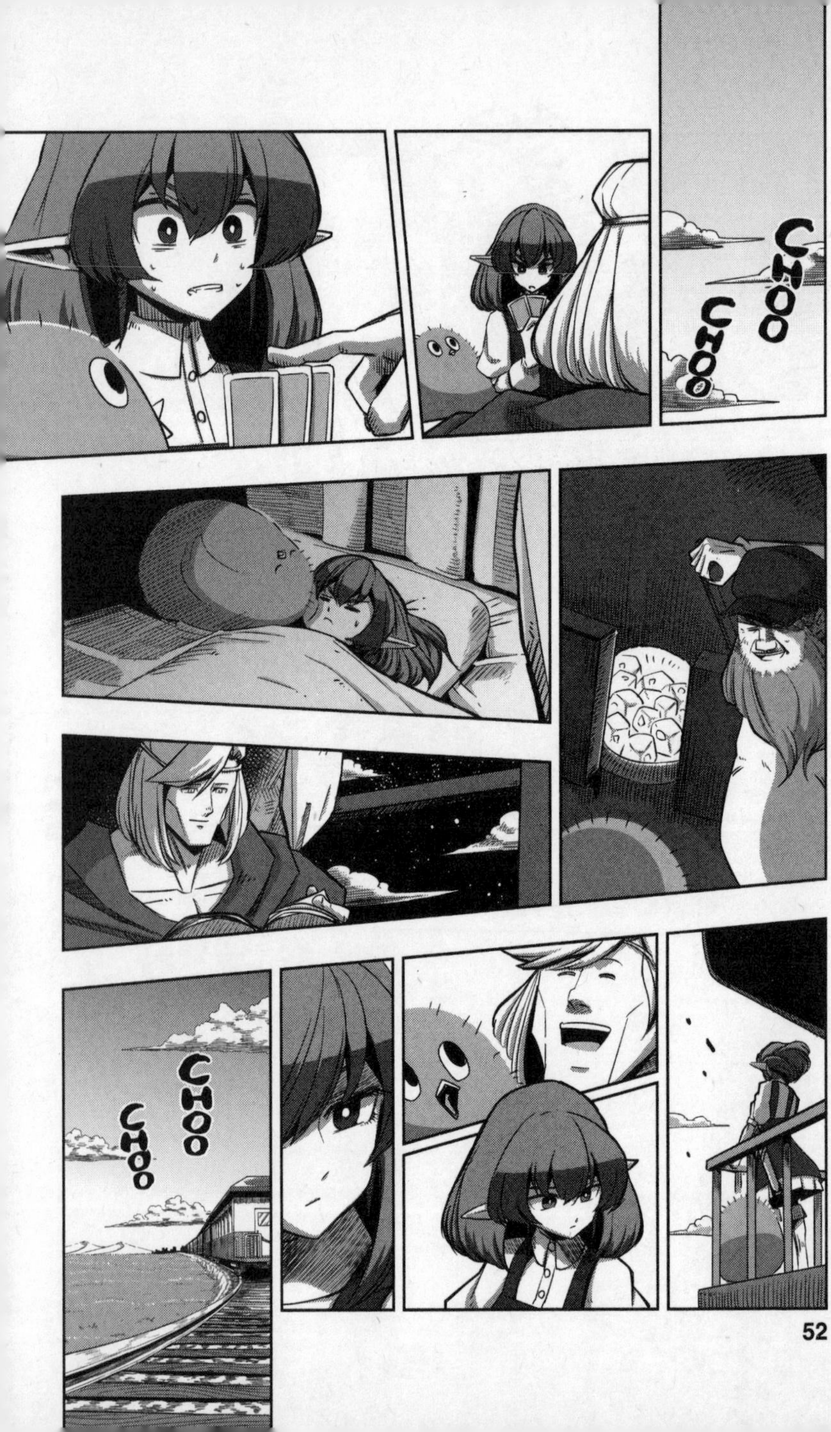
CHOO CHOO
CHOO CHOO

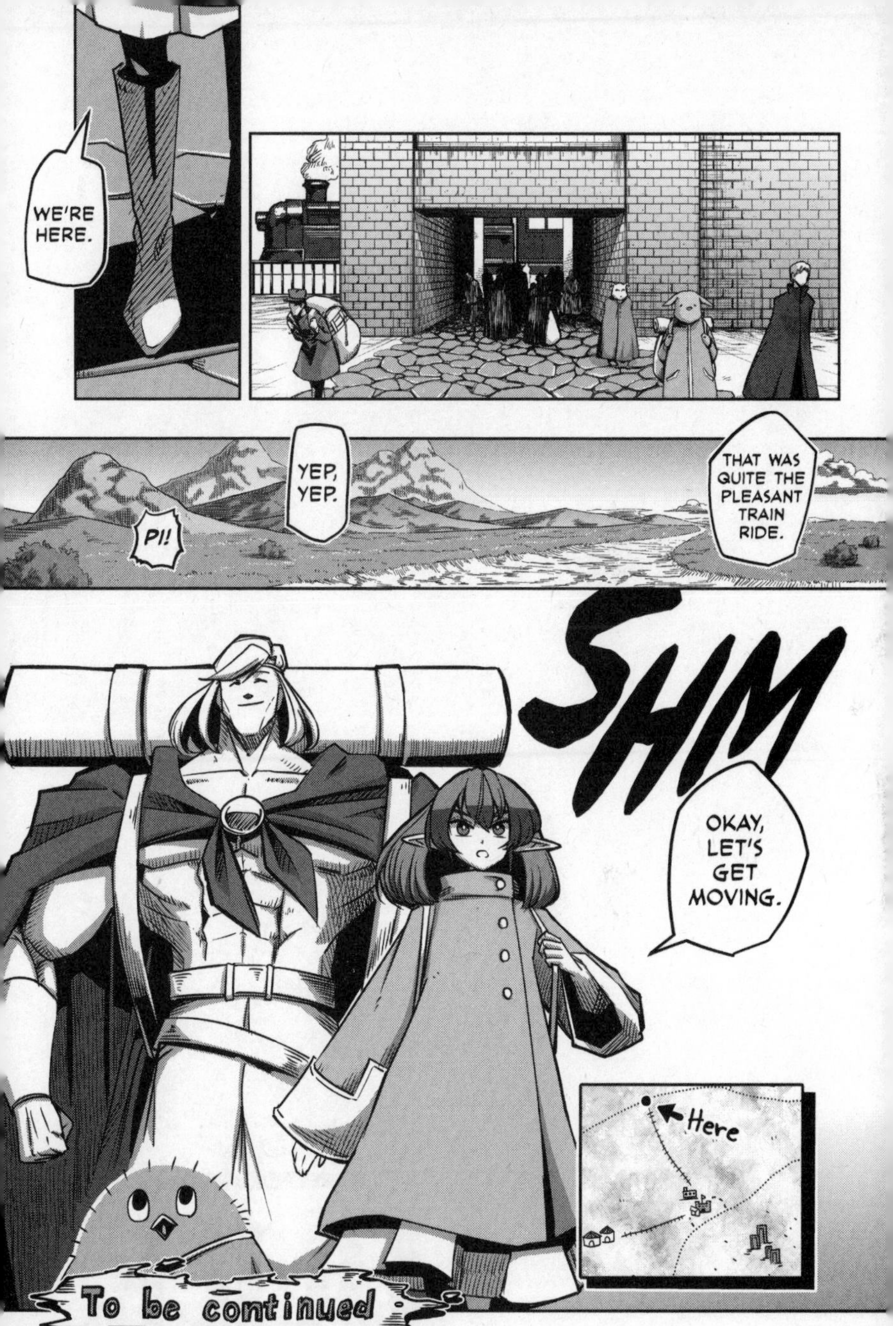
WE'RE HERE.
THAT WAS QUITE THE PLEASANT TRAIN RIDE.
YEP, YEP.
PI!
SHM
OKAY, LET'S GET MOVING.
Here
To be continued

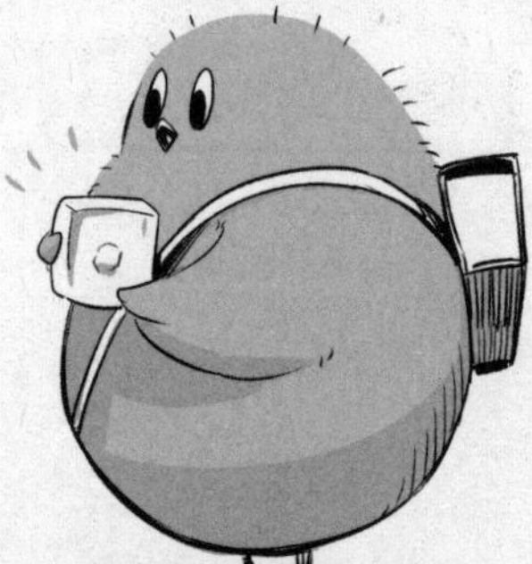

Helck

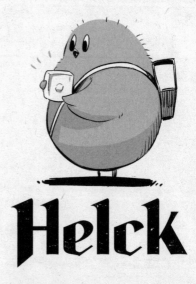

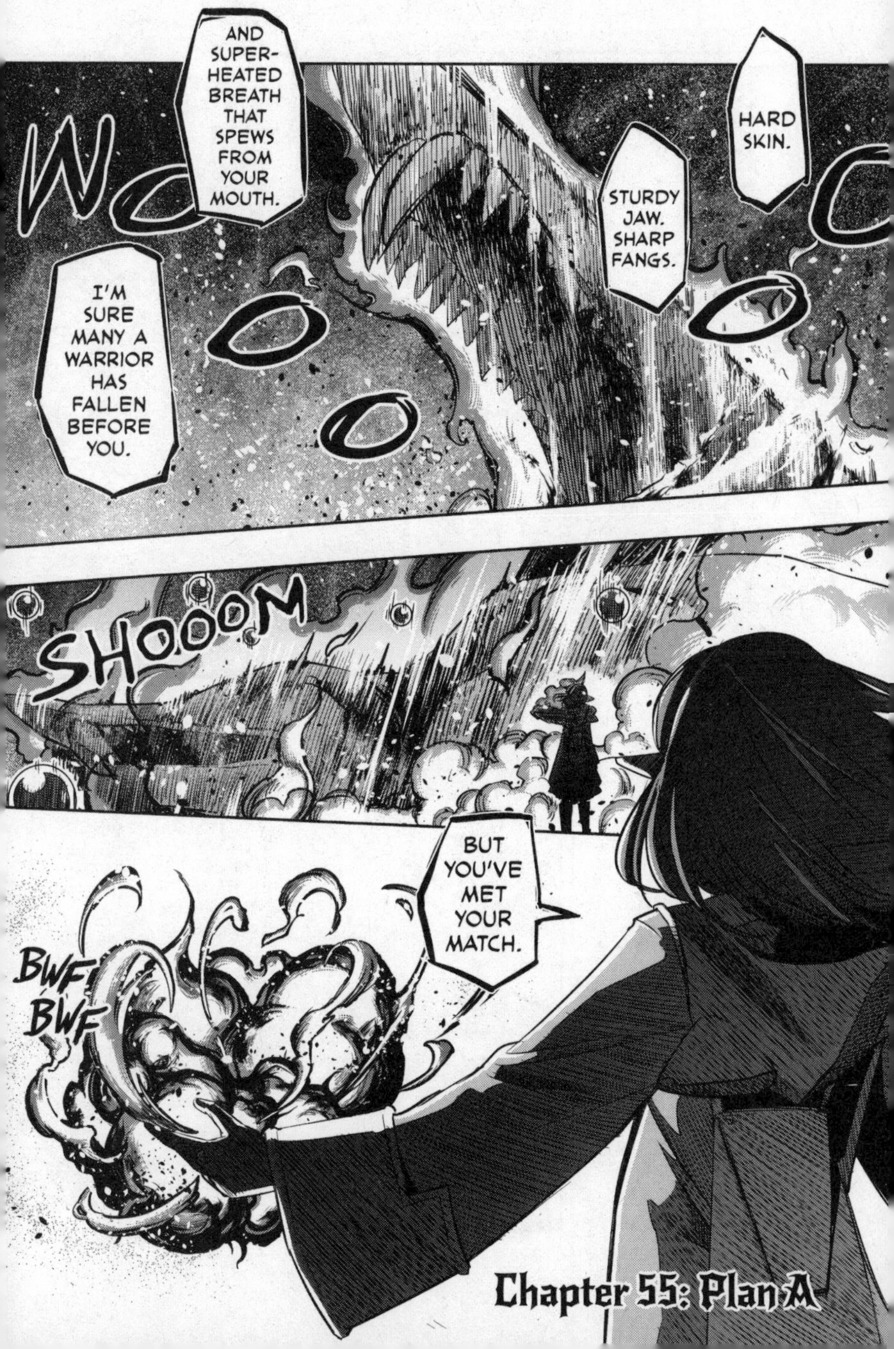
HARD SKIN.
STURDY JAW. SHARP FANGS.
AND SUPER-HEATED BREATH THAT SPEWS FROM YOUR MOUTH.
I'M SURE MANY A WARRIOR HAS FALLEN BEFORE YOU.
WOOOOO
SHOOOM
BUT YOU'VE MET YOUR MATCH.
BWF BWF

Chapter 55: Plan A

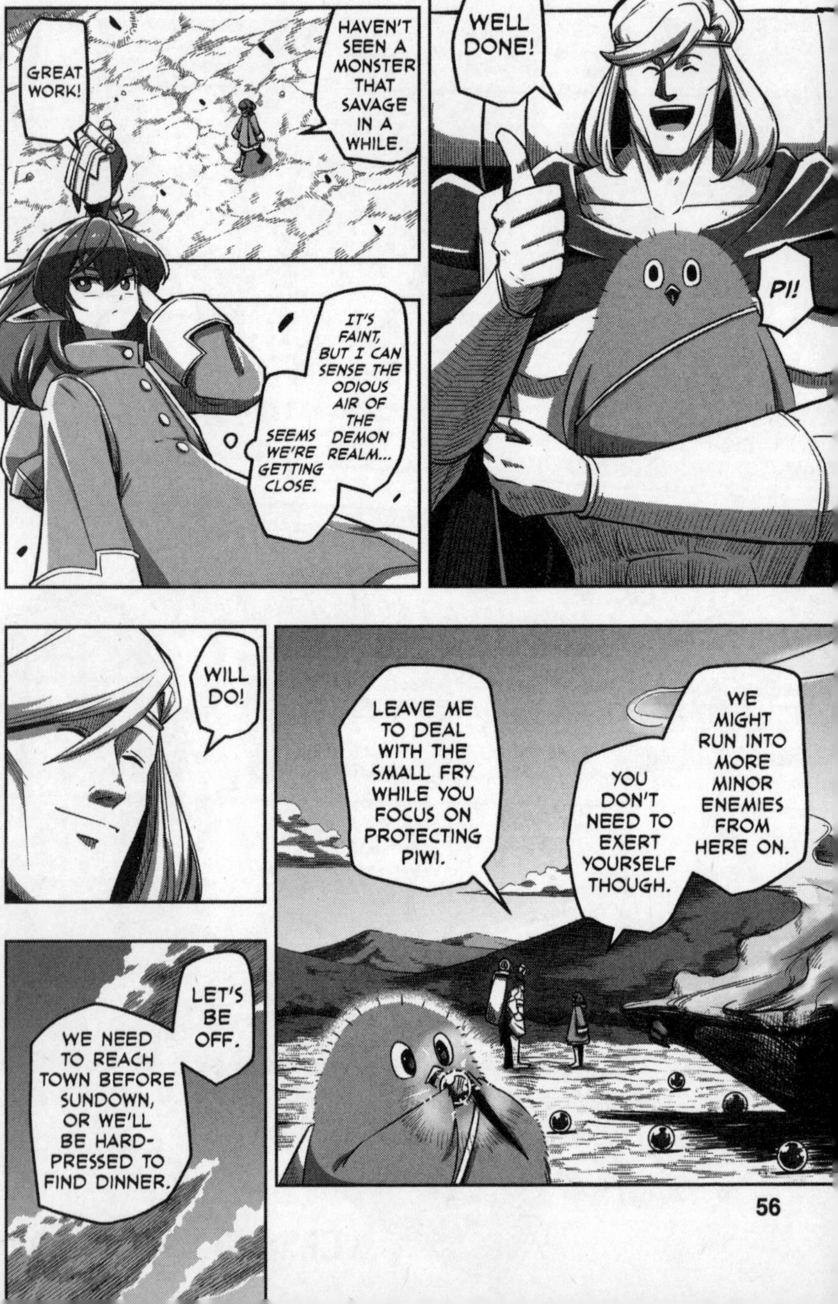

WELL DONE!
PI!
HAVEN'T SEEN A MONSTER THAT SAVAGE IN A WHILE.
GREAT WORK!
IT'S FAINT, BUT I CAN SENSE THE ODIOUS AIR OF THE DEMON REALM...
SEEMS WE'RE GETTING CLOSE.
WE MIGHT RUN INTO MORE MINOR ENEMIES FROM HERE ON.
YOU DON'T NEED TO EXERT YOURSELF THOUGH.
LEAVE ME TO DEAL WITH THE SMALL FRY WHILE YOU FOCUS ON PROTECTING PIWI.
WILL DO!
LET'S BE OFF.
WE NEED TO REACH TOWN BEFORE SUNDOWN, OR WE'LL BE HARD-PRESSED TO FIND DINNER.

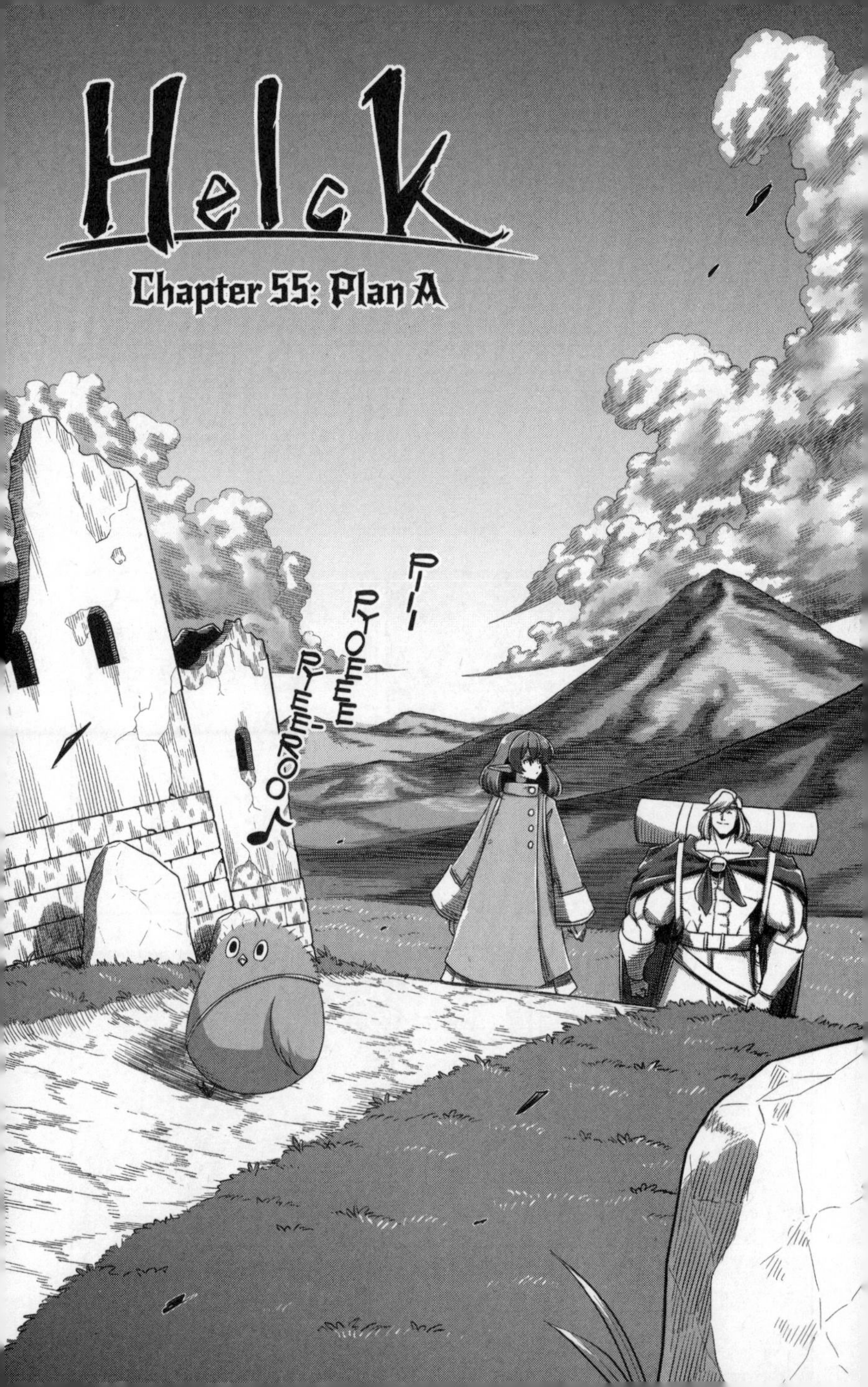
Helck
Chapter 55: Plan A
PIII
PYOEEE
PYEEROOO♪

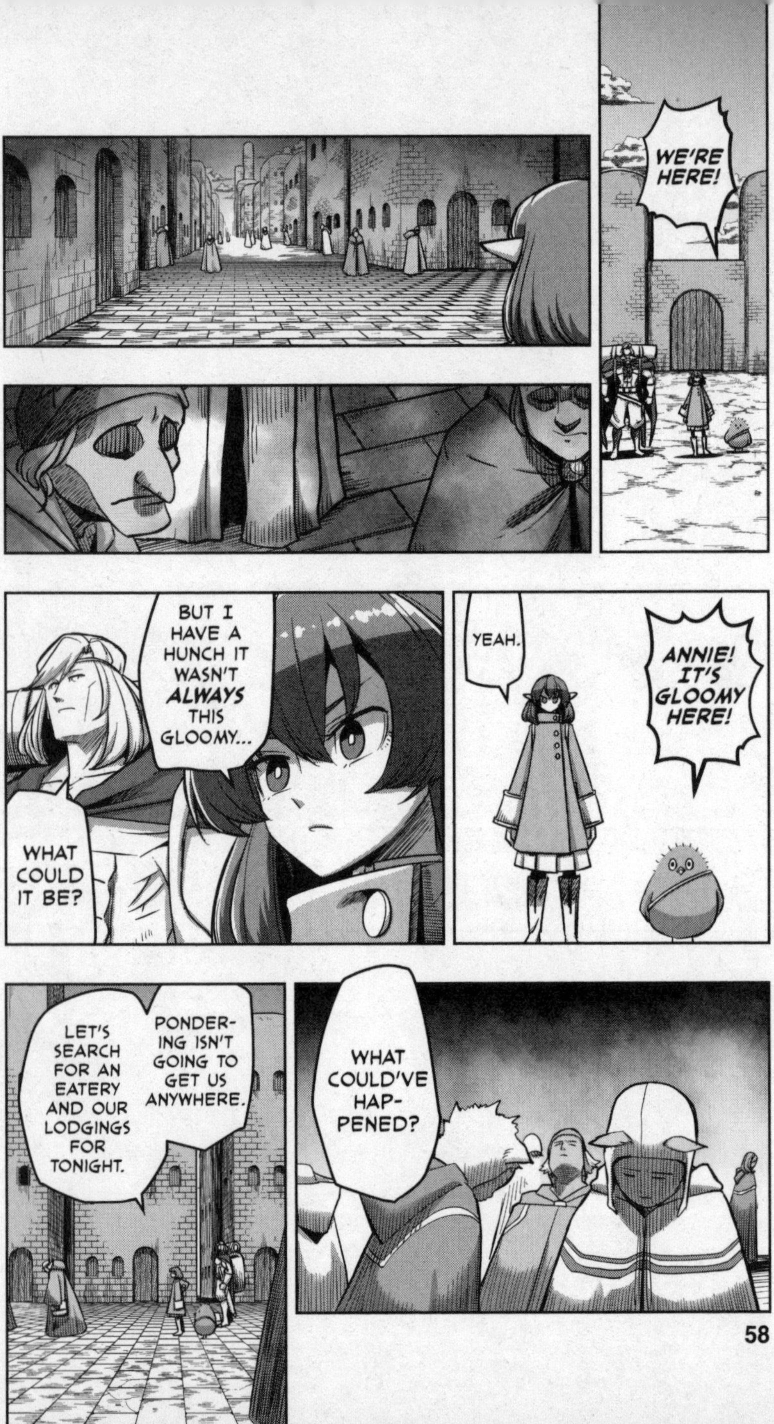
WE'RE HERE!
ANNIE! IT'S GLOOMY HERE!
YEAH.
BUT I HAVE A HUNCH IT WASN'T ALWAYS THIS GLOOMY...
WHAT COULD IT BE?
WHAT COULD'VE HAP-PENED?
PONDER-ING ISN'T GOING TO GET US ANYWHERE.
LET'S SEARCH FOR AN EATERY AND OUR LODGINGS FOR TONIGHT.

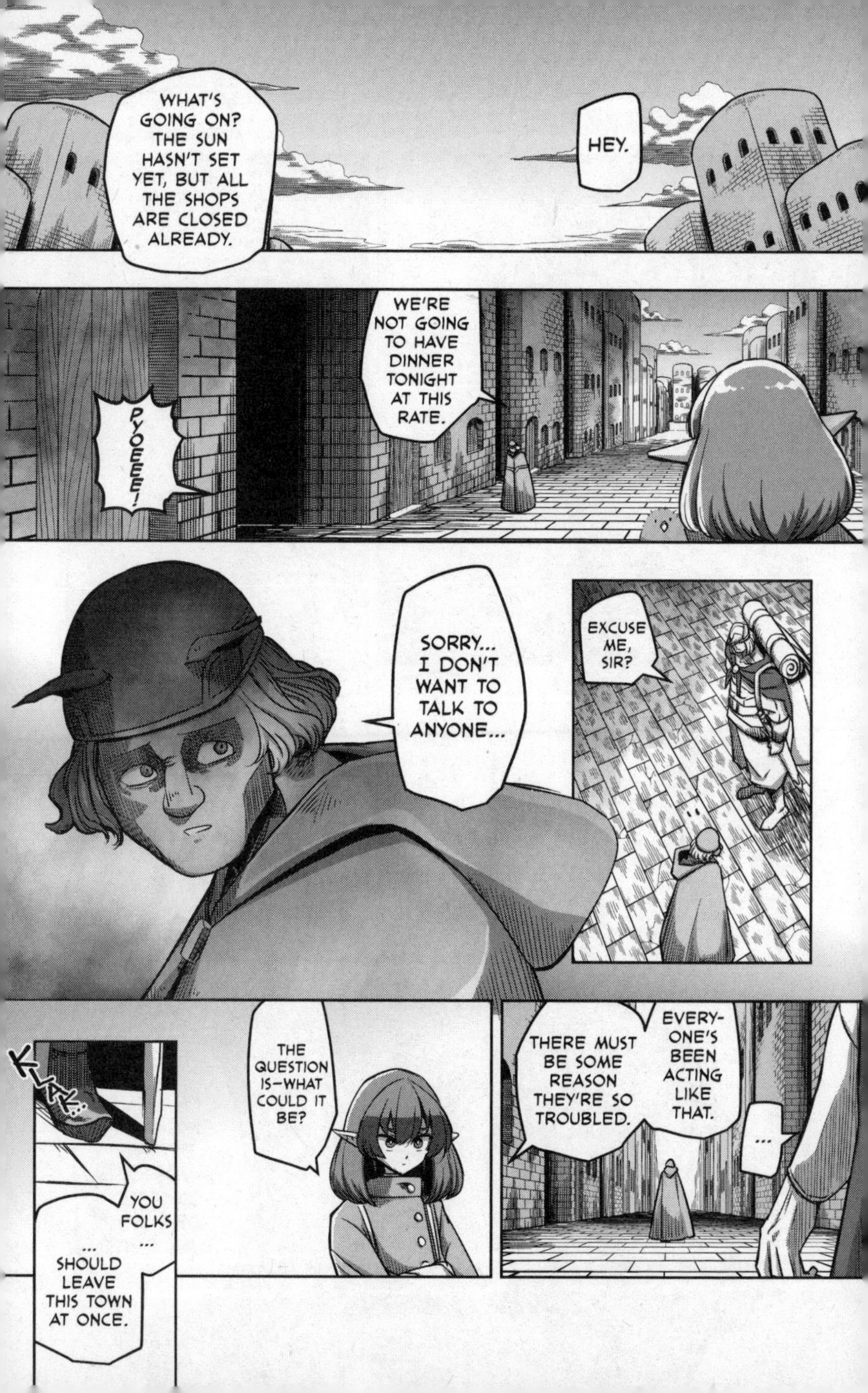
HEY.
WHAT'S GOING ON? THE SUN HASN'T SET YET, BUT ALL THE SHOPS ARE CLOSED ALREADY.
WE'RE NOT GOING TO HAVE DINNER TONIGHT AT THIS RATE.
PYOEEE!
EXCUSE ME, SIR?
SORRY... I DON'T WANT TO TALK TO ANYONE...
EVERY-ONE'S BEEN ACTING LIKE THAT.
THERE MUST BE SOME REASON THEY'RE SO TROUBLED.
...
THE QUESTION IS—WHAT COULD IT BE?
KLAK...
YOU FOLKS...
...SHOULD LEAVE THIS TOWN AT ONCE.

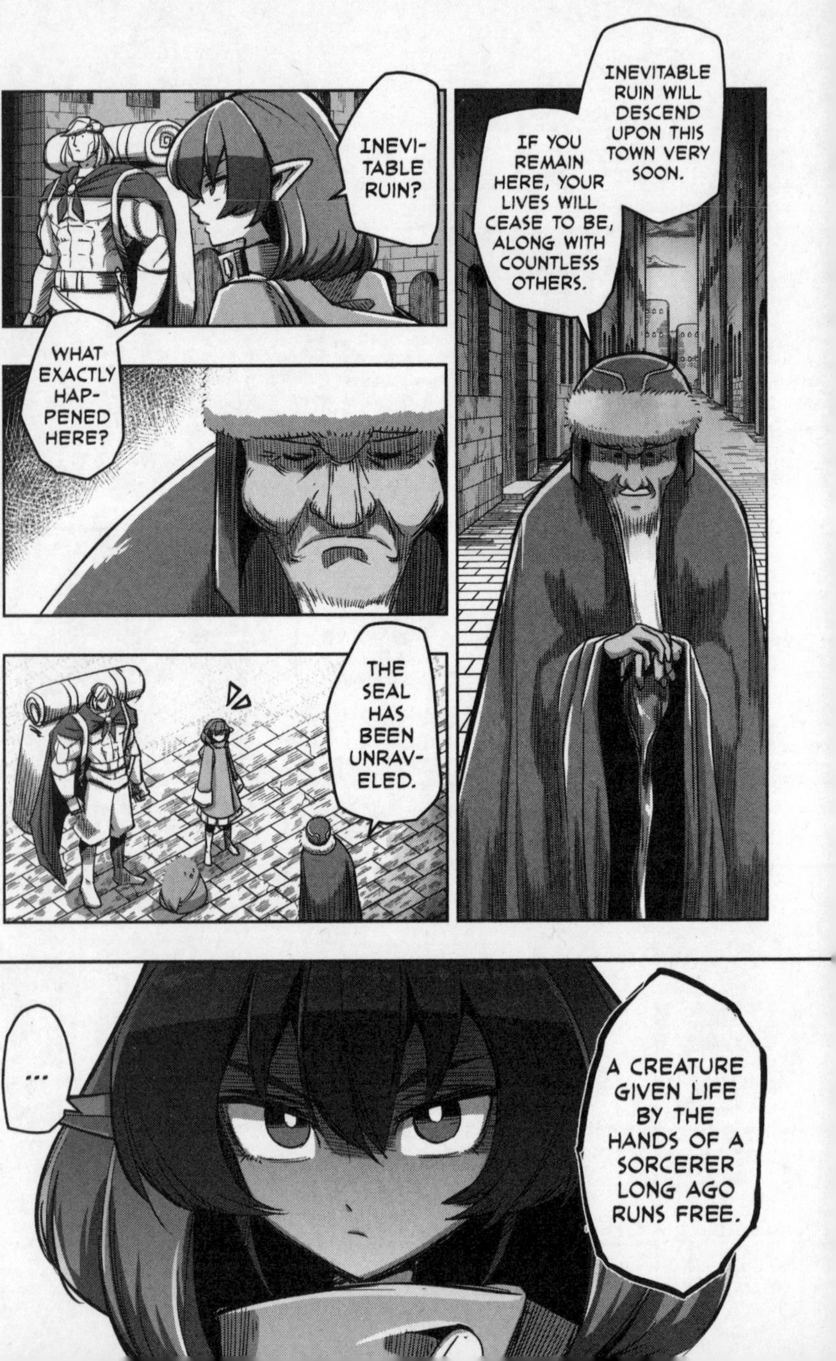
INEVITABLE RUIN WILL DESCEND UPON THIS TOWN VERY SOON.
IF YOU REMAIN HERE, YOUR LIVES WILL CEASE TO BE, ALONG WITH COUNTLESS OTHERS.
INEVI-TABLE RUIN?
WHAT EXACTLY HAP-PENED HERE?
THE SEAL HAS BEEN UNRAV-ELED.
A CREATURE GIVEN LIFE BY THE HANDS OF A SORCERER LONG AGO RUNS FREE.
...

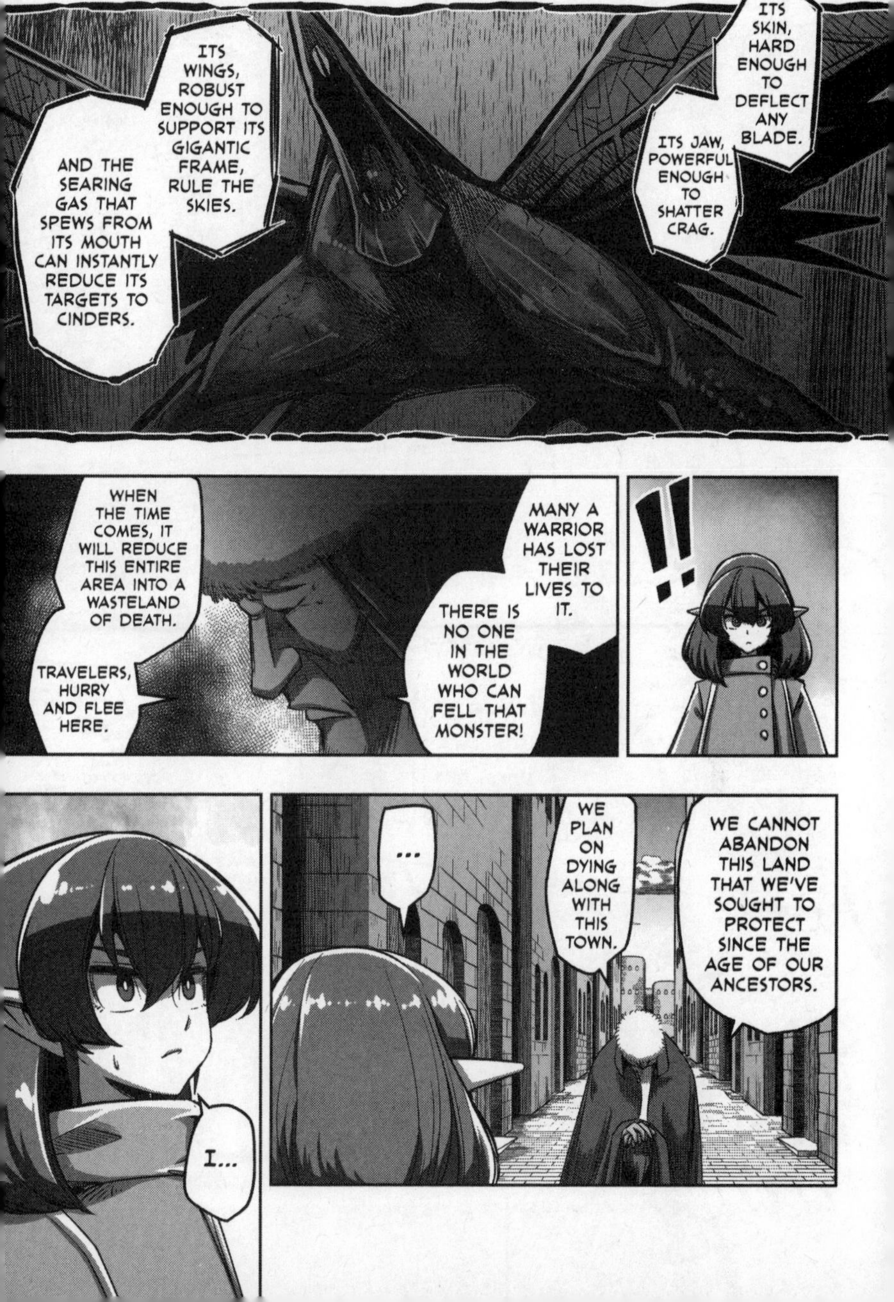
ITS SKIN, HARD ENOUGH TO DEFLECT ANY BLADE.
ITS JAW, POWERFUL ENOUGH TO SHATTER CRAG.
ITS WINGS, ROBUST ENOUGH TO SUPPORT ITS GIGANTIC FRAME, RULE THE SKIES.
AND THE SEARING GAS THAT SPEWS FROM ITS MOUTH CAN INSTANTLY REDUCE ITS TARGETS TO CINDERS.
!!
MANY A WARRIOR HAS LOST THEIR LIVES TO IT.
THERE IS NO ONE IN THE WORLD WHO CAN FELL THAT MONSTER!
WHEN THE TIME COMES, IT WILL REDUCE THIS ENTIRE AREA INTO A WASTELAND OF DEATH.
TRAVELERS, HURRY AND FLEE HERE.
WE CANNOT ABANDON THIS LAND THAT WE'VE SOUGHT TO PROTECT SINCE THE AGE OF OUR ANCESTORS.
WE PLAN ON DYING ALONG WITH THIS TOWN.
...
I...

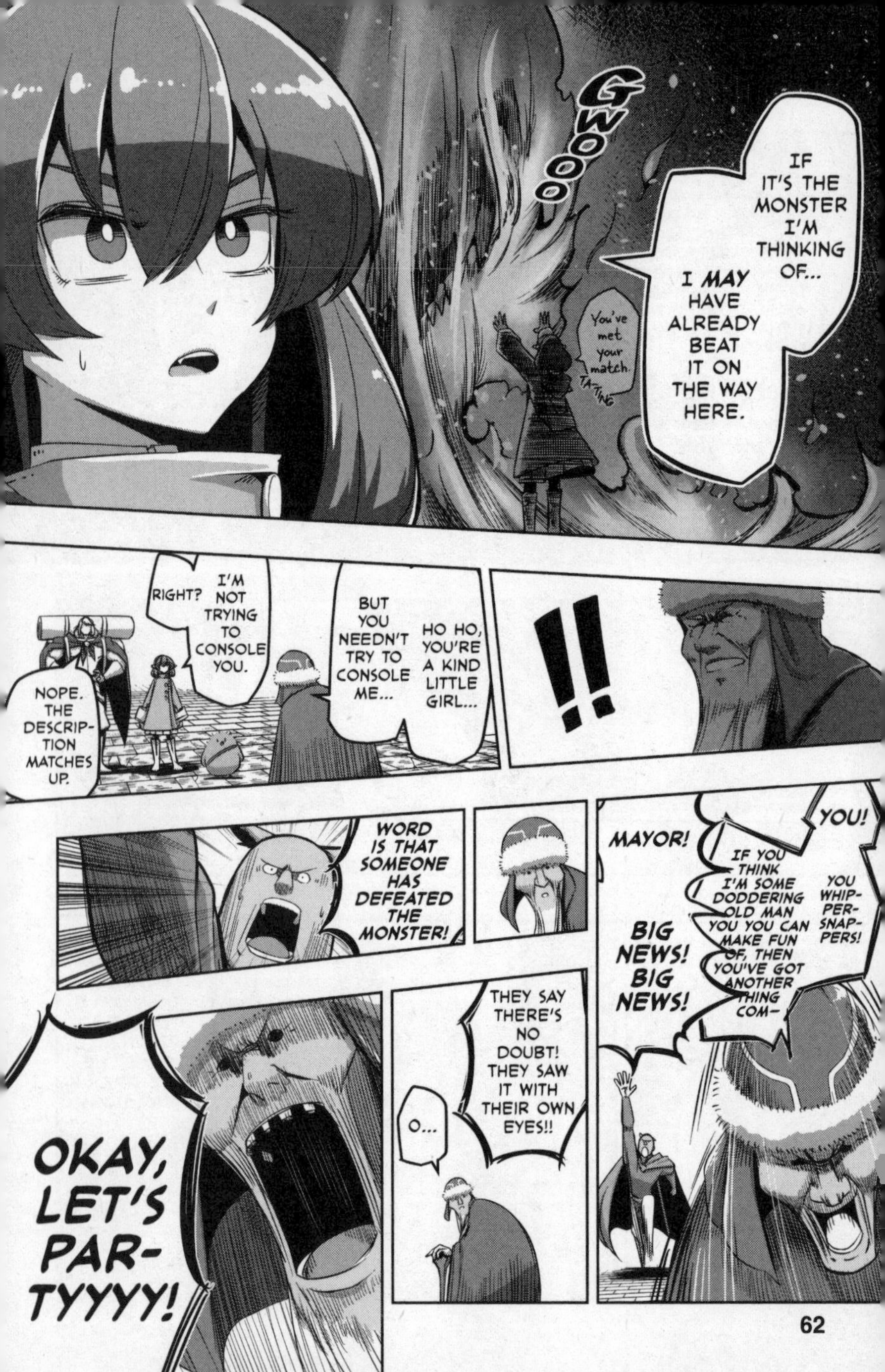
IF IT'S THE MONSTER I'M THINKING OF...
I *MAY* HAVE ALREADY BEAT IT ON THE WAY HERE.
You've met your match.
TA-TING
GWOOOO
!!
HO HO, YOU'RE A KIND LITTLE GIRL...
BUT YOU NEEDN'T TRY TO CONSOLE ME...
I'M NOT TRYING TO CONSOLE YOU.
RIGHT?
NOPE. THE DESCRIPTION MATCHES UP.
YOU!
YOU WHIPPERSNAPPERS!
IF YOU THINK I'M SOME DODDERING OLD MAN YOU YOU CAN MAKE FUN OF, THEN YOU'VE GOT ANOTHER THING COM—
MAYOR!
BIG NEWS! BIG NEWS!
WORD IS THAT SOMEONE HAS DEFEATED THE MONSTER!
THEY SAY THERE'S NO DOUBT! THEY SAW IT WITH THEIR OWN EYES!!
O...
OKAY, LET'S PAR-TYYYY!

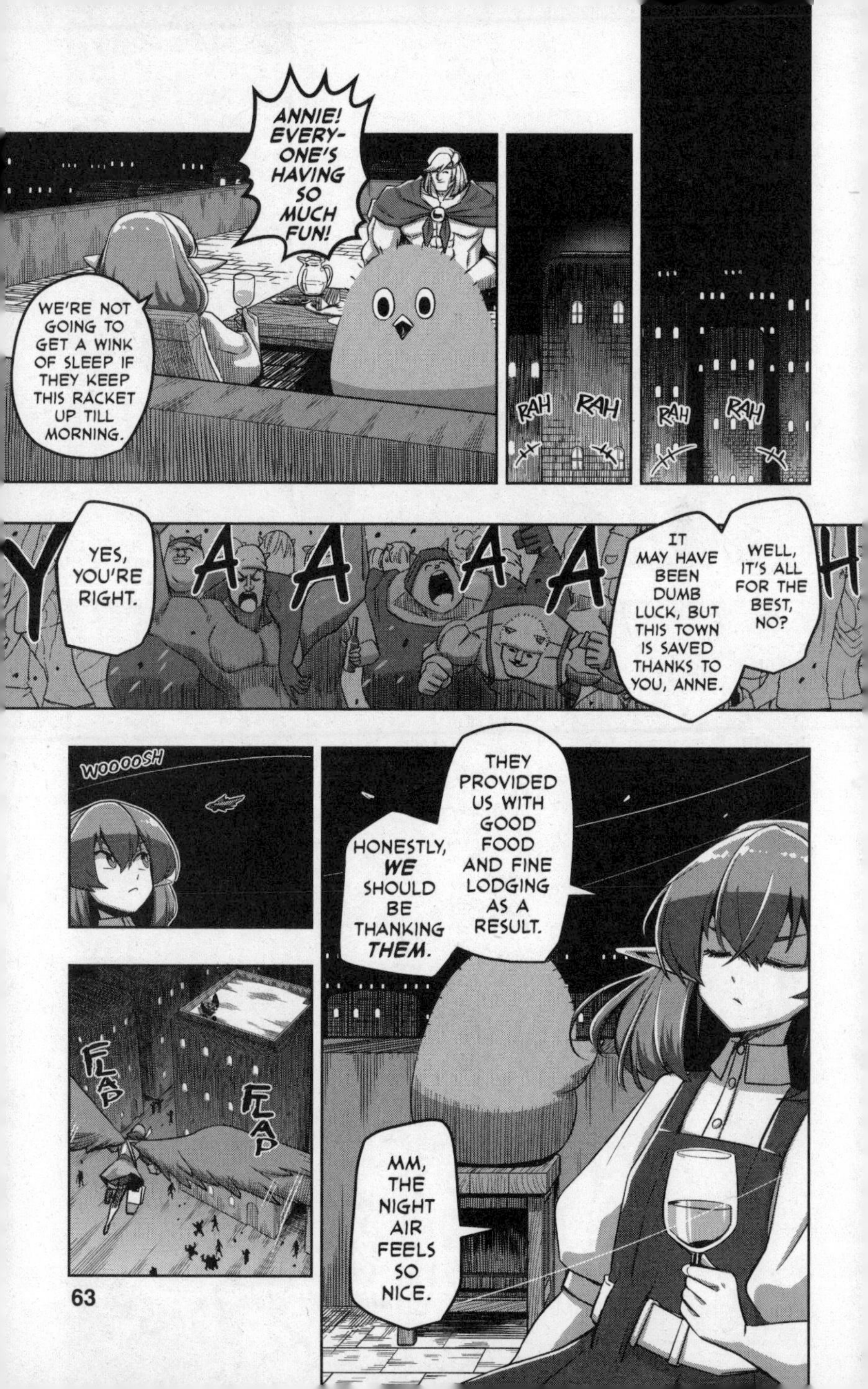
RAH RAH
RAH RAH
ANNIE! EVERYONE'S HAVING SO MUCH FUN!
WE'RE NOT GOING TO GET A WINK OF SLEEP IF THEY KEEP THIS RACKET UP TILL MORNING.
WELL, IT'S ALL FOR THE BEST, NO?
IT MAY HAVE BEEN DUMB LUCK, BUT THIS TOWN IS SAVED THANKS TO YOU, ANNE.
YAAAAH
YES, YOU'RE RIGHT.
THEY PROVIDED US WITH GOOD FOOD AND FINE LODGING AS A RESULT.
HONESTLY, *WE* SHOULD BE THANKING *THEM.*
MM, THE NIGHT AIR FEELS SO NICE.
WOOOOSH
FLAP
FLAP

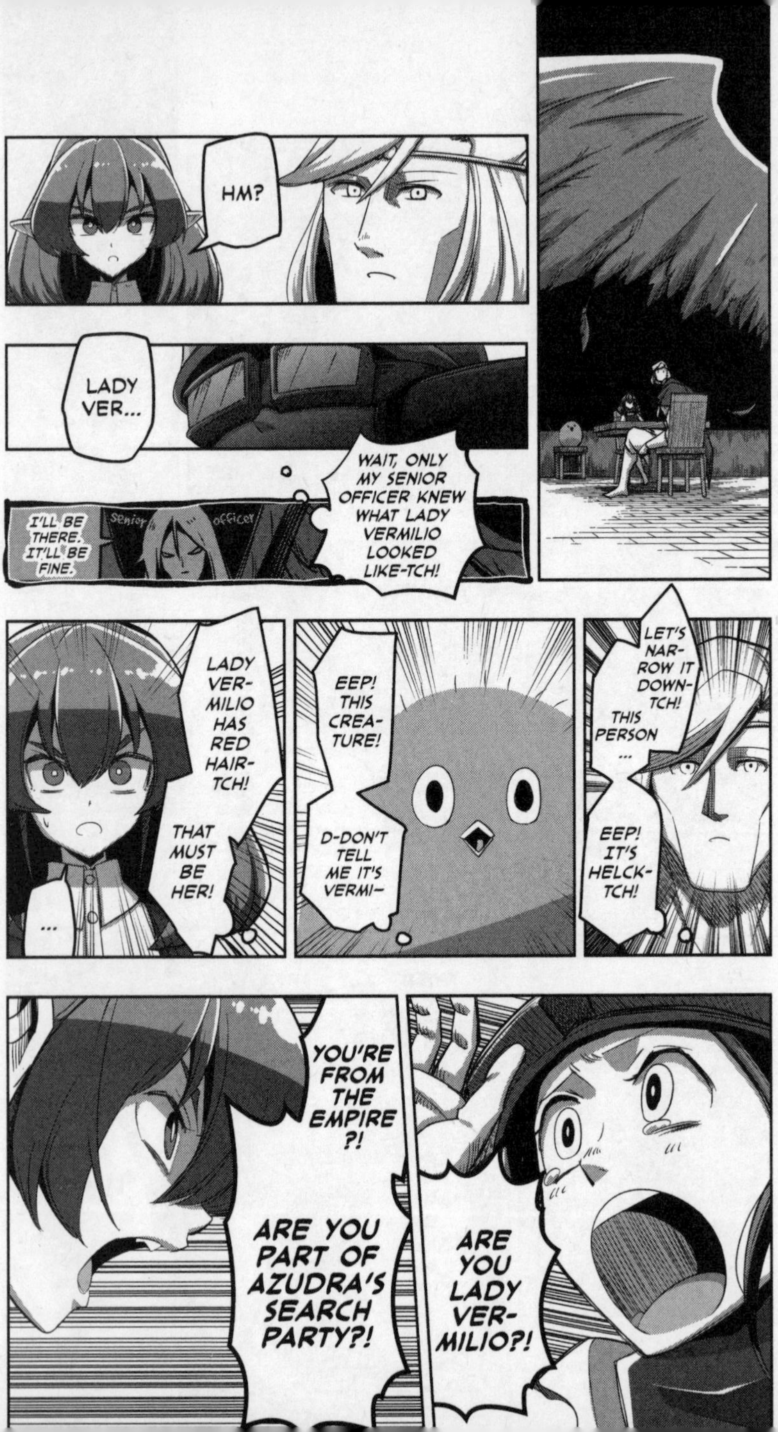
HM?
LADY VER...
WAIT, ONLY MY SENIOR OFFICER KNEW WHAT LADY VERMILIO LOOKED LIKE-TCH!
senior officer
I'LL BE THERE. IT'LL BE FINE.
LET'S NARROW IT DOWN-TCH!
THIS PERSON...
EEP! IT'S HELCK-TCH!
EEP! THIS CREATURE!
D-DON'T TELL ME IT'S VERMI-
LADY VERMILIO HAS RED HAIR-TCH!
THAT MUST BE HER!
...
ARE YOU LADY VERMILIO?!
YOU'RE FROM THE EMPIRE?!
ARE YOU PART OF AZUDRA'S SEARCH PARTY?!

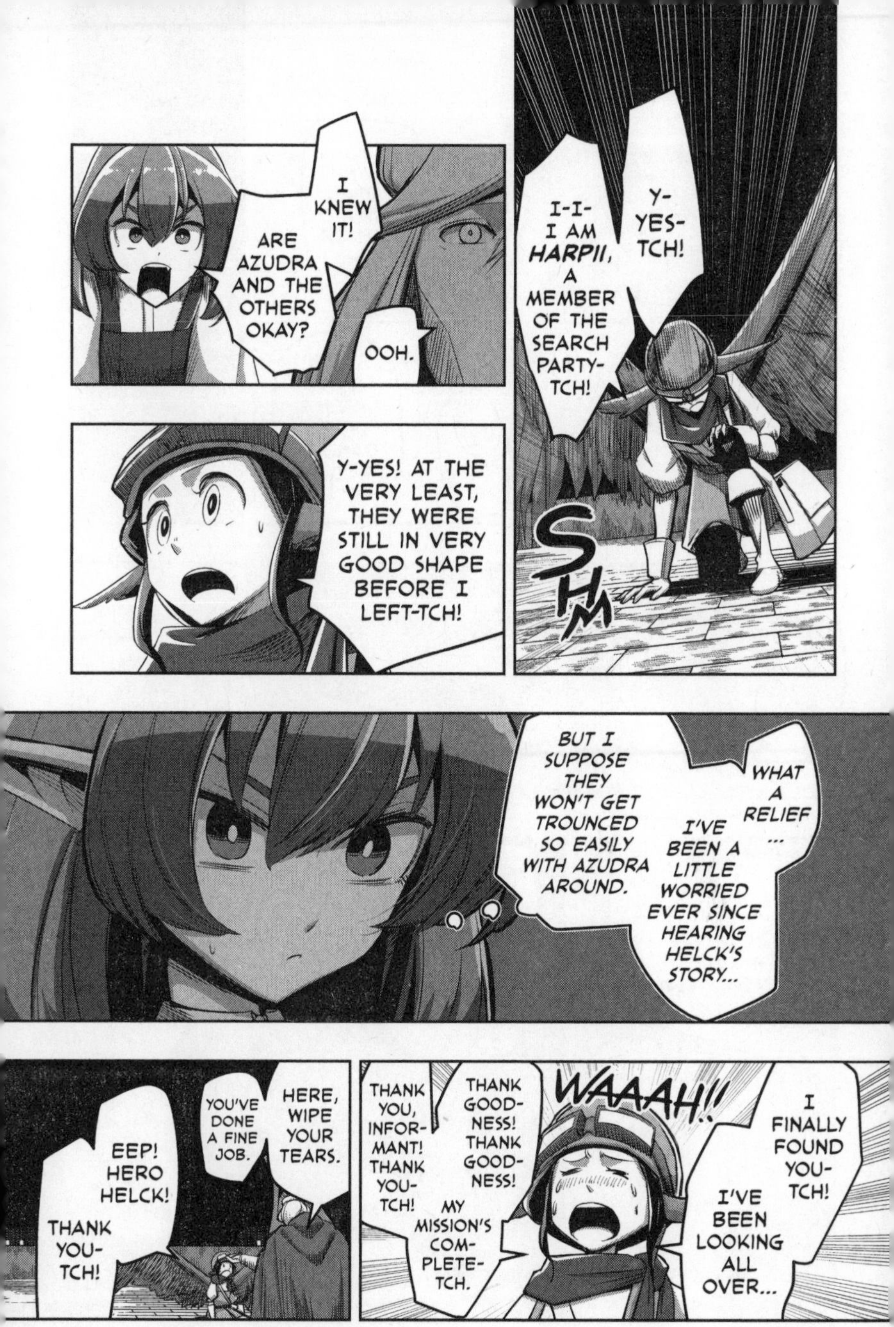
Y-YES-TCH!
I-I-I AM HARPII, A MEMBER OF THE SEARCH PARTY-TCH!
SHM
I KNEW IT!
ARE AZUDRA AND THE OTHERS OKAY?
OOH.
Y-YES! AT THE VERY LEAST, THEY WERE STILL IN VERY GOOD SHAPE BEFORE I LEFT-TCH!
WHAT A RELIEF...
I'VE BEEN A LITTLE WORRIED EVER SINCE HEARING HELCK'S STORY...
BUT I SUPPOSE THEY WON'T GET TROUNCED SO EASILY WITH AZUDRA AROUND.
WAAAH!!
I FINALLY FOUND YOU-TCH!
I'VE BEEN LOOKING ALL OVER...
THANK GOODNESS! THANK GOODNESS!
THANK YOU, INFORMANT! THANK YOU-TCH!
MY MISSION'S COMPLETE-TCH.
HERE, WIPE YOUR TEARS.
YOU'VE DONE A FINE JOB.
EEP! HERO HELCK!
THANK YOU-TCH!

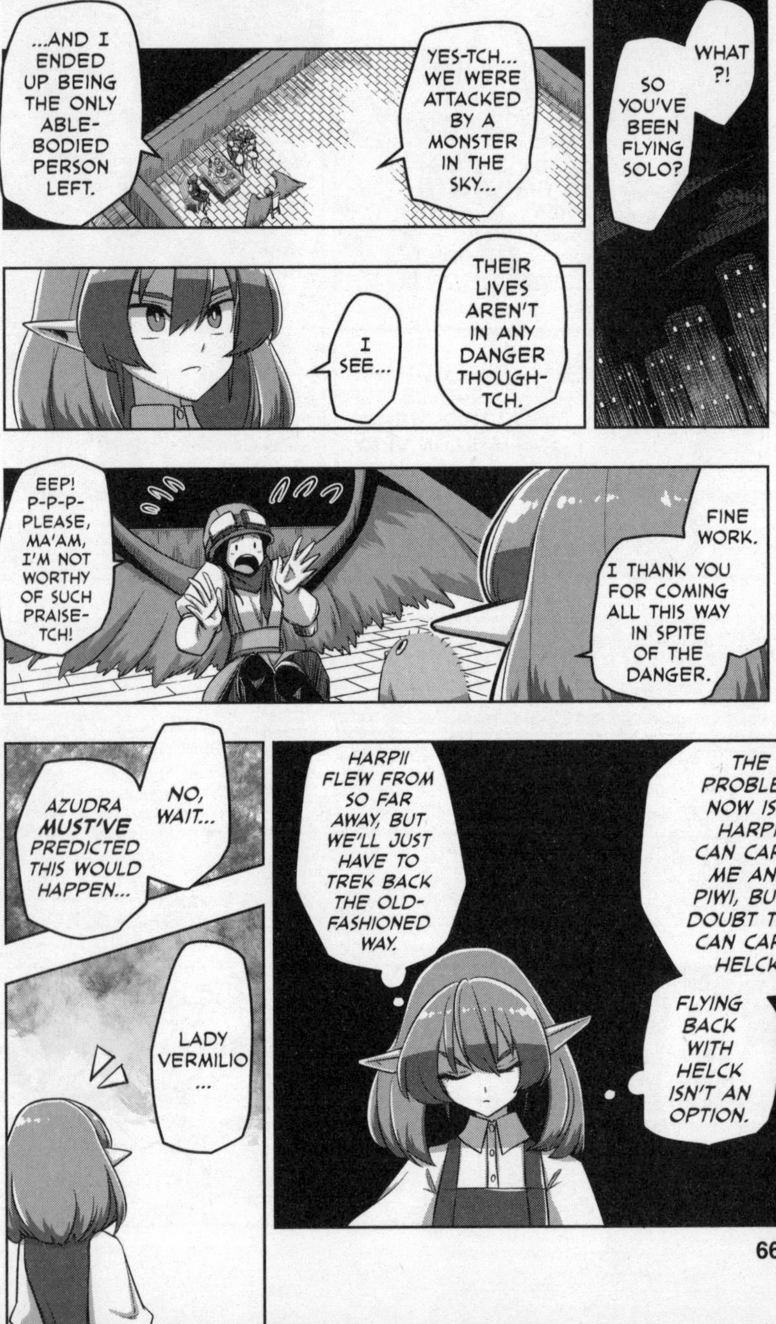
WHAT ?!
SO YOU'VE BEEN FLYING SOLO?
YES-TCH... WE WERE ATTACKED BY A MONSTER IN THE SKY...
...AND I ENDED UP BEING THE ONLY ABLE-BODIED PERSON LEFT.
THEIR LIVES AREN'T IN ANY DANGER THOUGH-TCH.
I SEE...
FINE WORK.
I THANK YOU FOR COMING ALL THIS WAY IN SPITE OF THE DANGER.
EEP! P-P-P-PLEASE, MA'AM, I'M NOT WORTHY OF SUCH PRAISE-TCH!
THE PROBLEM NOW IS... HARPII CAN CARRY ME AND PIWI, BUT I DOUBT THEY CAN CARRY HELCK.
FLYING BACK WITH HELCK ISN'T AN OPTION.
HARPII FLEW FROM SO FAR AWAY, BUT WE'LL JUST HAVE TO TREK BACK THE OLD-FASHIONED WAY.
NO, WAIT...
AZUDRA MUST'VE PREDICTED THIS WOULD HAPPEN...
LADY VERMILIO ...

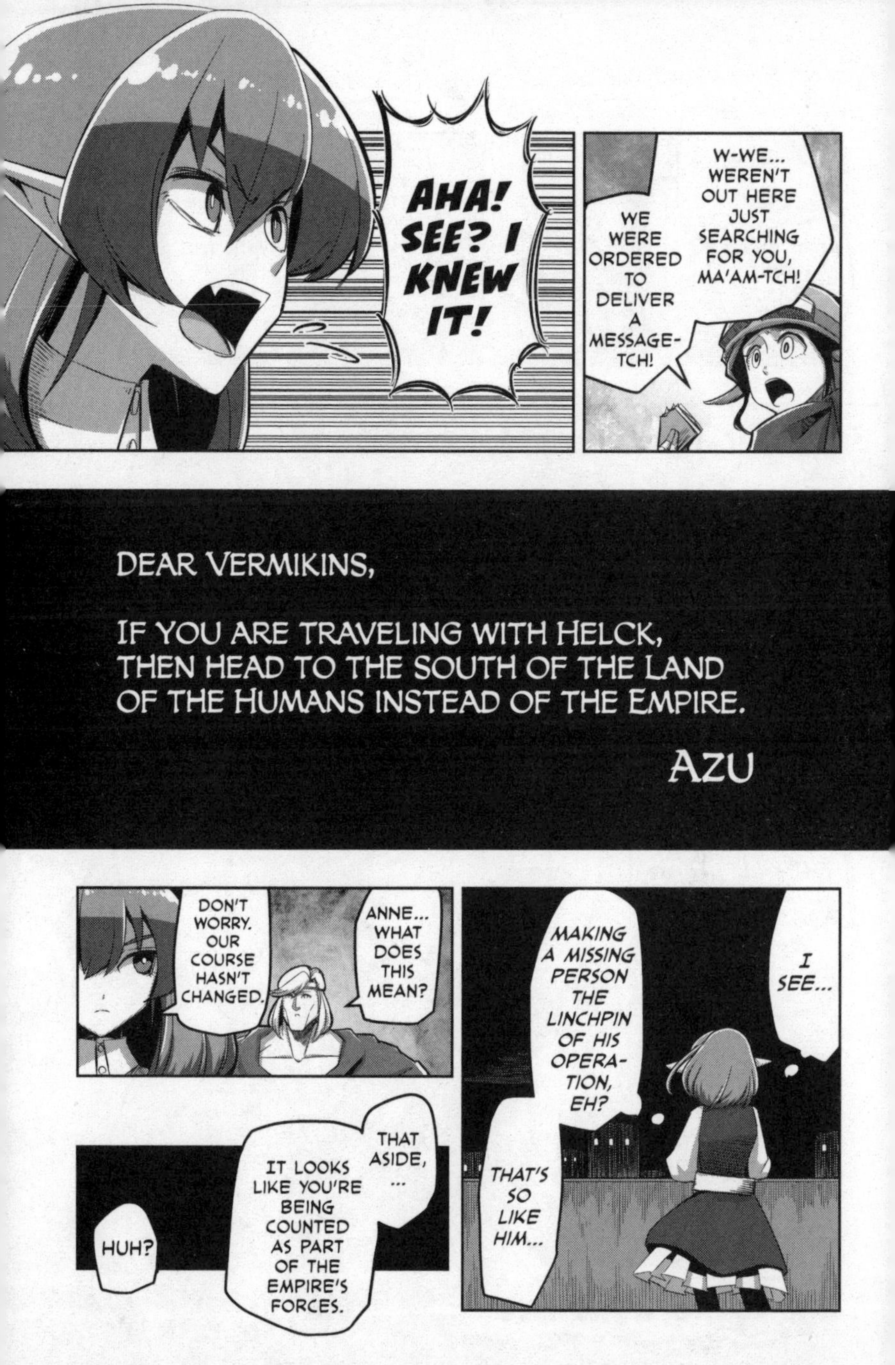
W-WE... WEREN'T OUT HERE JUST SEARCHING FOR YOU, MA'AM-TCH!
WE WERE ORDERED TO DELIVER A MESSAGE-TCH!
AHA! SEE? I KNEW IT!
DEAR VERMIKINS,
IF YOU ARE TRAVELING WITH HELCK, THEN HEAD TO THE SOUTH OF THE LAND OF THE HUMANS INSTEAD OF THE EMPIRE.
AZU
I SEE...
MAKING A MISSING PERSON THE LINCHPIN OF HIS OPERATION, EH?
THAT'S SO LIKE HIM...
ANNE... WHAT DOES THIS MEAN?
DON'T WORRY. OUR COURSE HASN'T CHANGED.
THAT ASIDE, ...
IT LOOKS LIKE YOU'RE BEING COUNTED AS PART OF THE EMPIRE'S FORCES.
HUH?

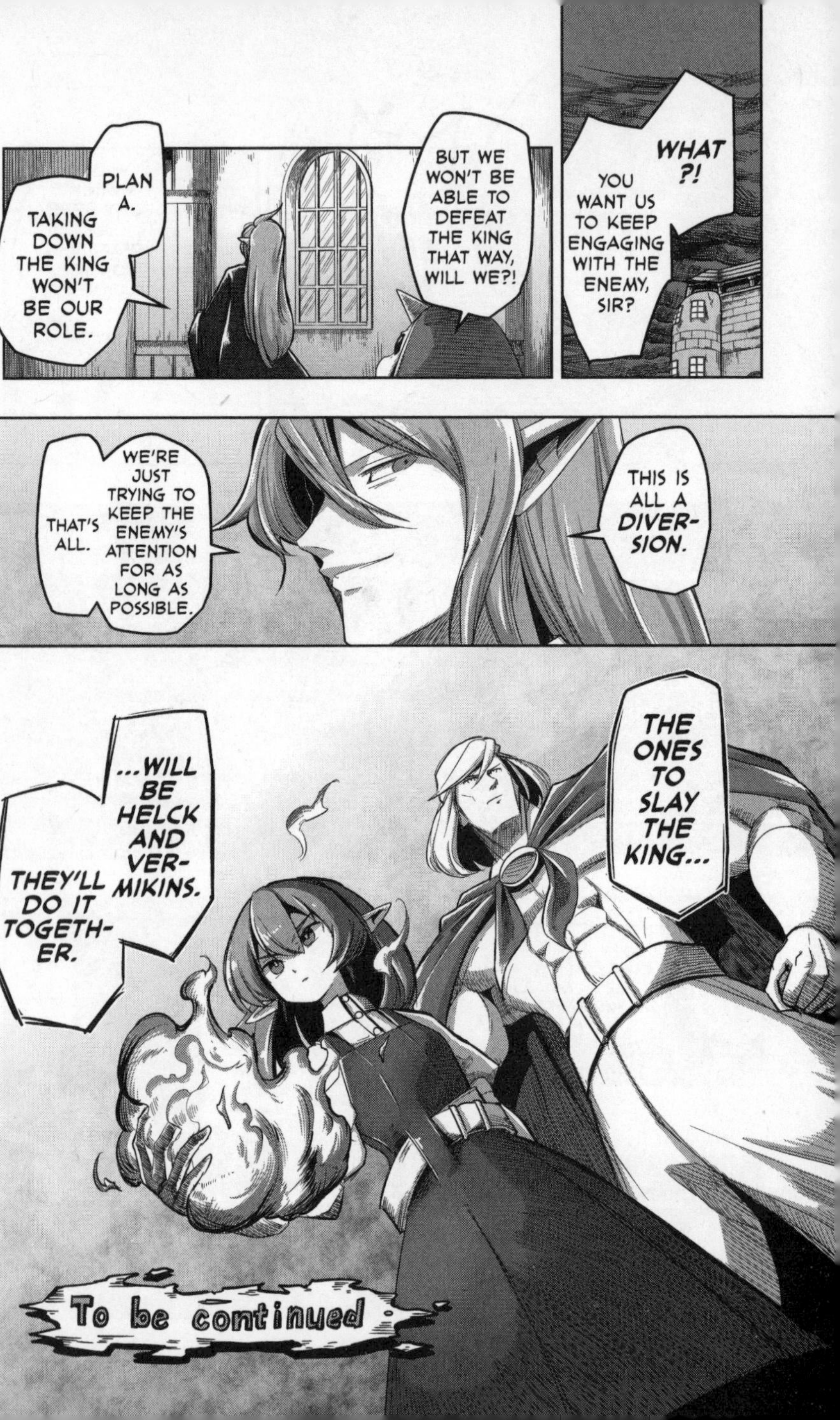
WHAT?!
YOU WANT US TO KEEP ENGAGING WITH THE ENEMY, SIR?
BUT WE WON'T BE ABLE TO DEFEAT THE KING THAT WAY, WILL WE?!
PLAN A.
TAKING DOWN THE KING WON'T BE OUR ROLE.
THIS IS ALL A DIVERSION.
WE'RE JUST TRYING TO KEEP THE ENEMY'S ATTENTION FOR AS LONG AS POSSIBLE.
THAT'S ALL.
THE ONES TO SLAY THE KING...
...WILL BE HELCK AND VERMIKINS.
THEY'LL DO IT TOGETHER.
To be continued

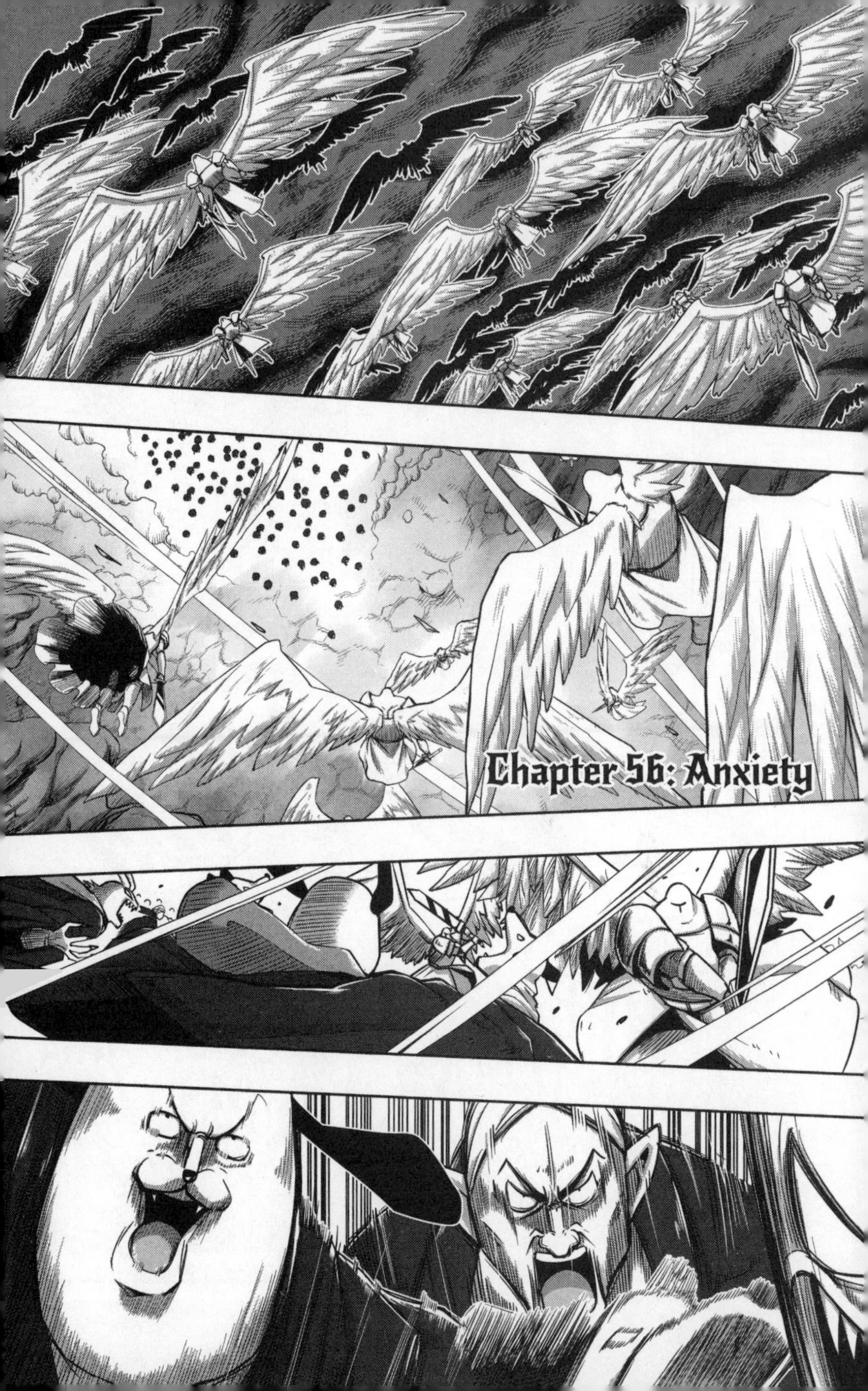
Chapter 56: Anxiety

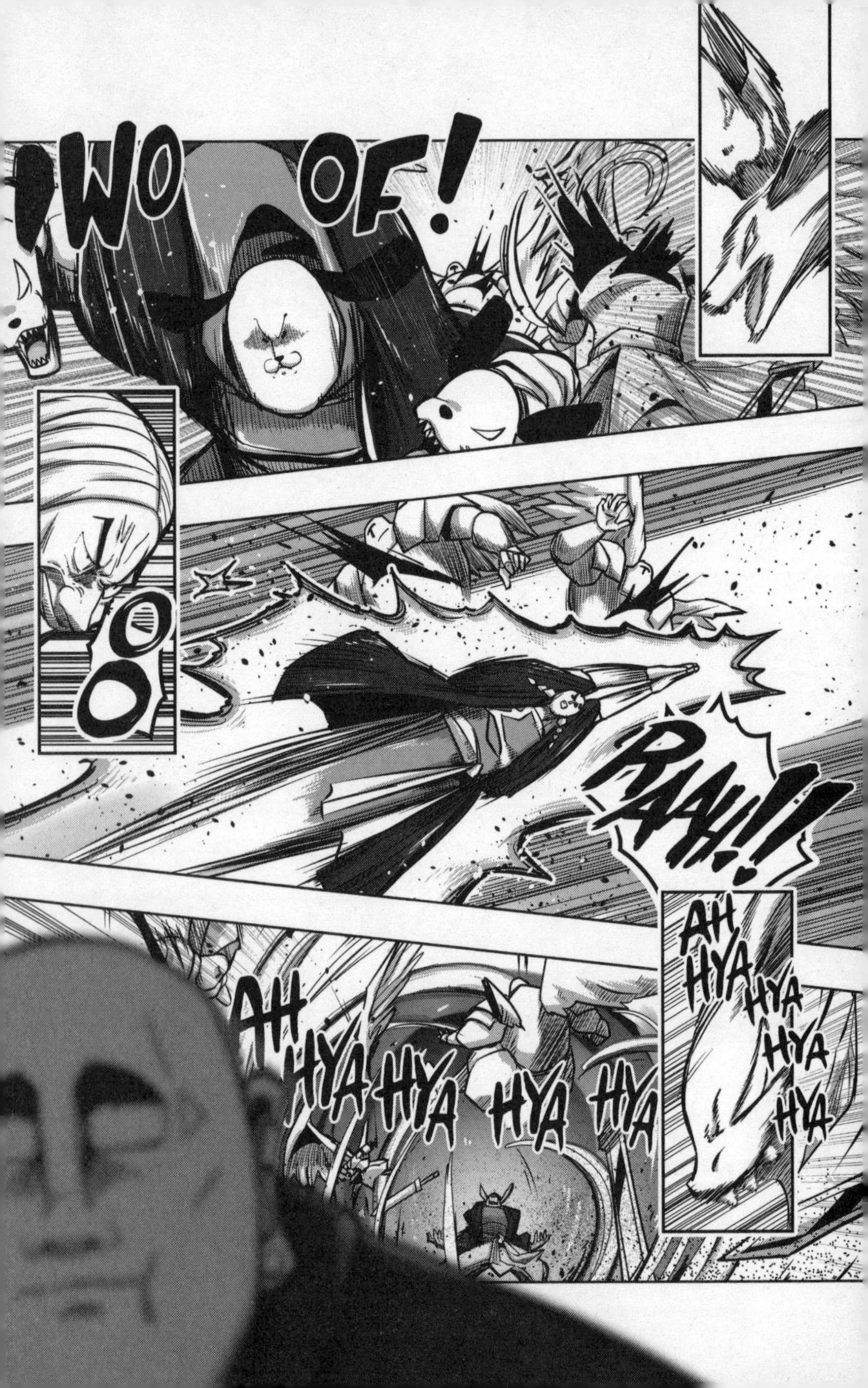
WOOF!
OOO
RAAH!!
AH HYA HYA HYA HYA
AH HYA HYA HYA HYA

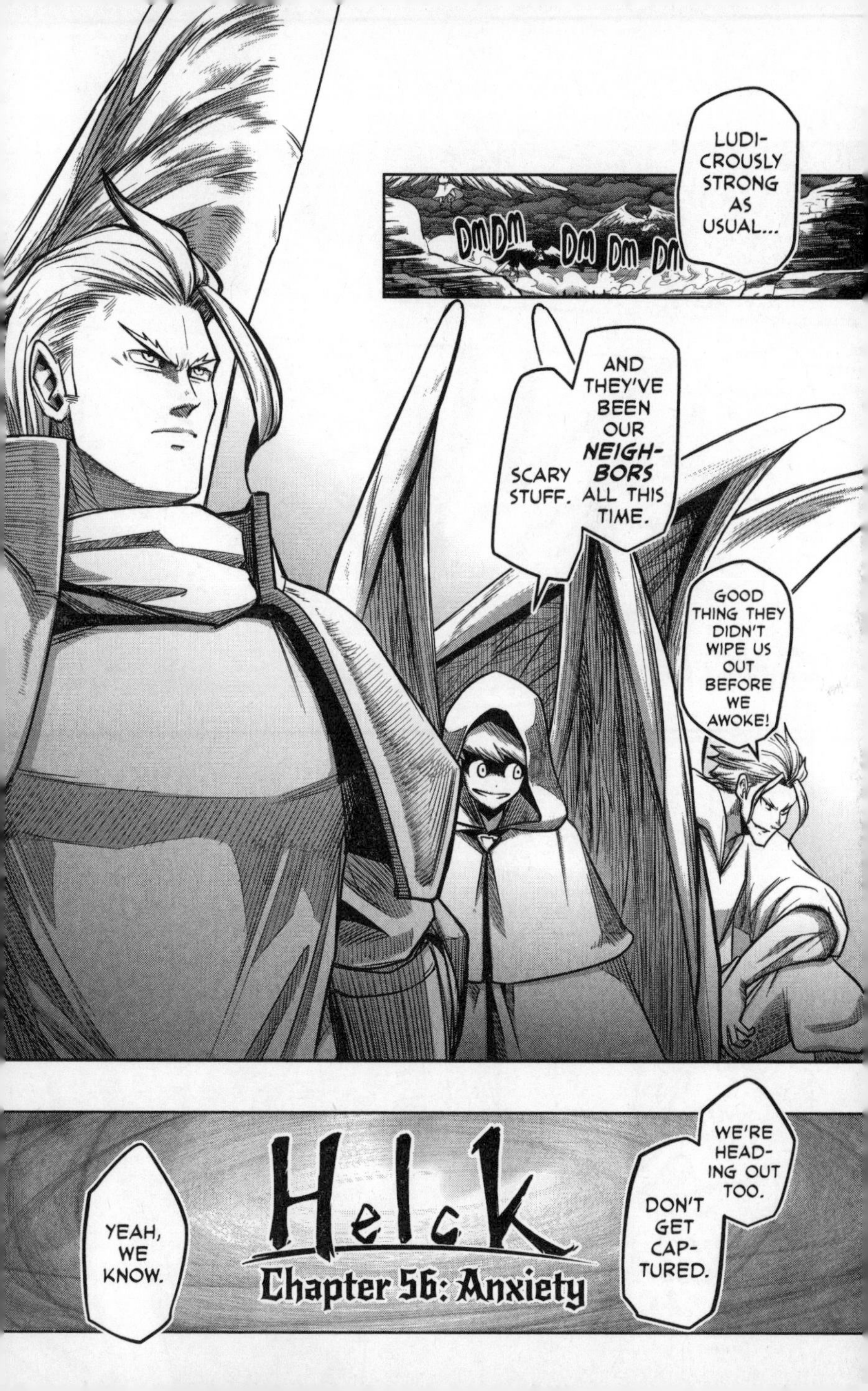
LUDI-CROUSLY STRONG AS USUAL...
DMDM DM DM DM
AND THEY'VE BEEN OUR NEIGHBORS ALL THIS TIME.
SCARY STUFF.
GOOD THING THEY DIDN'T WIPE US OUT BEFORE WE AWOKE!
WE'RE HEAD-ING OUT TOO.
DON'T GET CAP-TURED.
Helck
Chapter 56: Anxiety
YEAH, WE KNOW.

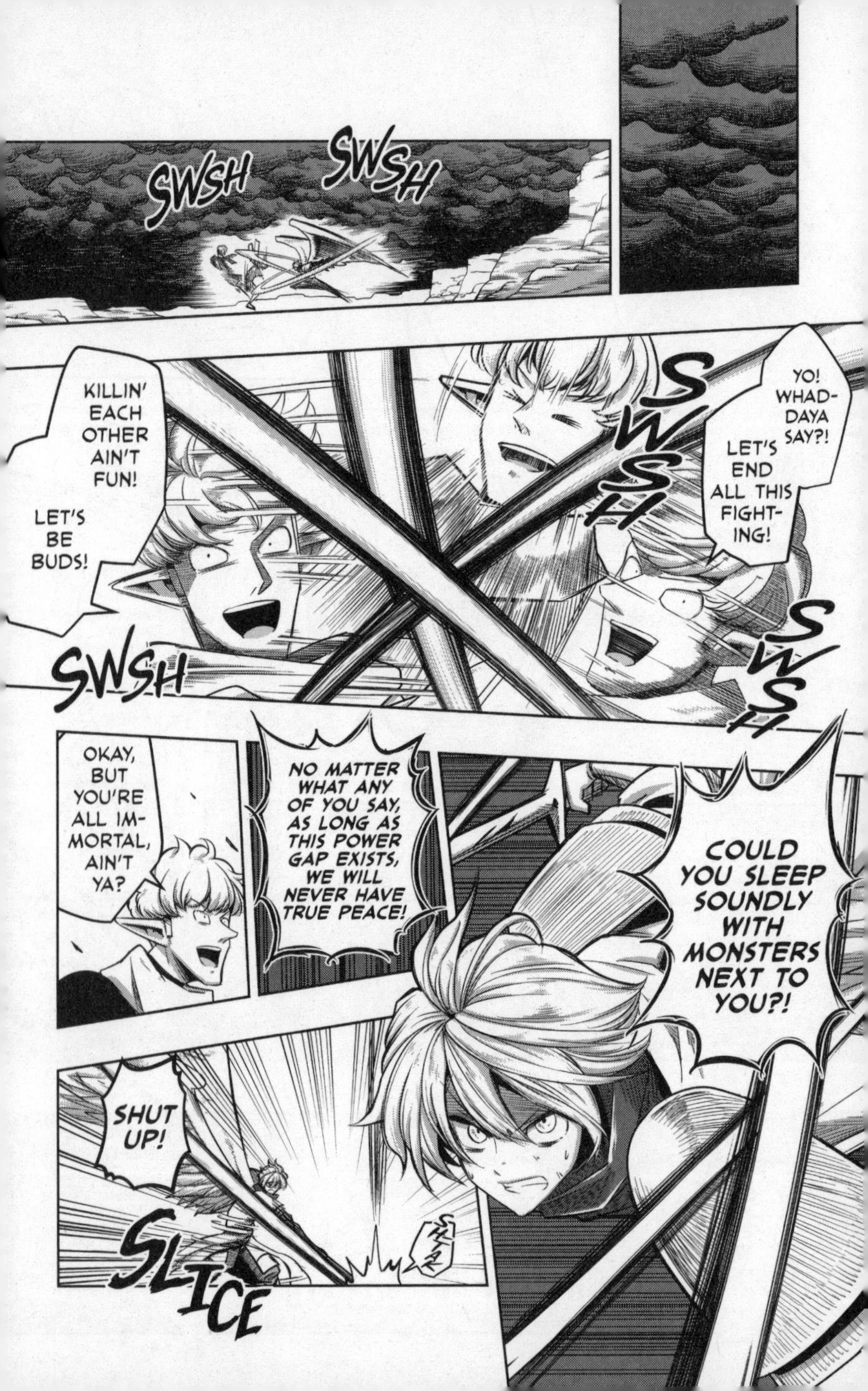
SWSH
SWSH
YO! WHADDAYA SAY?!
LET'S END ALL THIS FIGHTING!
SWSH
KILLIN' EACH OTHER AIN'T FUN!
LET'S BE BUDS!
SWSH
SWSH
COULD YOU SLEEP SOUNDLY WITH MONSTERS NEXT TO YOU?!
NO MATTER WHAT ANY OF YOU SAY, AS LONG AS THIS POWER GAP EXISTS, WE WILL NEVER HAVE TRUE PEACE!
OKAY, BUT YOU'RE ALL IMMORTAL, AIN'T YA?
SHUT UP!
SHAK
SLICE

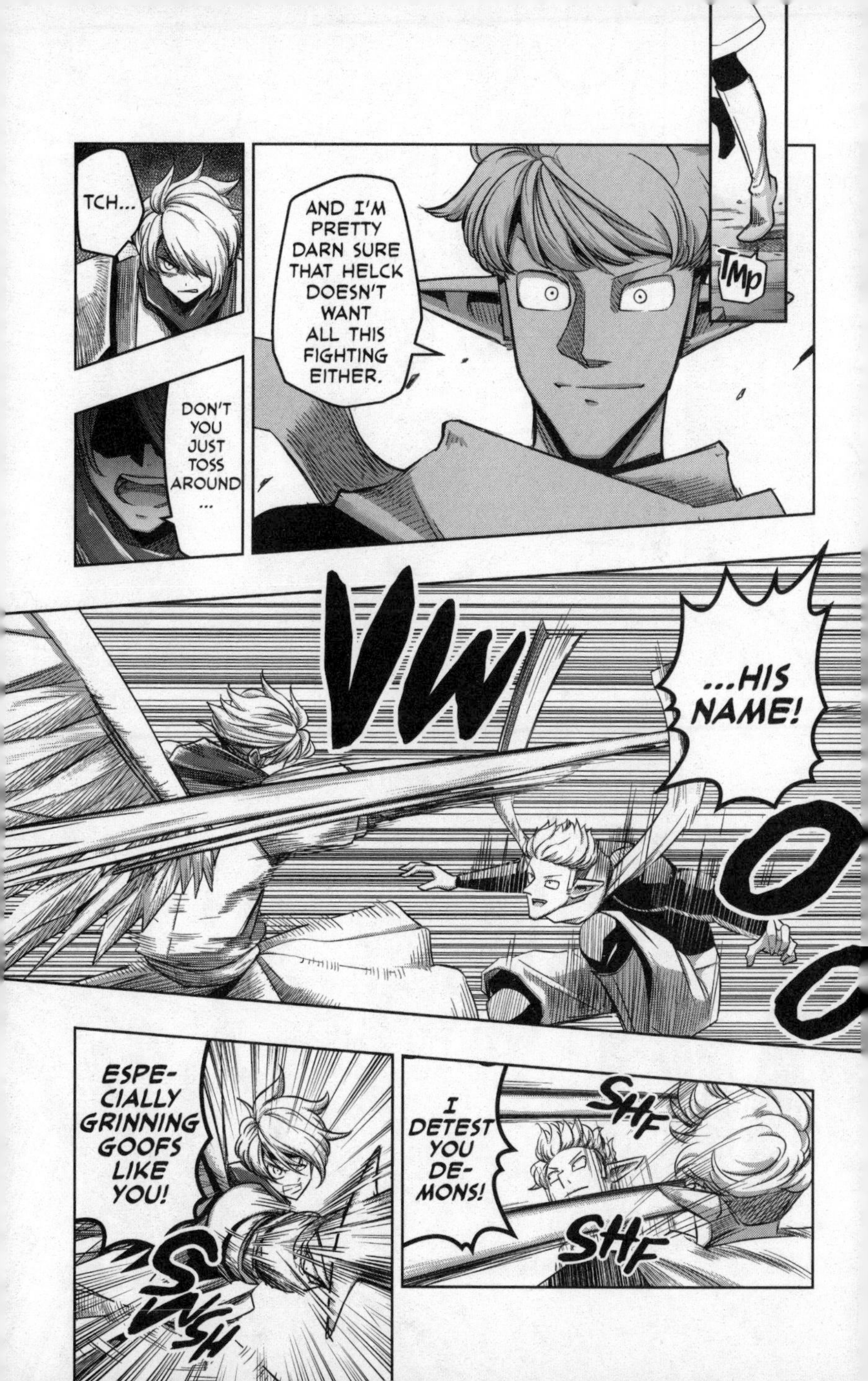
TMp
AND I'M PRETTY DARN SURE THAT HELCK DOESN'T WANT ALL THIS FIGHTING EITHER.
TCH...
DON'T YOU JUST TOSS AROUND ...
...HIS NAME!
VW
OOO
I DETEST YOU DE-MONS!
SHF
SHF
ESPE-CIALLY GRINNING GOOFS LIKE YOU!
SNSH

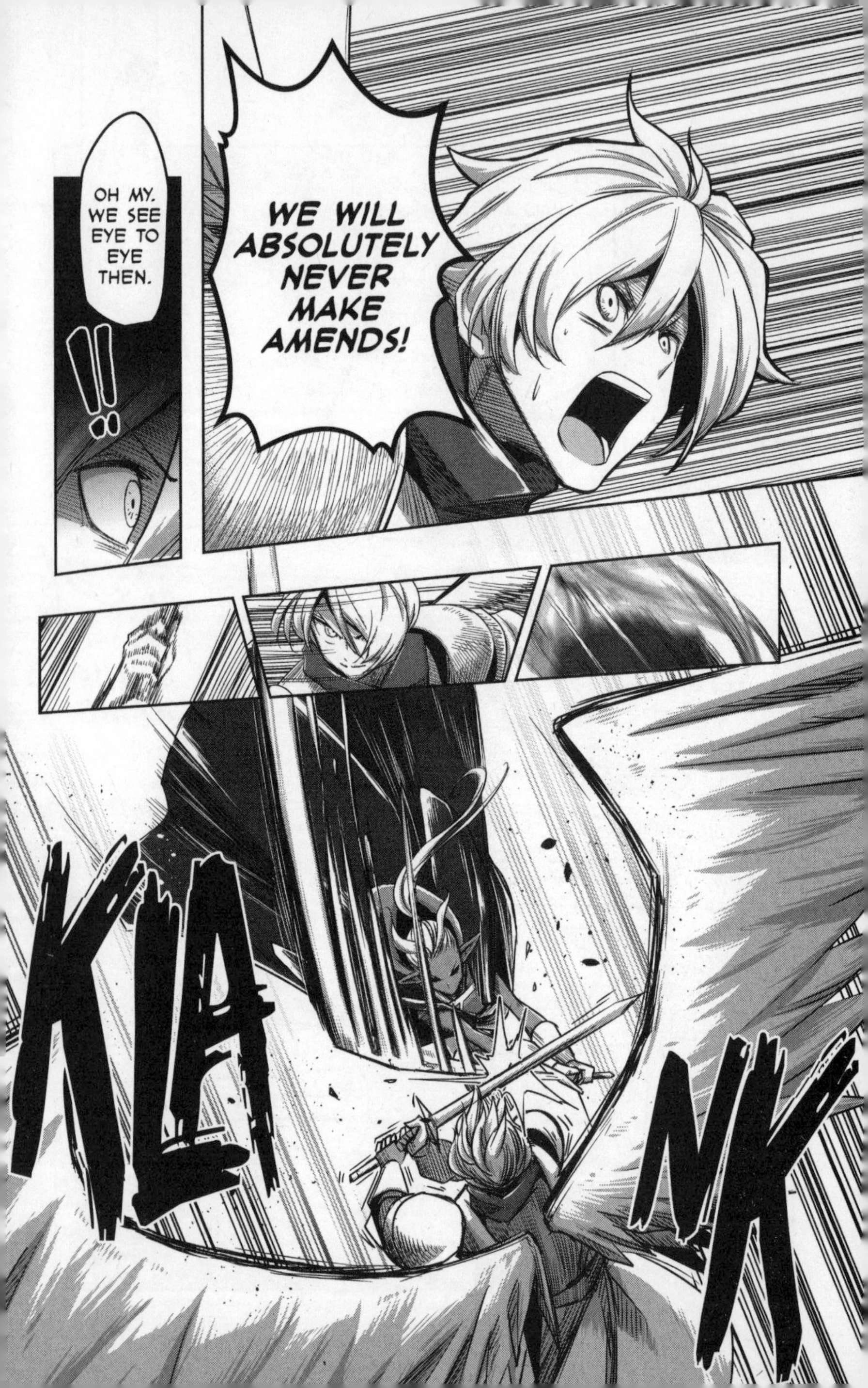
WE WILL ABSOLUTELY NEVER MAKE AMENDS!
OH MY. WE SEE EYE TO EYE THEN.
!!
KLANK

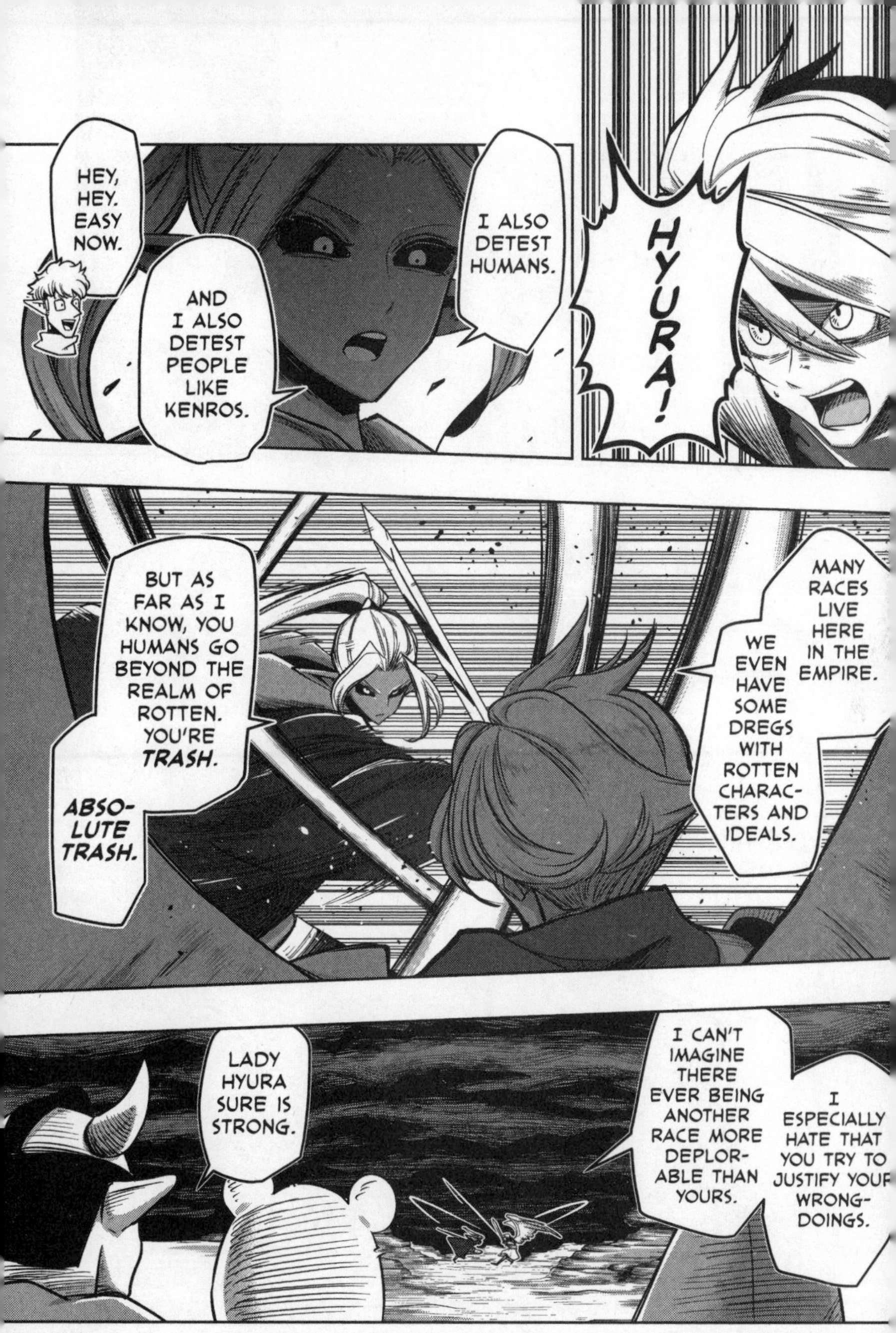
HYURA!
I ALSO DETEST HUMANS.
HEY, HEY. EASY NOW.
AND I ALSO DETEST PEOPLE LIKE KENROS.
MANY RACES LIVE HERE IN THE EMPIRE.
WE EVEN HAVE SOME DREGS WITH ROTTEN CHARACTERS AND IDEALS.
BUT AS FAR AS I KNOW, YOU HUMANS GO BEYOND THE REALM OF ROTTEN. YOU'RE **TRASH**.
ABSOLUTE TRASH.
I CAN'T IMAGINE THERE EVER BEING ANOTHER RACE MORE DEPLORABLE THAN YOURS.
I ESPECIALLY HATE THAT YOU TRY TO JUSTIFY YOUR WRONGDOINGS.
LADY HYURA SURE IS STRONG.

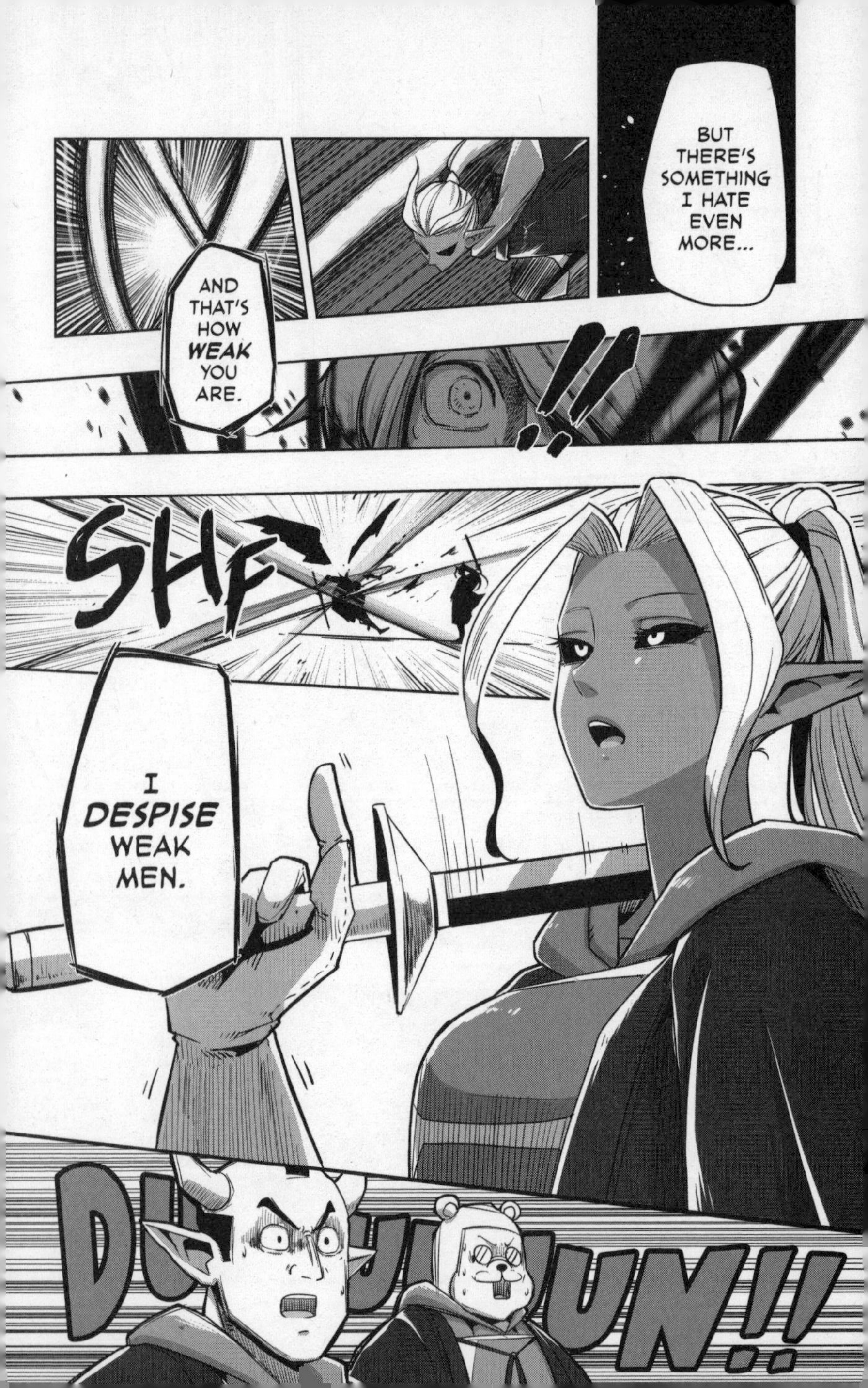
BUT THERE'S SOMETHING I HATE EVEN MORE...
AND THAT'S HOW WEAK YOU ARE.
!!
SHF
I DESPISE WEAK MEN.
UN!!

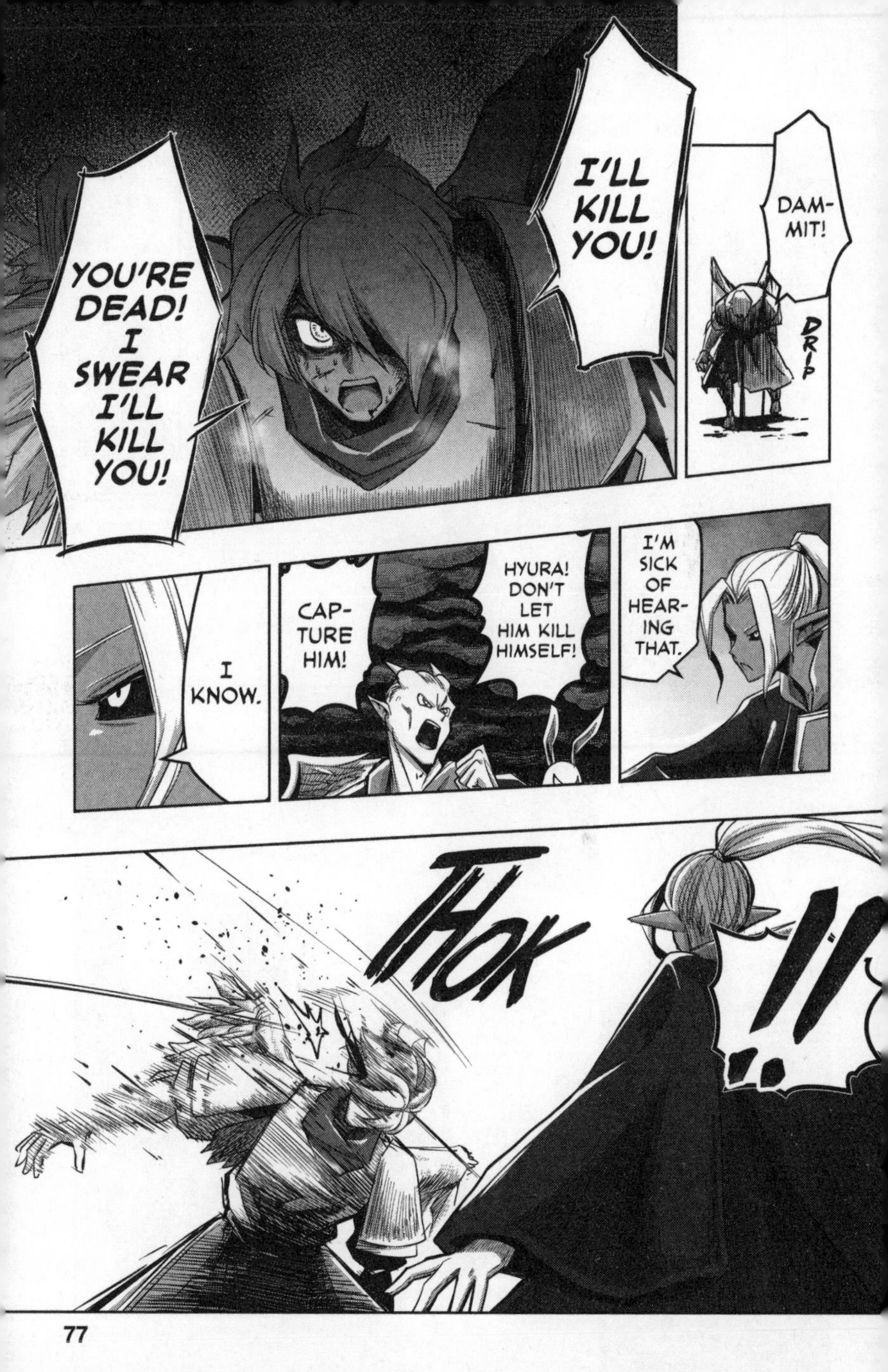
DAM-MIT!
DRIP
I'LL KILL YOU!
YOU'RE DEAD! I SWEAR I'LL KILL YOU!
I'M SICK OF HEARING THAT.
HYURA! DON'T LET HIM KILL HIMSELF!
CAPTURE HIM!
I KNOW.
THOK!!

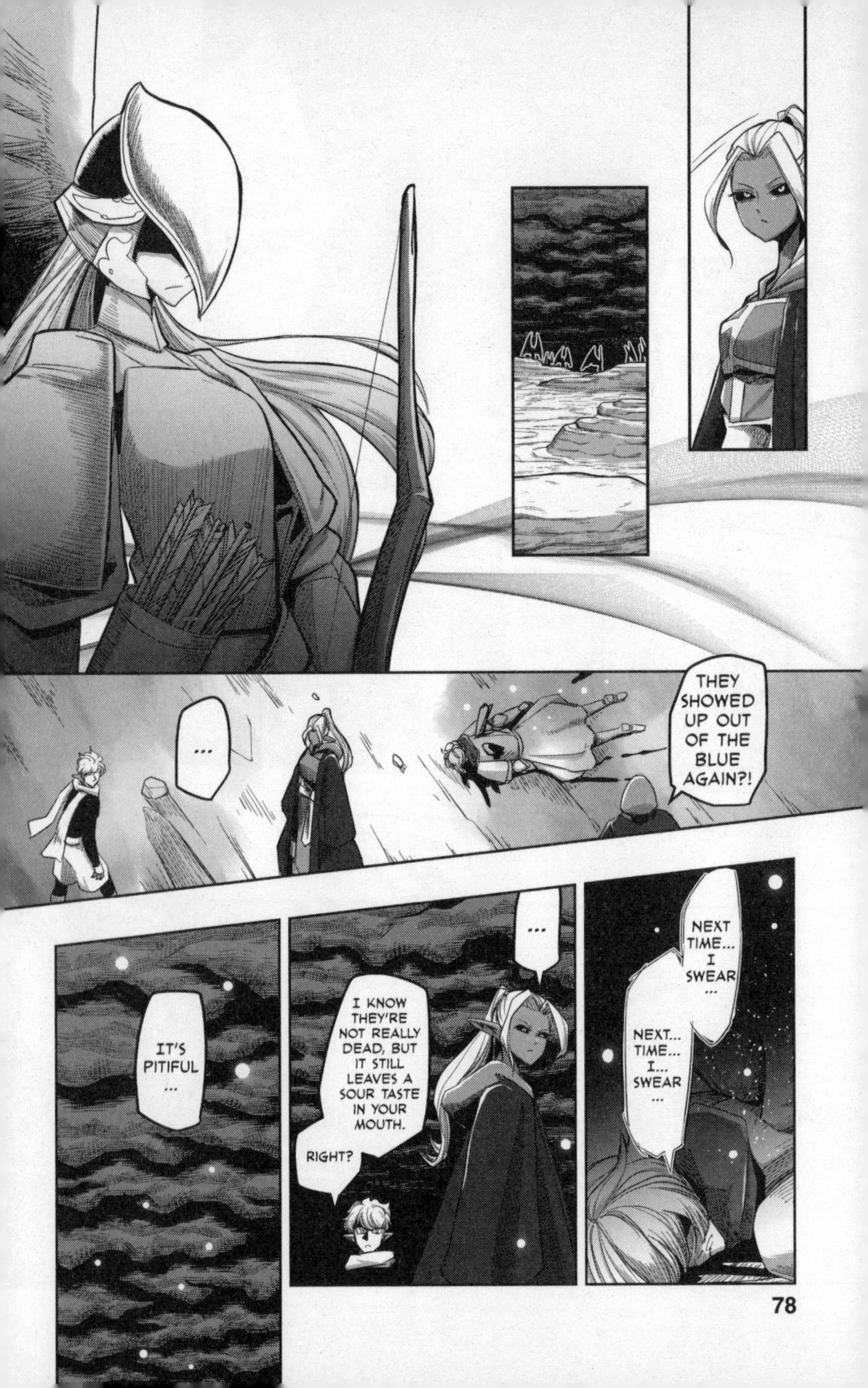
THEY SHOWED UP OUT OF THE BLUE AGAIN?!
...
NEXT TIME... I SWEAR ...
NEXT... TIME... I... SWEAR ...
...
I KNOW THEY'RE NOT REALLY DEAD, BUT IT STILL LEAVES A SOUR TASTE IN YOUR MOUTH.
RIGHT?
IT'S PITIFUL ...

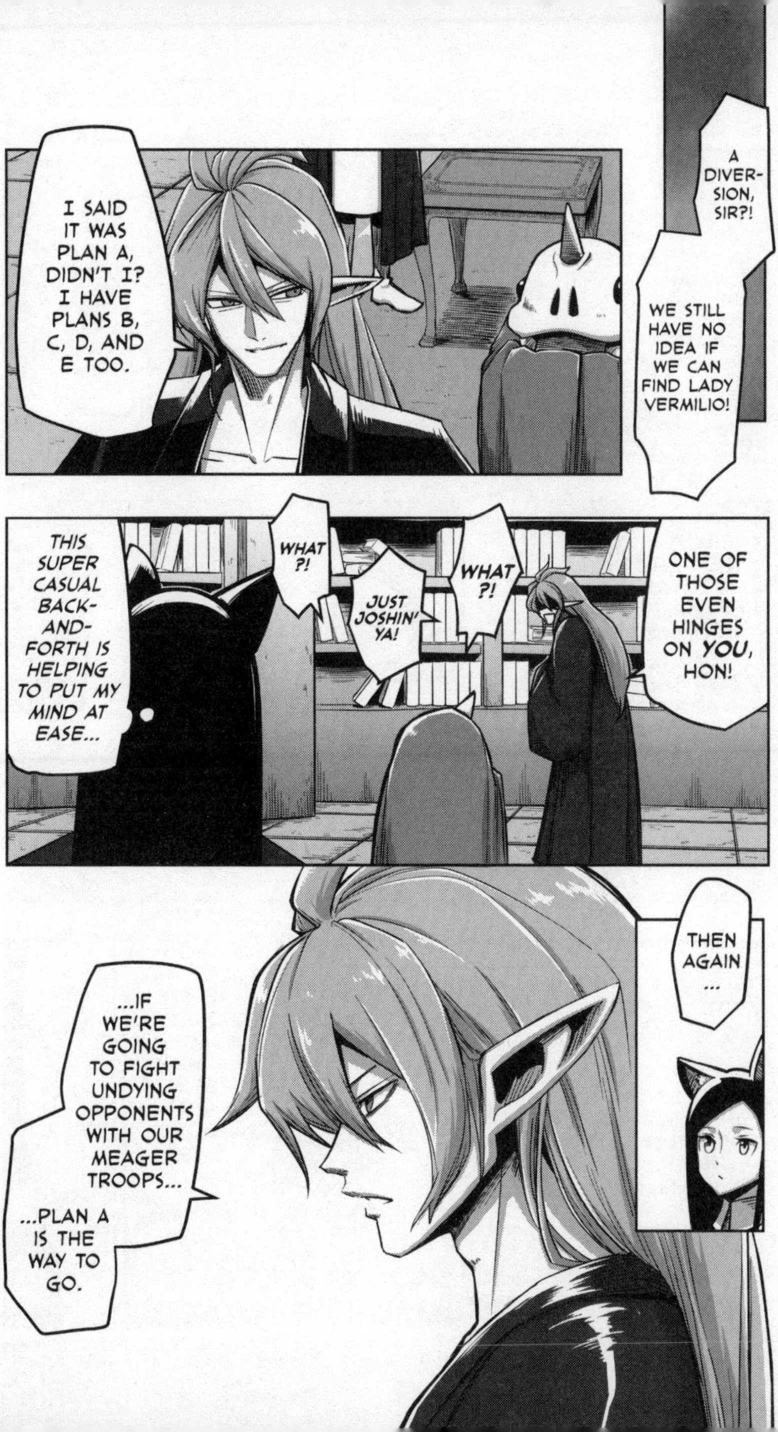
A DIVERSION, SIR?!
WE STILL HAVE NO IDEA IF WE CAN FIND LADY VERMILIO!
I SAID IT WAS PLAN A, DIDN'T I? I HAVE PLANS B, C, D, AND E TOO.
ONE OF THOSE EVEN HINGES ON *YOU*, HON!
WHAT?!
JUST JOSHIN' YA!
WHAT?!
THIS SUPER CASUAL BACK-AND-FORTH IS HELPING TO PUT MY MIND AT EASE...
THEN AGAIN...
...IF WE'RE GOING TO FIGHT UNDYING OPPONENTS WITH OUR MEAGER TROOPS...
...PLAN A IS THE WAY TO GO.

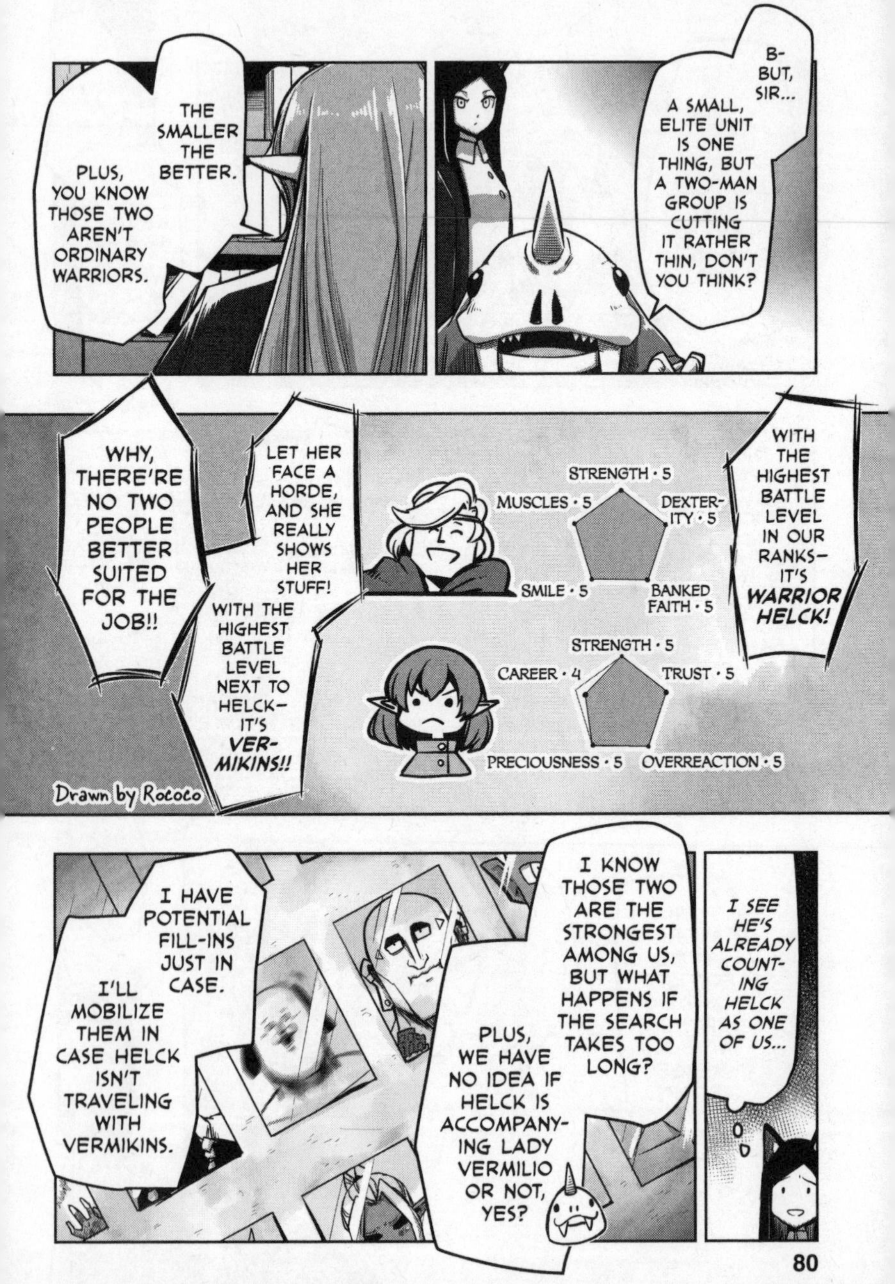
B- BUT, SIR...
A SMALL, ELITE UNIT IS ONE THING, BUT A TWO-MAN GROUP IS CUTTING IT RATHER THIN, DON'T YOU THINK?
THE SMALLER THE BETTER.
PLUS, YOU KNOW THOSE TWO AREN'T ORDINARY WARRIORS.
WITH THE HIGHEST BATTLE LEVEL IN OUR RANKS— IT'S ***WARRIOR HELCK!***
STRENGTH • 5
DEXTER-ITY • 5
BANKED FAITH • 5
SMILE • 5
MUSCLES • 5
STRENGTH • 5
TRUST • 5
OVERREACTION • 5
PRECIOUSNESS • 5
CAREER • 4
WITH THE HIGHEST BATTLE LEVEL NEXT TO HELCK— IT'S ***VER-MIKINS!!***
LET HER FACE A HORDE, AND SHE REALLY SHOWS HER STUFF!
WHY, THERE'RE NO TWO PEOPLE BETTER SUITED FOR THE JOB!!
Drawn by Rococo
I SEE HE'S ALREADY COUNTING HELCK AS ONE OF US...
I KNOW THOSE TWO ARE THE STRONGEST AMONG US, BUT WHAT HAPPENS IF THE SEARCH TAKES TOO LONG?
PLUS, WE HAVE NO IDEA IF HELCK IS ACCOMPANYING LADY VERMILIO OR NOT, YES?
I HAVE POTENTIAL FILL-INS JUST IN CASE.
I'LL MOBILIZE THEM IN CASE HELCK ISN'T TRAVELING WITH VERMIKINS.

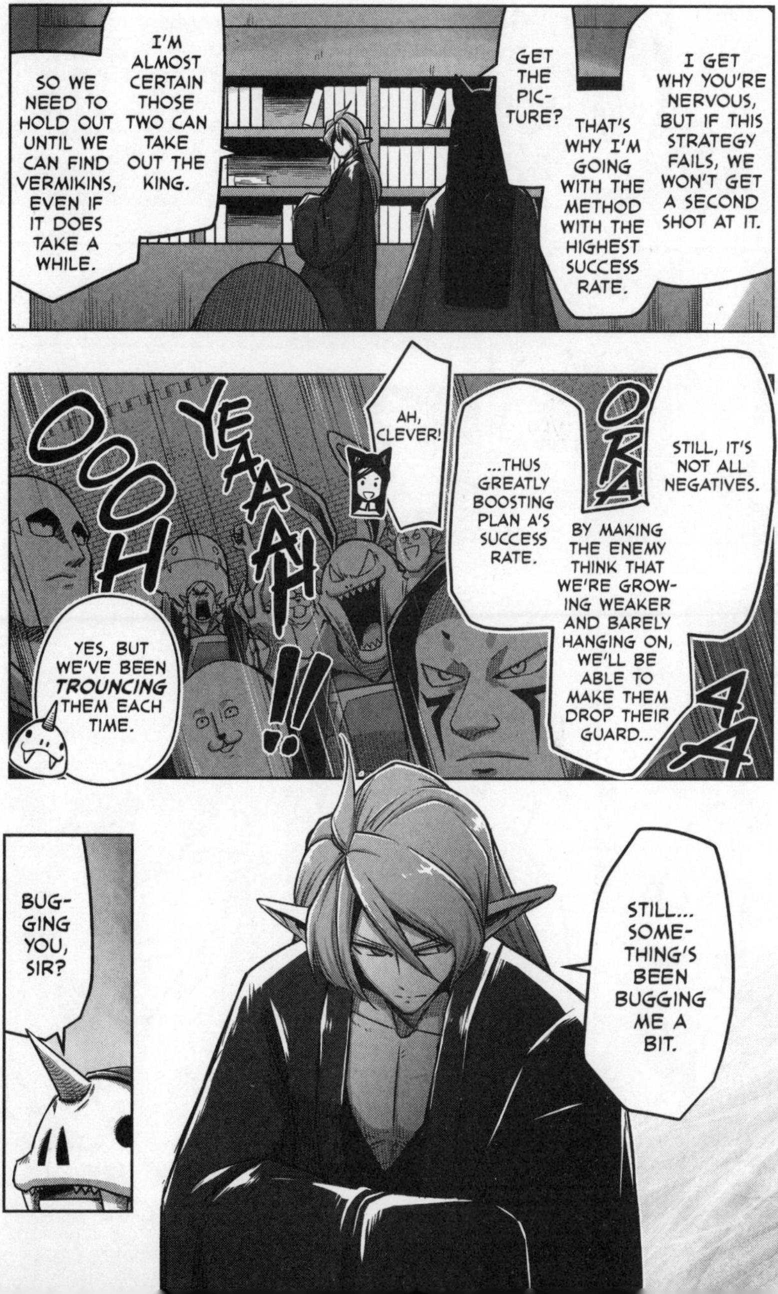
I GET WHY YOU'RE NERVOUS, BUT IF THIS STRATEGY FAILS, WE WON'T GET A SECOND SHOT AT IT.
THAT'S WHY I'M GOING WITH THE METHOD WITH THE HIGHEST SUCCESS RATE.
GET THE PIC-TURE?
I'M ALMOST CERTAIN THOSE TWO CAN TAKE OUT THE KING.
SO WE NEED TO HOLD OUT UNTIL WE CAN FIND VERMIKINS, EVEN IF IT DOES TAKE A WHILE.
STILL, IT'S NOT ALL NEGATIVES.
BY MAKING THE ENEMY THINK THAT WE'RE GROW-ING WEAKER AND BARELY HANGING ON, WE'LL BE ABLE TO MAKE THEM DROP THEIR GUARD...
...THUS GREATLY BOOSTING PLAN A'S SUCCESS RATE.
OKAAA
AH, CLEVER!
YEAAAH!!
OOOOH
YES, BUT WE'VE BEEN *TROUNCING* THEM EACH TIME.
STILL... SOME-THING'S BEEN BUGGING ME A BIT.
BUG-GING YOU, SIR?

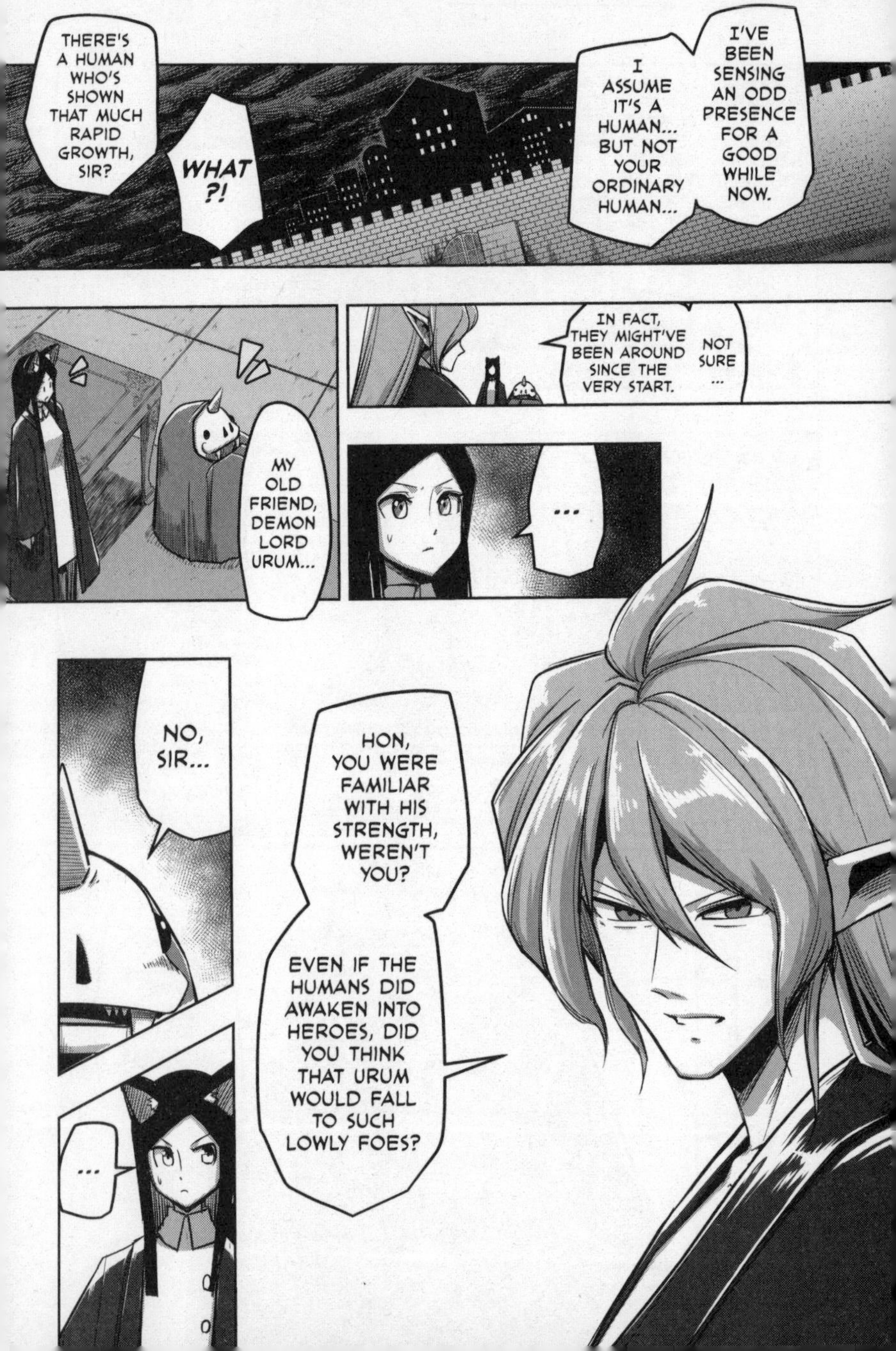
I'VE BEEN SENSING AN ODD PRESENCE FOR A GOOD WHILE NOW.
I ASSUME IT'S A HUMAN... BUT NOT YOUR ORDINARY HUMAN...
WHAT ?!
THERE'S A HUMAN WHO'S SHOWN THAT MUCH RAPID GROWTH, SIR?
NOT SURE ...
IN FACT, THEY MIGHT'VE BEEN AROUND SINCE THE VERY START.
...
MY OLD FRIEND, DEMON LORD URUM...
HON, YOU WERE FAMILIAR WITH HIS STRENGTH, WEREN'T YOU?
EVEN IF THE HUMANS DID AWAKEN INTO HEROES, DID YOU THINK THAT URUM WOULD FALL TO SUCH LOWLY FOES?
NO, SIR...
...

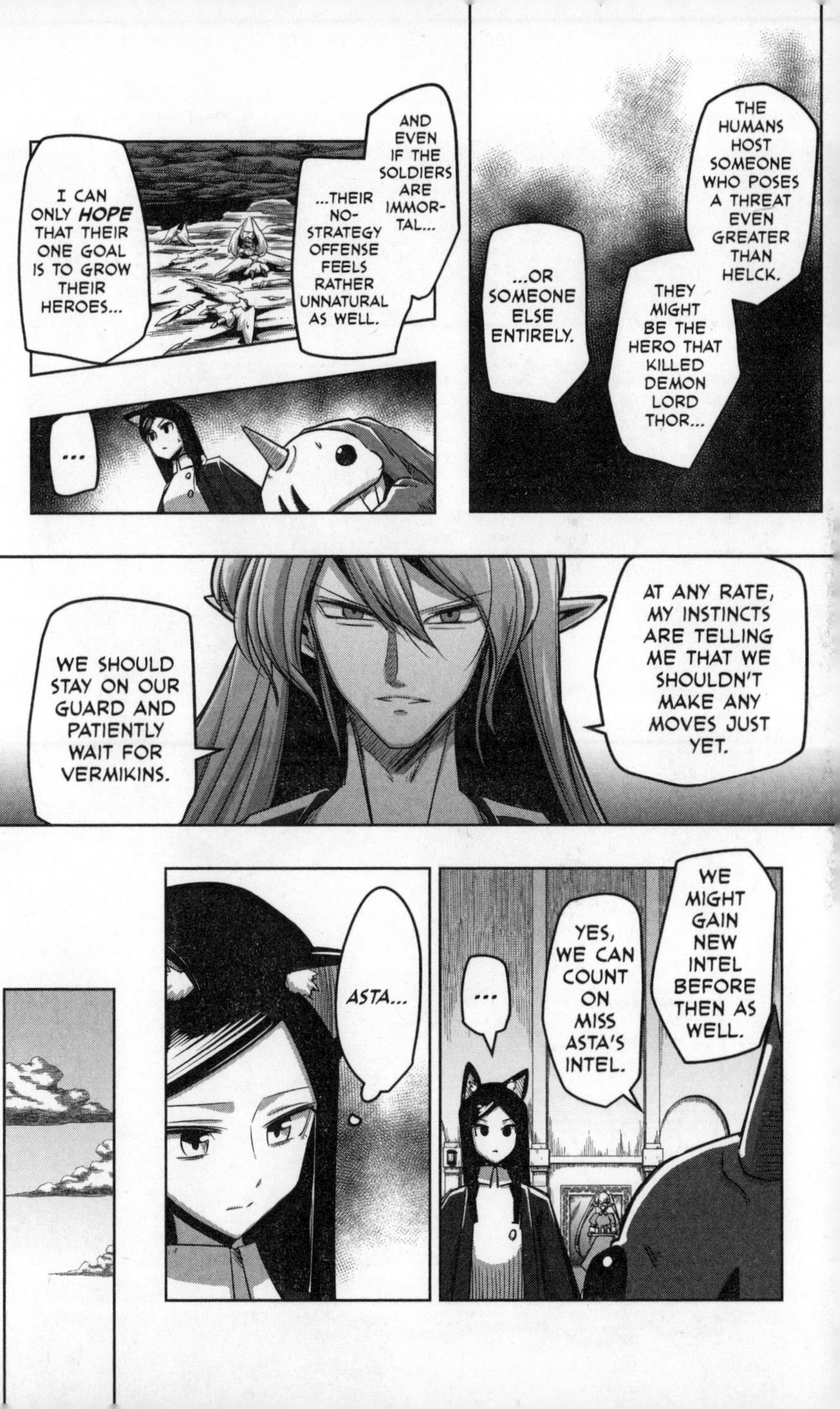
THE HUMANS HOST SOMEONE WHO POSES A THREAT EVEN GREATER THAN HELCK.
THEY MIGHT BE THE HERO THAT KILLED DEMON LORD THOR...
...OR SOMEONE ELSE ENTIRELY.
AND EVEN IF THE SOLDIERS ARE IMMORTAL...
...THEIR NO-STRATEGY OFFENSE FEELS RATHER UNNATURAL AS WELL.
I CAN ONLY ***HOPE*** THAT THEIR ONE GOAL IS TO GROW THEIR HEROES...
...
AT ANY RATE, MY INSTINCTS ARE TELLING ME THAT WE SHOULDN'T MAKE ANY MOVES JUST YET.
WE SHOULD STAY ON OUR GUARD AND PATIENTLY WAIT FOR VERMIKINS.
WE MIGHT GAIN NEW INTEL BEFORE THEN AS WELL.
YES, WE CAN COUNT ON MISS ASTA'S INTEL.
...
ASTA...

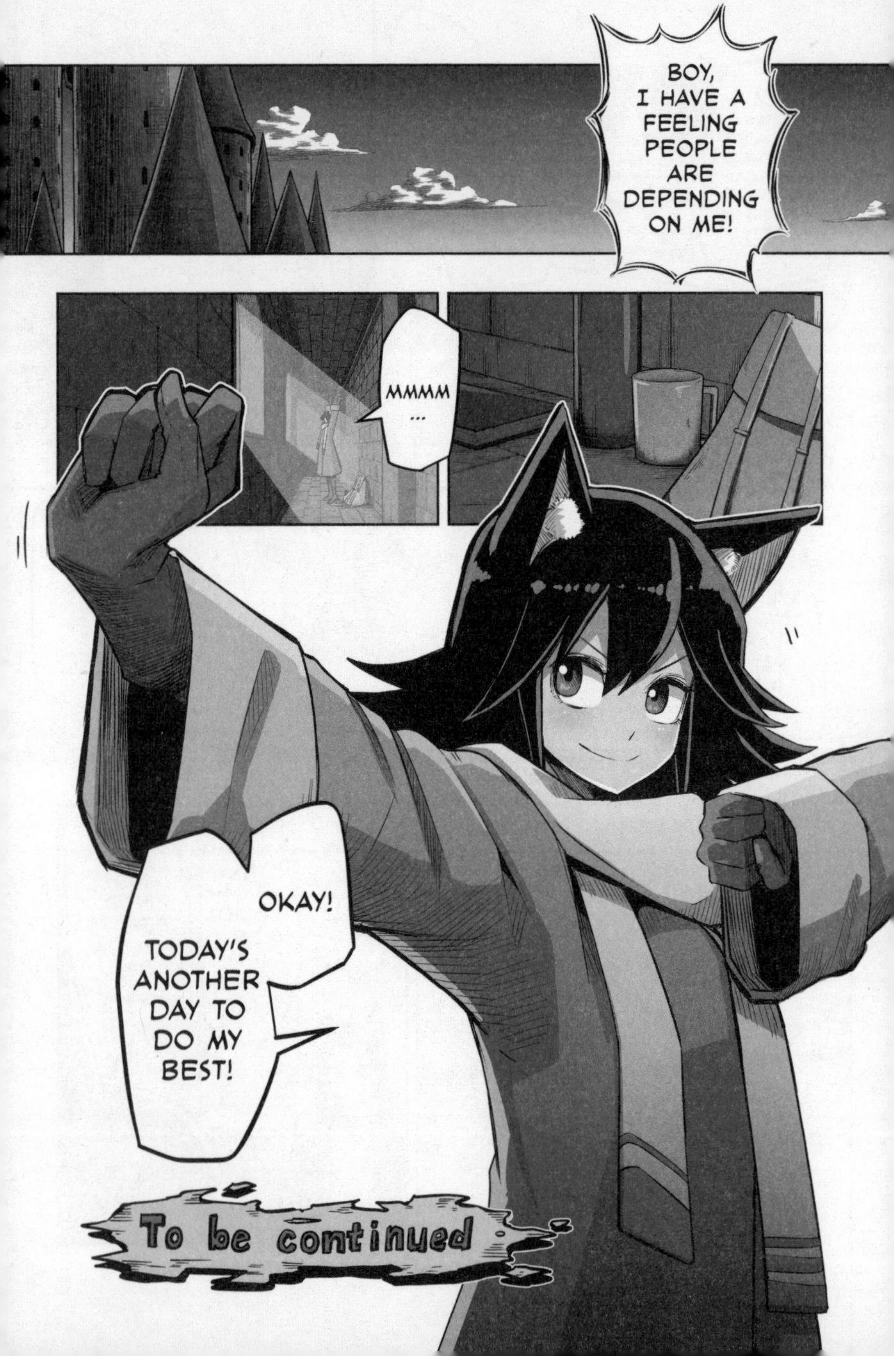
BOY, I HAVE A FEELING PEOPLE ARE DEPENDING ON ME!
MMMM ...
OKAY!
TODAY'S ANOTHER DAY TO DO MY BEST!
To be continued

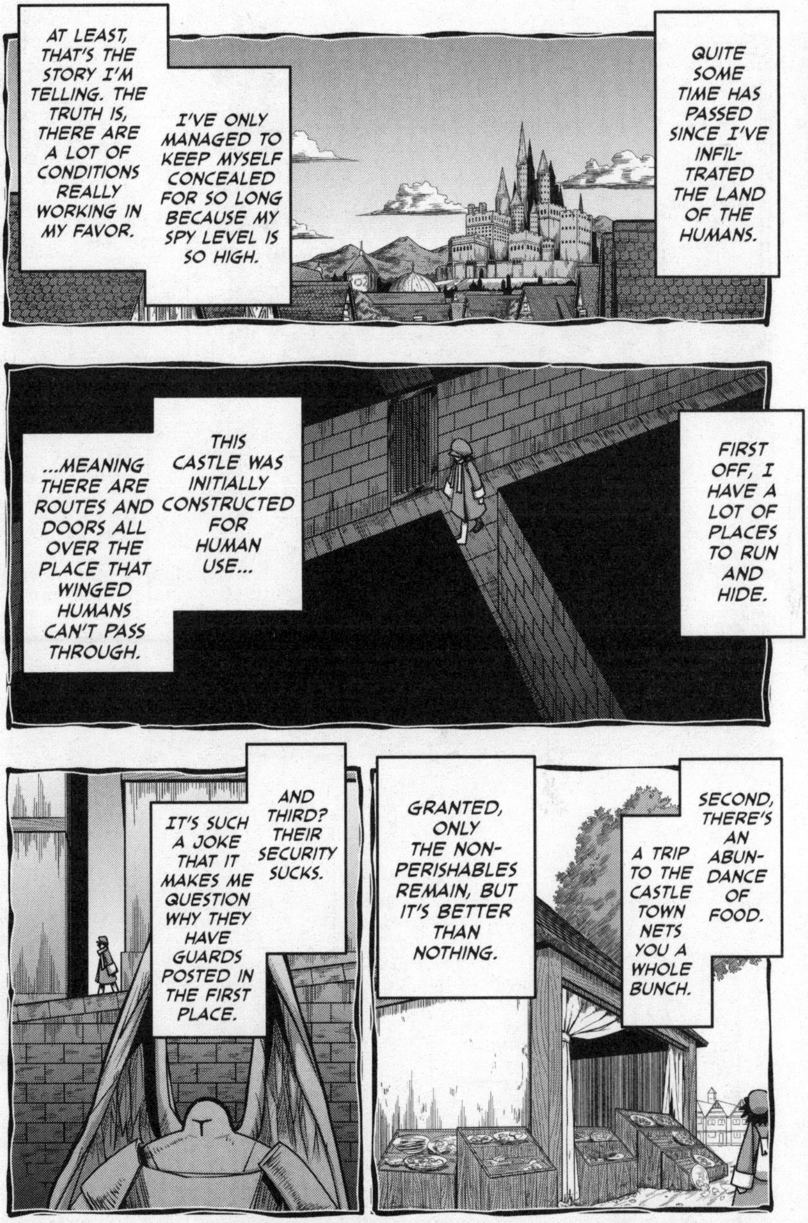
QUITE SOME TIME HAS PASSED SINCE I'VE INFILTRATED THE LAND OF THE HUMANS.
I'VE ONLY MANAGED TO KEEP MYSELF CONCEALED FOR SO LONG BECAUSE MY SPY LEVEL IS SO HIGH.
AT LEAST, THAT'S THE STORY I'M TELLING. THE TRUTH IS, THERE ARE A LOT OF CONDITIONS REALLY WORKING IN MY FAVOR.
FIRST OFF, I HAVE A LOT OF PLACES TO RUN AND HIDE.
THIS CASTLE WAS INITIALLY CONSTRUCTED FOR HUMAN USE...
...MEANING THERE ARE ROUTES AND DOORS ALL OVER THE PLACE THAT WINGED HUMANS CAN'T PASS THROUGH.
SECOND, THERE'S AN ABUNDANCE OF FOOD.
A TRIP TO THE CASTLE TOWN NETS YOU A WHOLE BUNCH.
GRANTED, ONLY THE NON-PERISHABLES REMAIN, BUT IT'S BETTER THAN NOTHING.
AND THIRD? THEIR SECURITY SUCKS.
IT'S SUCH A JOKE THAT IT MAKES ME QUESTION WHY THEY HAVE GUARDS POSTED IN THE FIRST PLACE.

Chapter 57: Exploring the Castle

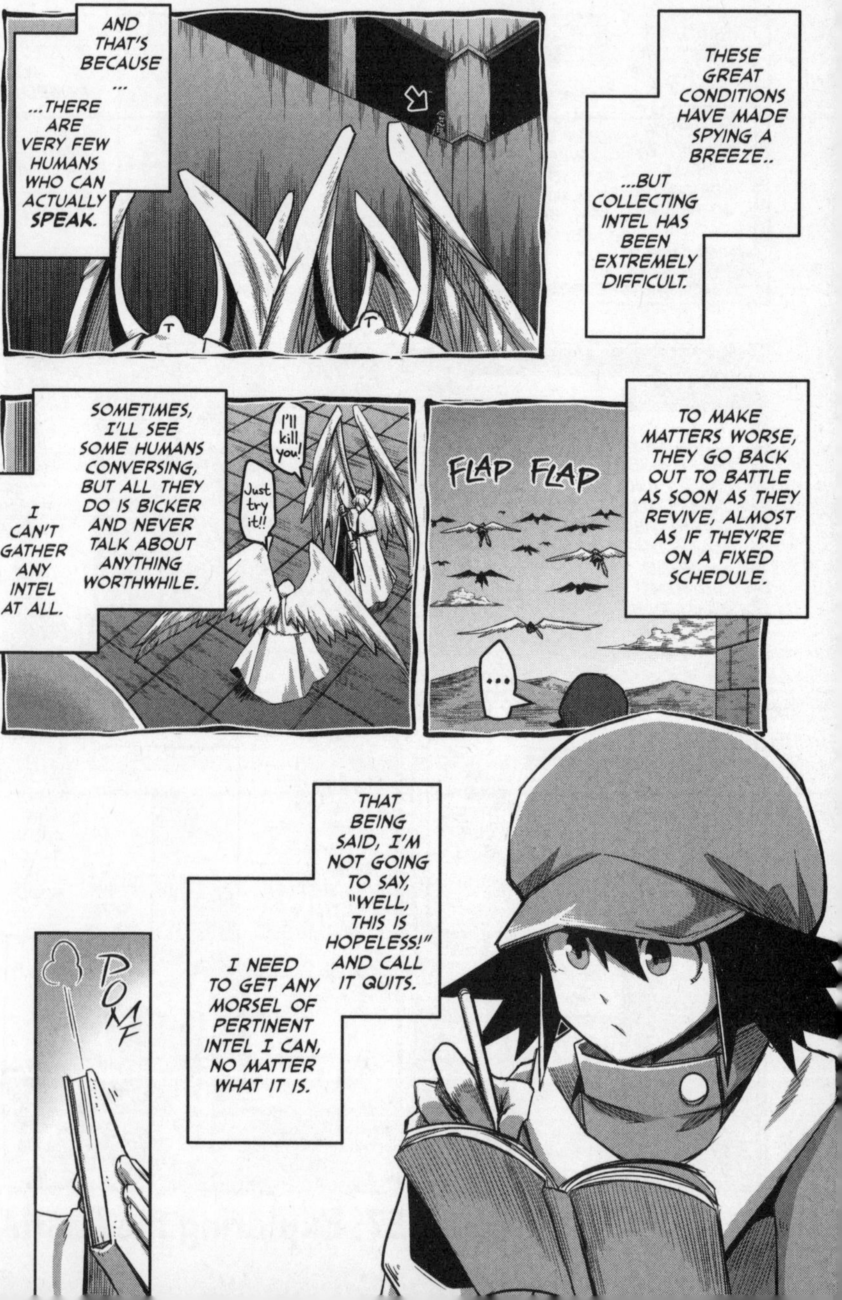
THESE GREAT CONDITIONS HAVE MADE SPYING A BREEZE..
...BUT COLLECTING INTEL HAS BEEN EXTREMELY DIFFICULT.
AND THAT'S BECAUSE...
...THERE ARE VERY FEW HUMANS WHO CAN ACTUALLY **SPEAK**.
TO MAKE MATTERS WORSE, THEY GO BACK OUT TO BATTLE AS SOON AS THEY REVIVE, ALMOST AS IF THEY'RE ON A FIXED SCHEDULE.
FLAP FLAP
...
SOMETIMES, I'LL SEE SOME HUMANS CONVERSING, BUT ALL THEY DO IS BICKER AND NEVER TALK ABOUT ANYTHING WORTHWHILE.
I'll kill you!
Just try it!!
I CAN'T GATHER ANY INTEL AT ALL.
THAT BEING SAID, I'M NOT GOING TO SAY, "WELL, THIS IS HOPELESS!" AND CALL IT QUITS.
I NEED TO GET ANY MORSEL OF PERTINENT INTEL I CAN, NO MATTER WHAT IT IS.
POMF

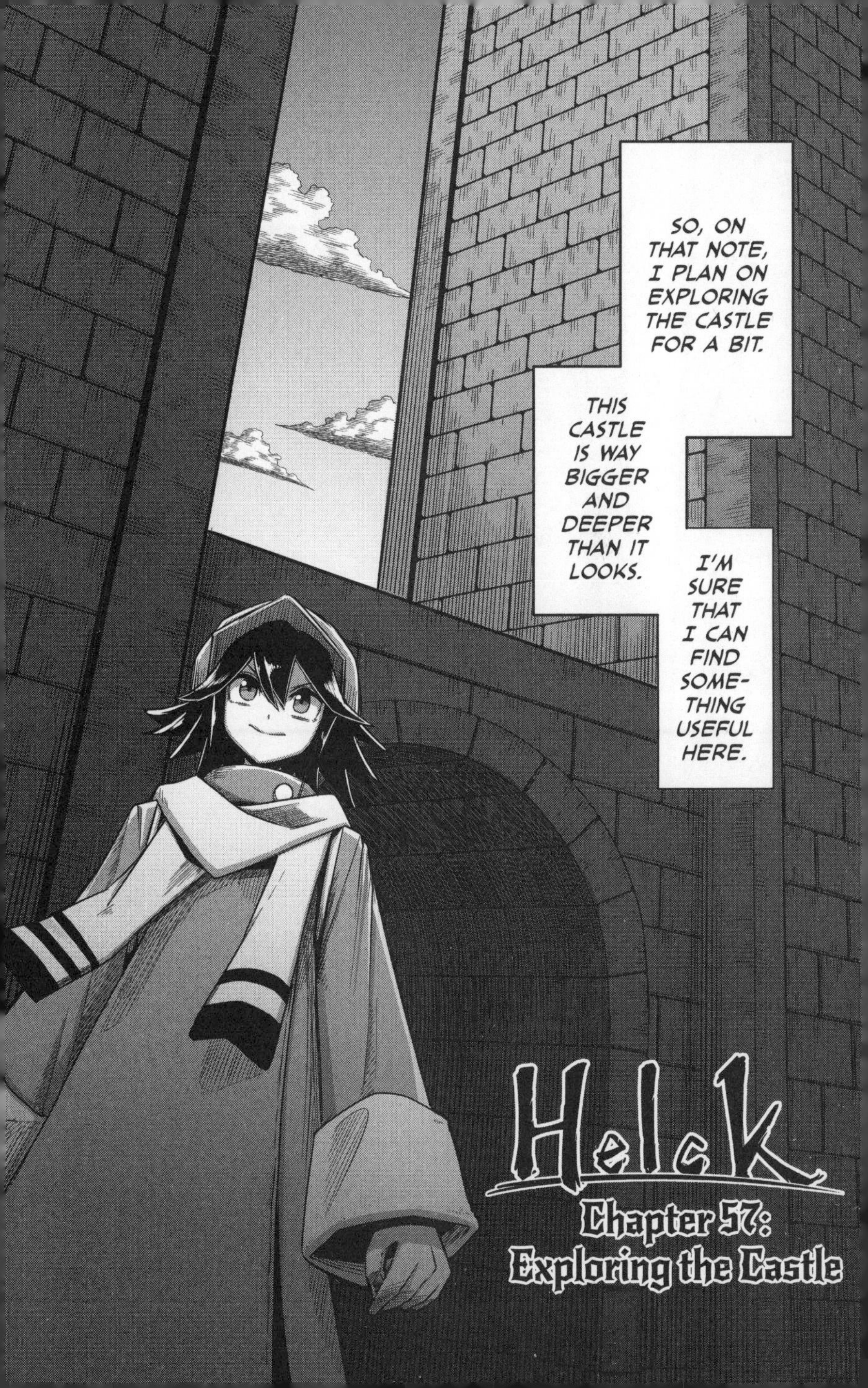
SO, ON THAT NOTE, I PLAN ON EXPLORING THE CASTLE FOR A BIT.
THIS CASTLE IS WAY BIGGER AND DEEPER THAN IT LOOKS.
I'M SURE THAT I CAN FIND SOME-THING USEFUL HERE.
Helck
Chapter 57: Exploring the Castle

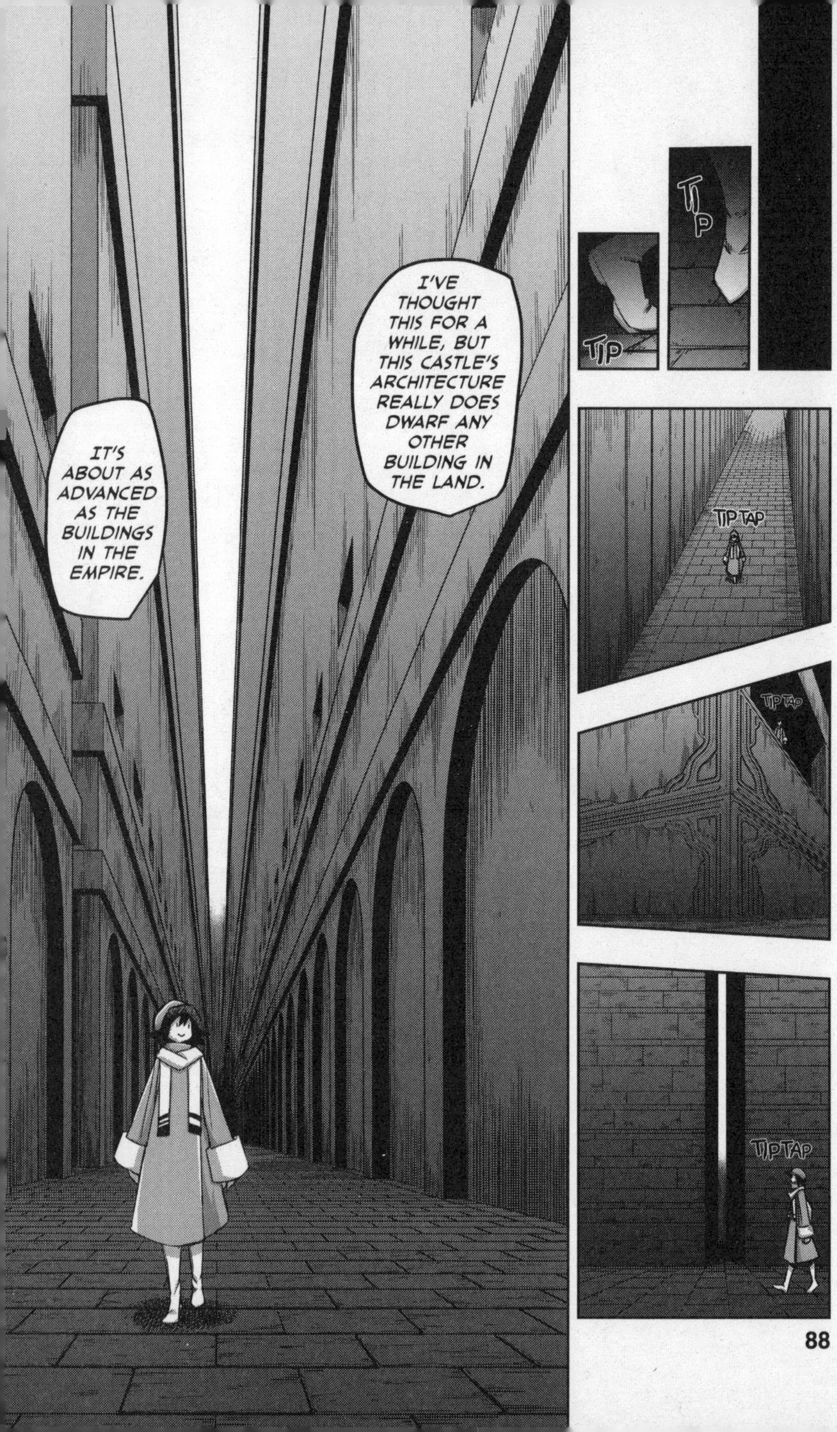
TIP
TIP
TIP TAP
TIP TAP
TIP TAP
I'VE THOUGHT THIS FOR A WHILE, BUT THIS CASTLE'S ARCHITECTURE REALLY DOES DWARF ANY OTHER BUILDING IN THE LAND.
IT'S ABOUT AS ADVANCED AS THE BUILDINGS IN THE EMPIRE.

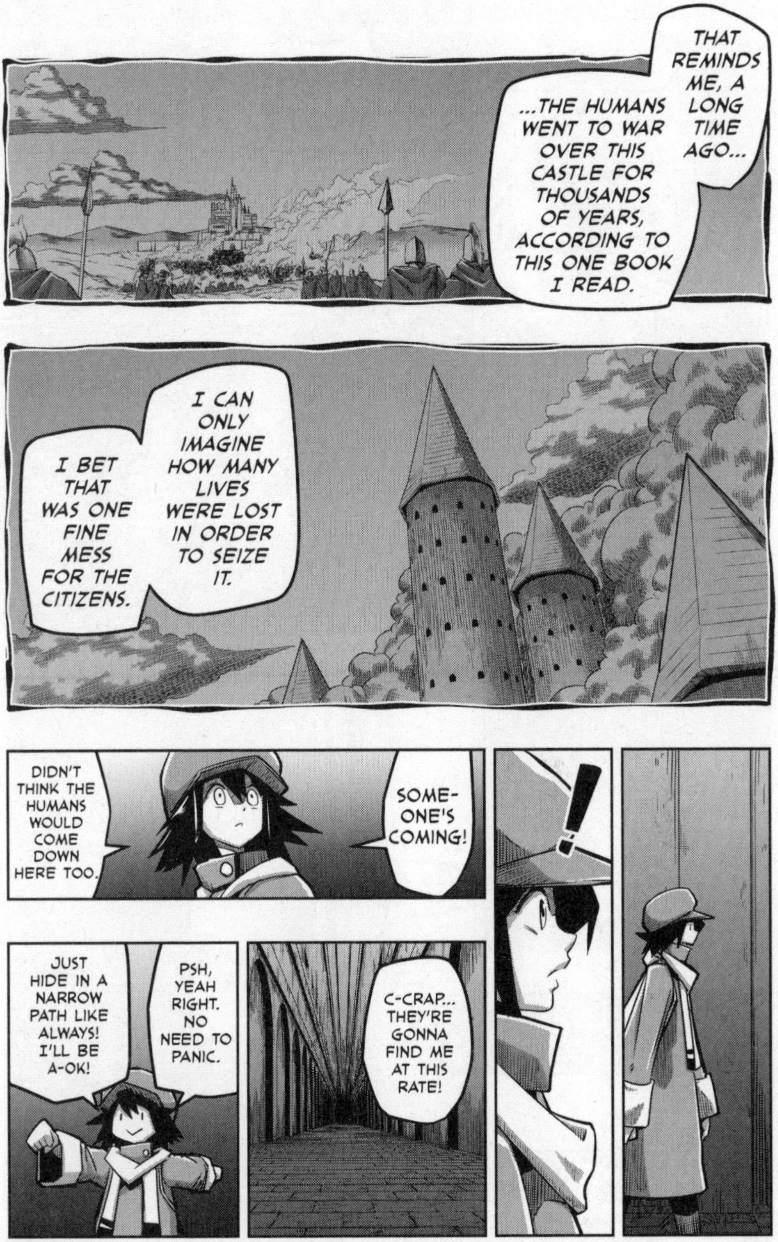
THAT REMINDS ME, A LONG TIME AGO...
...THE HUMANS WENT TO WAR OVER THIS CASTLE FOR THOUSANDS OF YEARS, ACCORDING TO THIS ONE BOOK I READ.
I CAN ONLY IMAGINE HOW MANY LIVES WERE LOST IN ORDER TO SEIZE IT.
I BET THAT WAS ONE FINE MESS FOR THE CITIZENS.
!
SOME-ONE'S COMING!
DIDN'T THINK THE HUMANS WOULD COME DOWN HERE TOO.
C-CRAP... THEY'RE GONNA FIND ME AT THIS RATE!
PSH, YEAH RIGHT. NO NEED TO PANIC.
JUST HIDE IN A NARROW PATH LIKE ALWAYS! I'LL BE A-OK!

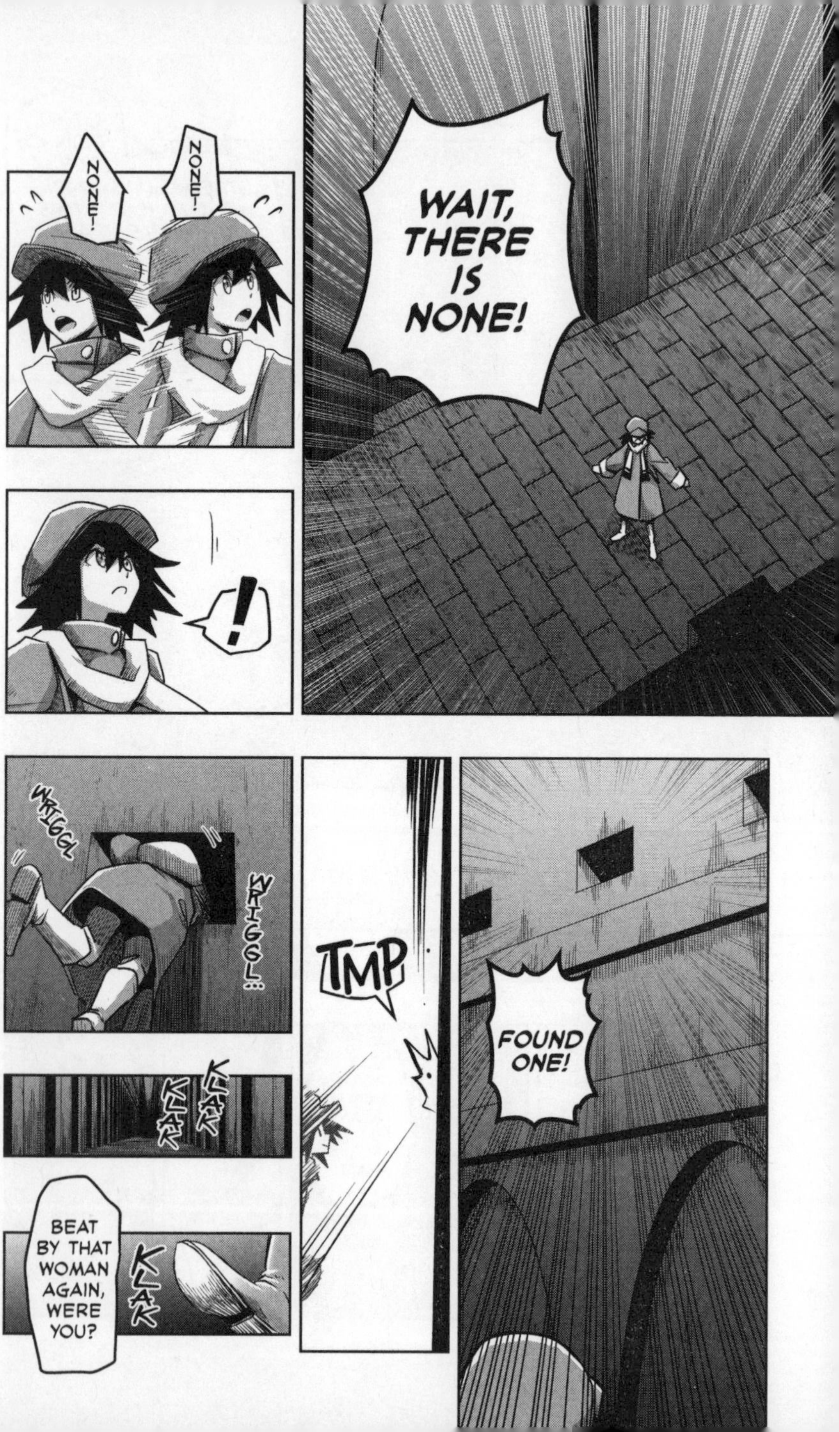
WAIT, THERE IS NONE!
NONE!
NONE!
!
FOUND ONE!
TMP
WRIGGL
WRIGGL...
KLAK
KLAK
KLAK
BEAT BY THAT WOMAN AGAIN, WERE YOU?

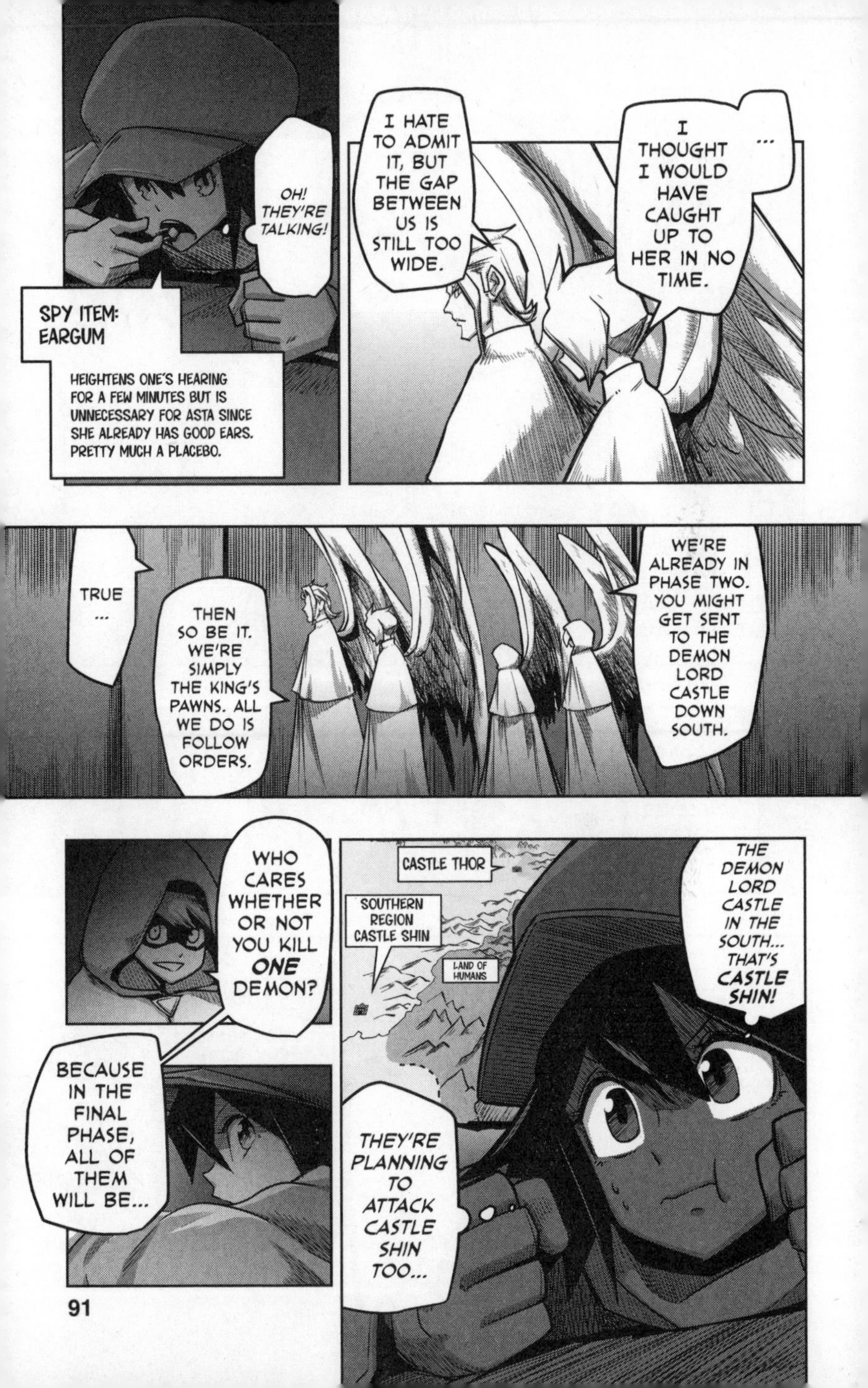
...
I THOUGHT I WOULD HAVE CAUGHT UP TO HER IN NO TIME.
I HATE TO ADMIT IT, BUT THE GAP BETWEEN US IS STILL TOO WIDE.
OH! THEY'RE TALKING!
SPY ITEM: EARGUM
HEIGHTENS ONE'S HEARING FOR A FEW MINUTES BUT IS UNNECESSARY FOR ASTA SINCE SHE ALREADY HAS GOOD EARS. PRETTY MUCH A PLACEBO.
WE'RE ALREADY IN PHASE TWO. YOU MIGHT GET SENT TO THE DEMON LORD CASTLE DOWN SOUTH.
THEN SO BE IT. WE'RE SIMPLY THE KING'S PAWNS. ALL WE DO IS FOLLOW ORDERS.
TRUE ...
THE DEMON LORD CASTLE IN THE SOUTH... THAT'S CASTLE SHIN!
CASTLE THOR
SOUTHERN REGION CASTLE SHIN
LAND OF HUMANS
THEY'RE PLANNING TO ATTACK CASTLE SHIN TOO...
WHO CARES WHETHER OR NOT YOU KILL ONE DEMON?
BECAUSE IN THE FINAL PHASE, ALL OF THEM WILL BE...

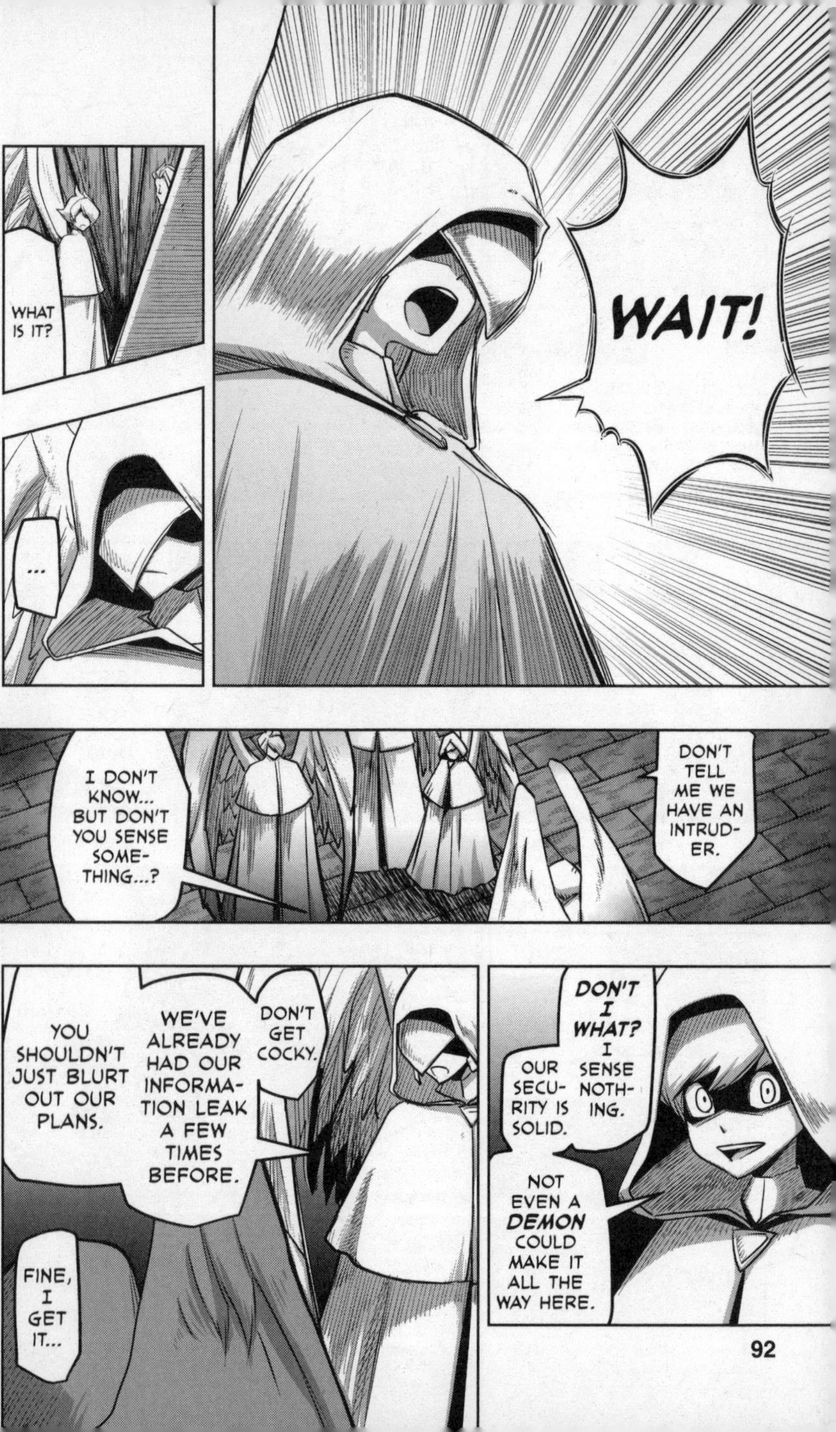
WAIT!
WHAT IS IT?
...
DON'T TELL ME WE HAVE AN INTRUDER.
I DON'T KNOW... BUT DON'T YOU SENSE SOMETHING...?
DON'T I WHAT? I SENSE NOTHING.
OUR SECURITY IS SOLID.
NOT EVEN A DEMON COULD MAKE IT ALL THE WAY HERE.
DON'T GET COCKY.
WE'VE ALREADY HAD OUR INFORMATION LEAK A FEW TIMES BEFORE.
YOU SHOULDN'T JUST BLURT OUT OUR PLANS.
FINE, I GET IT...

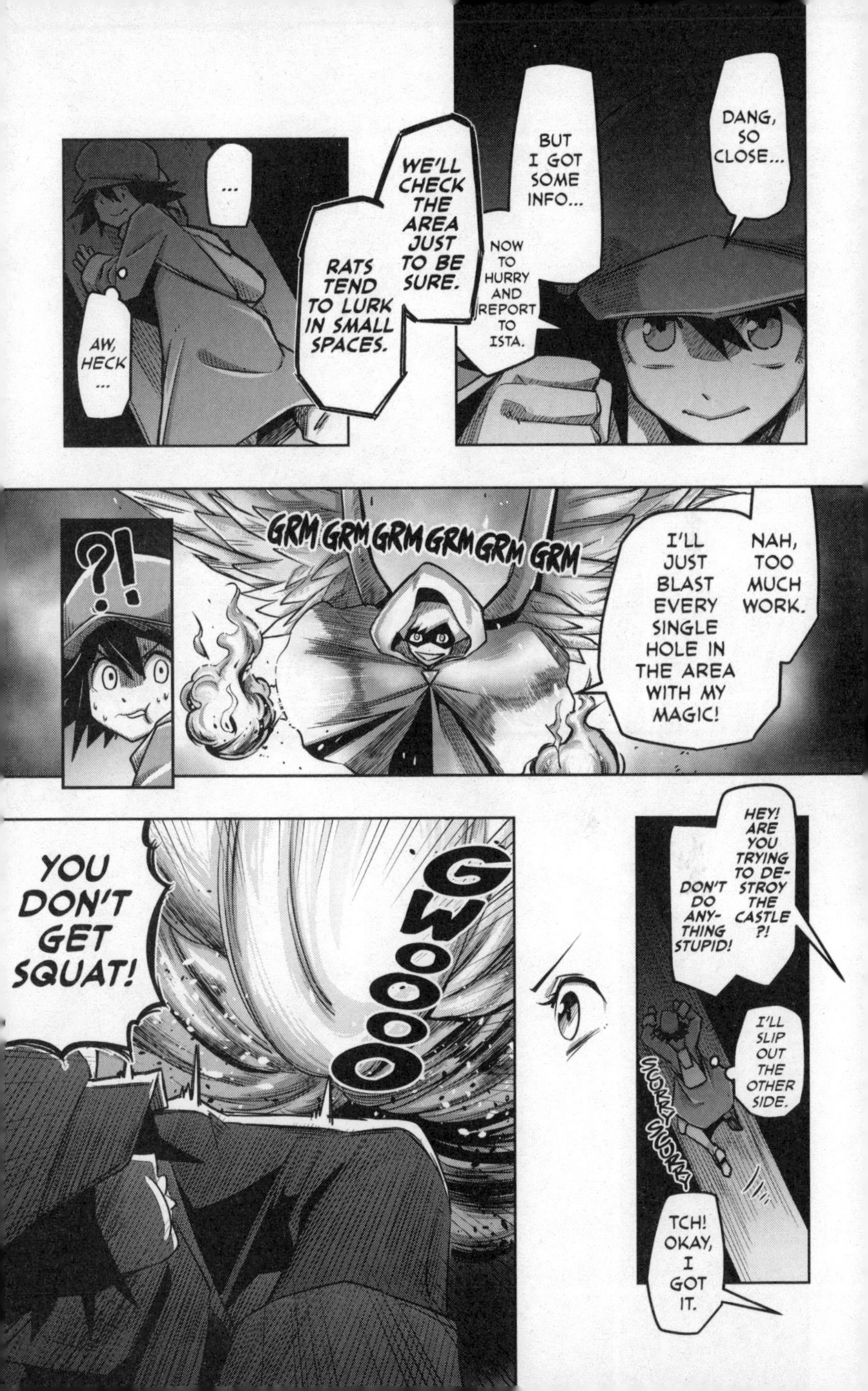
DANG, SO CLOSE...
BUT I GOT SOME INFO...
NOW TO HURRY AND REPORT TO ISTA.
WE'LL CHECK THE AREA JUST TO BE SURE.
RATS TEND TO LURK IN SMALL SPACES.
...
AW, HECK ...
NAH, TOO MUCH WORK.
I'LL JUST BLAST EVERY SINGLE HOLE IN THE AREA WITH MY MAGIC!
GRM GRM GRM GRM GRM GRM
?!
HEY! ARE YOU TRYING TO DE-STROY THE CASTLE ?!
DON'T DO ANY-THING STUPID!
I'LL SLIP OUT THE OTHER SIDE.
TCH! OKAY, I GOT IT.
GWOOOO
YOU DON'T GET SQUAT!

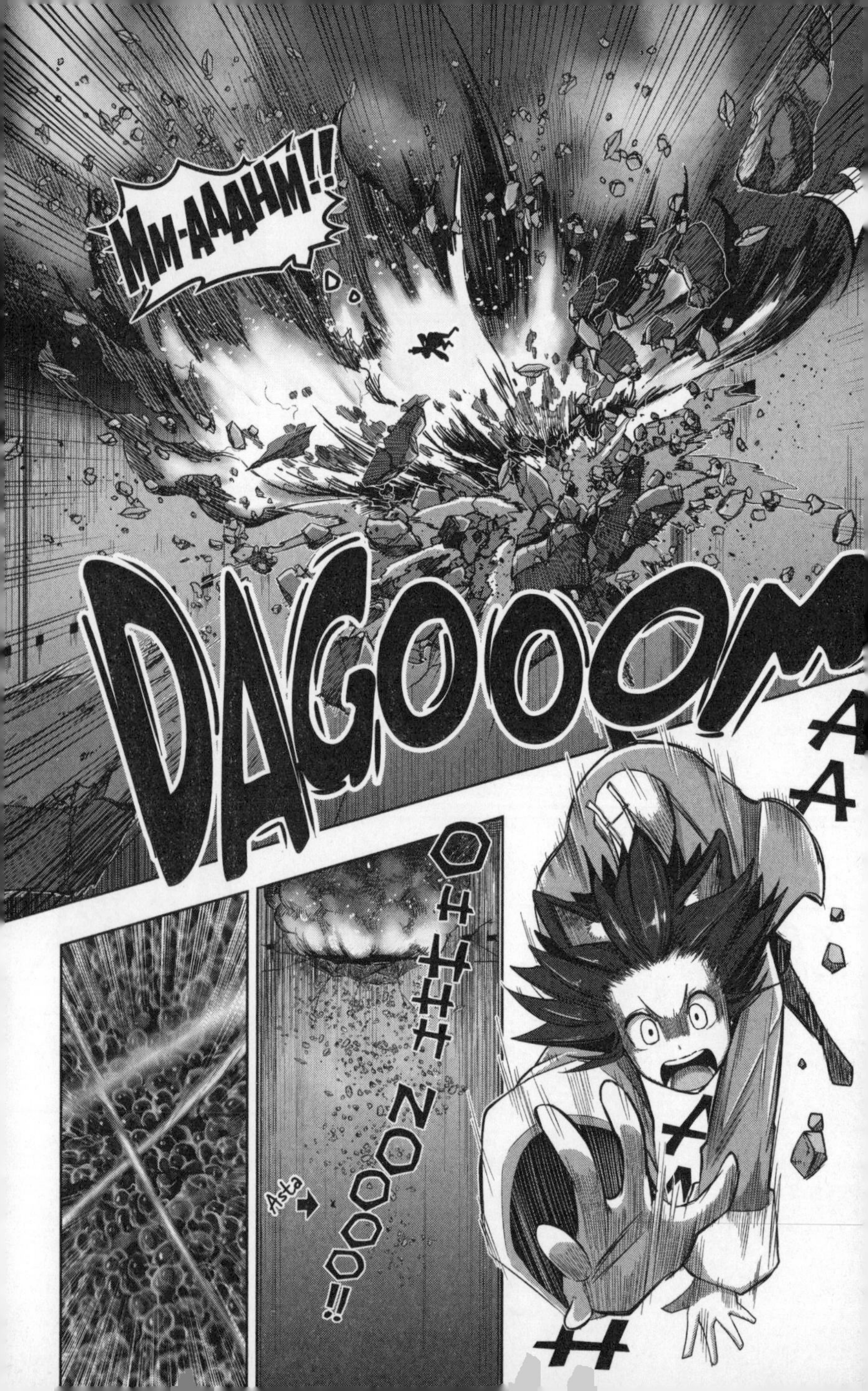
MM-AAAHM!!
DAGOOOM
AAAAH
OHHHH NOOOOO!!
Asta

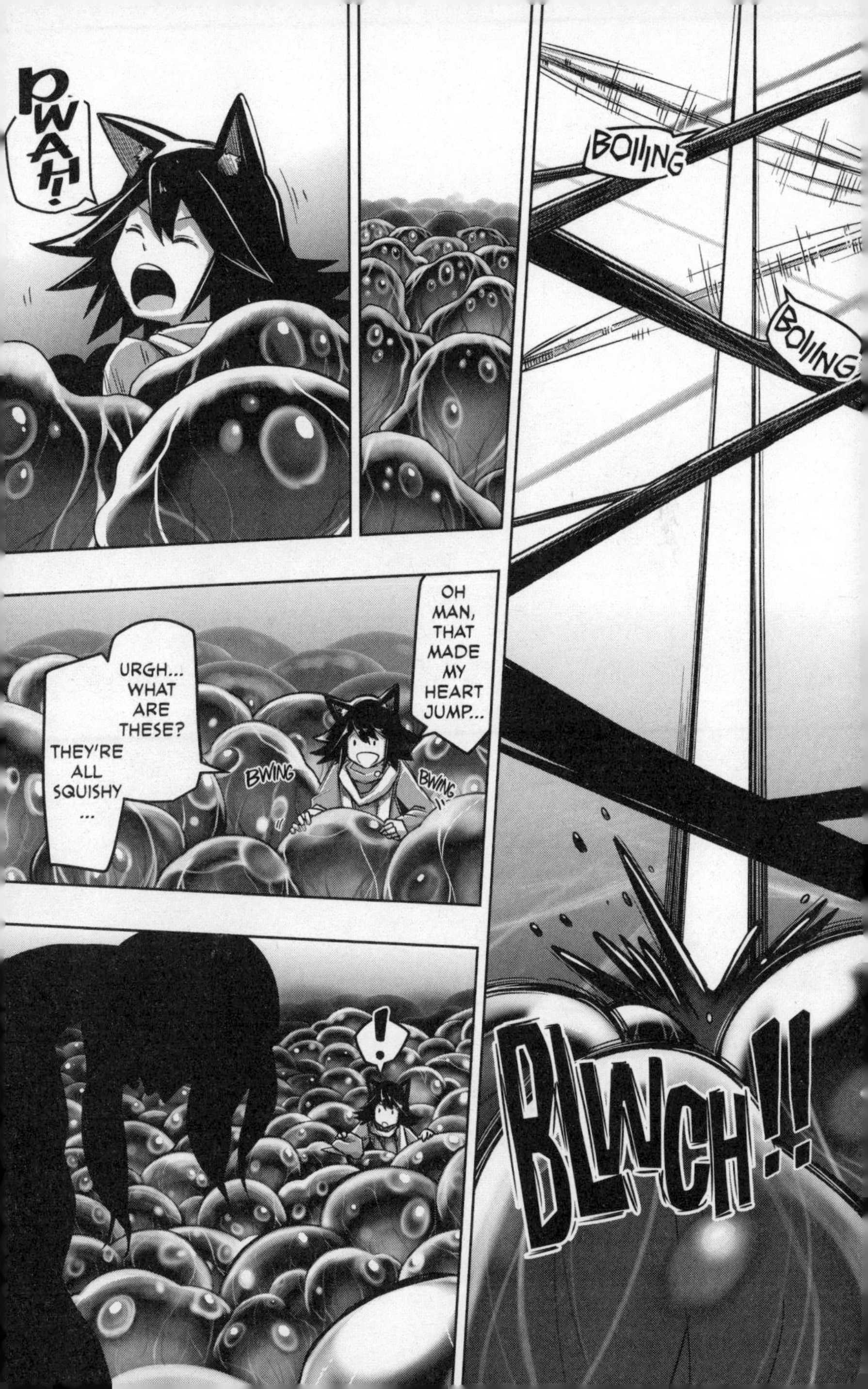
BOIIING
BOIIING
BLWCH!!
PWAH!
OH MAN, THAT MADE MY HEART JUMP...
URGH... WHAT ARE THESE? THEY'RE ALL SQUISHY ...
BWING
BWING
!

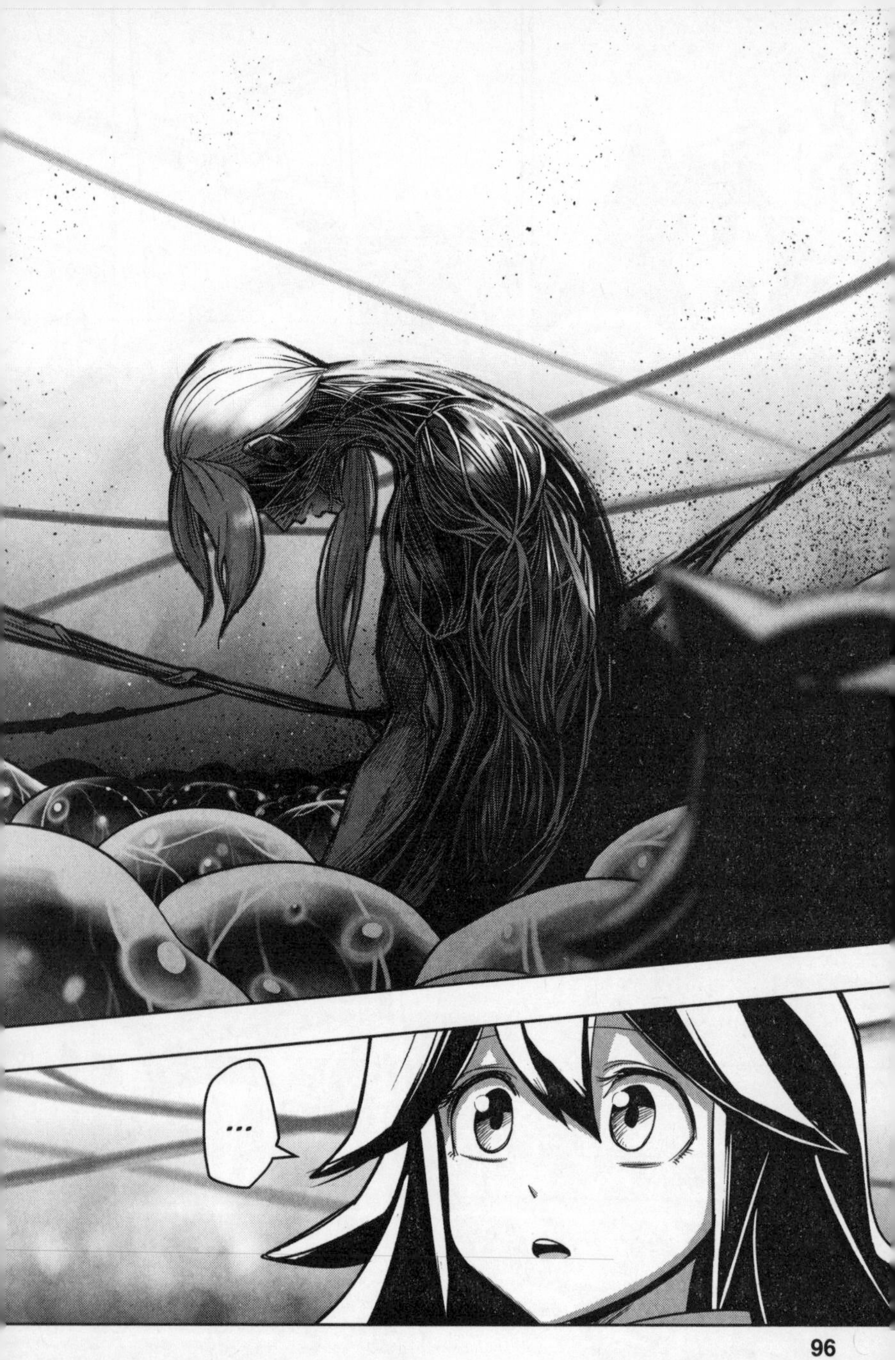
...

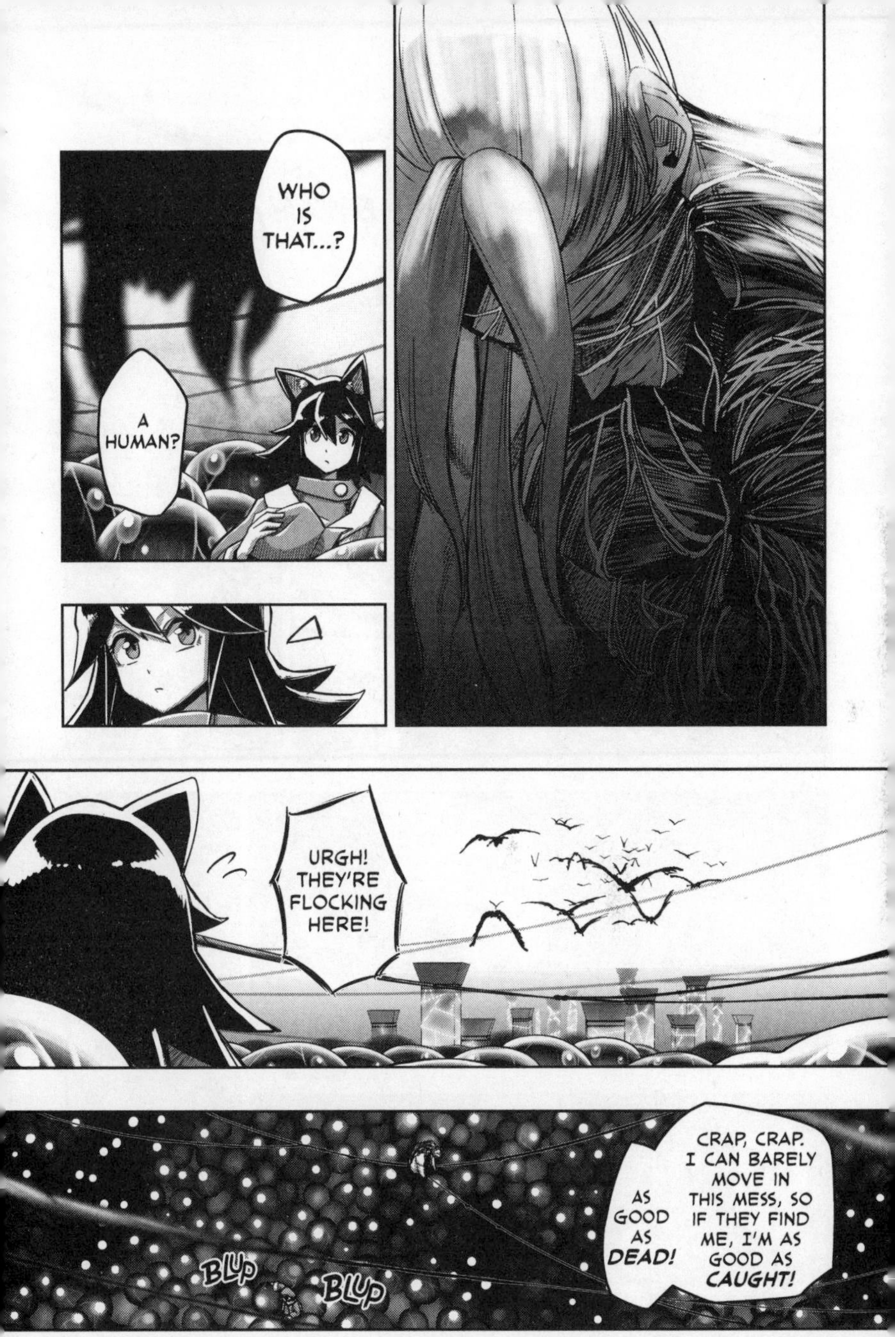
WHO IS THAT...?
A HUMAN?
URGH! THEY'RE FLOCKING HERE!
CRAP, CRAP. I CAN BARELY MOVE IN THIS MESS, SO IF THEY FIND ME, I'M AS GOOD AS *CAUGHT!*
AS GOOD AS *DEAD!*
BLUP
BLUP

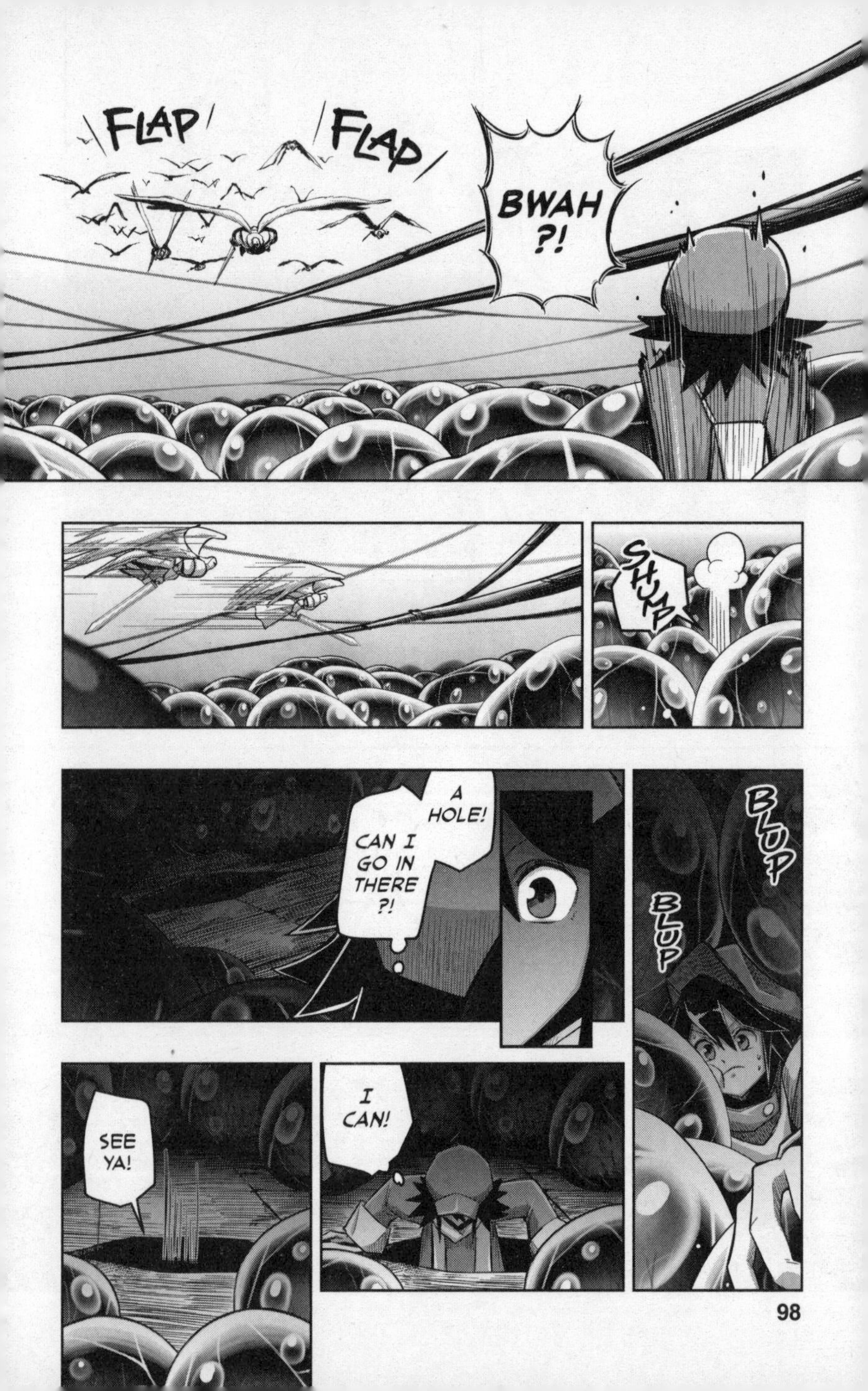
BWAH ?!
FLAP
FLAP
SHUMP
BLUP
BLUP
A HOLE!
CAN I GO IN THERE ?!
I CAN!
SEE YA!

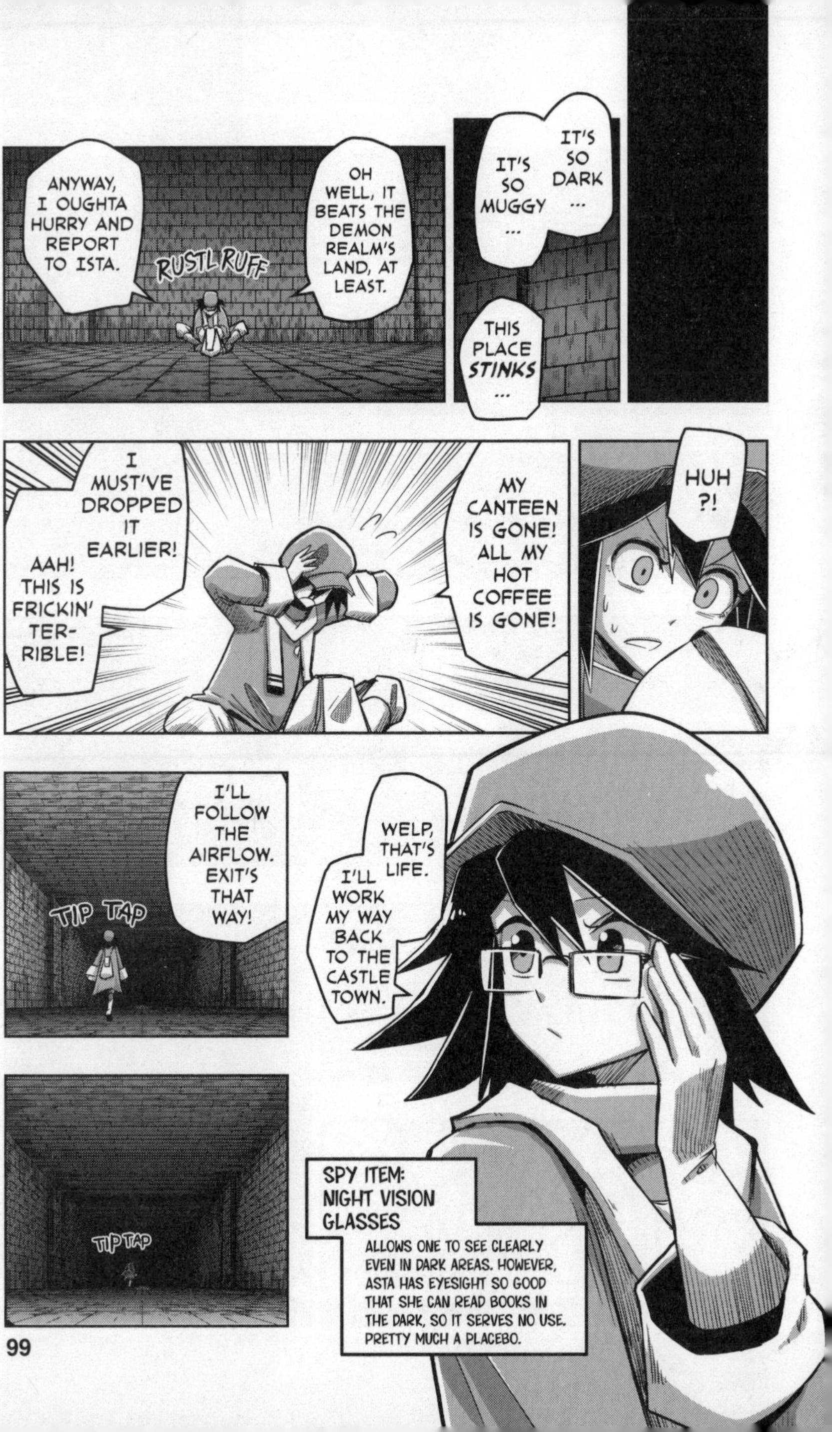

IT'S SO DARK ...
IT'S SO MUGGY ...
THIS PLACE STINKS ...
OH WELL, IT BEATS THE DEMON REALM'S LAND, AT LEAST.
RUSTL RUFF
ANYWAY, I OUGHTA HURRY AND REPORT TO ISTA.
HUH ?!
MY CANTEEN IS GONE! ALL MY HOT COFFEE IS GONE!
I MUST'VE DROPPED IT EARLIER!
AAH! THIS IS FRICKIN' TER-RIBLE!
WELP, THAT'S LIFE.
I'LL WORK MY WAY BACK TO THE CASTLE TOWN.
SPY ITEM: NIGHT VISION GLASSES
ALLOWS ONE TO SEE CLEARLY EVEN IN DARK AREAS. HOWEVER, ASTA HAS EYESIGHT SO GOOD THAT SHE CAN READ BOOKS IN THE DARK, SO IT SERVES NO USE. PRETTY MUCH A PLACEBO.
I'LL FOLLOW THE AIRFLOW. EXIT'S THAT WAY!
TIP TAP
TIP TAP

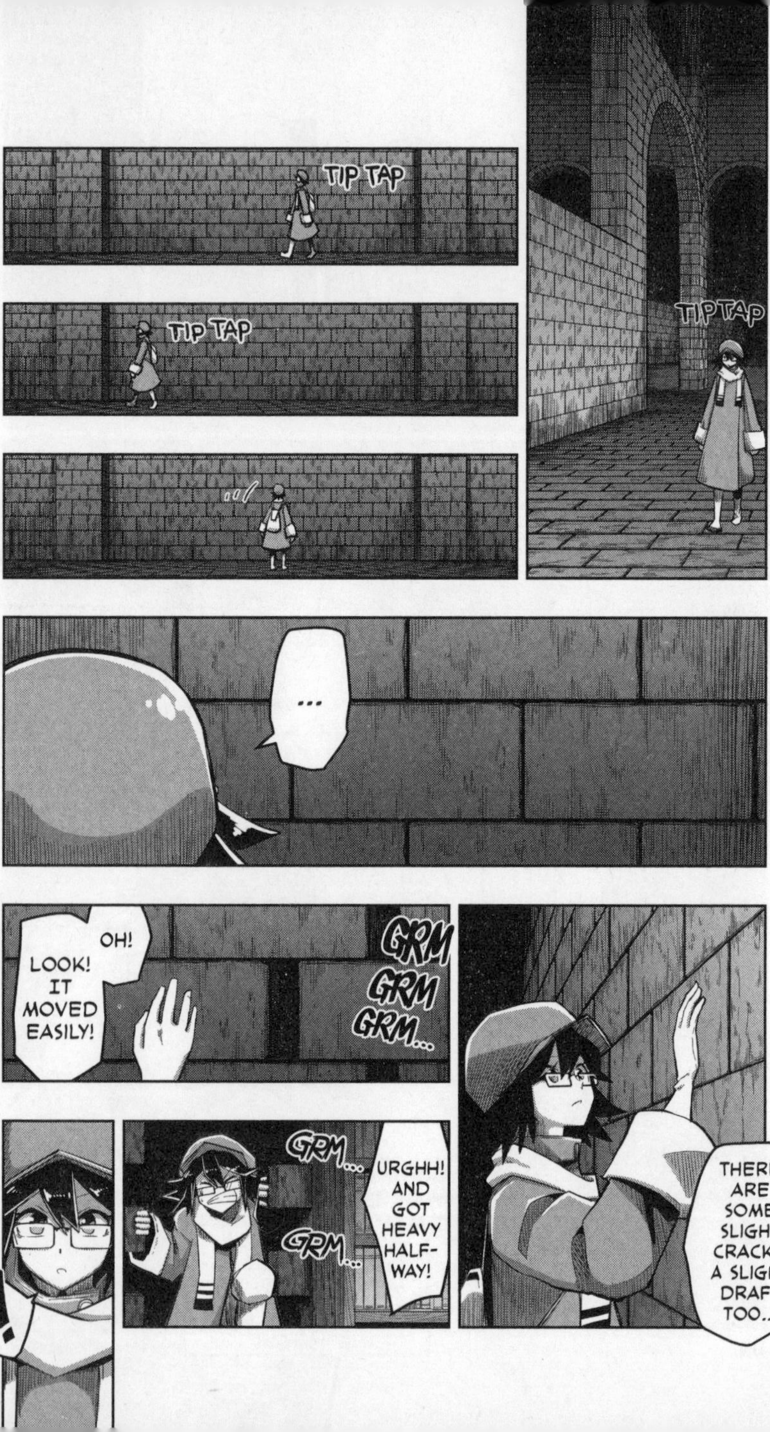
TIPTAP
TIP TAP
TIP TAP
...
THERE ARE SOME SLIGHT CRACKS. A SLIGHT DRAFT TOO...
GRM GRM GRM...
OH! LOOK! IT MOVED EASILY!
GRM...
URGHH! AND GOT HEAVY HALF-WAY!
GRM...
!

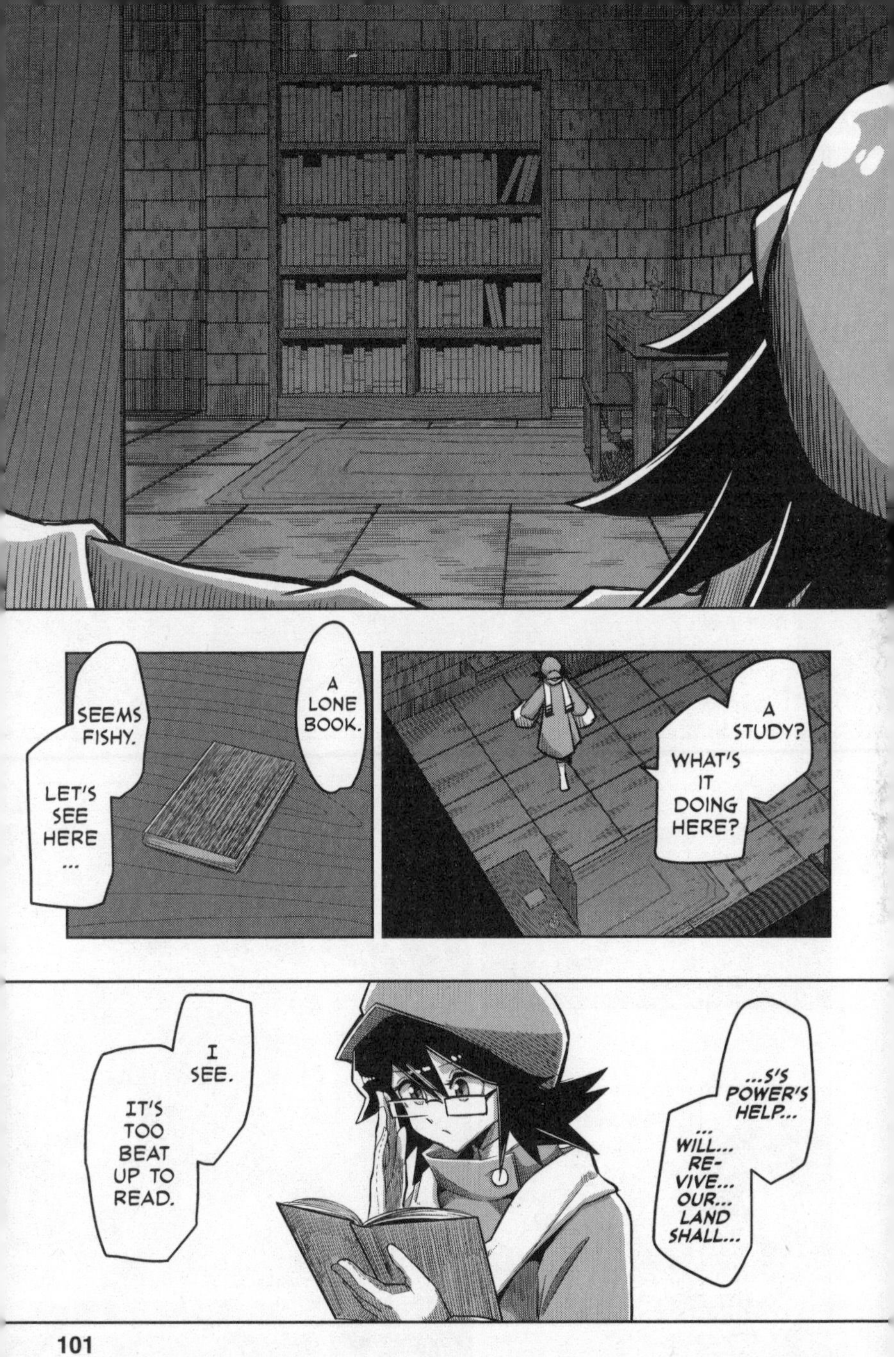
A STUDY?
WHAT'S IT DOING HERE?
A LONE BOOK.
SEEMS FISHY.
LET'S SEE HERE ...
...S'S POWER'S HELP...
... WILL... RE-VIVE... OUR... LAND SHALL...
I SEE.
IT'S TOO BEAT UP TO READ.

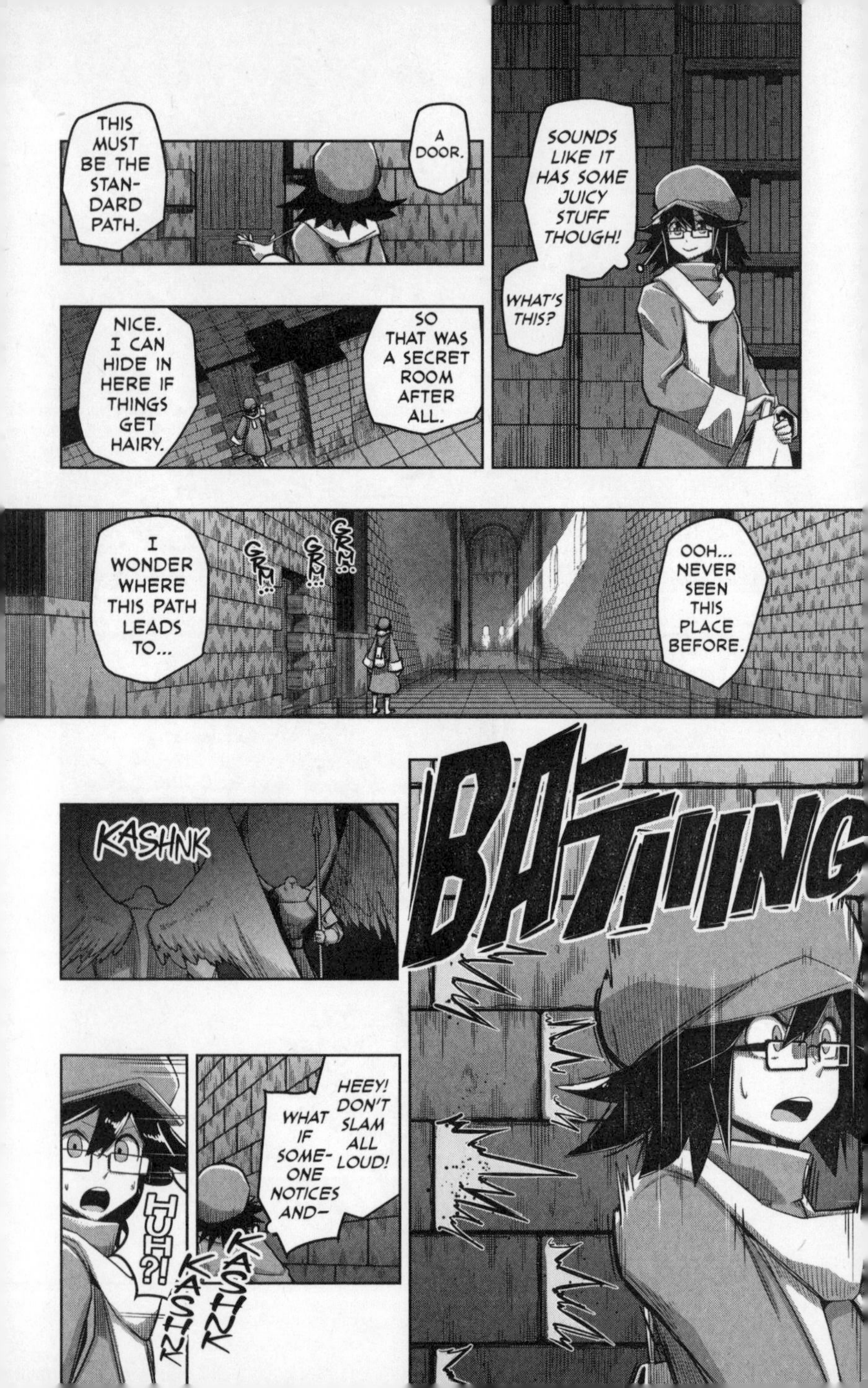
SOUNDS LIKE IT HAS SOME JUICY STUFF THOUGH!
WHAT'S THIS?
A DOOR.
THIS MUST BE THE STAN-DARD PATH.
SO THAT WAS A SECRET ROOM AFTER ALL.
NICE. I CAN HIDE IN HERE IF THINGS GET HAIRY.
OOH... NEVER SEEN THIS PLACE BEFORE.
GRM..
GRM..
GRM..
I WONDER WHERE THIS PATH LEADS TO...
BA-TIIING
KASHNK
HEEY! DON'T SLAM ALL LOUD!
WHAT IF SOME-ONE NOTICES AND—
KASHNK
KASHNK
HUH?!

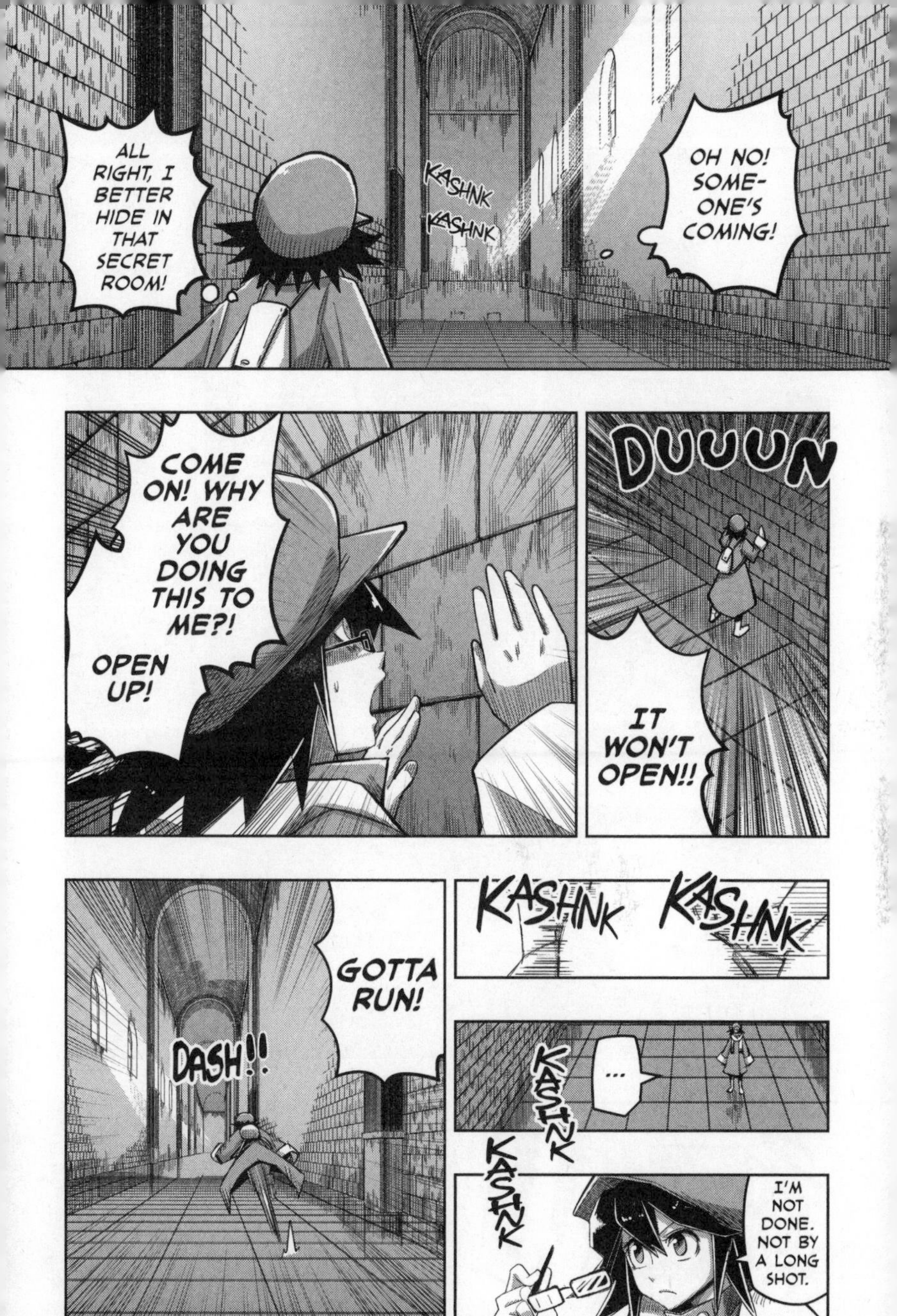
KASHNK
KASHNK
OH NO! SOME-ONE'S COMING!
ALL RIGHT, I BETTER HIDE IN THAT SECRET ROOM!
DUUUN
IT WON'T OPEN!!
COME ON! WHY ARE YOU DOING THIS TO ME?!
OPEN UP!
KASHNK KASHNK
KASHNK
...
KASHNK
I'M NOT DONE. NOT BY A LONG SHOT.
GOTTA RUN!
DASH!!

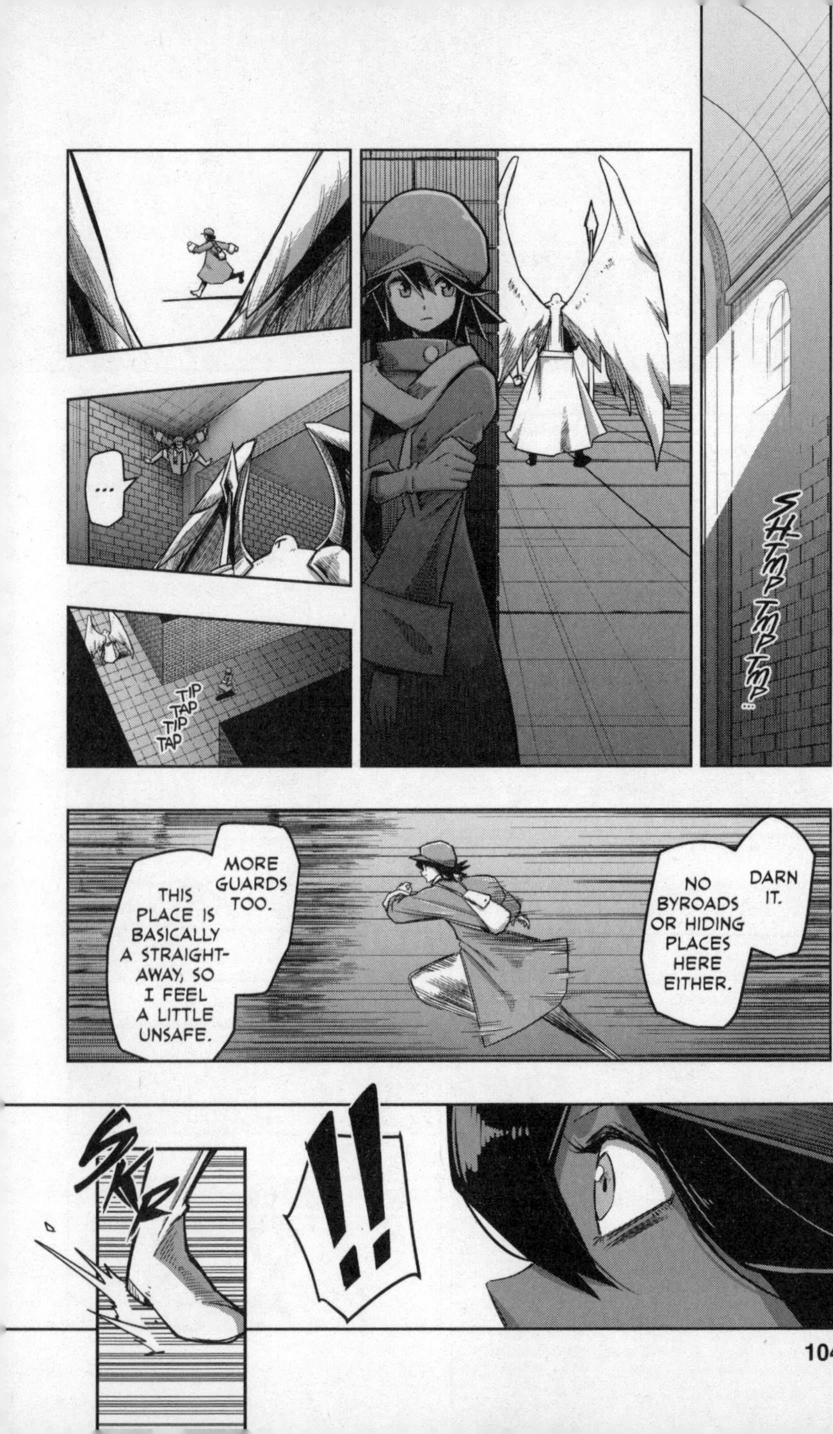

SHTMP TMP TMP
...
TIP TAP TIP TAP
DARN IT.
NO BYROADS OR HIDING PLACES HERE EITHER.
MORE GUARDS TOO.
THIS PLACE IS BASICALLY A STRAIGHT-AWAY, SO I FEEL A LITTLE UNSAFE.
!!
SKR

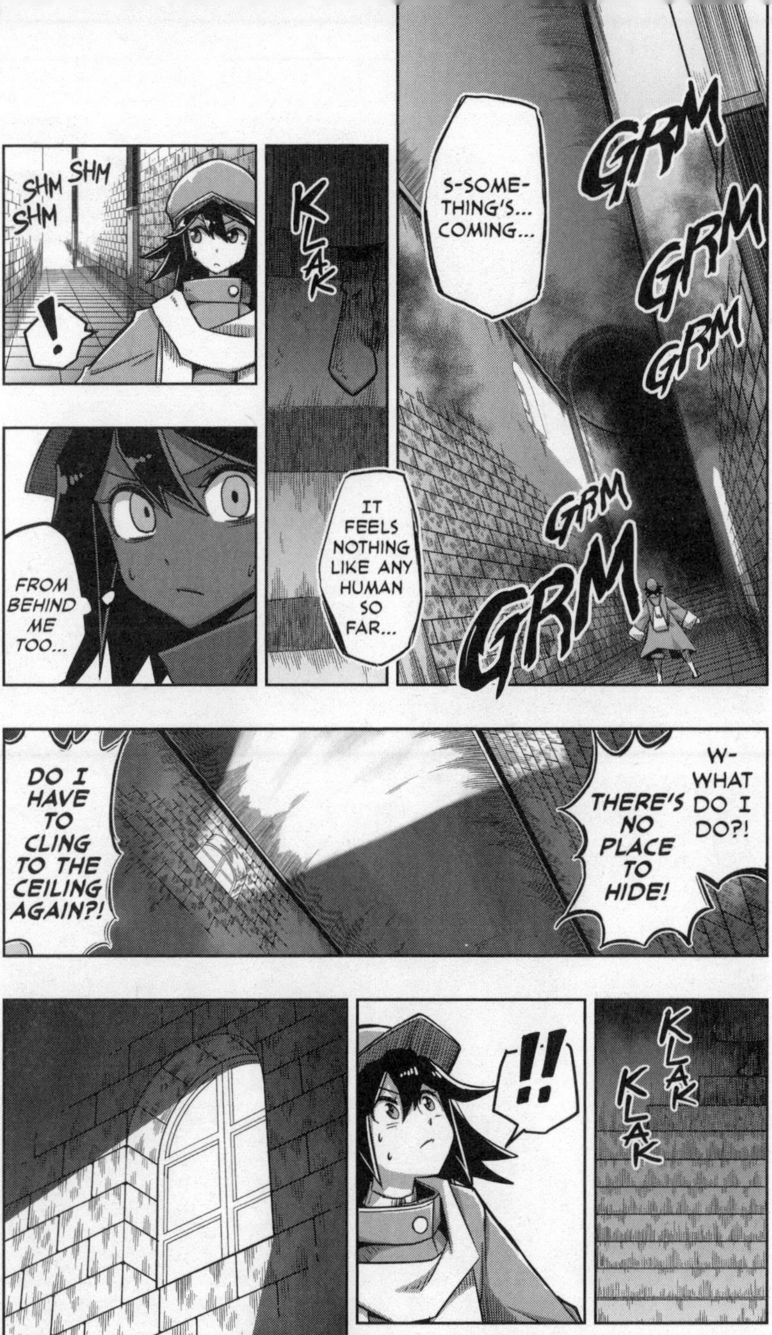
GRM GRM GRM
S-SOMETHING'S... COMING...
GRM GRM
IT FEELS NOTHING LIKE ANY HUMAN SO FAR...
KLAK
SHM SHM SHM
!
FROM BEHIND ME TOO...
W- WHAT DO I DO?!
THERE'S NO PLACE TO HIDE!
DO I HAVE TO CLING TO THE CEILING AGAIN?!
KLAK KLAK
!!

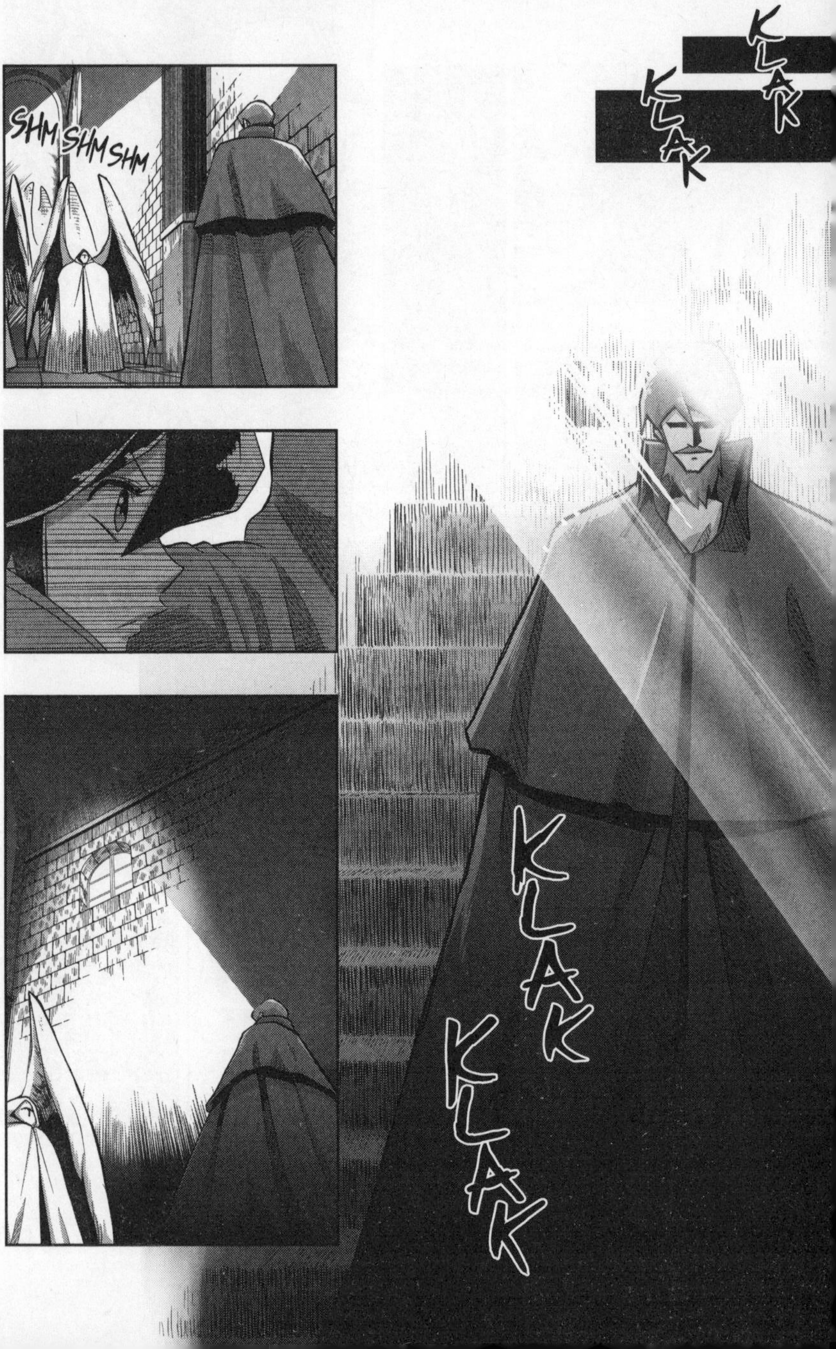
KLAK
KLAK
KLAK
KLAK
SHM SHM SHM

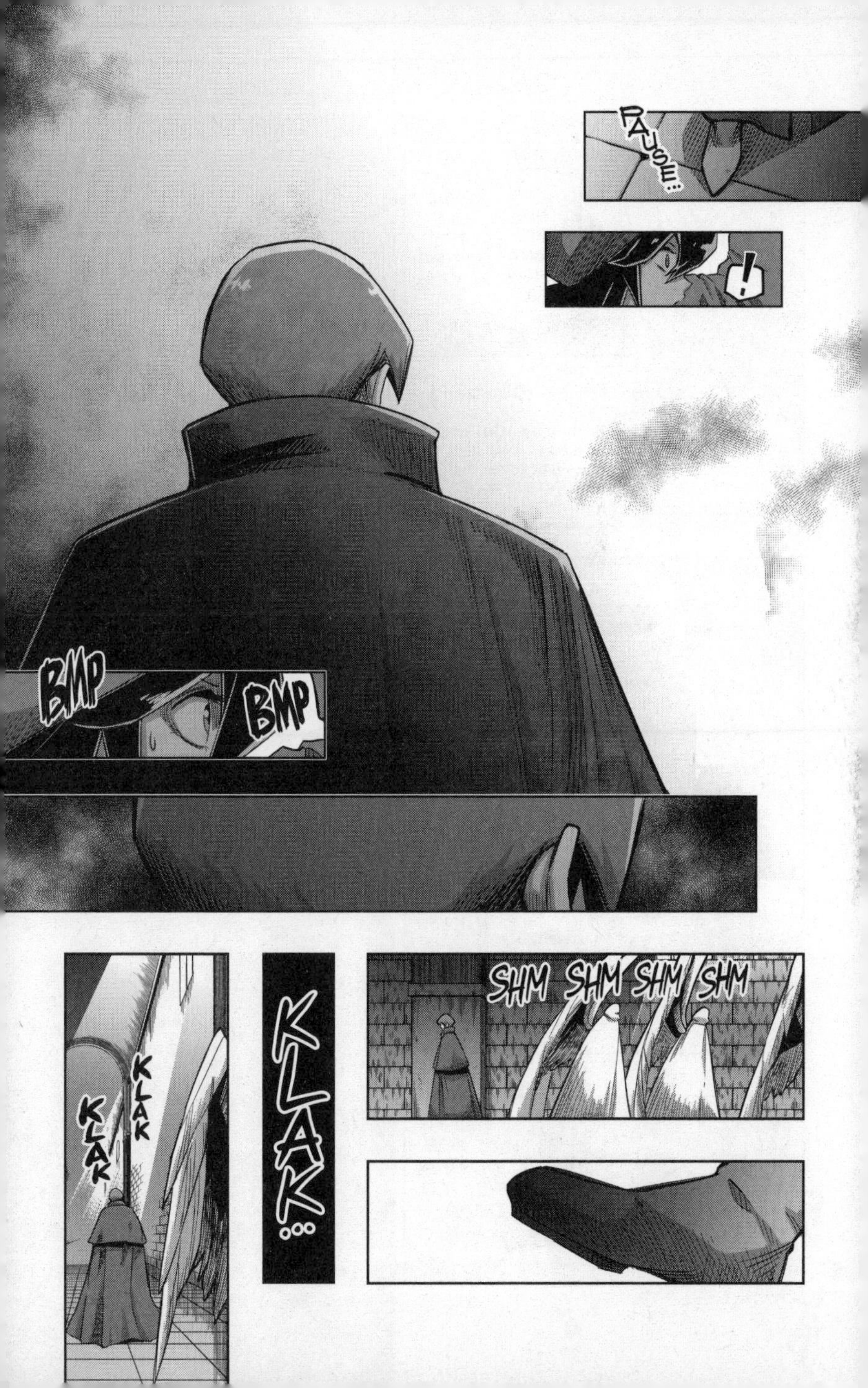
PAUSE...
!
BMP
BMP
SHM SHM SHM SHM
KLAK...
KLAK
KLAK

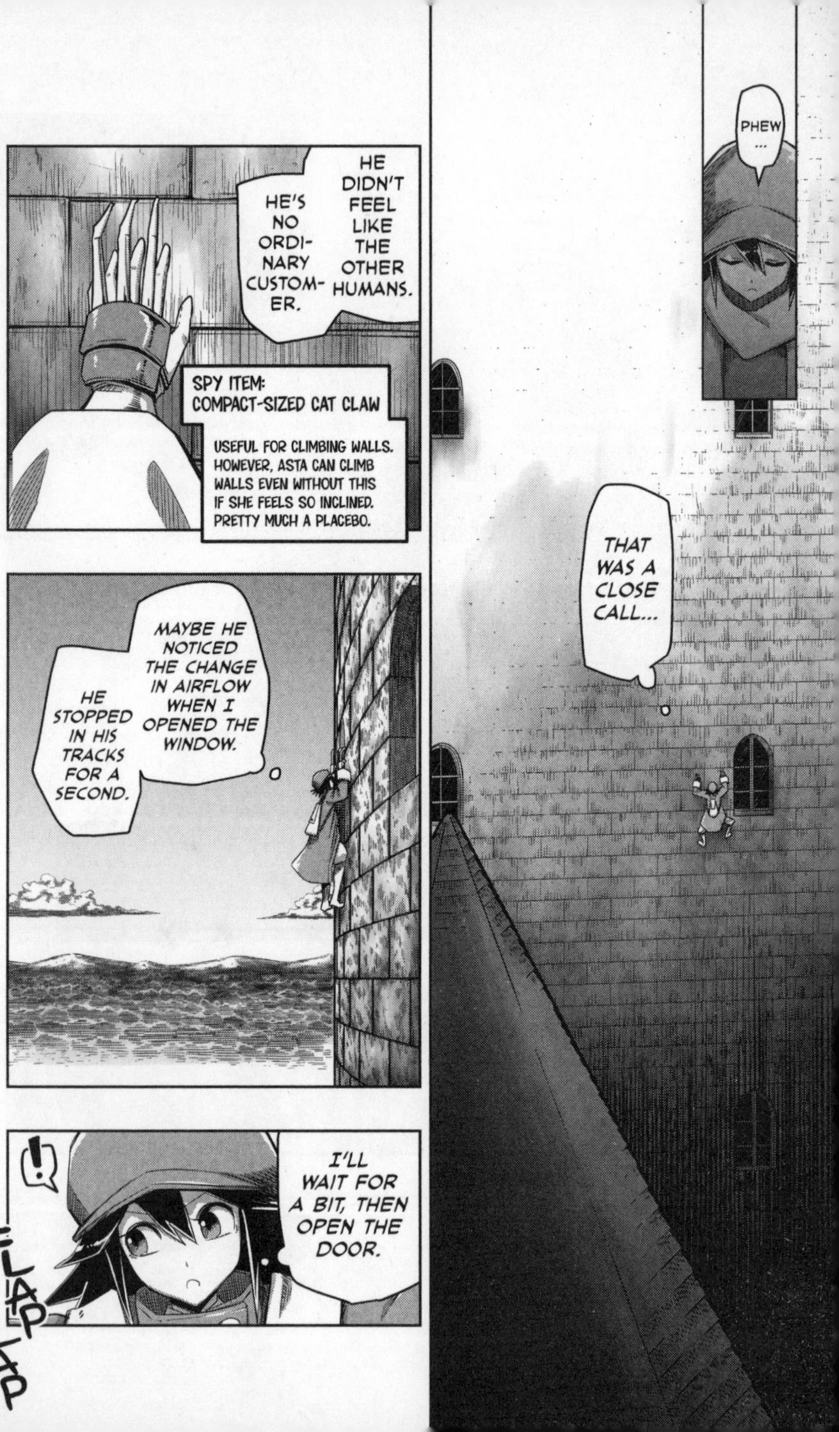
PHEW...
THAT WAS A CLOSE CALL...
HE DIDN'T FEEL LIKE THE OTHER HUMANS.
HE'S NO ORDINARY CUSTOMER.
SPY ITEM: COMPACT-SIZED CAT CLAW
USEFUL FOR CLIMBING WALLS. HOWEVER, ASTA CAN CLIMB WALLS EVEN WITHOUT THIS IF SHE FEELS SO INCLINED. PRETTY MUCH A PLACEBO.
MAYBE HE NOTICED THE CHANGE IN AIRFLOW WHEN I OPENED THE WINDOW.
HE STOPPED IN HIS TRACKS FOR A SECOND.
I'LL WAIT FOR A BIT, THEN OPEN THE DOOR.
!
FLAP
FLAP

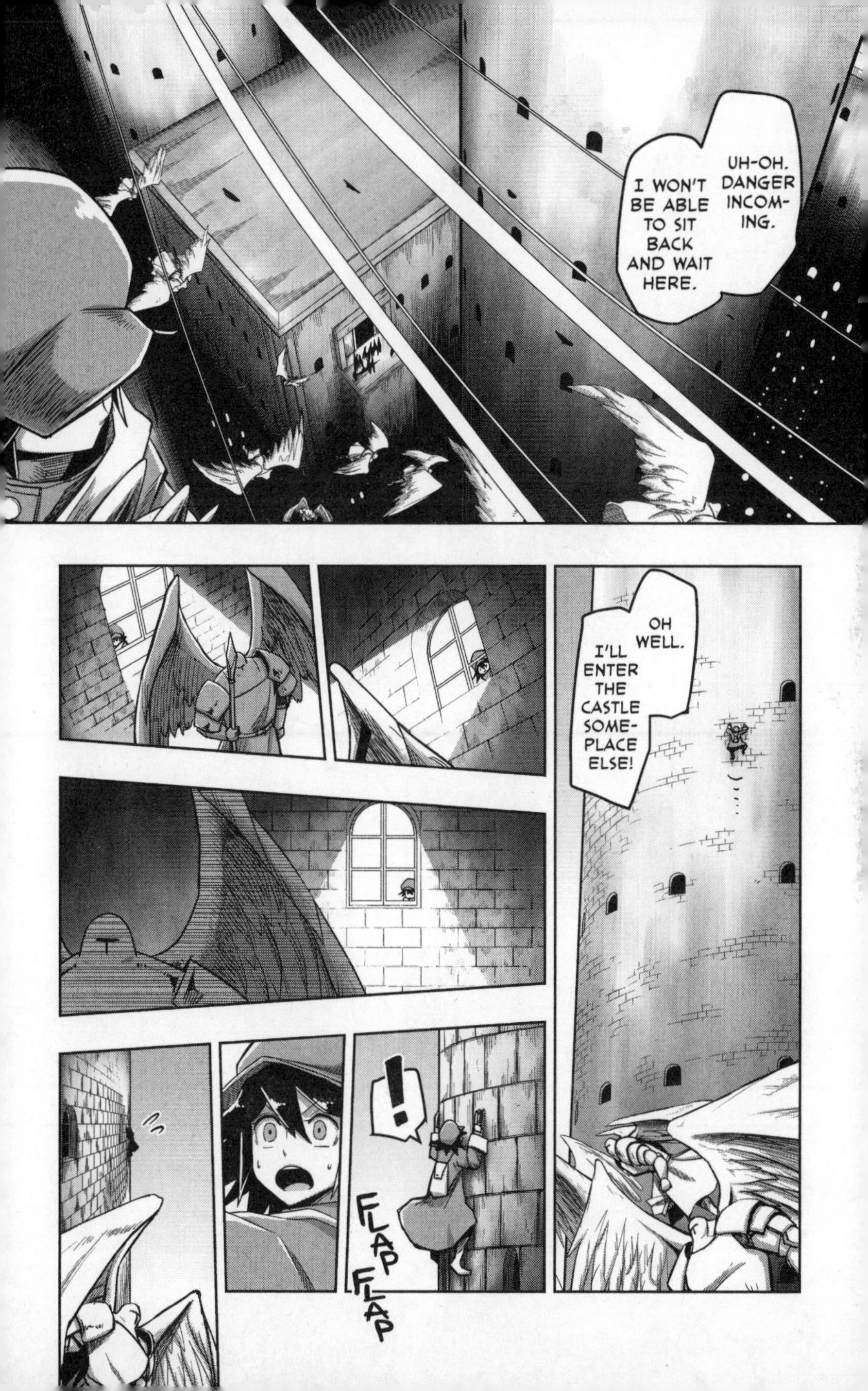
UH-OH. DANGER INCOMING.
I WON'T BE ABLE TO SIT BACK AND WAIT HERE.
OH WELL. I'LL ENTER THE CASTLE SOME-PLACE ELSE!
!
FLAP FLAP

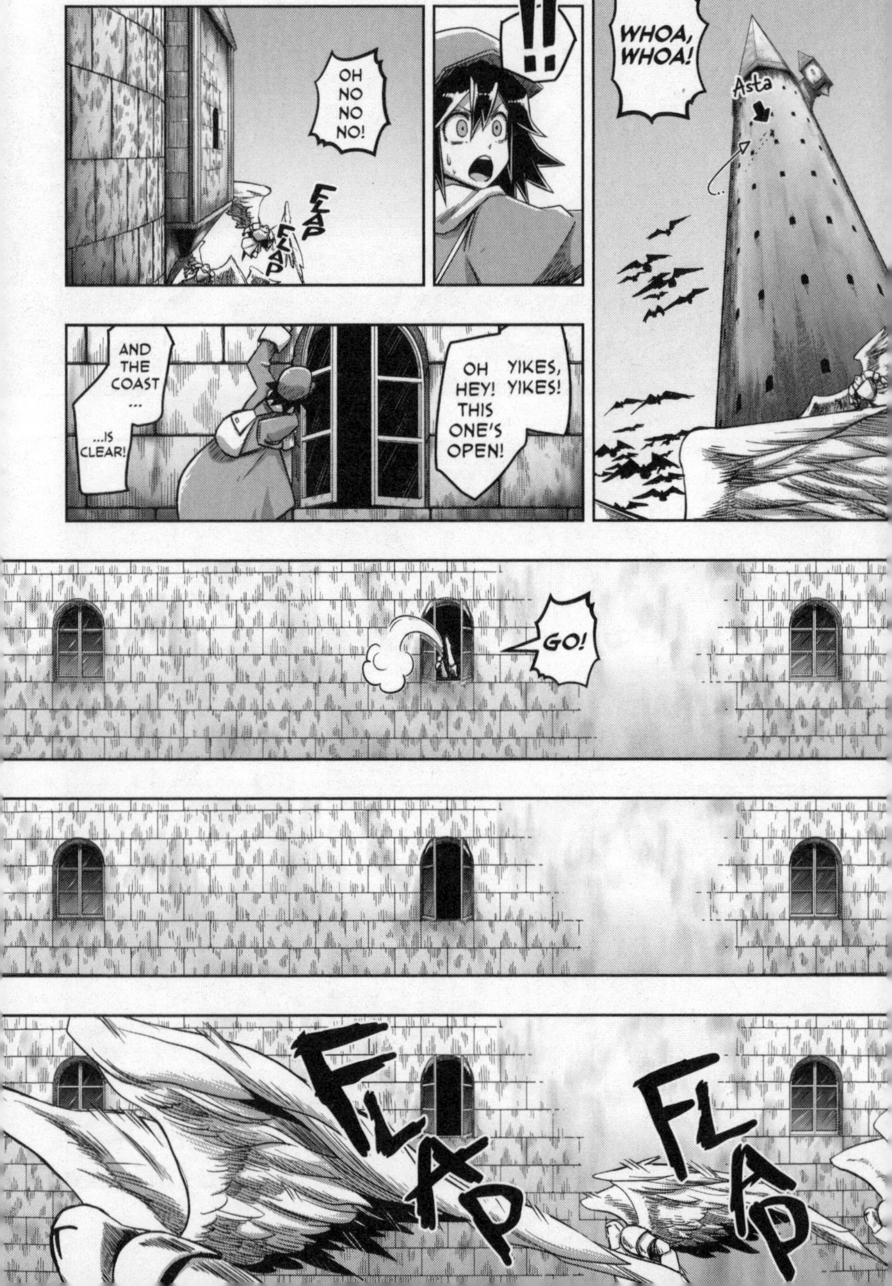
WHOA, WHOA!
Asta
!!
OH NO NO NO!
FLAP
FLAP
YIKES, YIKES!
OH HEY! THIS ONE'S OPEN!
AND THE COAST...
...IS CLEAR!
GO!
FLAP
FLAP

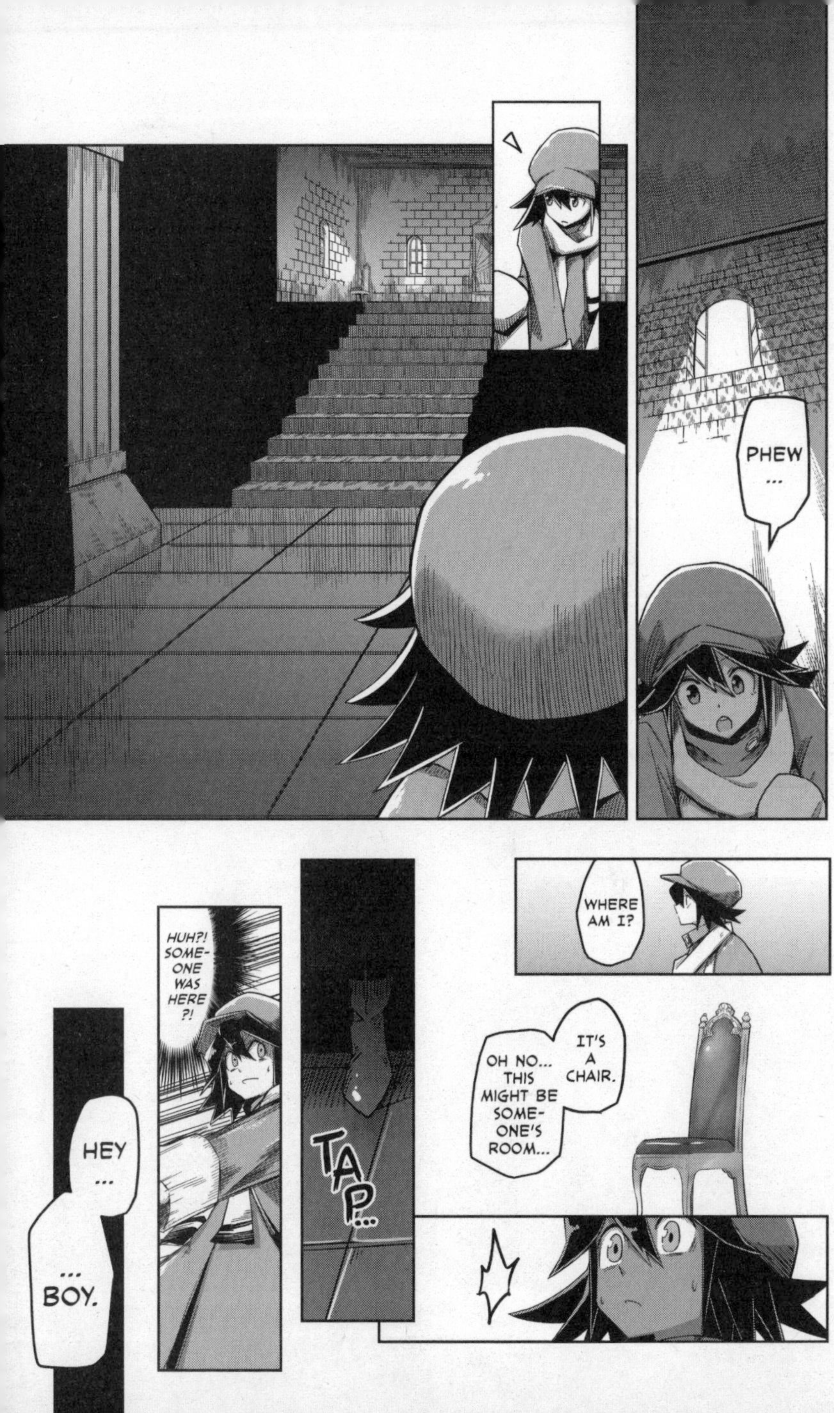
PHEW ...
WHERE AM I?
IT'S A CHAIR.
OH NO... THIS MIGHT BE SOME-ONE'S ROOM...
TAP...
HUH?! SOME-ONE WAS HERE?!
HEY ...
... BOY.

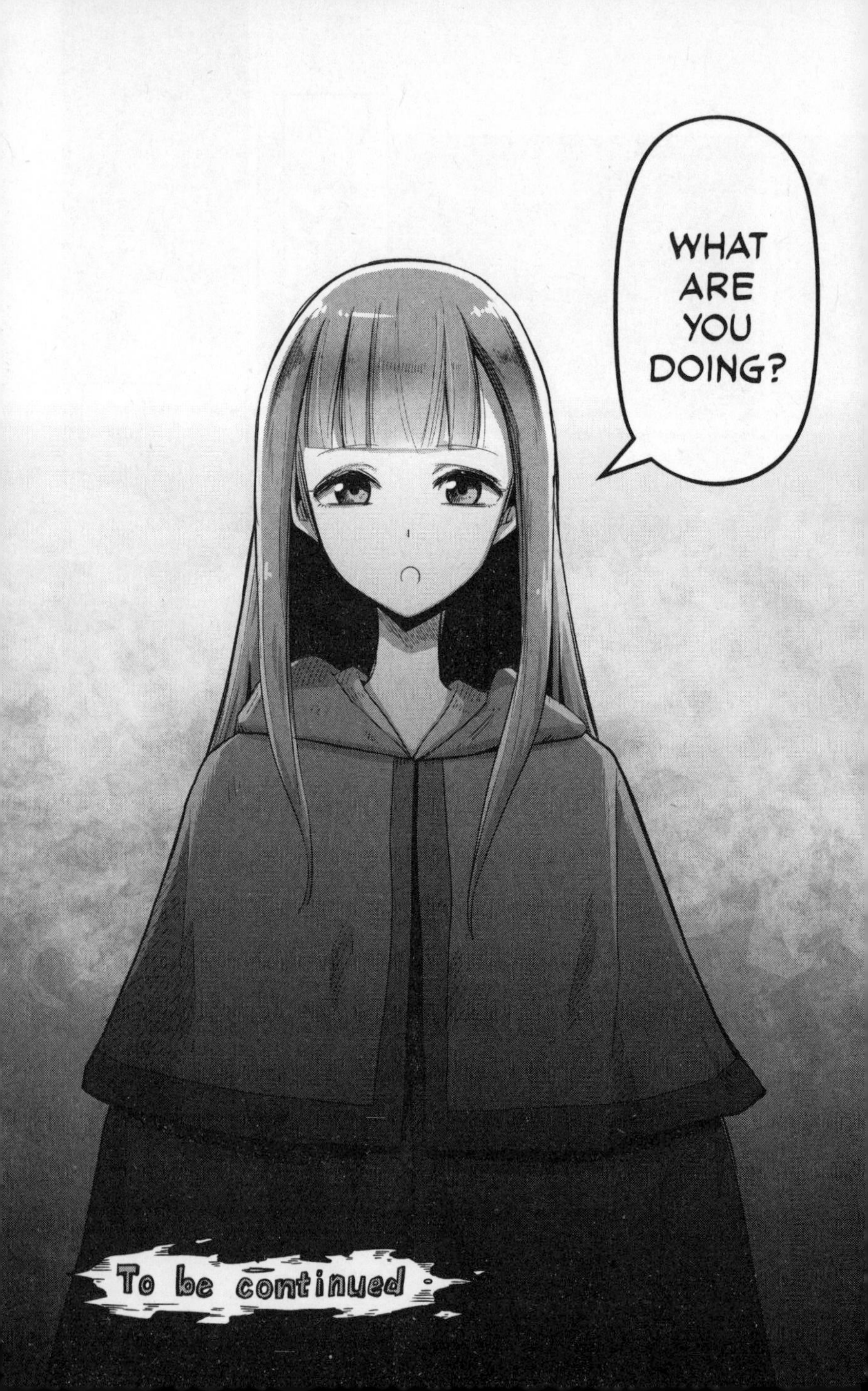
WHAT ARE YOU DOING?
To be continued

Chapter 58: The Mysterious Girl

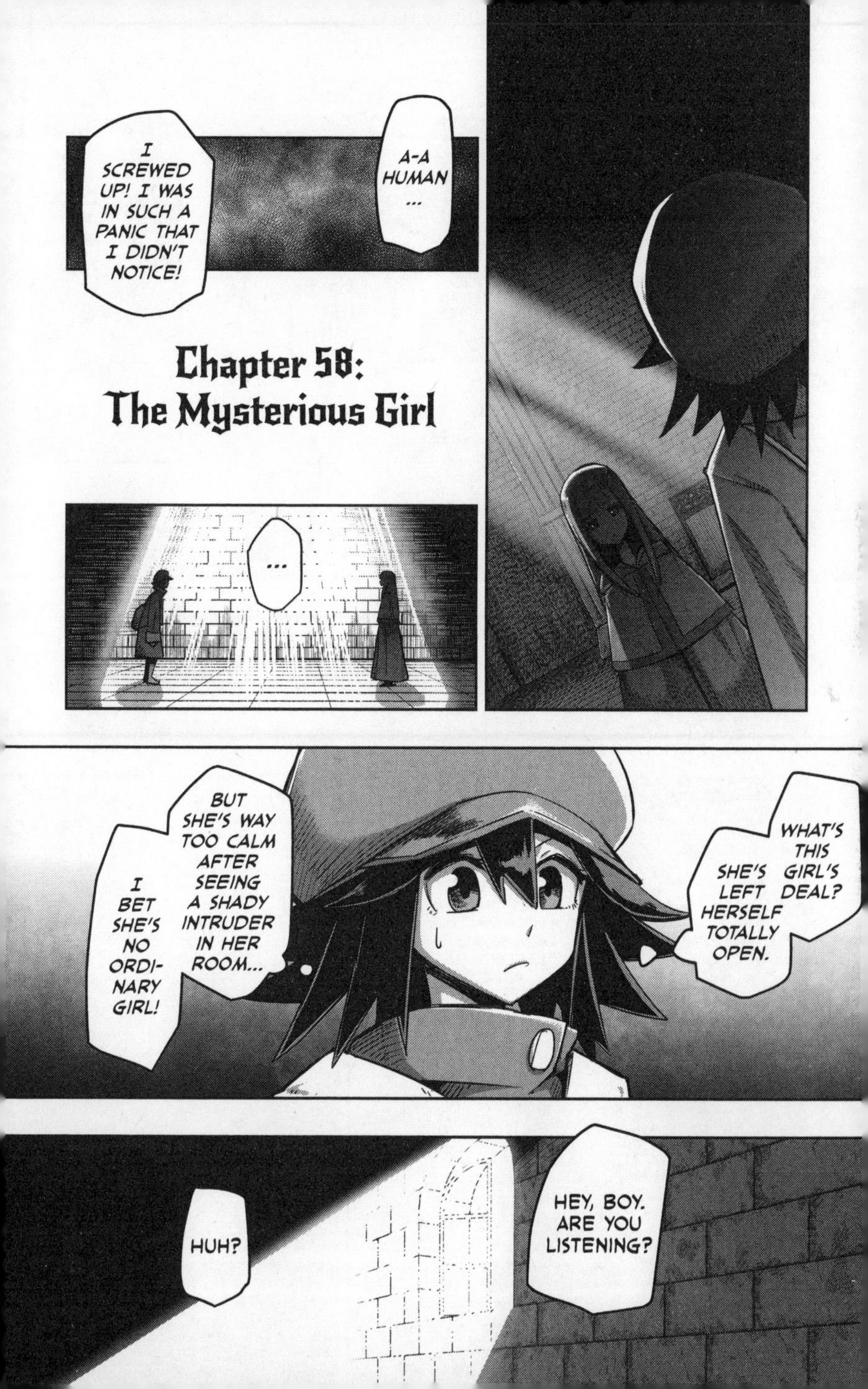

A-A HUMAN ...
I SCREWED UP! I WAS IN SUCH A PANIC THAT I DIDN'T NOTICE!
...
WHAT'S THIS GIRL'S DEAL? SHE'S LEFT HERSELF TOTALLY OPEN.
BUT SHE'S WAY TOO CALM AFTER SEEING A SHADY INTRUDER IN HER ROOM...
I BET SHE'S NO ORDINARY GIRL!
HEY, BOY. ARE YOU LISTENING?
HUH?

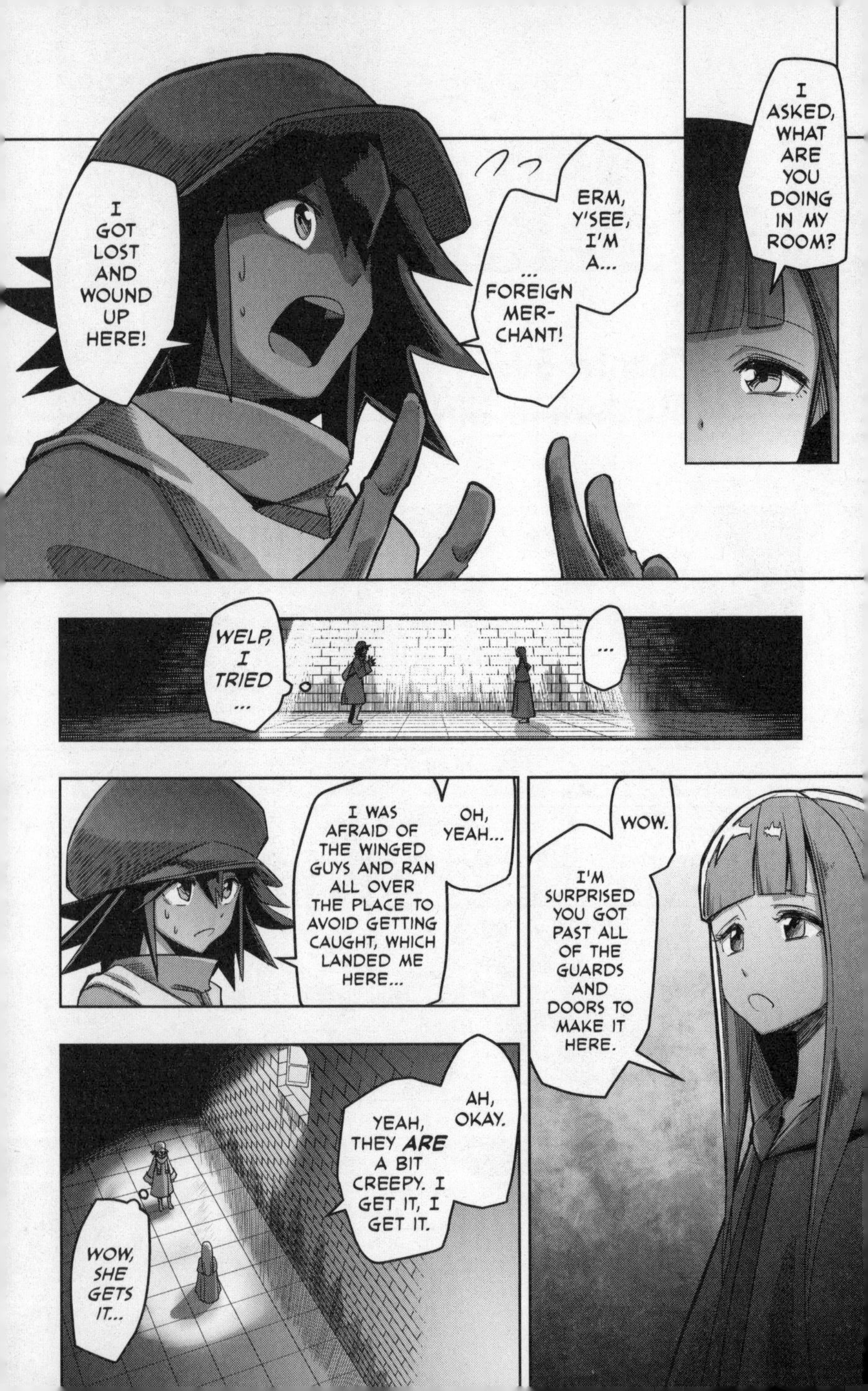
I ASKED, WHAT ARE YOU DOING IN MY ROOM?
ERM, Y'SEE, I'M A... ...FOREIGN MER-CHANT!
I GOT LOST AND WOUND UP HERE!
...
WELP, I TRIED...
WOW.
I'M SURPRISED YOU GOT PAST ALL OF THE GUARDS AND DOORS TO MAKE IT HERE.
OH, YEAH...
I WAS AFRAID OF THE WINGED GUYS AND RAN ALL OVER THE PLACE TO AVOID GETTING CAUGHT, WHICH LANDED ME HERE...
AH, OKAY.
YEAH, THEY *ARE* A BIT CREEPY. I GET IT, I GET IT.
WOW, SHE GETS IT...

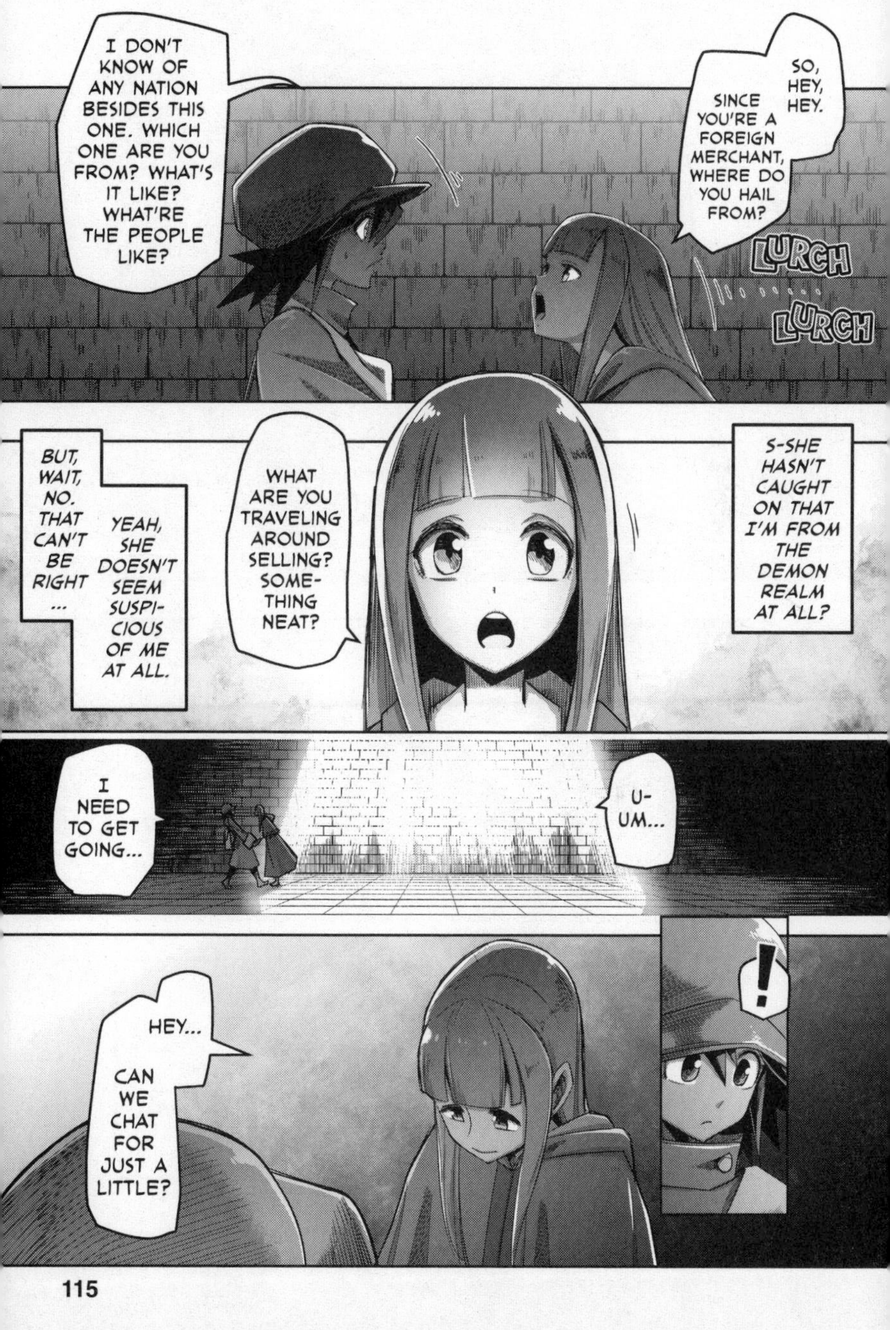
SO, HEY, HEY.
SINCE YOU'RE A FOREIGN MERCHANT, WHERE DO YOU HAIL FROM?
LURCH
LURCH
I DON'T KNOW OF ANY NATION BESIDES THIS ONE. WHICH ONE ARE YOU FROM? WHAT'S IT LIKE? WHAT'RE THE PEOPLE LIKE?
S-SHE HASN'T CAUGHT ON THAT I'M FROM THE DEMON REALM AT ALL?
WHAT ARE YOU TRAVELING AROUND SELLING? SOME-THING NEAT?
YEAH, SHE DOESN'T SEEM SUSPICIOUS OF ME AT ALL.
BUT, WAIT, NO. THAT CAN'T BE RIGHT...
U-UM...
I NEED TO GET GOING...
!
HEY...
CAN WE CHAT FOR JUST A LITTLE?

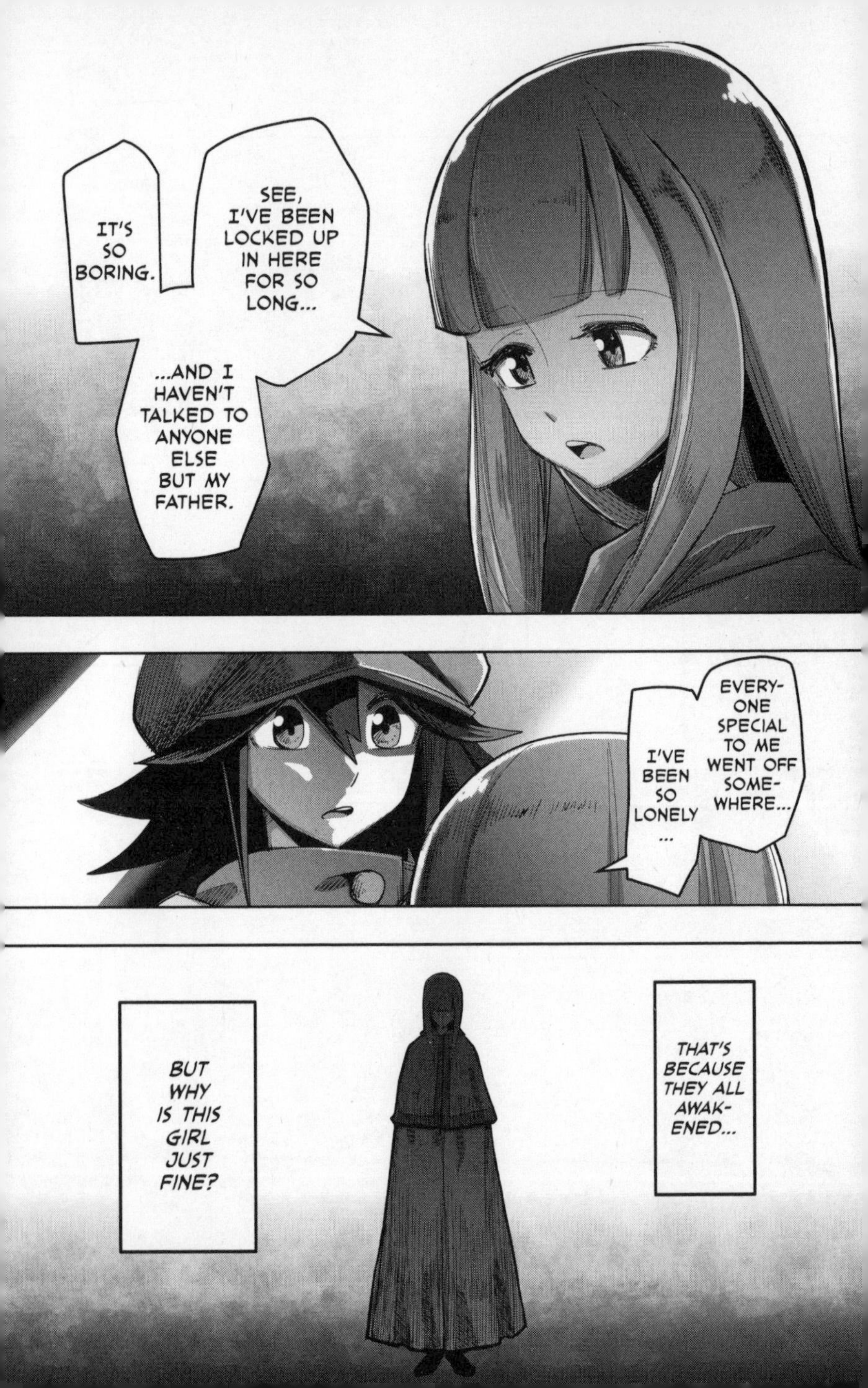
SEE, I'VE BEEN LOCKED UP IN HERE FOR SO LONG...
IT'S SO BORING.
...AND I HAVEN'T TALKED TO ANYONE ELSE BUT MY FATHER.
EVERY-ONE SPECIAL TO ME WENT OFF SOME-WHERE...
I'VE BEEN SO LONELY...
THAT'S BECAUSE THEY ALL AWAK-ENED...
BUT WHY IS THIS GIRL JUST FINE?

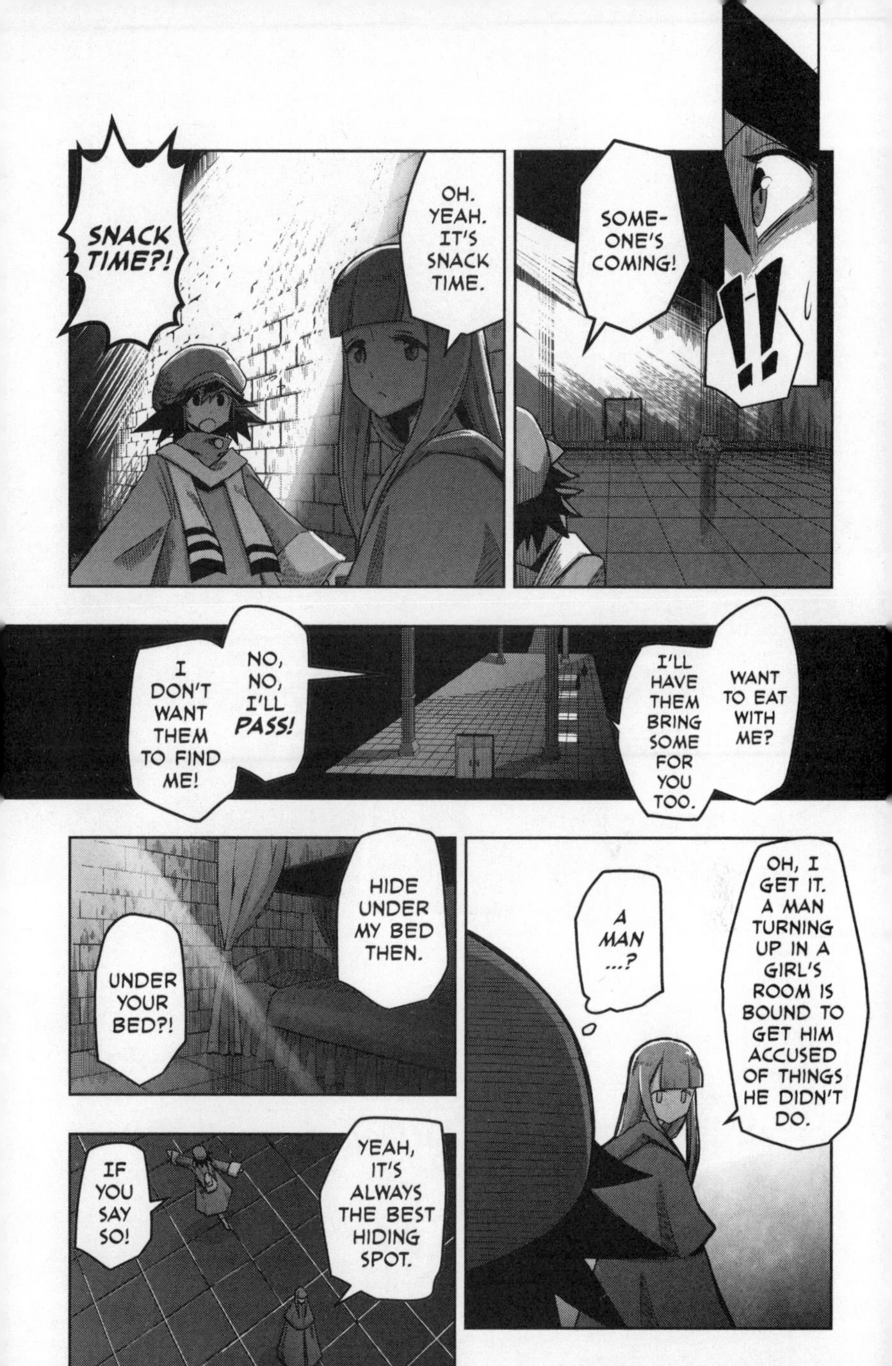
SOME-ONE'S COMING!
!!
OH. YEAH. IT'S SNACK TIME.
SNACK TIME?!
WANT TO EAT WITH ME?
I'LL HAVE THEM BRING SOME FOR YOU TOO.
NO, NO, I'LL *PASS!*
I DON'T WANT THEM TO FIND ME!
OH, I GET IT. A MAN TURNING UP IN A GIRL'S ROOM IS BOUND TO GET HIM ACCUSED OF THINGS HE DIDN'T DO.
A MAN ...?
HIDE UNDER MY BED THEN.
UNDER YOUR BED?!
YEAH, IT'S ALWAYS THE BEST HIDING SPOT.
IF YOU SAY SO!

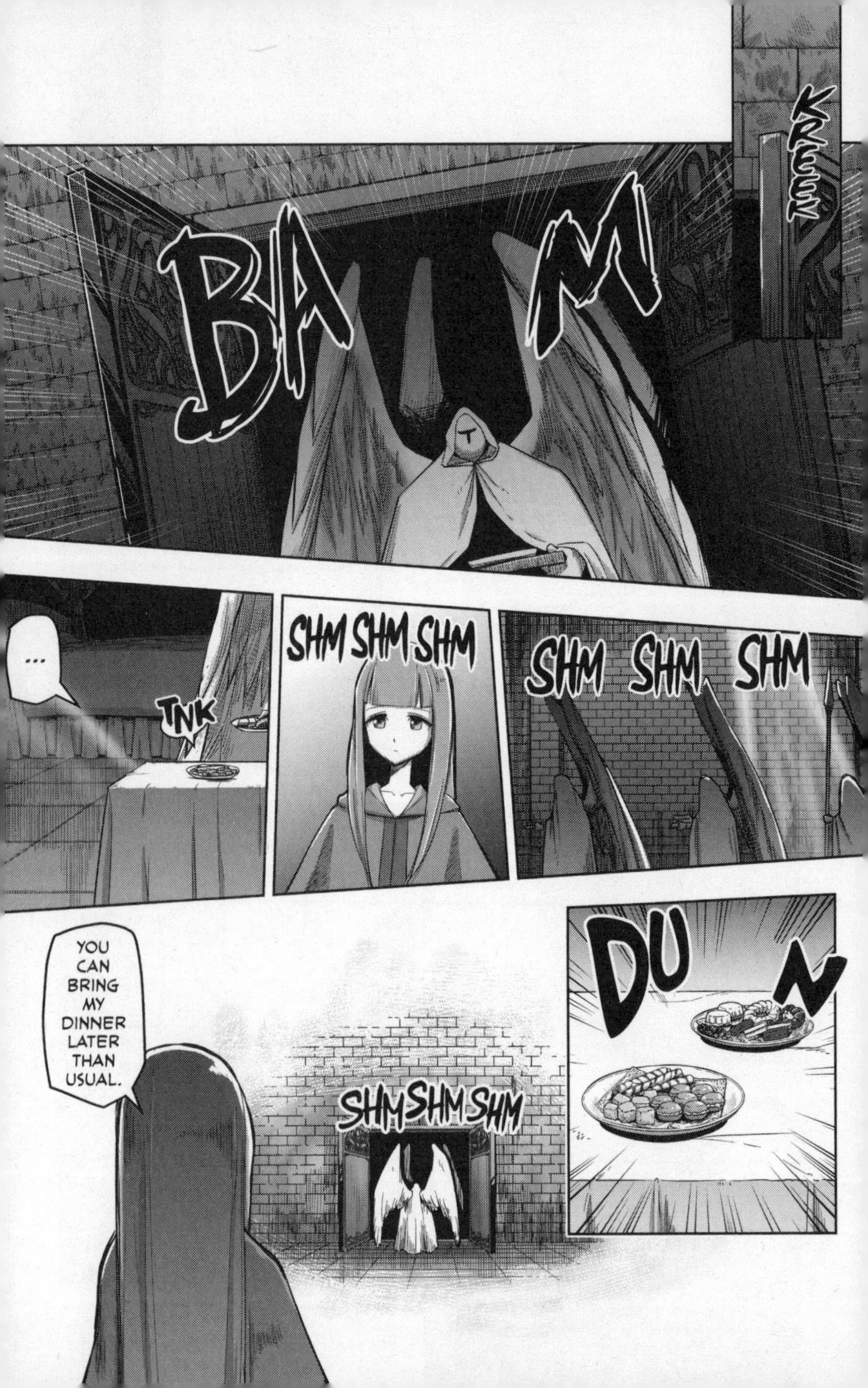
KREEEK
BAM
SHM SHM SHM
SHM SHM SHM
...
TNK
DUN
YOU CAN BRING MY DINNER LATER THAN USUAL.
SHM SHM SHM

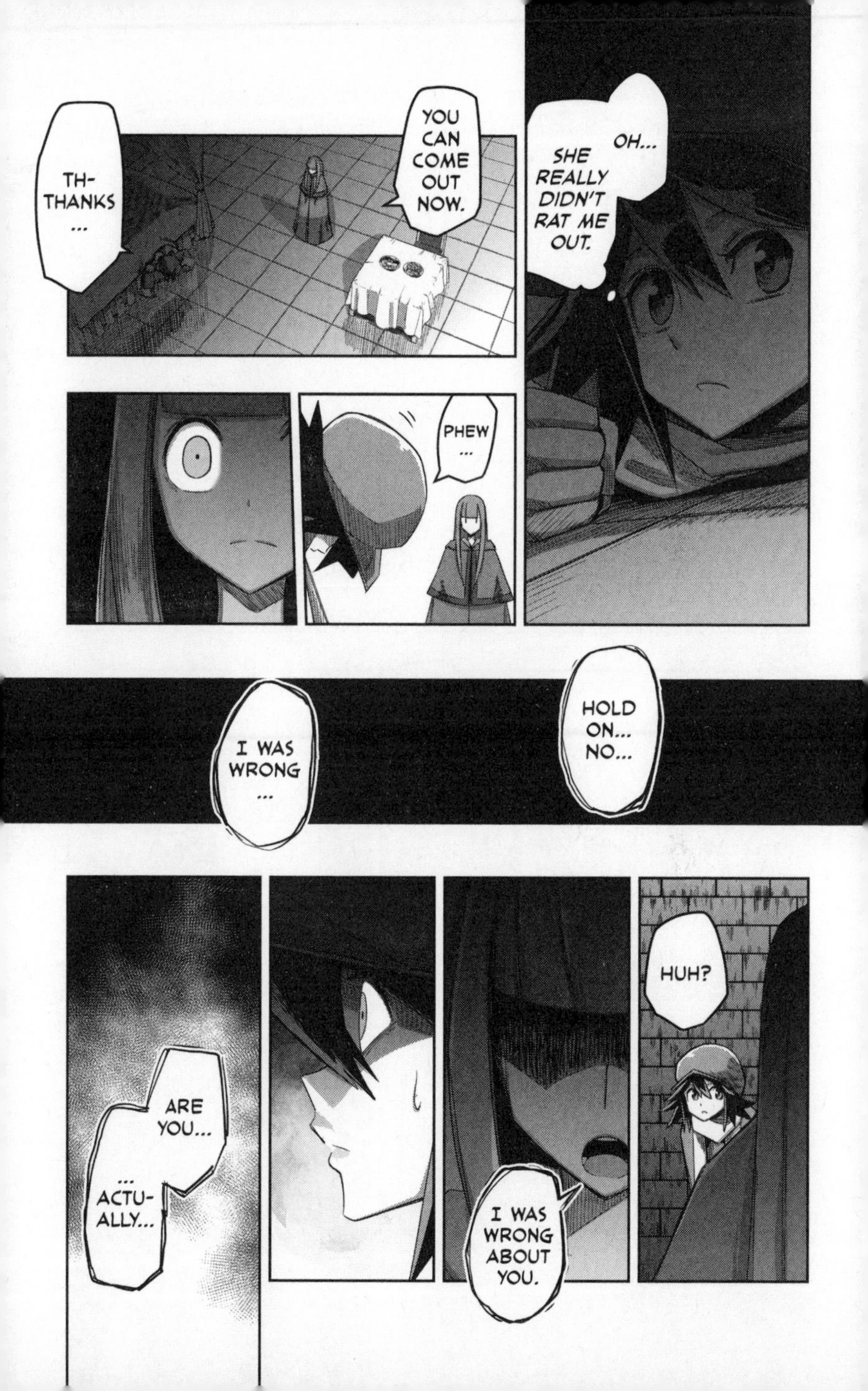
OH...
SHE REALLY DIDN'T RAT ME OUT.
YOU CAN COME OUT NOW.
TH-THANKS...
PHEW...
HOLD ON... NO...
I WAS WRONG...
HUH?
I WAS WRONG ABOUT YOU.
ARE YOU...
...ACTUALLY...

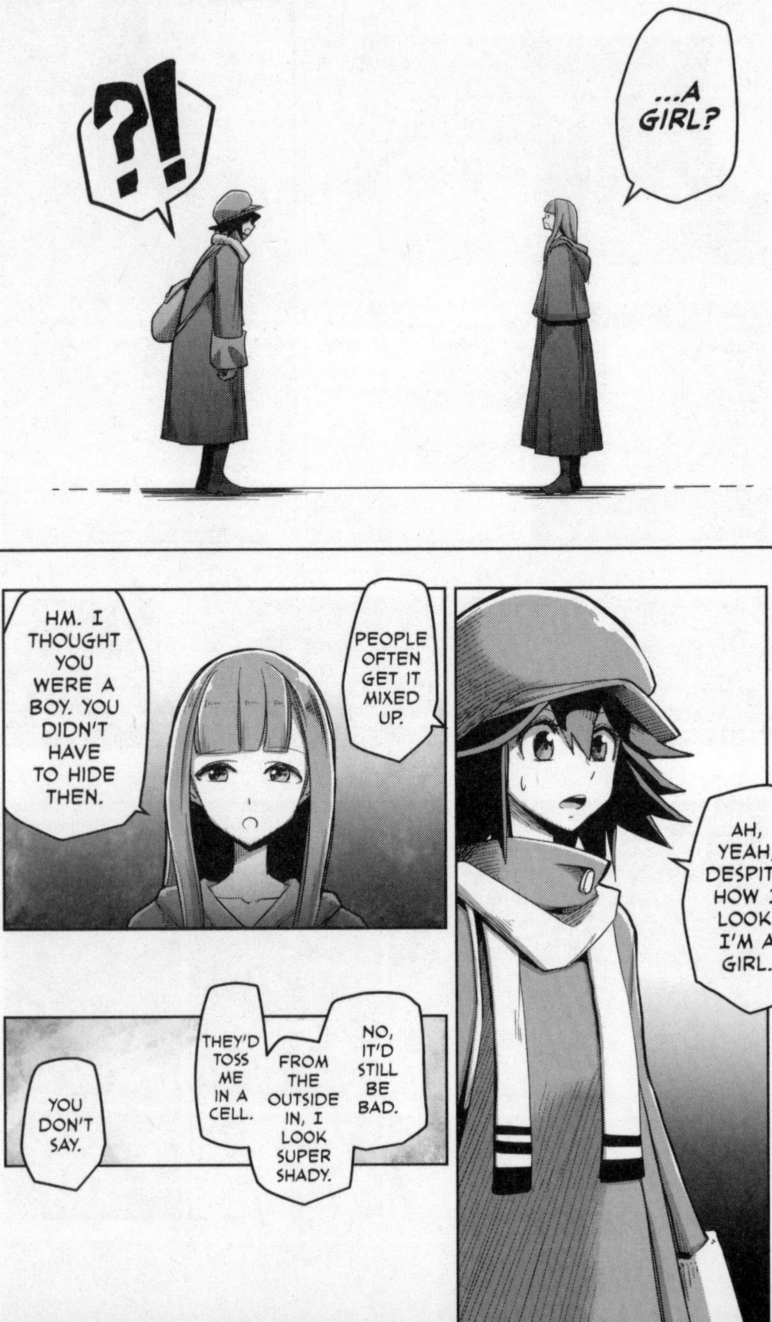
...A GIRL?
?!
AH, YEAH, DESPITE HOW I LOOK, I'M A GIRL.
PEOPLE OFTEN GET IT MIXED UP.
HM. I THOUGHT YOU WERE A BOY. YOU DIDN'T HAVE TO HIDE THEN.
NO, IT'D STILL BE BAD.
FROM THE OUTSIDE IN, I LOOK SUPER SHADY.
THEY'D TOSS ME IN A CELL.
YOU DON'T SAY.

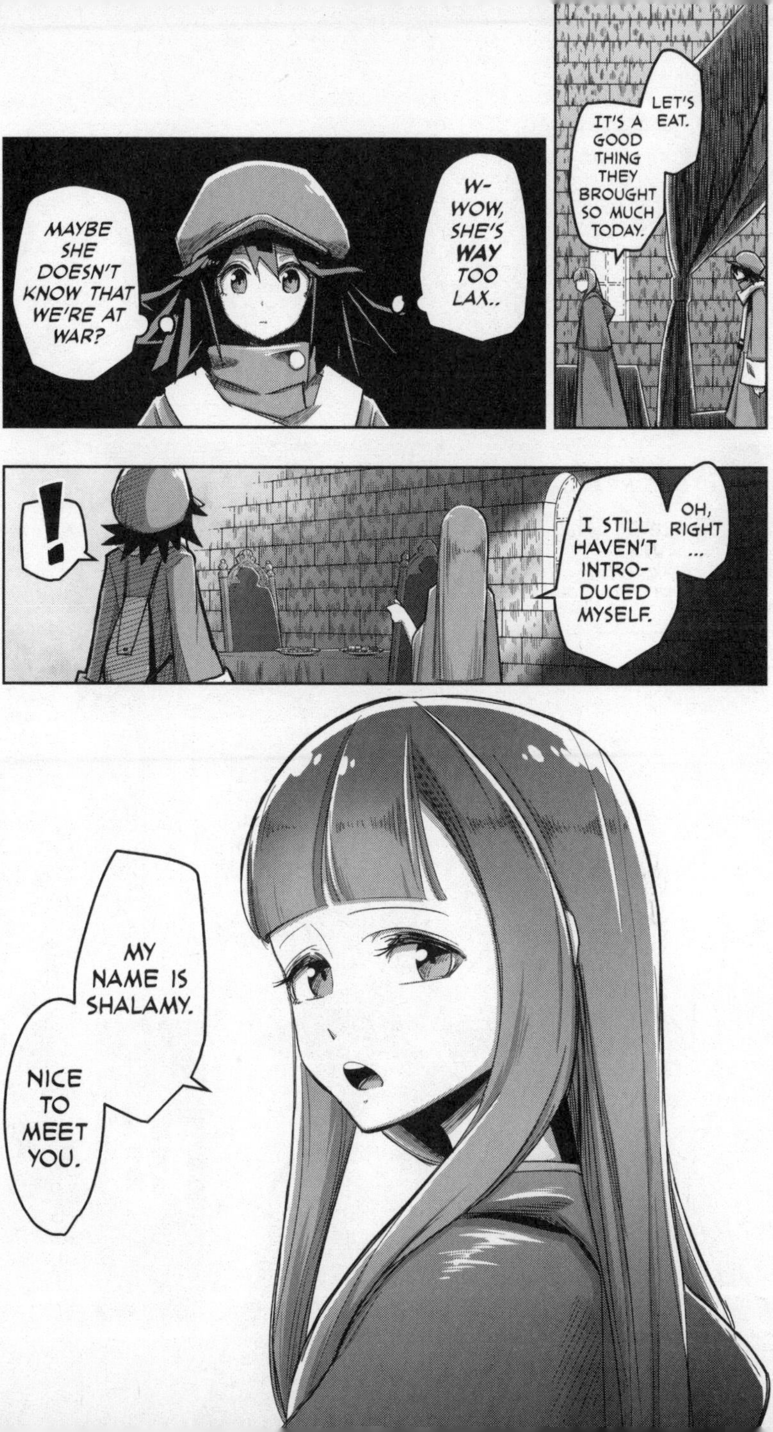
LET'S EAT.
IT'S A GOOD THING THEY BROUGHT SO MUCH TODAY.
W-WOW, SHE'S **WAY** TOO LAX..
MAYBE SHE DOESN'T KNOW THAT WE'RE AT WAR?
OH, RIGHT...
I STILL HAVEN'T INTRODUCED MYSELF.
!
MY NAME IS SHALAMY.
NICE TO MEET YOU.

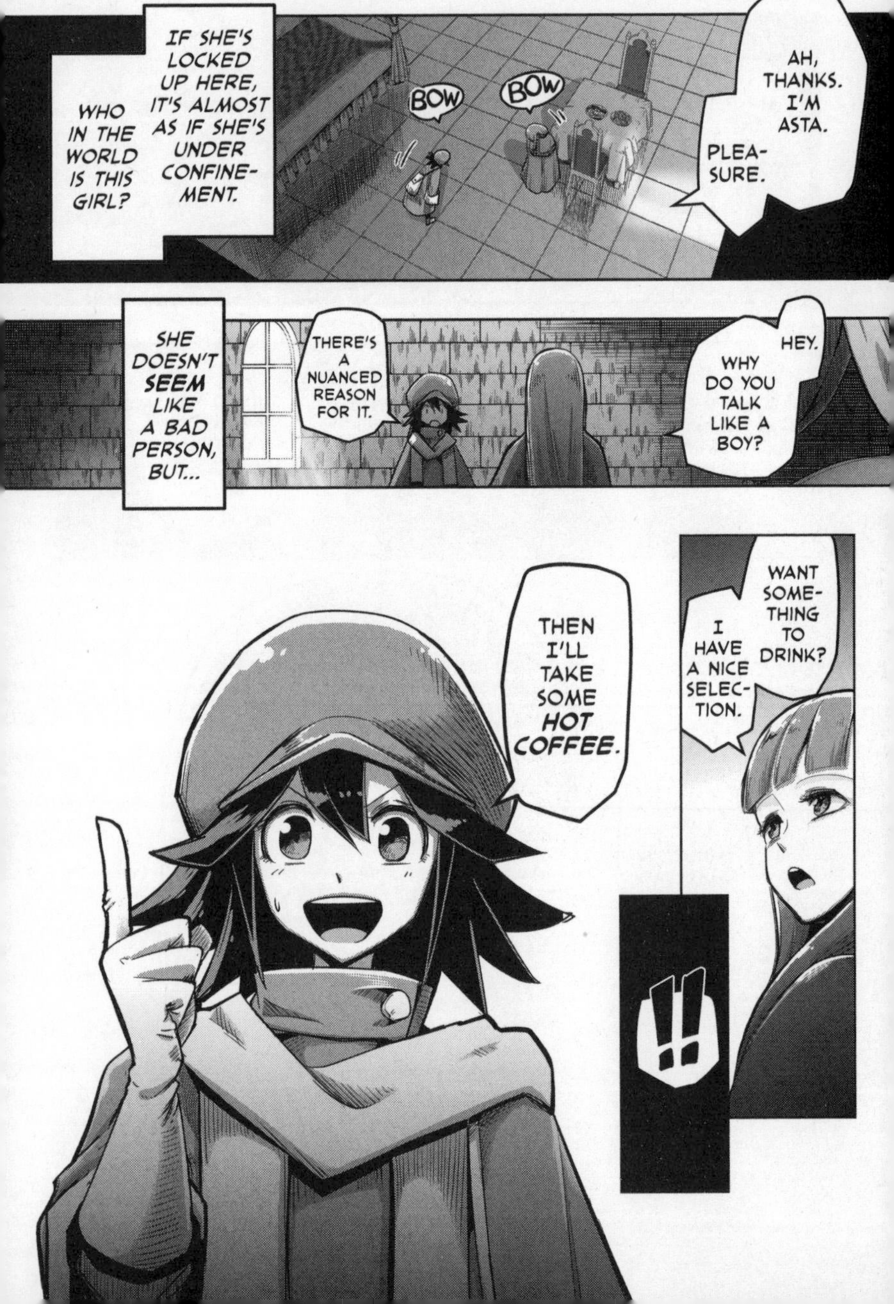
AH, THANKS. I'M ASTA.
PLEASURE.
BOW
BOW
IF SHE'S LOCKED UP HERE, IT'S ALMOST AS IF SHE'S UNDER CONFINEMENT.
WHO IN THE WORLD IS THIS GIRL?
HEY.
WHY DO YOU TALK LIKE A BOY?
THERE'S A NUANCED REASON FOR IT.
SHE DOESN'T SEEM LIKE A BAD PERSON, BUT...
WANT SOMETHING TO DRINK?
I HAVE A NICE SELECTION.
!!
THEN I'LL TAKE SOME HOT COFFEE.

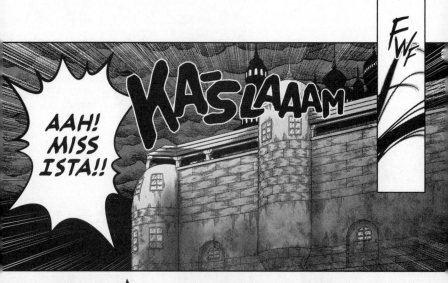

AAH! MISS ISTA!!

KA-SLAAAM

FWF

SHE COLLAPSED DURING HER CALL WITH MISS ASTA!

W-WHAT'S WRONG?!

S...

COULD SOMETHING HAVE HAPPENED TO OPERATIVE ASTA?!

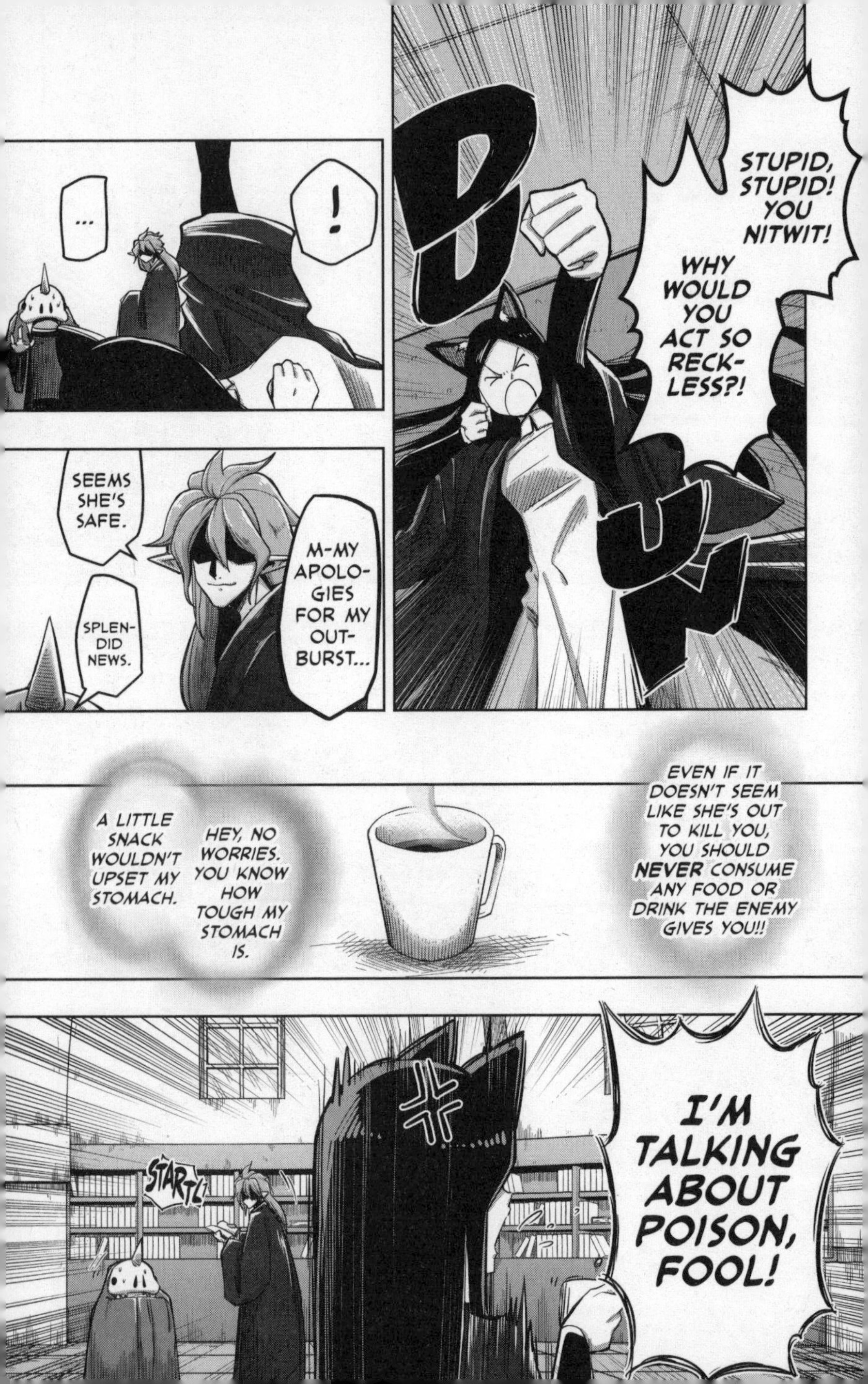
STUPID, STUPID! YOU NITWIT!
WHY WOULD YOU ACT SO RECK-LESS?!
!
...
M-MY APOLO-GIES FOR MY OUT-BURST...
SEEMS SHE'S SAFE.
SPLEN-DID NEWS.
EVEN IF IT DOESN'T SEEM LIKE SHE'S OUT TO KILL YOU, YOU SHOULD **NEVER** CONSUME ANY FOOD OR DRINK THE ENEMY GIVES YOU!!
HEY, NO WORRIES. YOU KNOW HOW TOUGH MY STOMACH IS.
A LITTLE SNACK WOULDN'T UPSET MY STOMACH.
I'M TALKING ABOUT POISON, FOOL!
STARTL

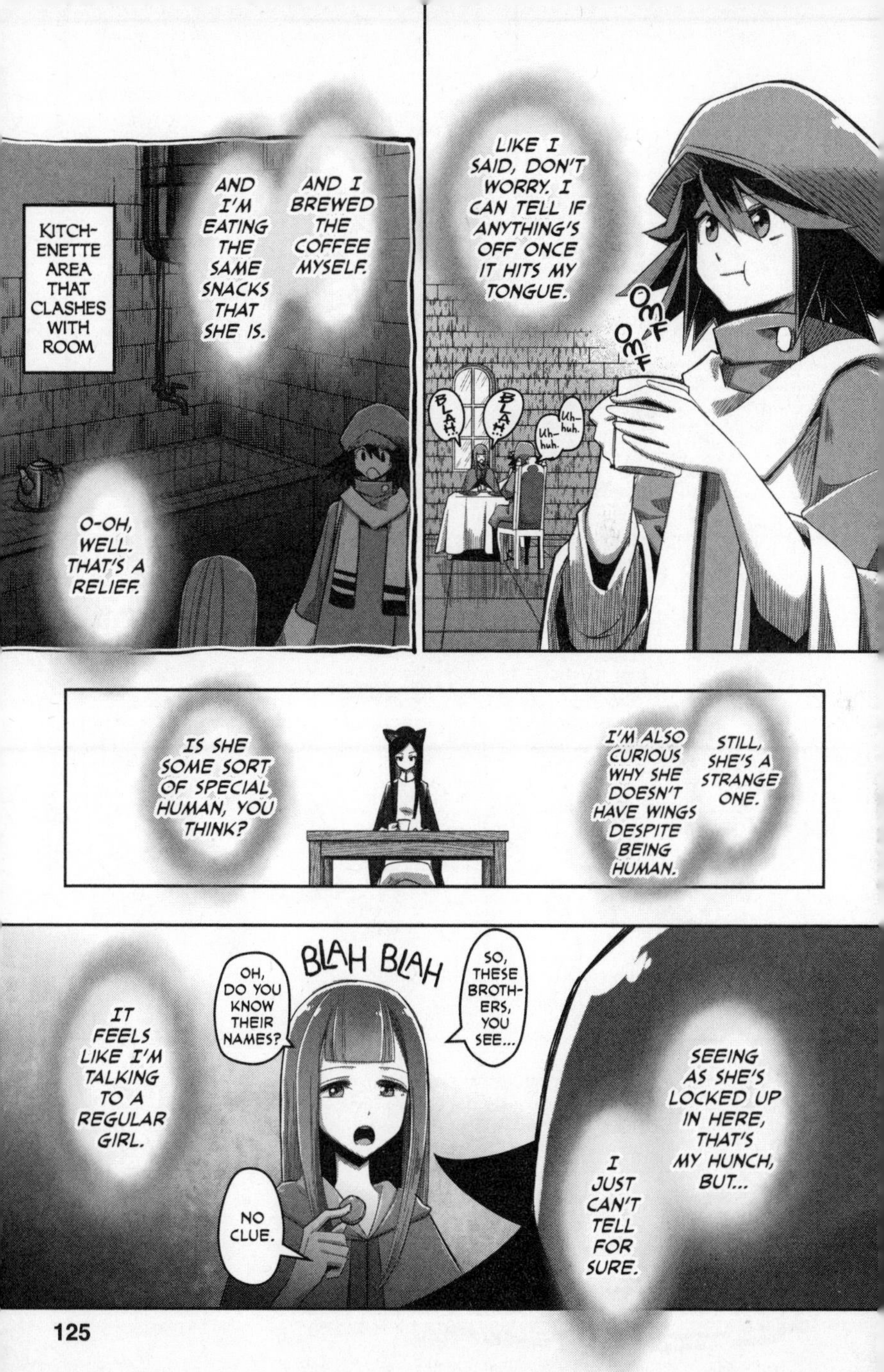

LIKE I SAID, DON'T WORRY. I CAN TELL IF ANYTHING'S OFF ONCE IT HITS MY TONGUE.
OMF OMF
BLAH...
BLAH...
Uh-huh.
Uh-huh.
AND I BREWED THE COFFEE MYSELF.
AND I'M EATING THE SAME SNACKS THAT SHE IS.
KITCHENETTE AREA THAT CLASHES WITH ROOM
O-OH, WELL. THAT'S A RELIEF.
STILL, SHE'S A STRANGE ONE.
I'M ALSO CURIOUS WHY SHE DOESN'T HAVE WINGS DESPITE BEING HUMAN.
IS SHE SOME SORT OF SPECIAL HUMAN, YOU THINK?
SEEING AS SHE'S LOCKED UP IN HERE, THAT'S MY HUNCH, BUT...
I JUST CAN'T TELL FOR SURE.
SO, THESE BROTHERS, YOU SEE...
BLAH BLAH
OH, DO YOU KNOW THEIR NAMES?
NO CLUE.
IT FEELS LIKE I'M TALKING TO A REGULAR GIRL.

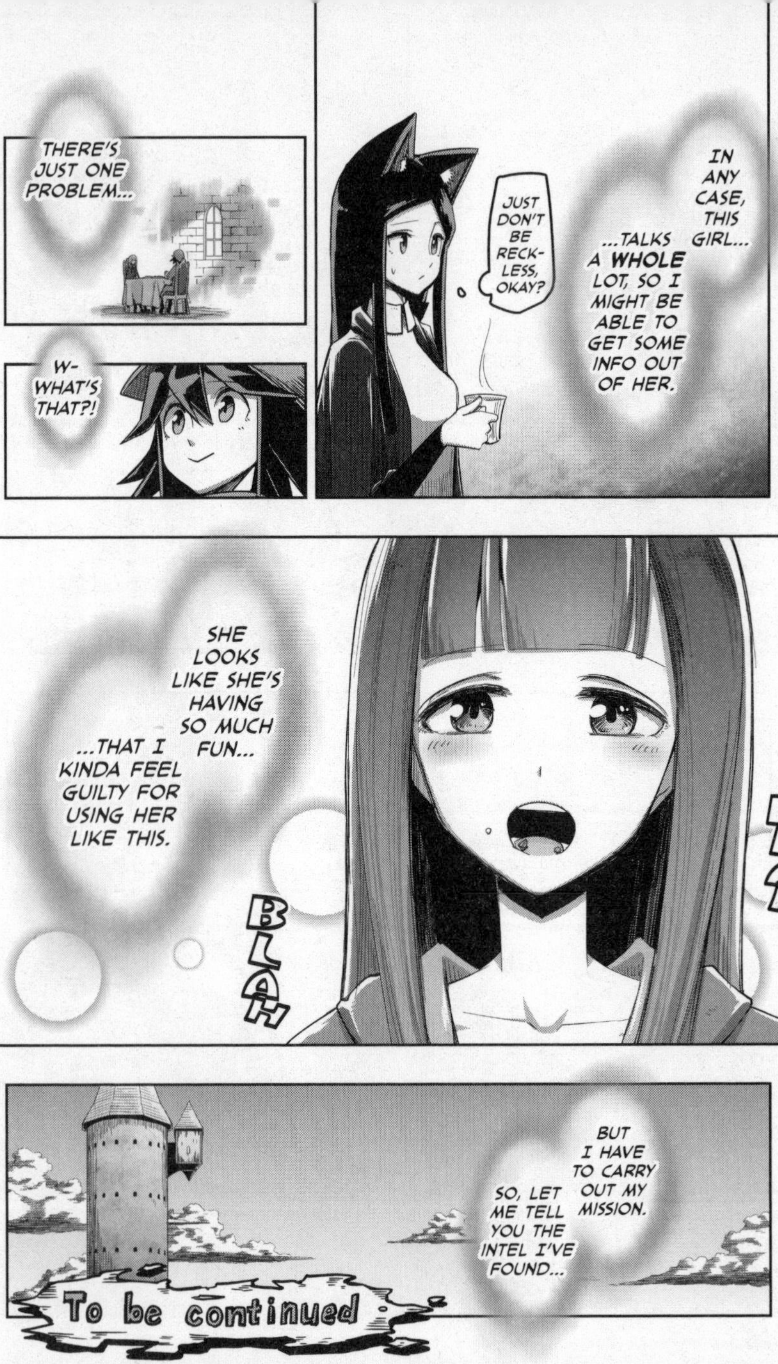
IN ANY CASE, THIS GIRL...
...TALKS A WHOLE LOT, SO I MIGHT BE ABLE TO GET SOME INFO OUT OF HER.
JUST DON'T BE RECK-LESS, OKAY?
THERE'S JUST ONE PROBLEM...
W-WHAT'S THAT?!
SHE LOOKS LIKE SHE'S HAVING SO MUCH FUN...
...THAT I KINDA FEEL GUILTY FOR USING HER LIKE THIS.
BLAH
BLAH
BUT I HAVE TO CARRY OUT MY MISSION.
SO, LET ME TELL YOU THE INTEL I'VE FOUND...
To be continued

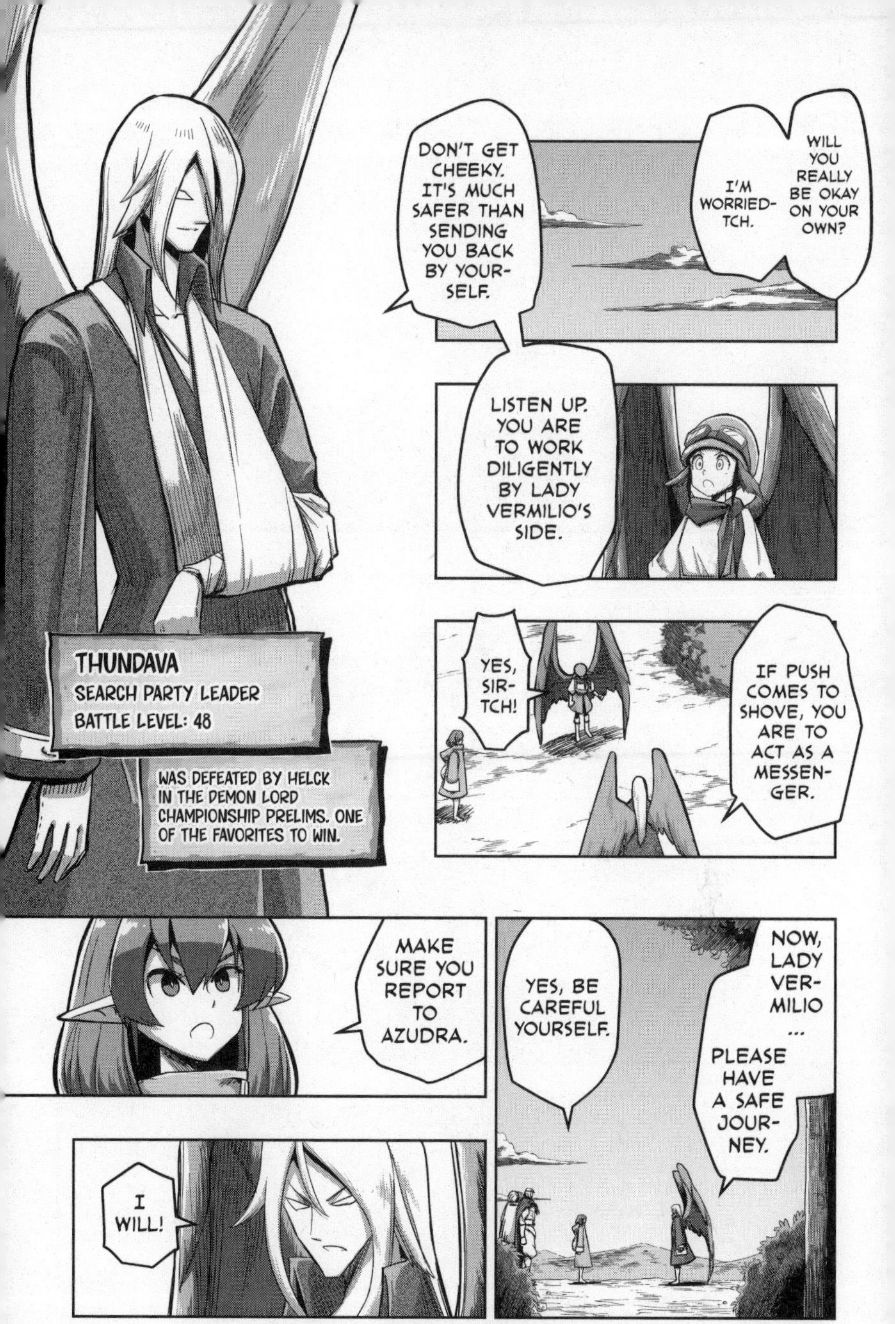
WILL YOU REALLY BE OKAY ON YOUR OWN?
I'M WORRIED-TCH.
DON'T GET CHEEKY. IT'S MUCH SAFER THAN SENDING YOU BACK BY YOURSELF.
LISTEN UP. YOU ARE TO WORK DILIGENTLY BY LADY VERMILIO'S SIDE.
IF PUSH COMES TO SHOVE, YOU ARE TO ACT AS A MESSENGER.
YES, SIR-TCH!
THUNDAVA
SEARCH PARTY LEADER
BATTLE LEVEL: 48
WAS DEFEATED BY HELCK IN THE DEMON LORD CHAMPIONSHIP PRELIMS. ONE OF THE FAVORITES TO WIN.
NOW, LADY VERMILIO...
PLEASE HAVE A SAFE JOURNEY.
YES, BE CAREFUL YOURSELF.
MAKE SURE YOU REPORT TO AZUDRA.
I WILL!

Chapter 59: Phase 2, Part 1

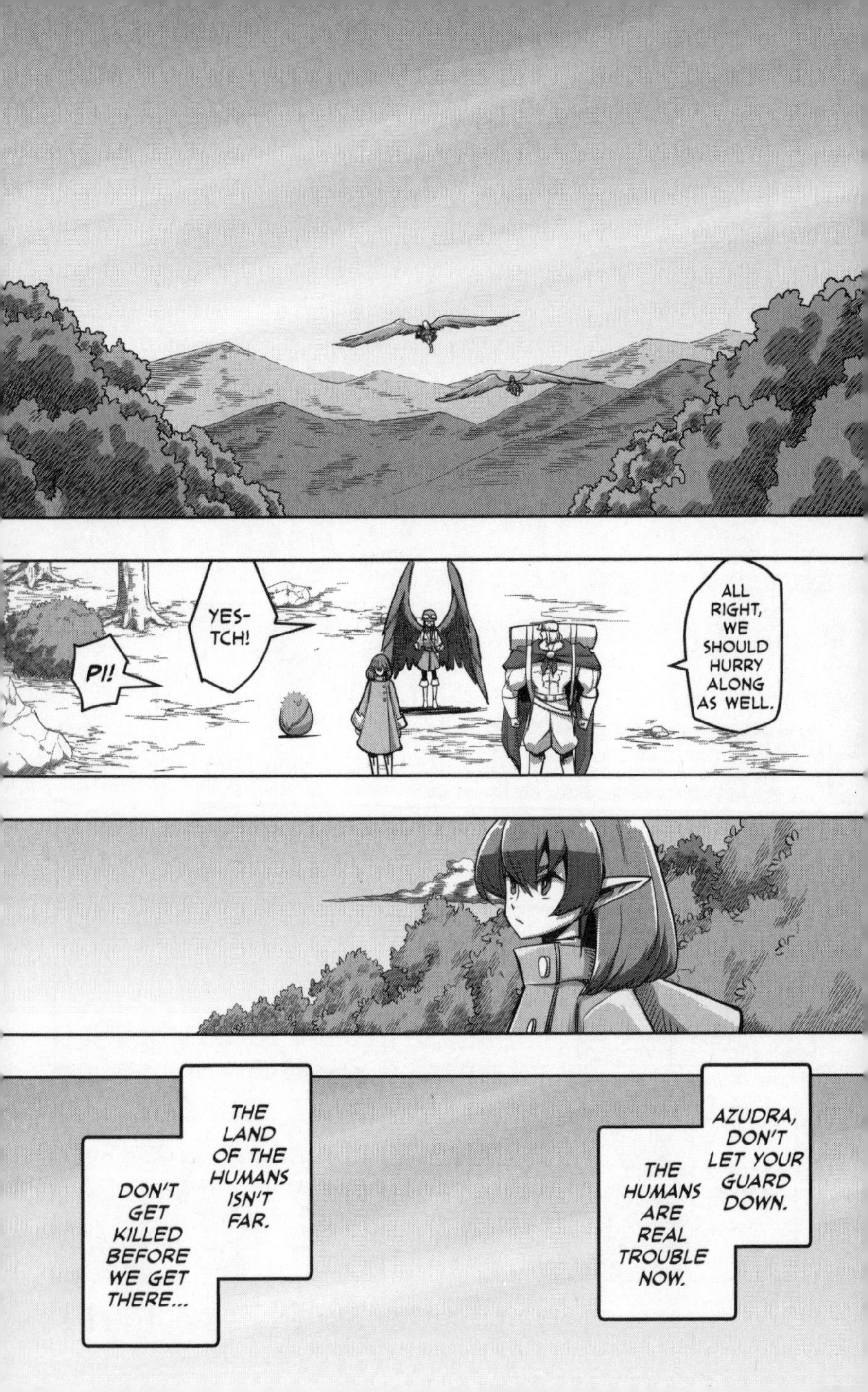
ALL RIGHT, WE SHOULD HURRY ALONG AS WELL.
YES-TCH!
PI!
AZUDRA, DON'T LET YOUR GUARD DOWN.
THE HUMANS ARE REAL TROUBLE NOW.
THE LAND OF THE HUMANS ISN'T FAR.
DON'T GET KILLED BEFORE WE GET THERE...

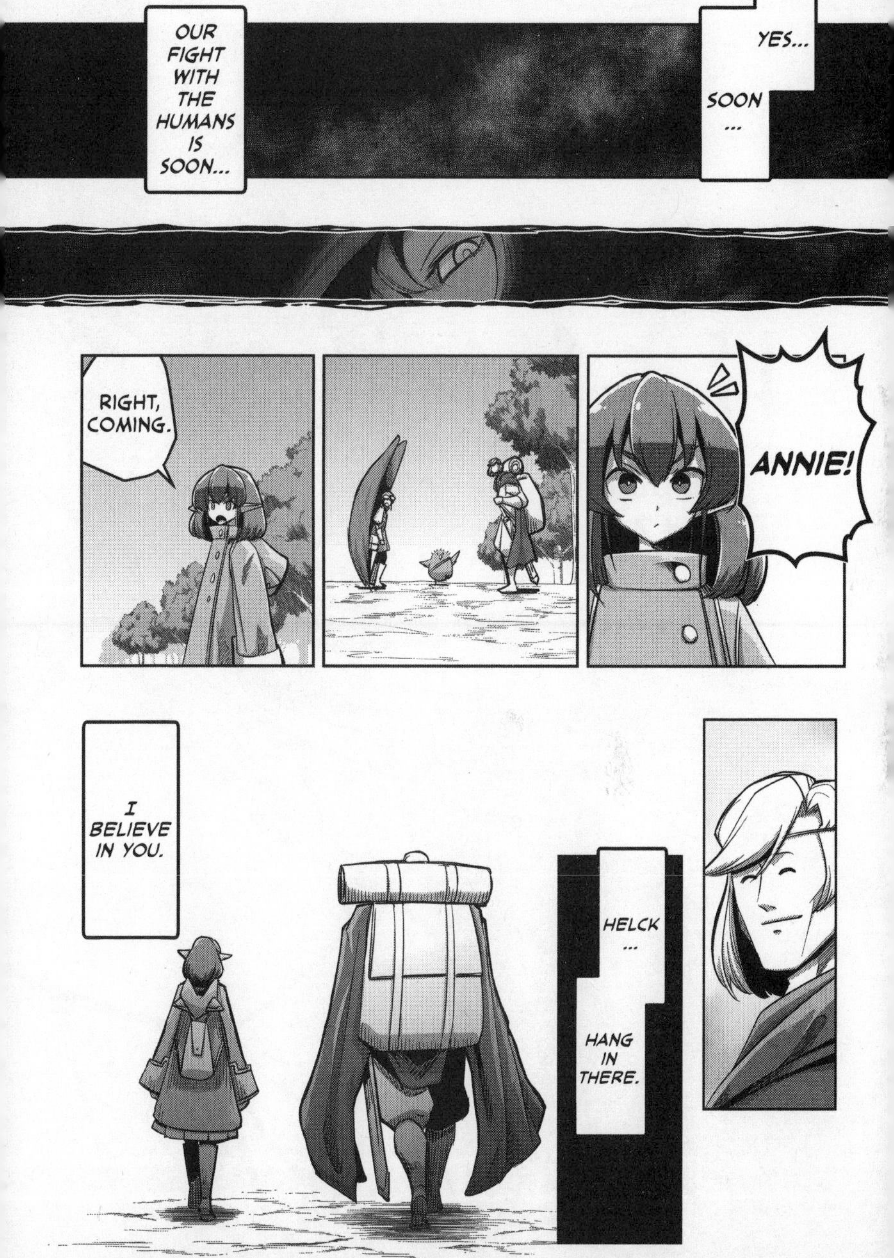
YES...
SOON ...
OUR FIGHT WITH THE HUMANS IS SOON...
ANNIE!
RIGHT, COMING.
HELCK ...
HANG IN THERE.
I BELIEVE IN YOU.

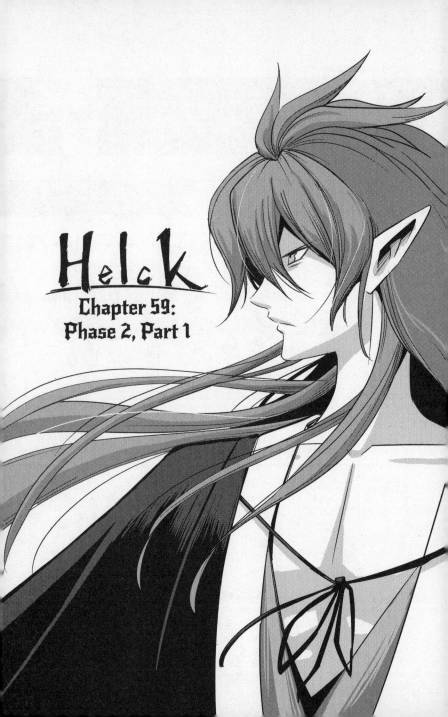

Helck

Chapter 59:
Phase 2, Part 1

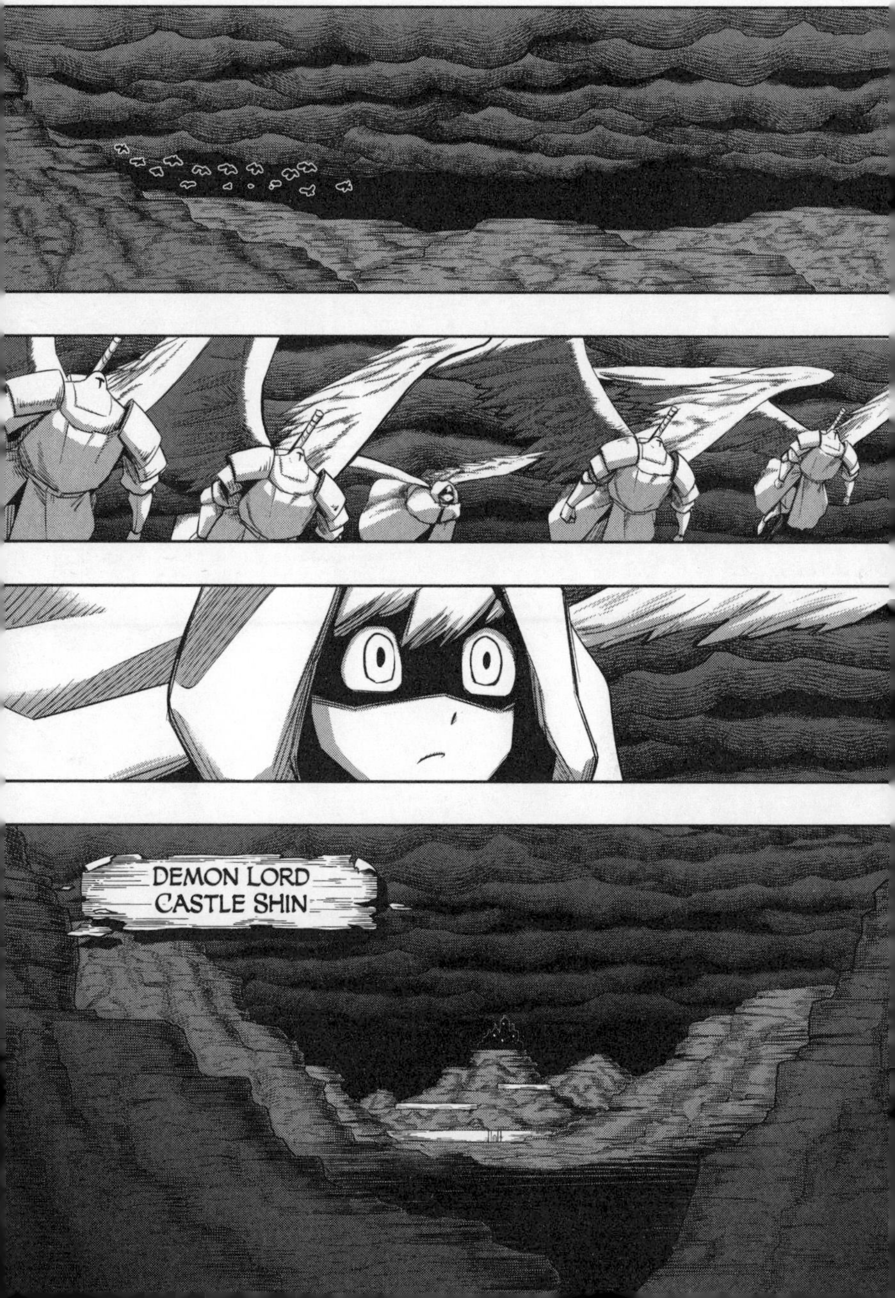
DEMON LORD CASTLE SHIN

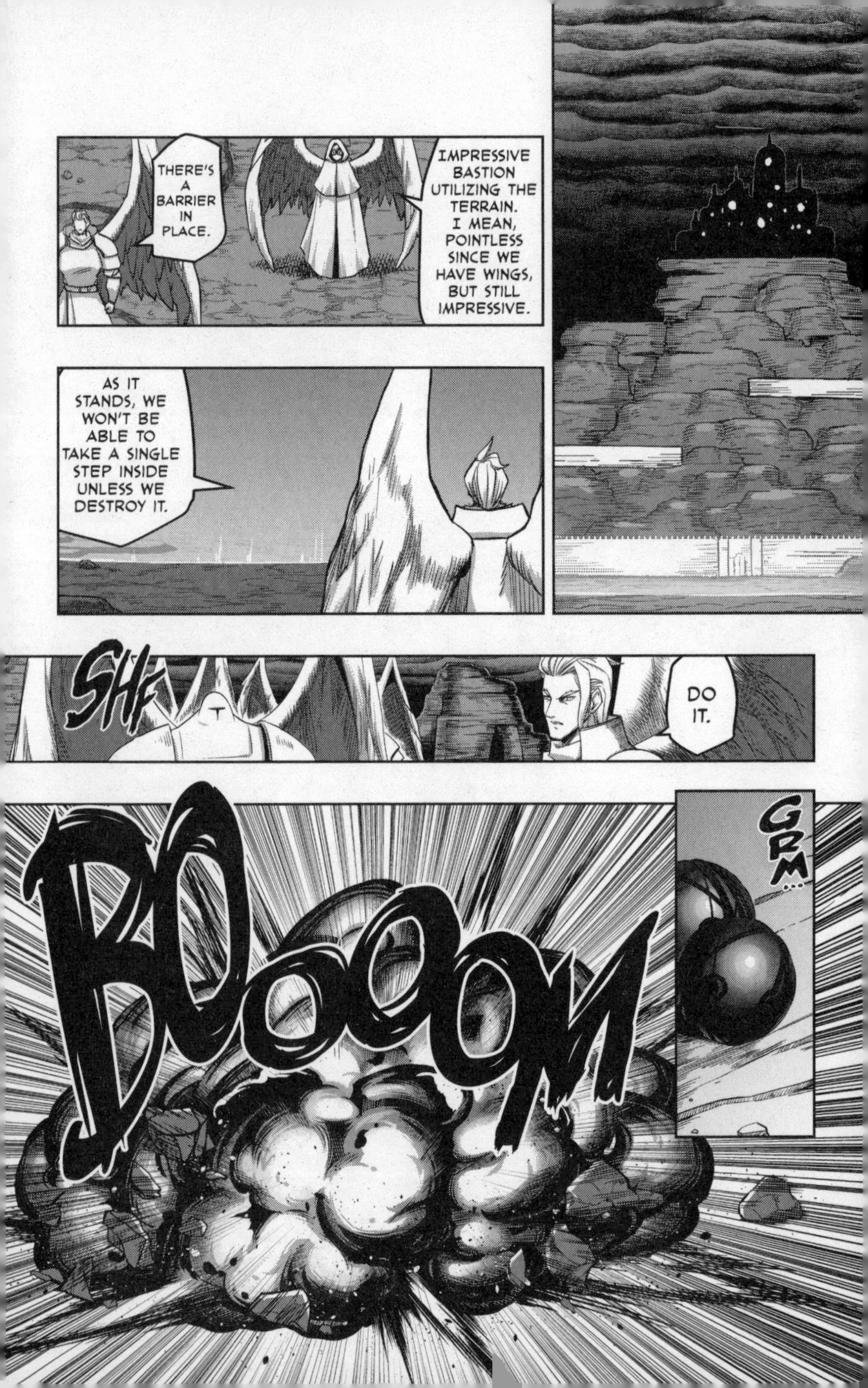
IMPRESSIVE BASTION UTILIZING THE TERRAIN. I MEAN, POINTLESS SINCE WE HAVE WINGS, BUT STILL IMPRESSIVE.
THERE'S A BARRIER IN PLACE.
AS IT STANDS, WE WON'T BE ABLE TO TAKE A SINGLE STEP INSIDE UNLESS WE DESTROY IT.
DO IT.
SHF
GRM..
BOOOOM

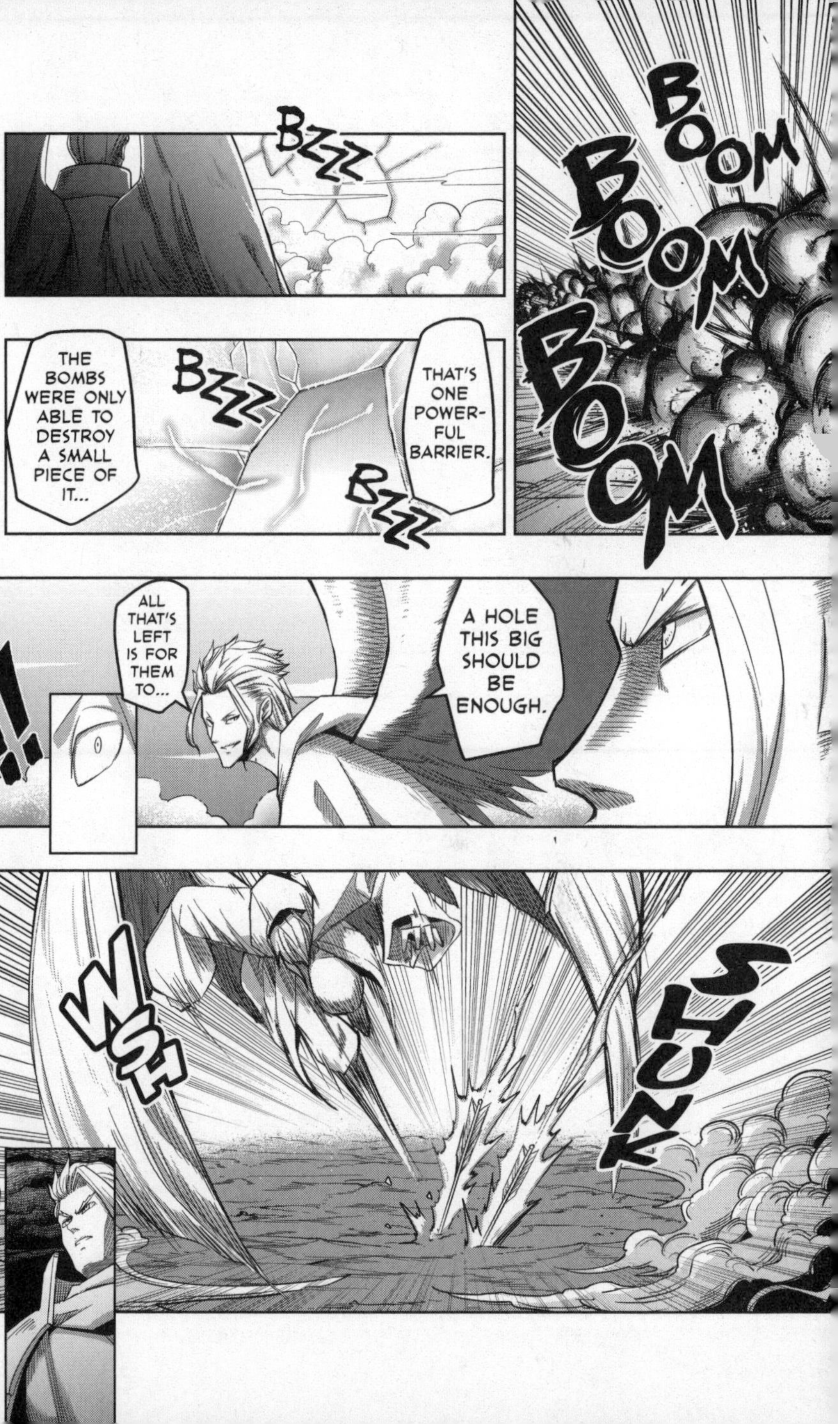
BOOM
BOOM
BOOM
BZZZ
THAT'S ONE POWERFUL BARRIER.
BZZZ
BZZZ
THE BOMBS WERE ONLY ABLE TO DESTROY A SMALL PIECE OF IT...
BZZZ
A HOLE THIS BIG SHOULD BE ENOUGH.
ALL THAT'S LEFT IS FOR THEM TO...
!!
SHUNK
WSH

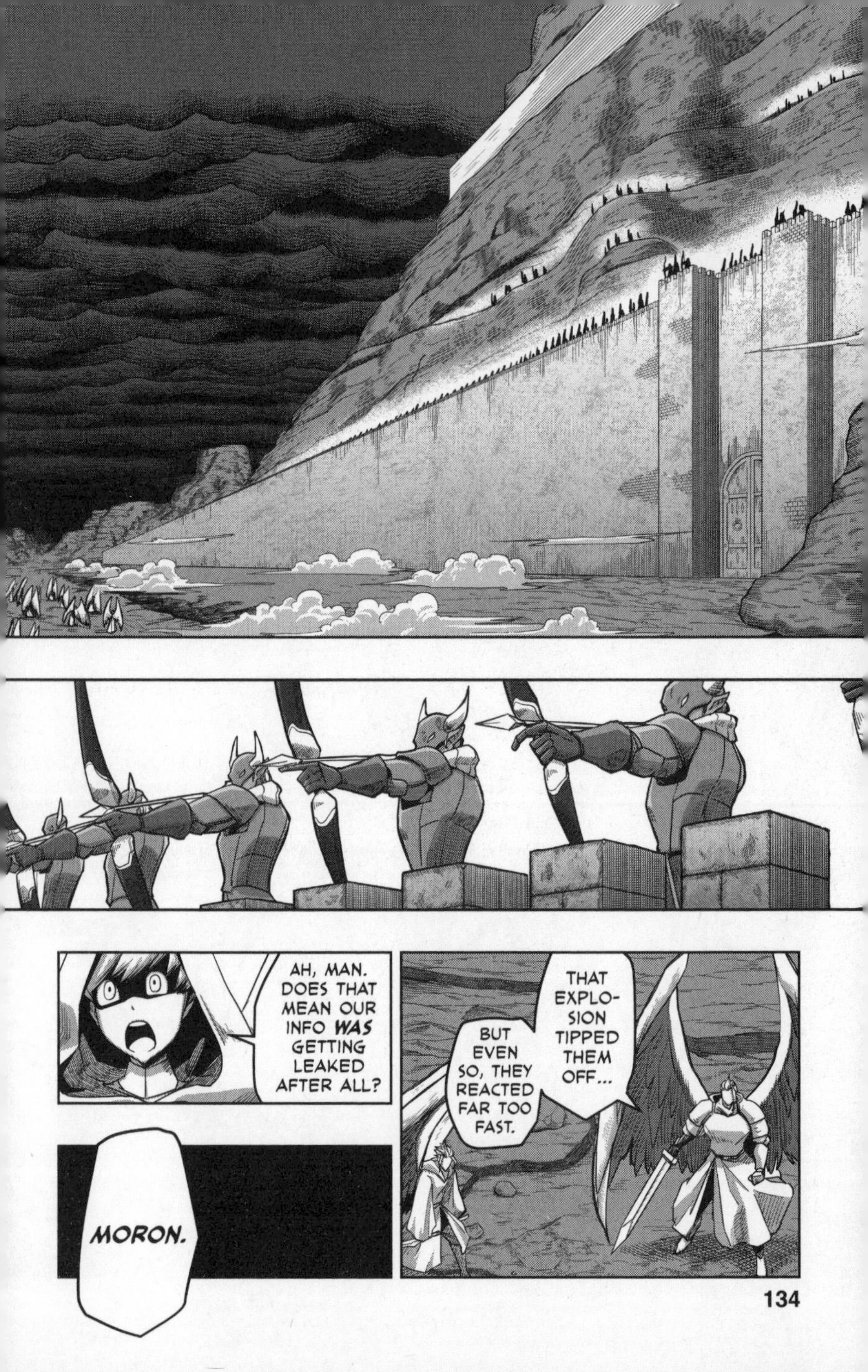
THAT EXPLOSION TIPPED THEM OFF...
BUT EVEN SO, THEY REACTED FAR TOO FAST.
AH, MAN. DOES THAT MEAN OUR INFO *WAS* GETTING LEAKED AFTER ALL?
MORON.

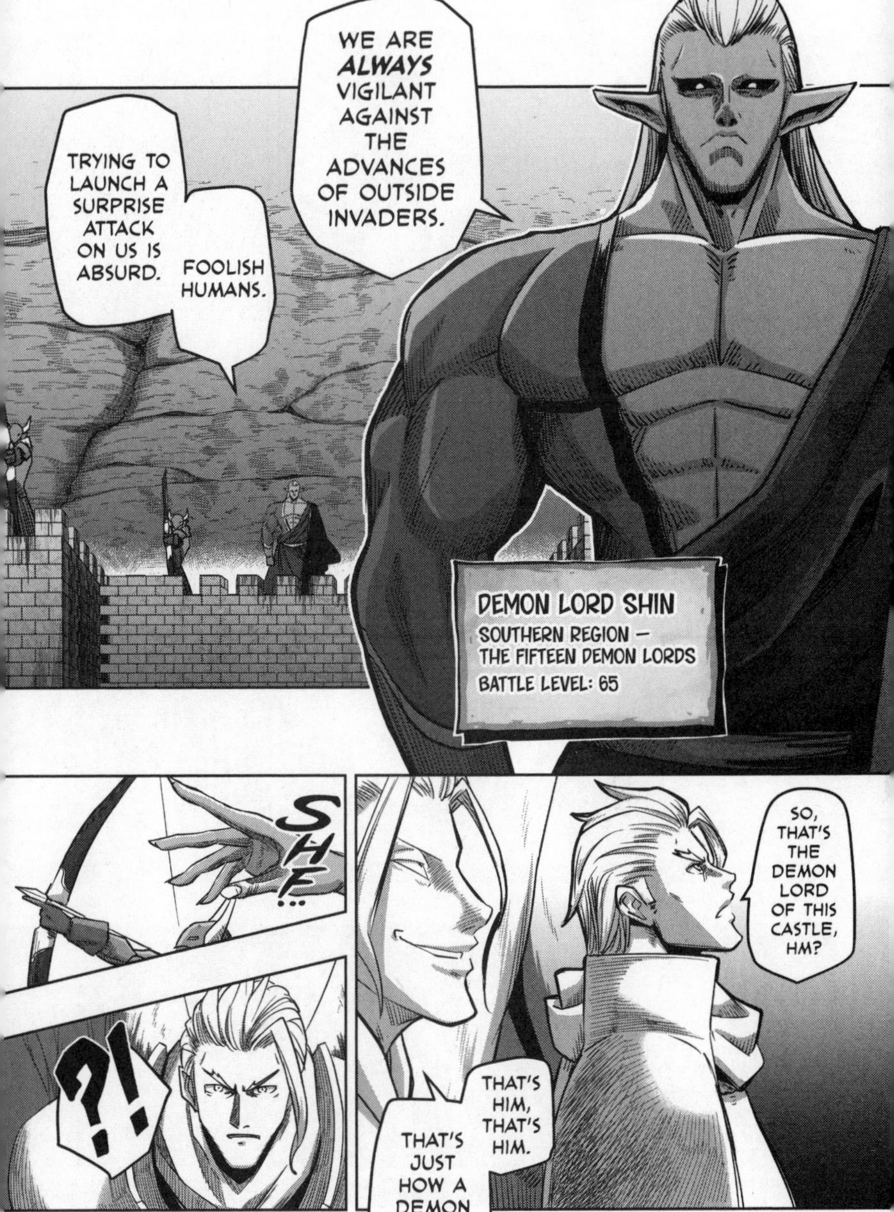
WE ARE *ALWAYS* VIGILANT AGAINST THE ADVANCES OF OUTSIDE INVADERS.
TRYING TO LAUNCH A SURPRISE ATTACK ON US IS ABSURD.
FOOLISH HUMANS.
DEMON LORD SHIN
SOUTHERN REGION — THE FIFTEEN DEMON LORDS
BATTLE LEVEL: 65
SO, THAT'S THE DEMON LORD OF THIS CASTLE, HM?
THAT'S HIM, THAT'S HIM.
THAT'S JUST HOW A DEMON LORD ACTS.
SHF...
?!

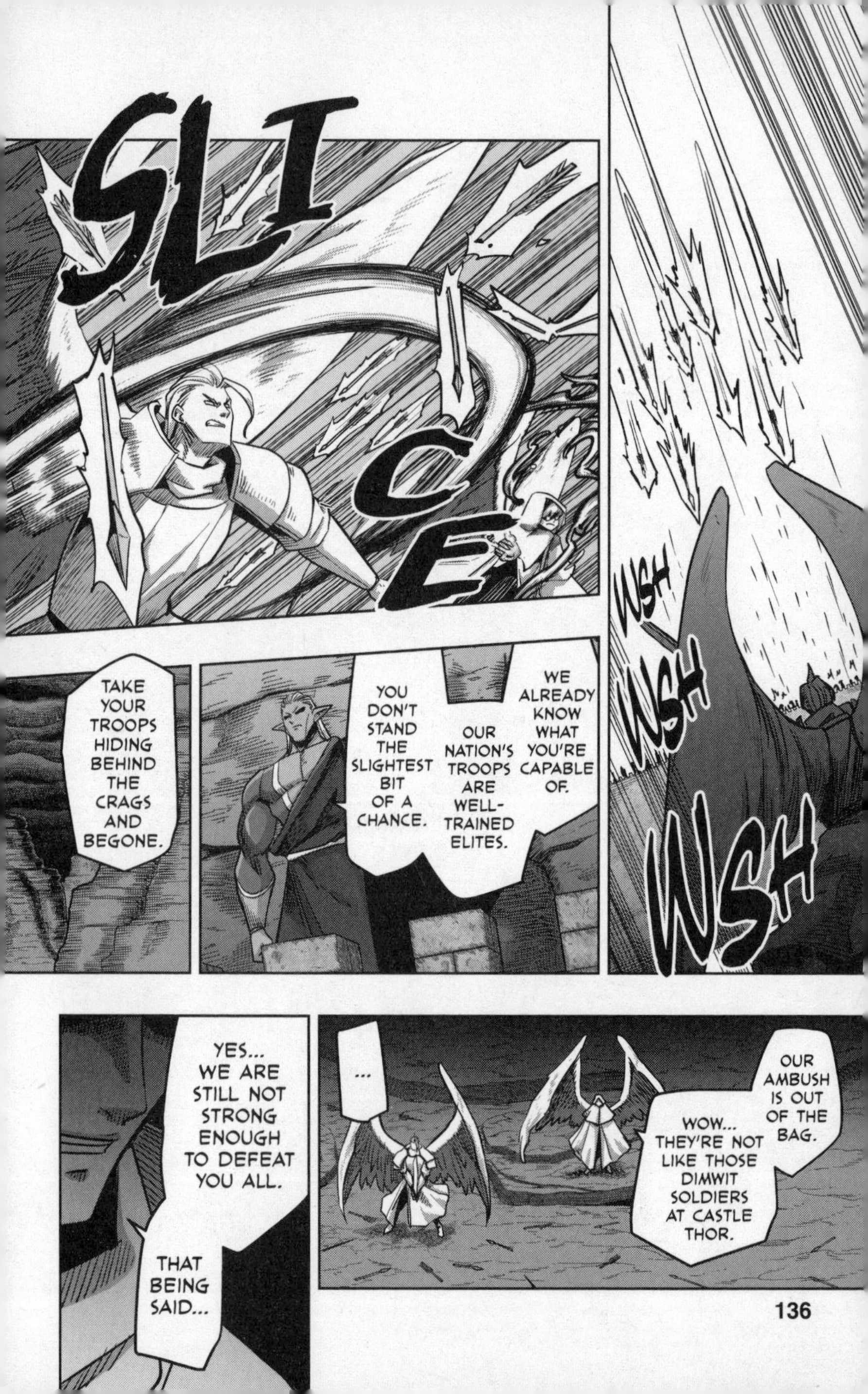
WSH
WSH
WSH
SLICE
WE ALREADY KNOW WHAT YOU'RE CAPABLE OF.
OUR NATION'S TROOPS ARE WELL-TRAINED ELITES.
YOU DON'T STAND THE SLIGHTEST BIT OF A CHANCE.
TAKE YOUR TROOPS HIDING BEHIND THE CRAGS AND BEGONE.
OUR AMBUSH IS OUT OF THE BAG.
WOW... THEY'RE NOT LIKE THOSE DIMWIT SOLDIERS AT CASTLE THOR.
...
YES... WE ARE STILL NOT STRONG ENOUGH TO DEFEAT YOU ALL.
THAT BEING SAID...

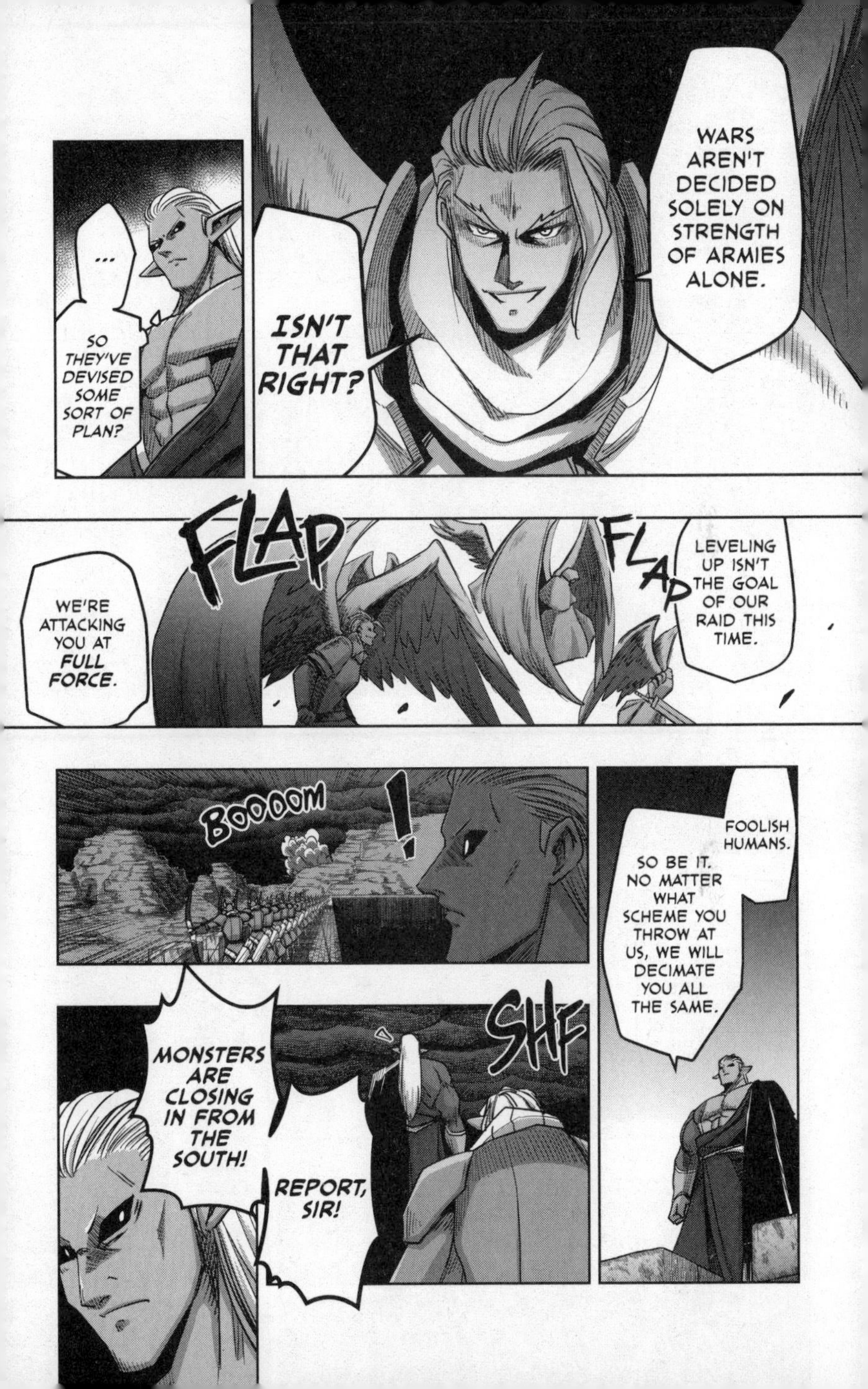
WARS AREN'T DECIDED SOLELY ON STRENGTH OF ARMIES ALONE.
ISN'T THAT RIGHT?
...
SO THEY'VE DEVISED SOME SORT OF PLAN?
LEVELING UP ISN'T THE GOAL OF OUR RAID THIS TIME.
FLAP
FLAP
WE'RE ATTACKING YOU AT FULL FORCE.
FOOLISH HUMANS.
SO BE IT. NO MATTER WHAT SCHEME YOU THROW AT US, WE WILL DECIMATE YOU ALL THE SAME.
!
BOOOOM
SHF
REPORT, SIR!
MONSTERS ARE CLOSING IN FROM THE SOUTH!

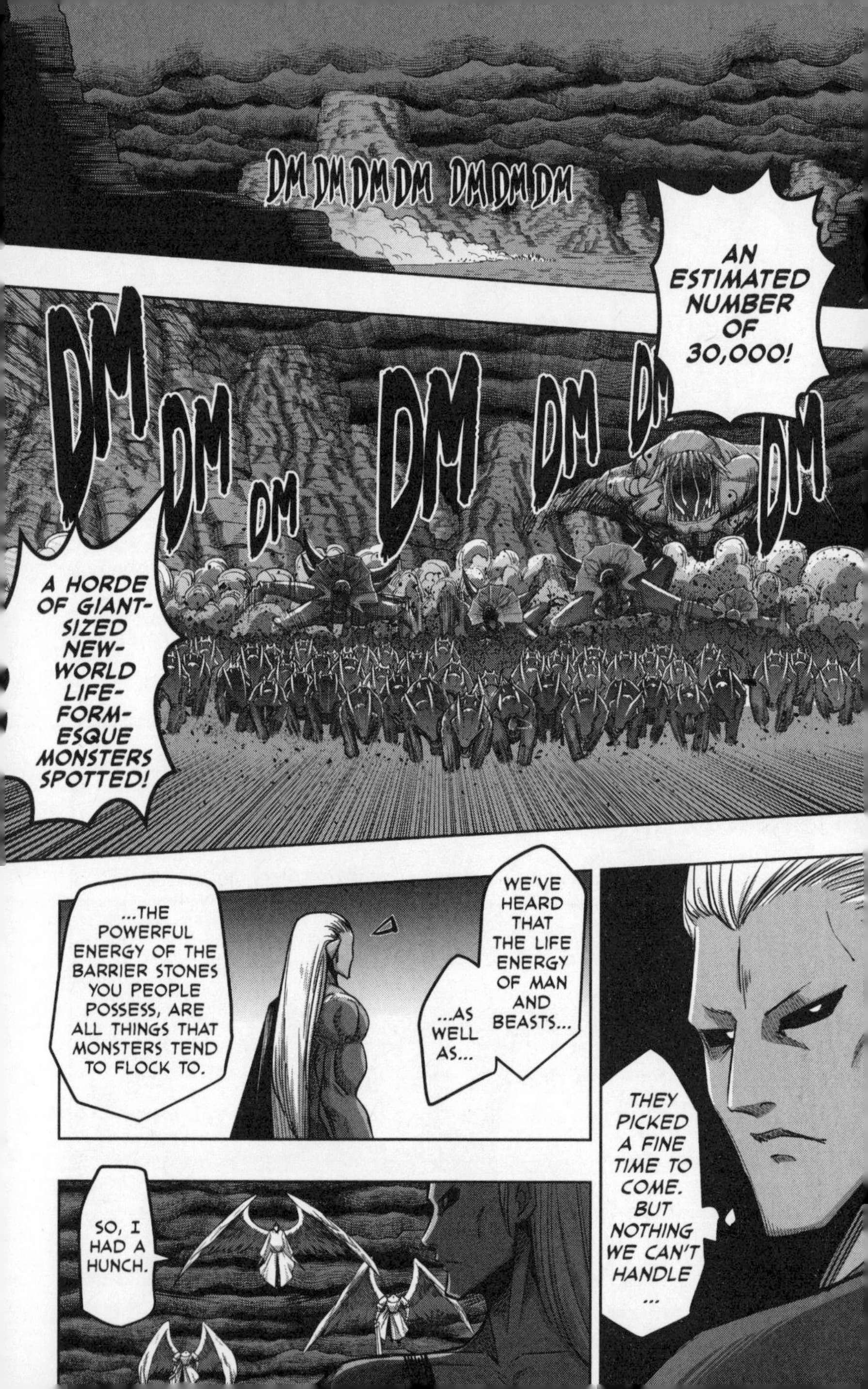
DM DM DM DM DM DM DM
AN ESTIMATED NUMBER OF 30,000!
DM DM DM DM DM DM DM
A HORDE OF GIANT-SIZED NEW-WORLD LIFE-FORM-ESQUE MONSTERS SPOTTED!
THEY PICKED A FINE TIME TO COME. BUT NOTHING WE CAN'T HANDLE ...
WE'VE HEARD THAT THE LIFE ENERGY OF MAN AND BEASTS...
...AS WELL AS...
...THE POWERFUL ENERGY OF THE BARRIER STONES YOU PEOPLE POSSESS, ARE ALL THINGS THAT MONSTERS TEND TO FLOCK TO.
SO, I HAD A HUNCH.

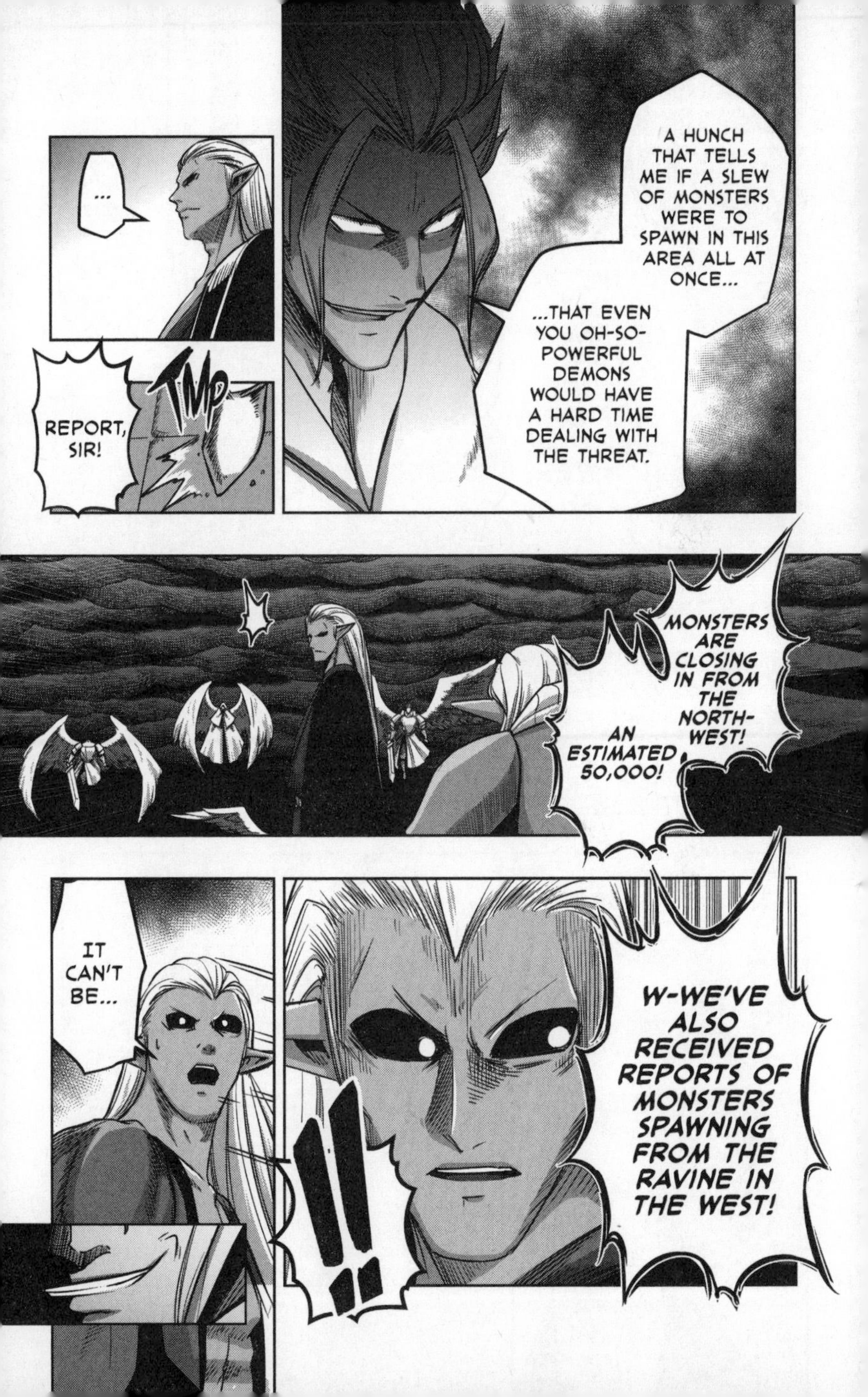
A HUNCH THAT TELLS ME IF A SLEW OF MONSTERS WERE TO SPAWN IN THIS AREA ALL AT ONCE...
...THAT EVEN YOU OH-SO-POWERFUL DEMONS WOULD HAVE A HARD TIME DEALING WITH THE THREAT.
...
TMP
REPORT, SIR!
MONSTERS ARE CLOSING IN FROM THE NORTH-WEST!
AN ESTIMATED 50,000!
W-WE'VE ALSO RECEIVED REPORTS OF MONSTERS SPAWNING FROM THE RAVINE IN THE WEST!
!!
IT CAN'T BE...

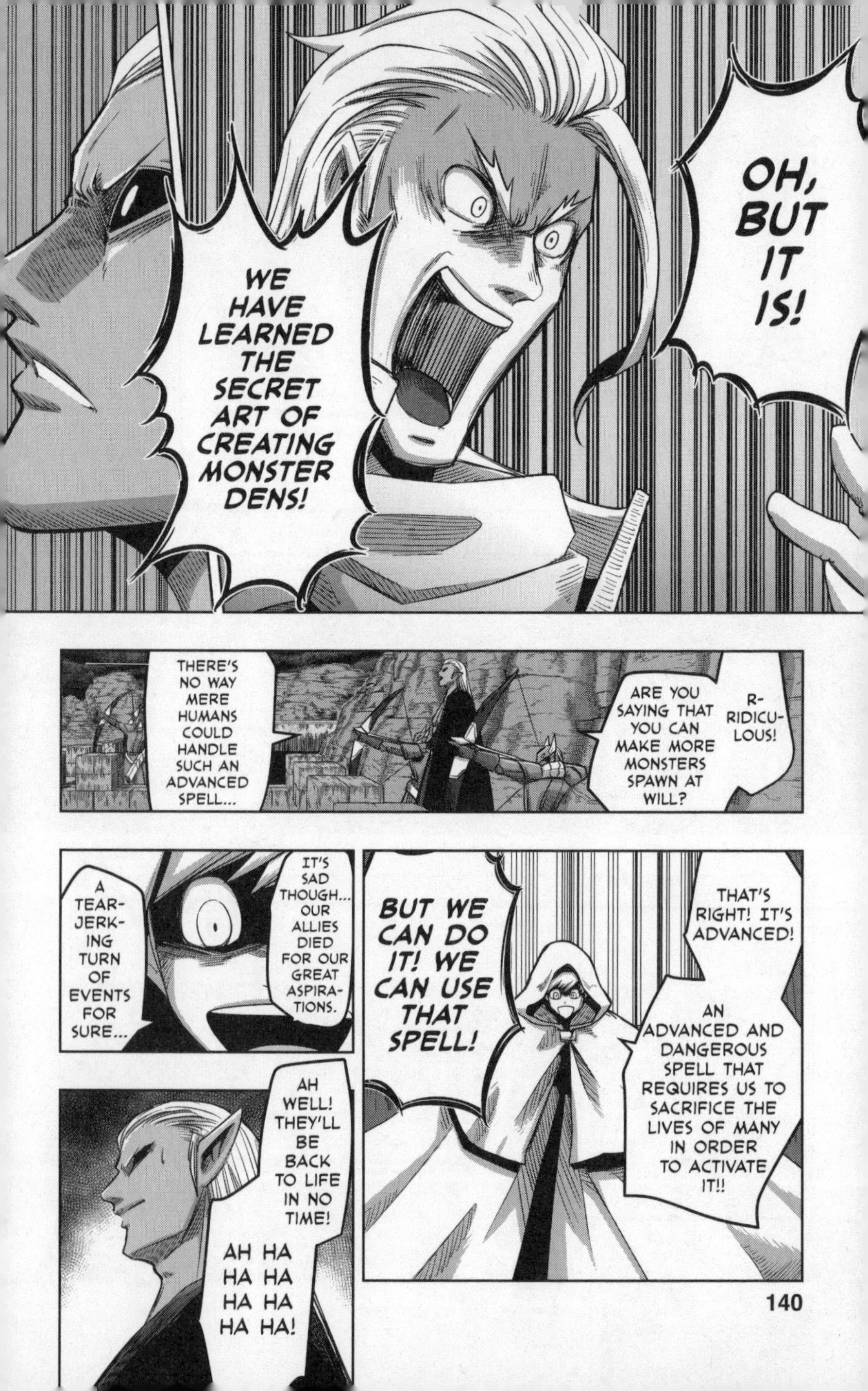
OH, BUT IT IS!
WE HAVE LEARNED THE SECRET ART OF CREATING MONSTER DENS!
R-RIDICULOUS!
ARE YOU SAYING THAT YOU CAN MAKE MORE MONSTERS SPAWN AT WILL?
THERE'S NO WAY MERE HUMANS COULD HANDLE SUCH AN ADVANCED SPELL...
THAT'S RIGHT! IT'S ADVANCED!
AN ADVANCED AND DANGEROUS SPELL THAT REQUIRES US TO SACRIFICE THE LIVES OF MANY IN ORDER TO ACTIVATE IT!!
BUT WE CAN DO IT! WE CAN USE THAT SPELL!
IT'S SAD THOUGH... OUR ALLIES DIED FOR OUR GREAT ASPIRATIONS.
A TEAR-JERKING TURN OF EVENTS FOR SURE...
AH WELL! THEY'LL BE BACK TO LIFE IN NO TIME!
AH HA HA HA HA HA HA HA HA!

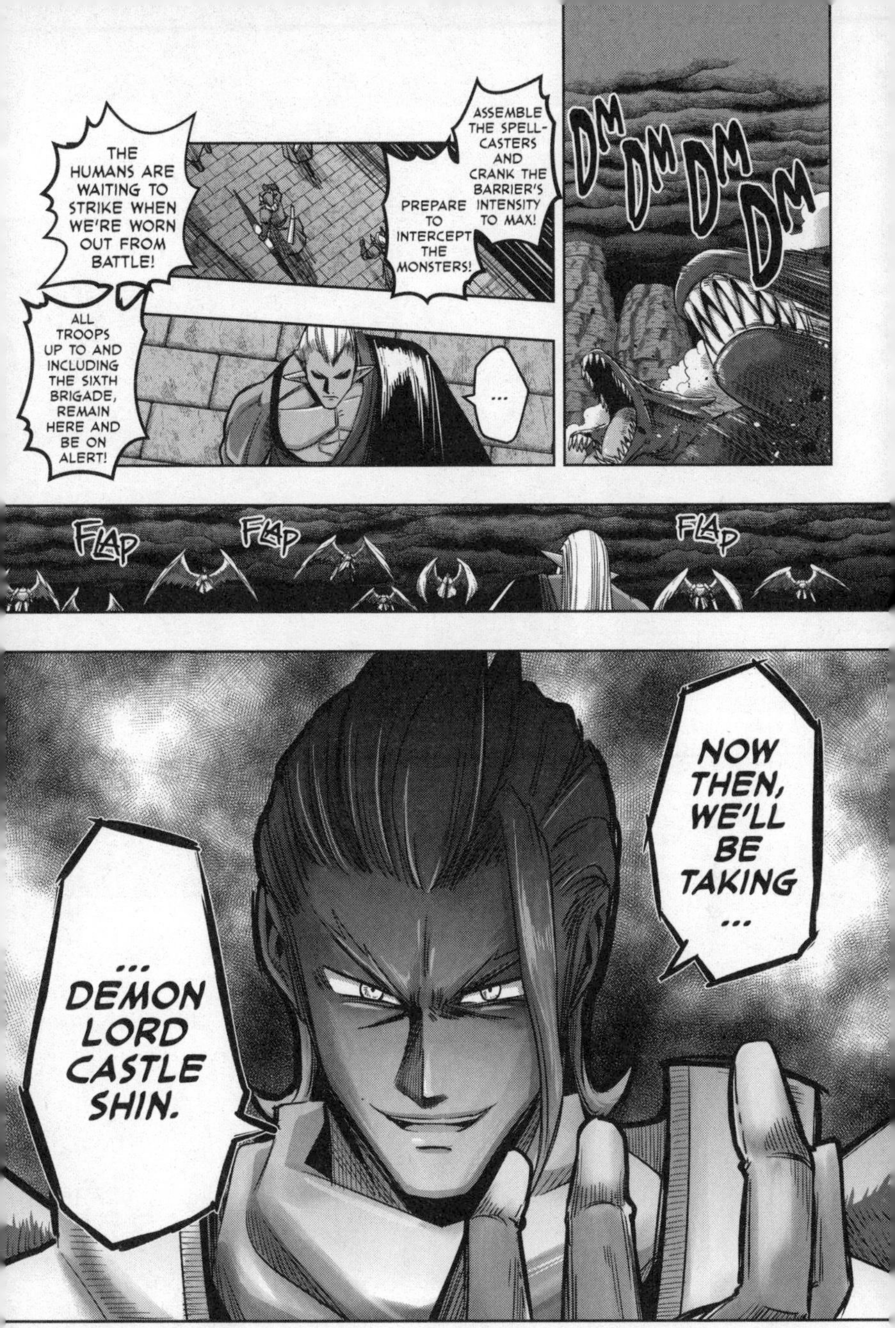
DM DM DM DM DM
ASSEMBLE THE SPELL-CASTERS AND CRANK THE BARRIER'S INTENSITY TO MAX!
PREPARE TO INTERCEPT THE MONSTERS!
THE HUMANS ARE WAITING TO STRIKE WHEN WE'RE WORN OUT FROM BATTLE!
ALL TROOPS UP TO AND INCLUDING THE SIXTH BRIGADE, REMAIN HERE AND BE ON ALERT!
...
FLAP
FLAP
FLAP
NOW THEN, WE'LL BE TAKING ...
... DEMON LORD CASTLE SHIN.

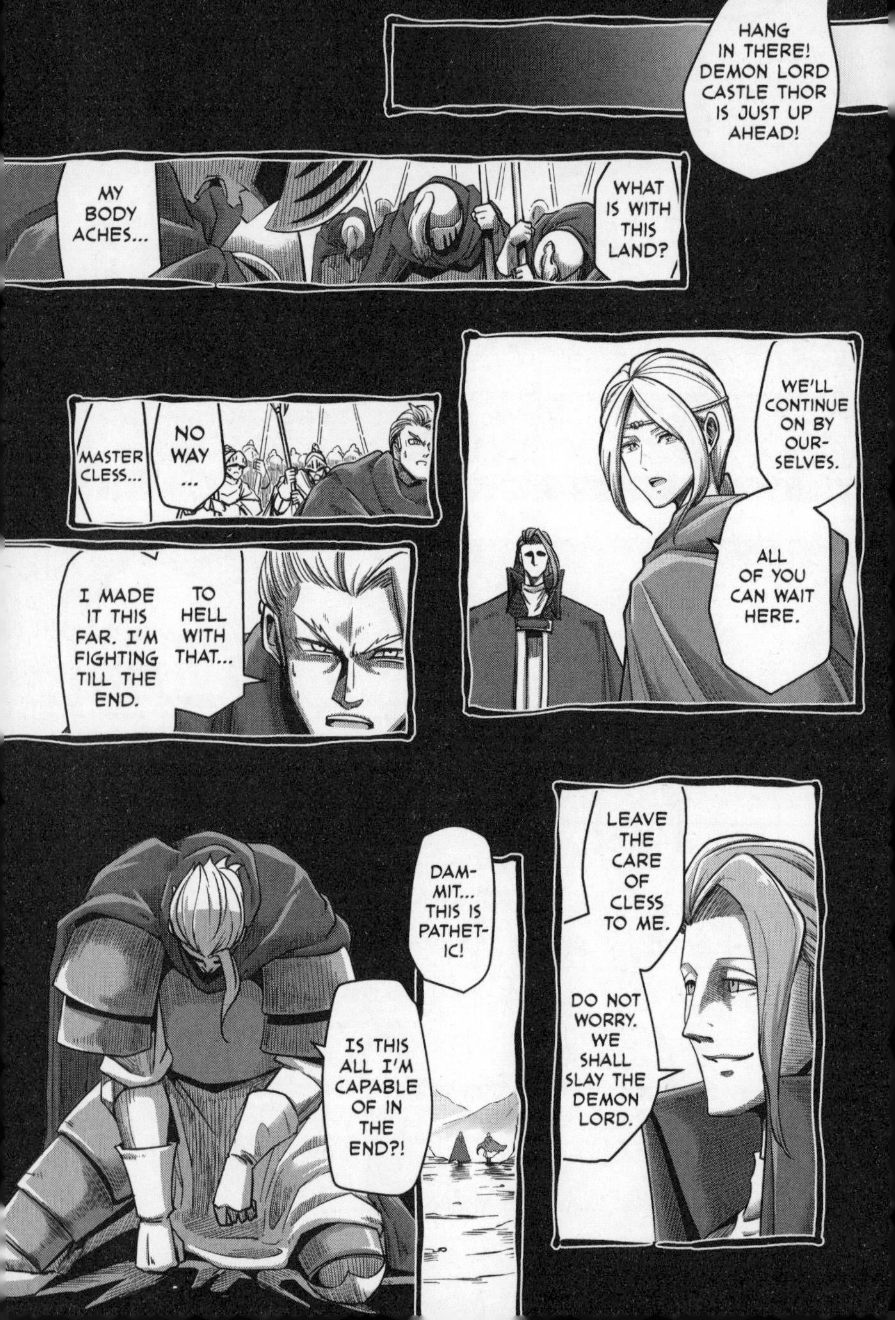
HANG IN THERE! DEMON LORD CASTLE THOR IS JUST UP AHEAD!
WHAT IS WITH THIS LAND?
MY BODY ACHES...
WE'LL CONTINUE ON BY OURSELVES.
ALL OF YOU CAN WAIT HERE.
NO WAY...
MASTER CLESS...
TO HELL WITH THAT...
I MADE IT THIS FAR. I'M FIGHTING TILL THE END.
LEAVE THE CARE OF CLESS TO ME.
DO NOT WORRY. WE SHALL SLAY THE DEMON LORD.
DAMMIT... THIS IS PATHETIC!
IS THIS ALL I'M CAPABLE OF IN THE END?!

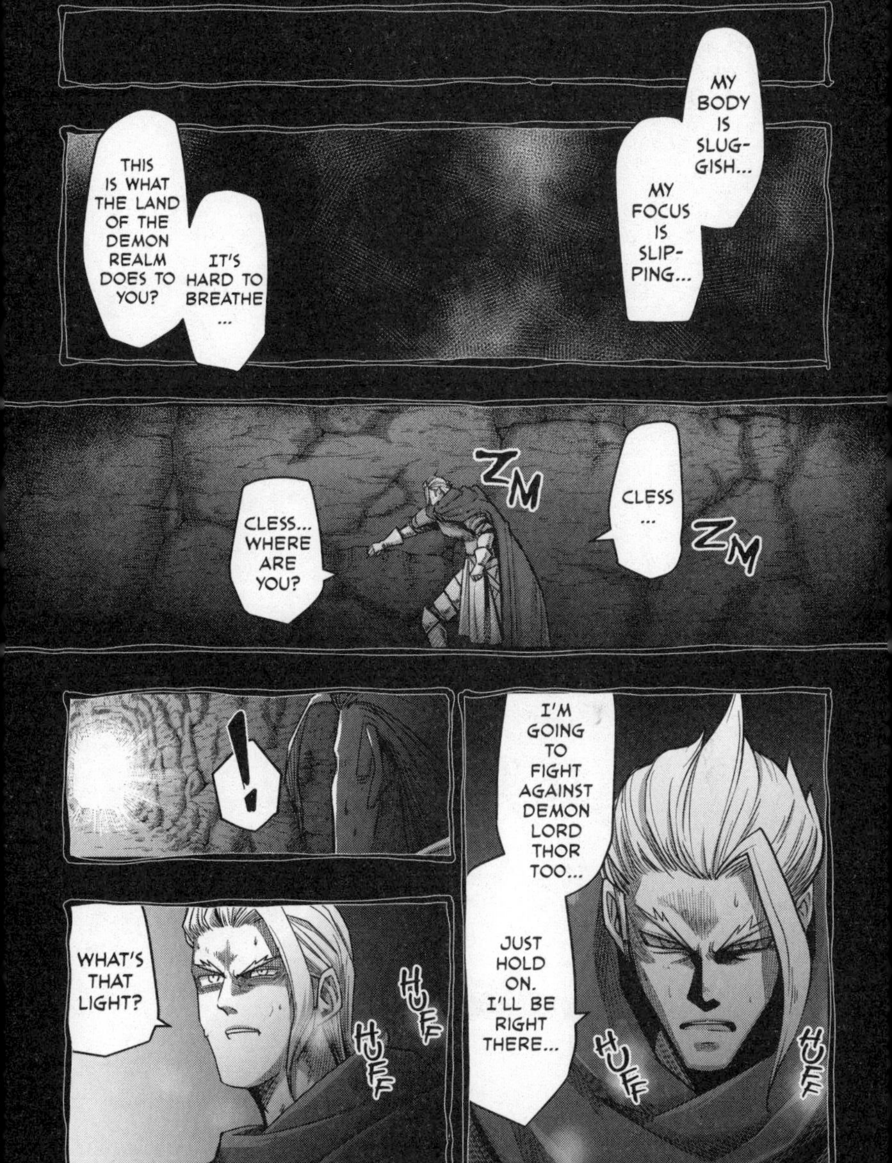
MY BODY IS SLUG-GISH...
MY FOCUS IS SLIP-PING...
IT'S HARD TO BREATHE...
THIS IS WHAT THE LAND OF THE DEMON REALM DOES TO YOU?
ZM
CLESS...
ZM
CLESS... WHERE ARE YOU?
I'M GOING TO FIGHT AGAINST DEMON LORD THOR TOO...
JUST HOLD ON. I'LL BE RIGHT THERE...
HUFF
HUFF
!
WHAT'S THAT LIGHT?
HUFF
HUFF

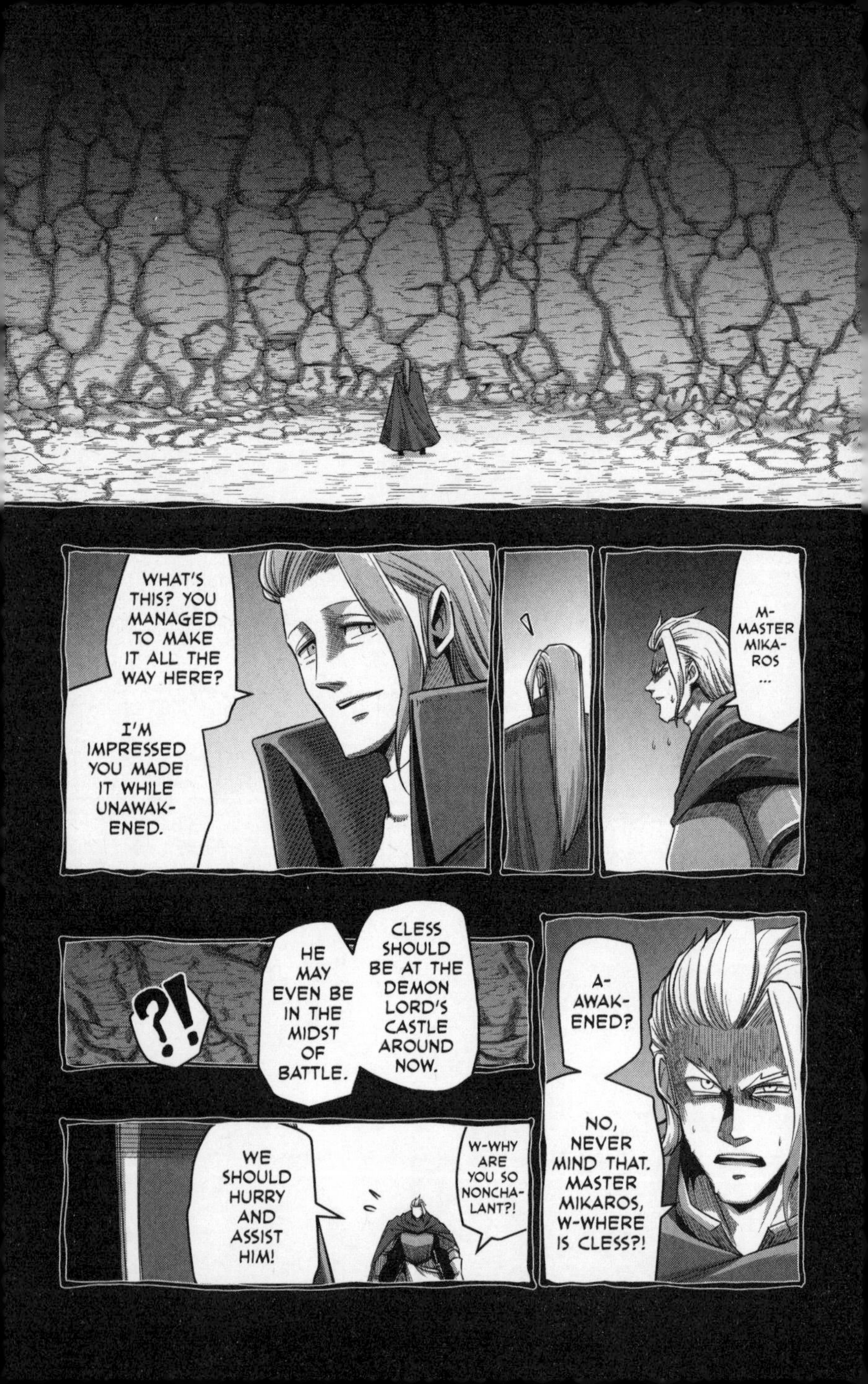
M-MASTER MIKAROS...
WHAT'S THIS? YOU MANAGED TO MAKE IT ALL THE WAY HERE?
I'M IMPRESSED YOU MADE IT WHILE UNAWAKENED.
A-AWAKENED?
NO, NEVER MIND THAT. MASTER MIKAROS, W-WHERE IS CLESS?!
CLESS SHOULD BE AT THE DEMON LORD'S CASTLE AROUND NOW.
HE MAY EVEN BE IN THE MIDST OF BATTLE.
?!
W-WHY ARE YOU SO NONCHALANT?!
WE SHOULD HURRY AND ASSIST HIM!

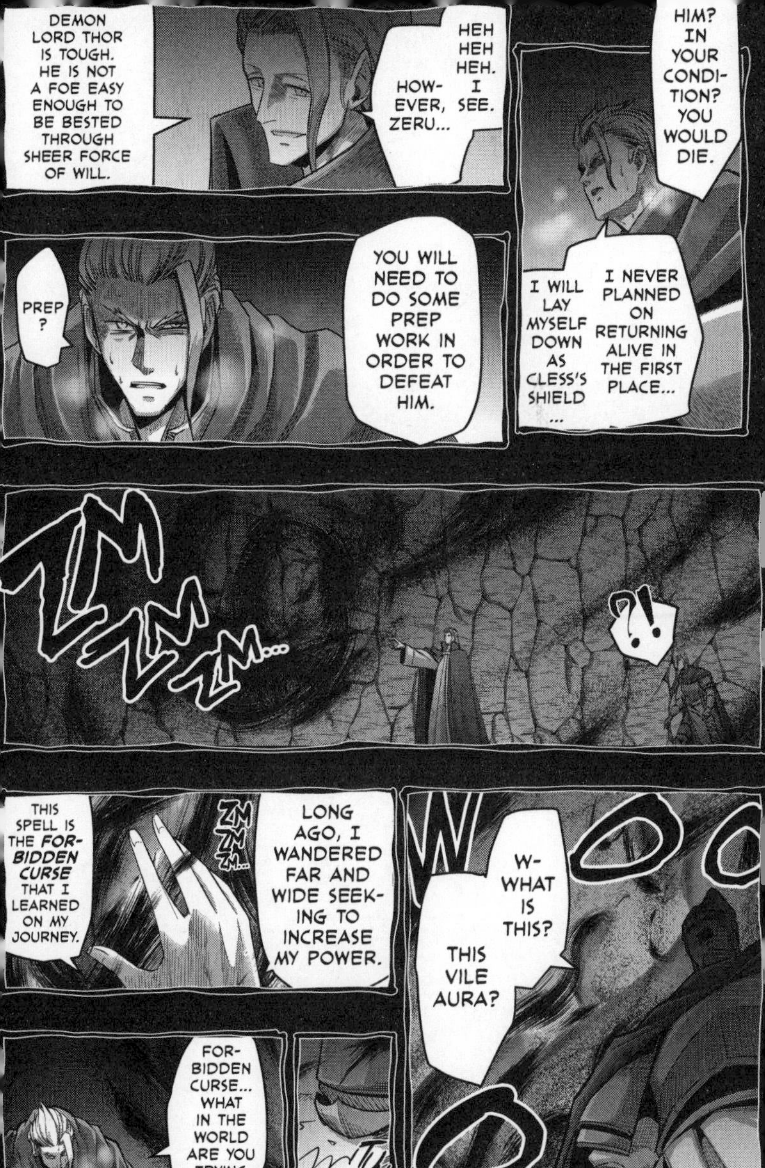
HIM? IN YOUR CONDITION? YOU WOULD DIE.
I NEVER PLANNED ON RETURNING ALIVE IN THE FIRST PLACE...
I WILL LAY MYSELF DOWN AS CLESS'S SHIELD...
HEH HEH HEH. I SEE.
HOWEVER, ZERU...
DEMON LORD THOR IS TOUGH. HE IS NOT A FOE EASY ENOUGH TO BE BESTED THROUGH SHEER FORCE OF WILL.
YOU WILL NEED TO DO SOME PREP WORK IN ORDER TO DEFEAT HIM.
PREP?
?!
ZM ZM ZM...
W-WHAT IS THIS?
THIS VILE AURA?
ZM ZM ZM...
LONG AGO, I WANDERED FAR AND WIDE SEEKING TO INCREASE MY POWER.
THIS SPELL IS THE *FORBIDDEN CURSE* THAT I LEARNED ON MY JOURNEY.
FORBIDDEN CURSE... WHAT IN THE WORLD ARE YOU TRYING

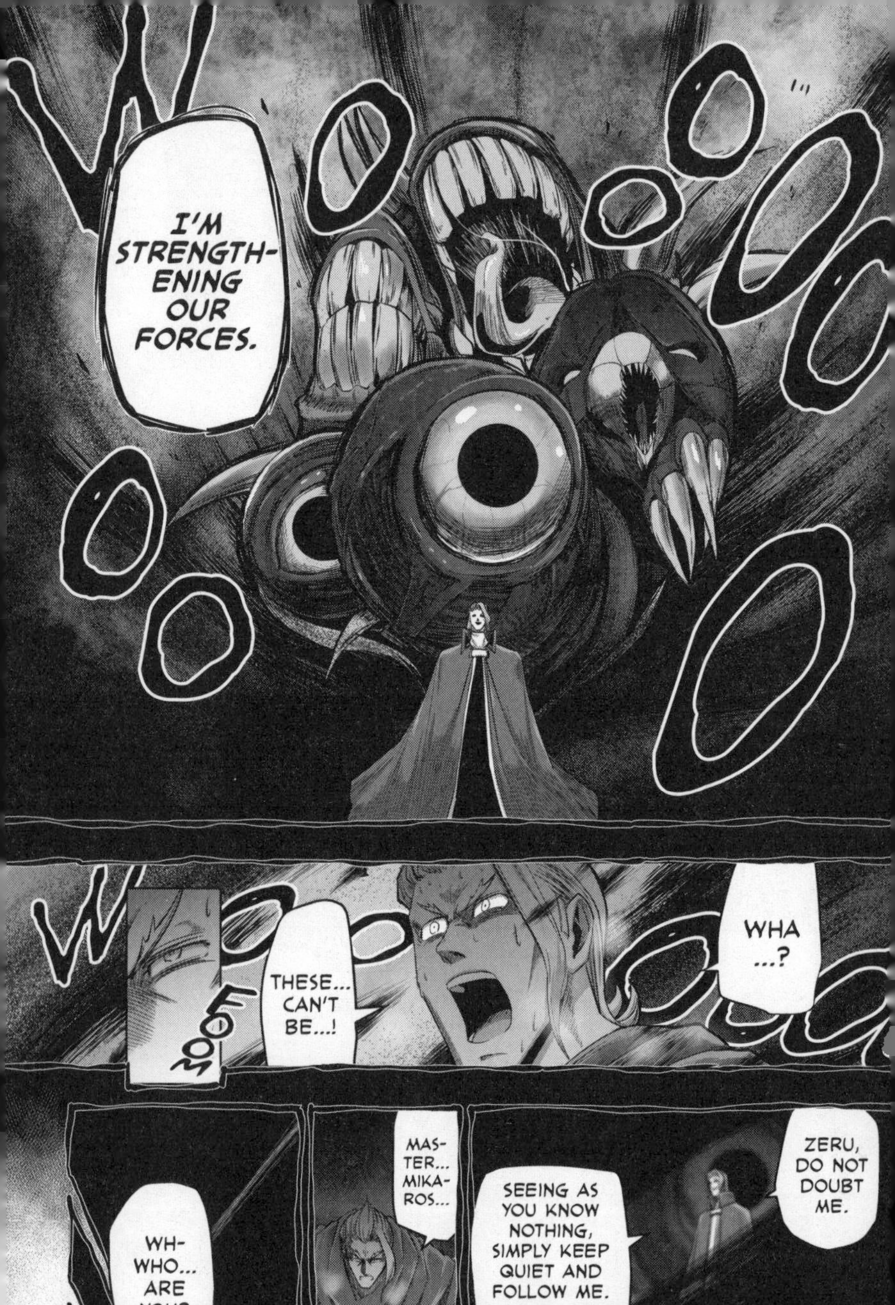
I'M STRENGTH-ENING OUR FORCES.
WHA ...?
THESE... CAN'T BE...!
FOOM
ZERU, DO NOT DOUBT ME.
SEEING AS YOU KNOW NOTHING, SIMPLY KEEP QUIET AND FOLLOW ME.
MAS-TER... MIKA-ROS...
WH-WHO... ARE YOU?

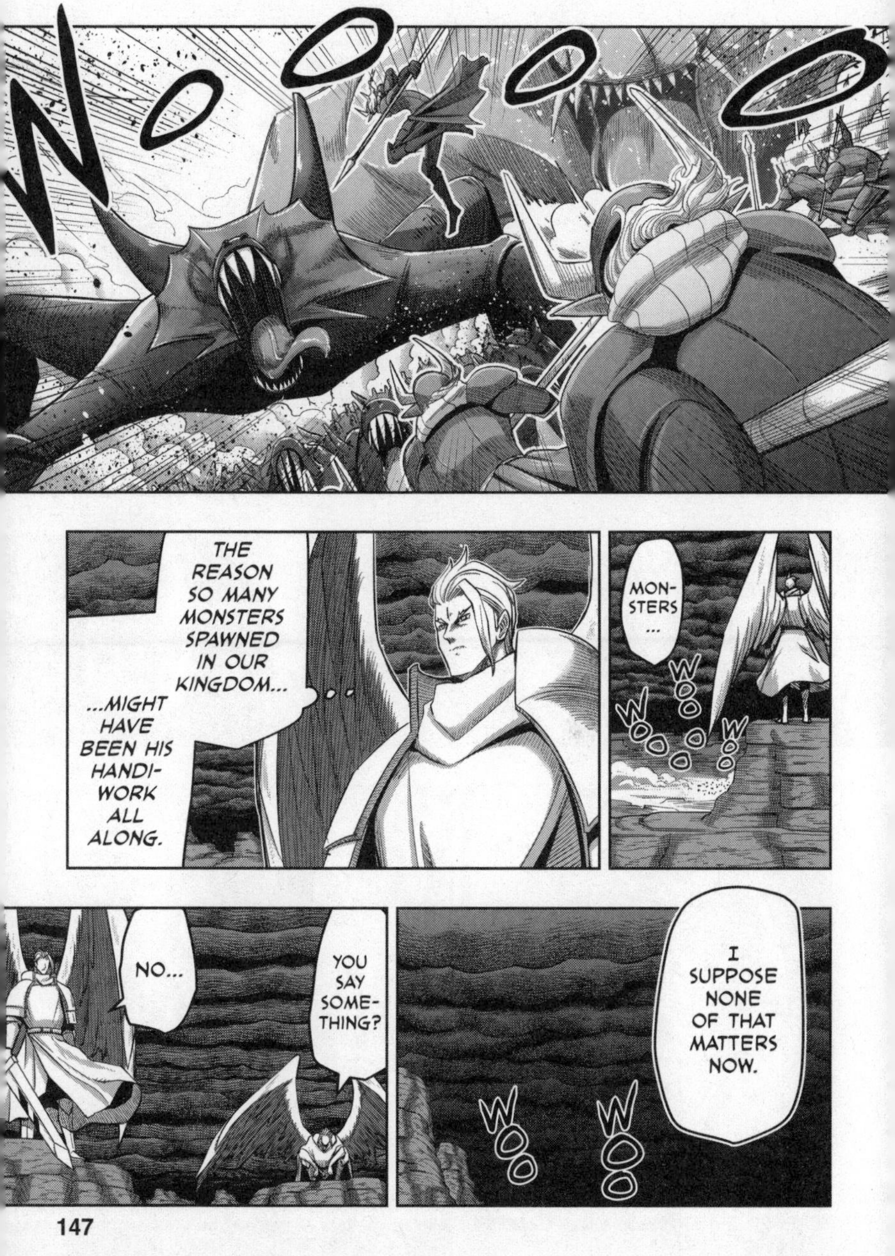
WOOOOOO
MON-STERS...
WOOO
WOOOO
WOO
THE REASON SO MANY MONSTERS SPAWNED IN OUR KINGDOM...
...MIGHT HAVE BEEN HIS HANDI-WORK ALL ALONG.
I SUPPOSE NONE OF THAT MATTERS NOW.
WOO
WOO
YOU SAY SOME-THING?
NO...

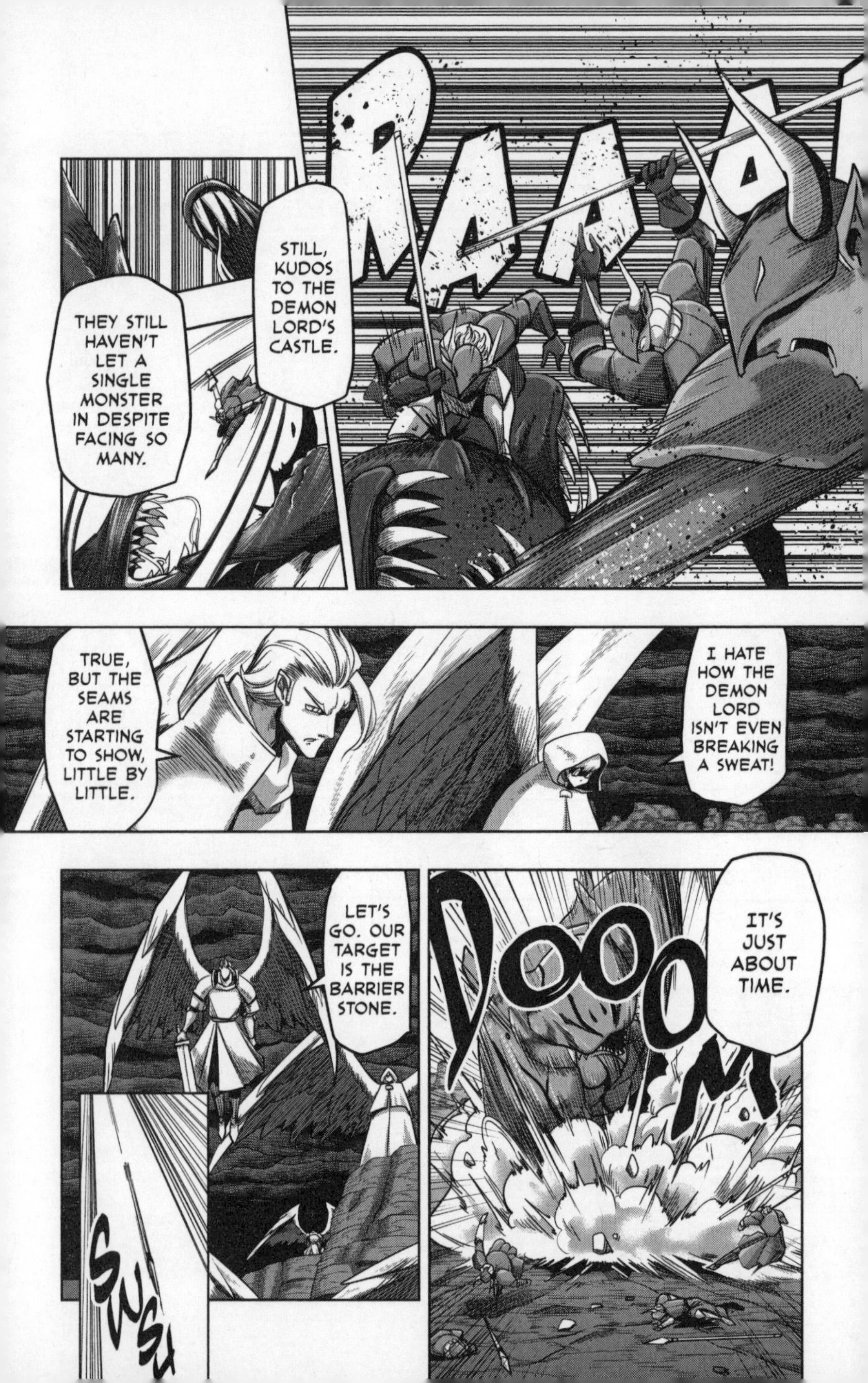
STILL, KUDOS TO THE DEMON LORD'S CASTLE.
THEY STILL HAVEN'T LET A SINGLE MONSTER IN DESPITE FACING SO MANY.
I HATE HOW THE DEMON LORD ISN'T EVEN BREAKING A SWEAT!
TRUE, BUT THE SEAMS ARE STARTING TO SHOW, LITTLE BY LITTLE.
IT'S JUST ABOUT TIME.
DOOOM
LET'S GO. OUR TARGET IS THE BARRIER STONE.

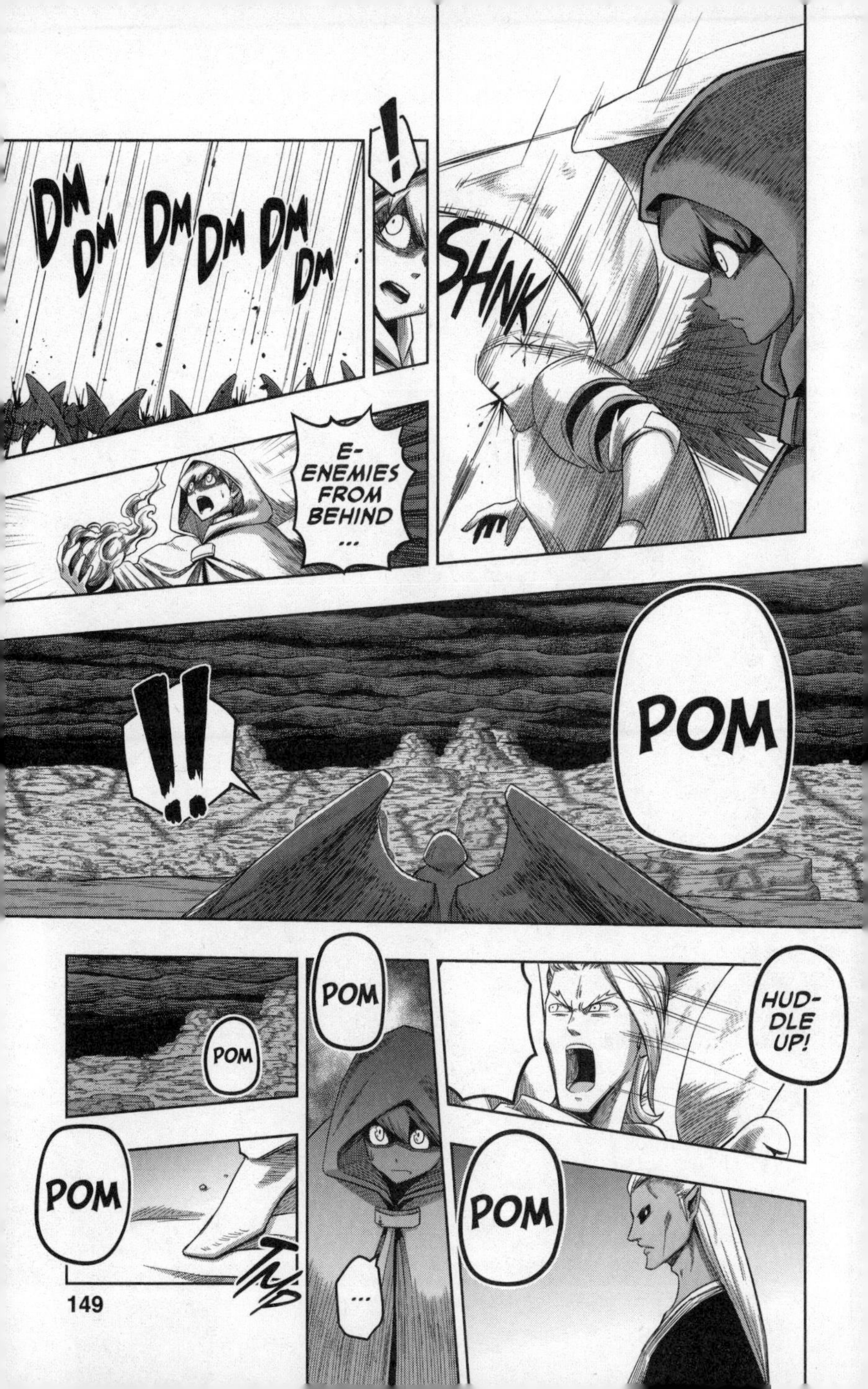
SHNK
!
DM DM DM DM DM DM
E-ENEMIES FROM BEHIND ...
POM
!!
HUD-DLE UP!
POM
POM
...
POM
POM
TMP

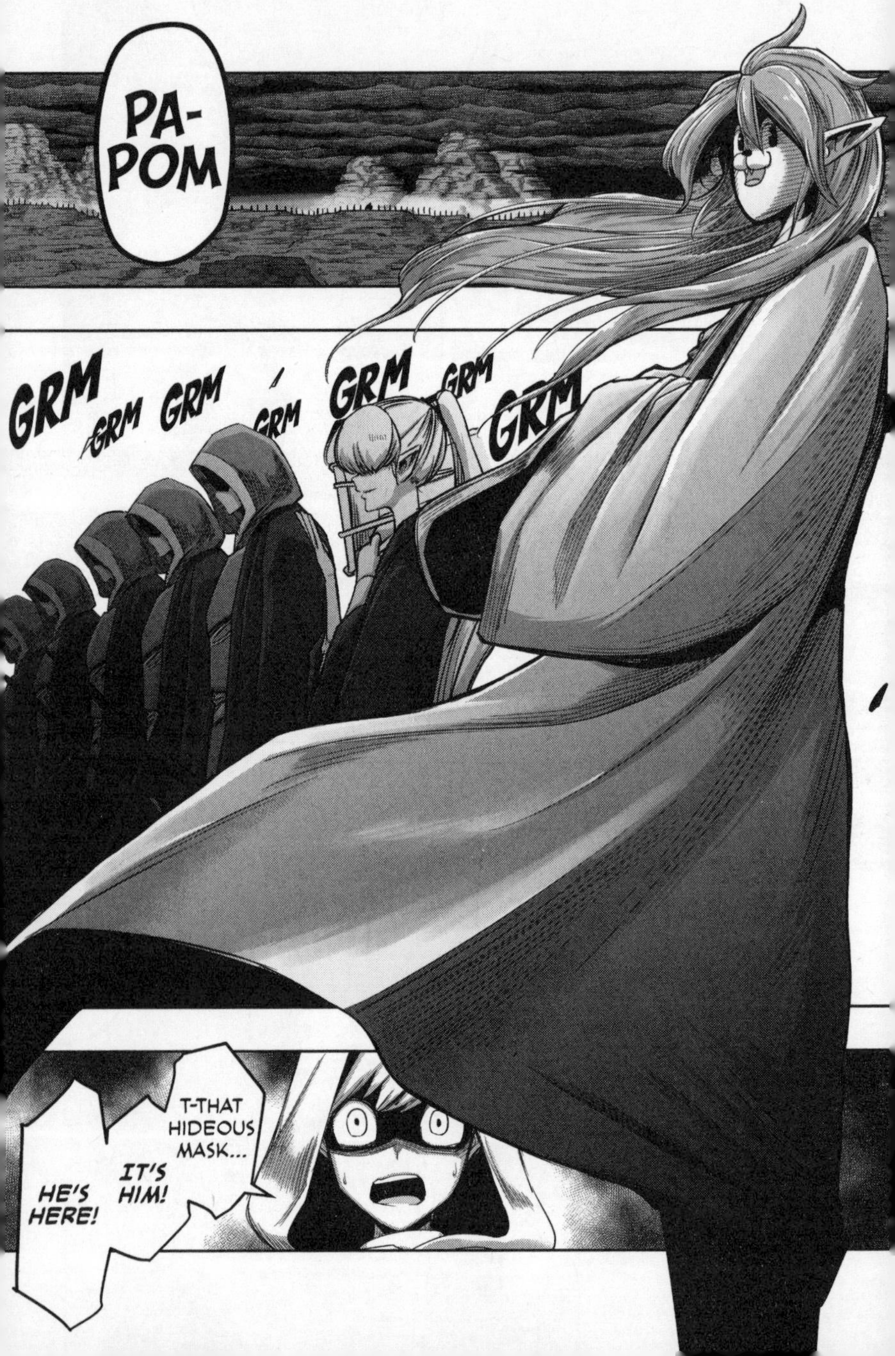
PA-
POM
GRM GRM GRM GRM GRM GRM GRM
T-THAT HIDEOUS MASK...
IT'S HIM!
HE'S HERE!

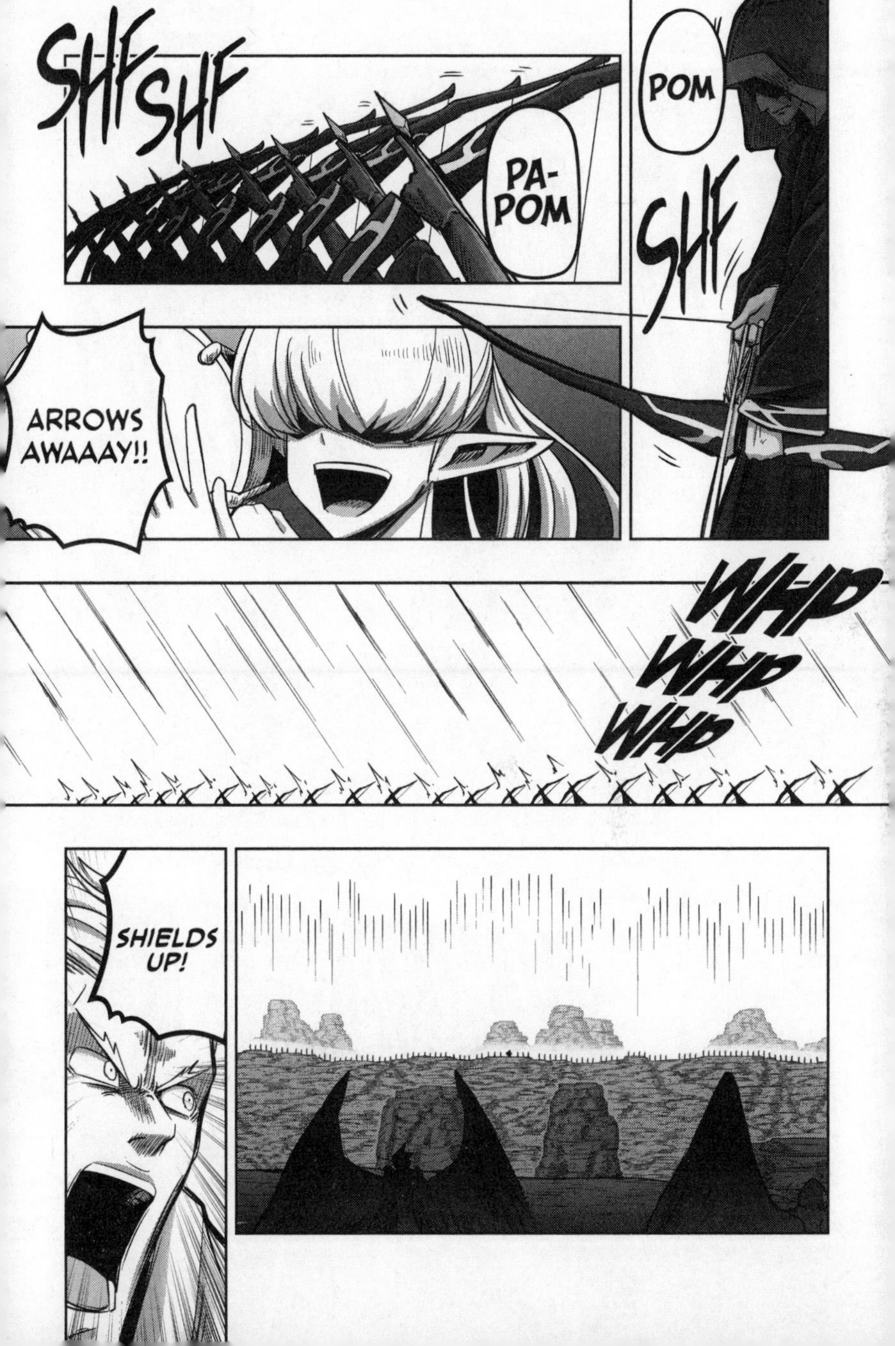
POM
SHF
PA-POM
SHF SHF
ARROWS AWAAAY!!
WHP WHP WHP
SHIELDS UP!

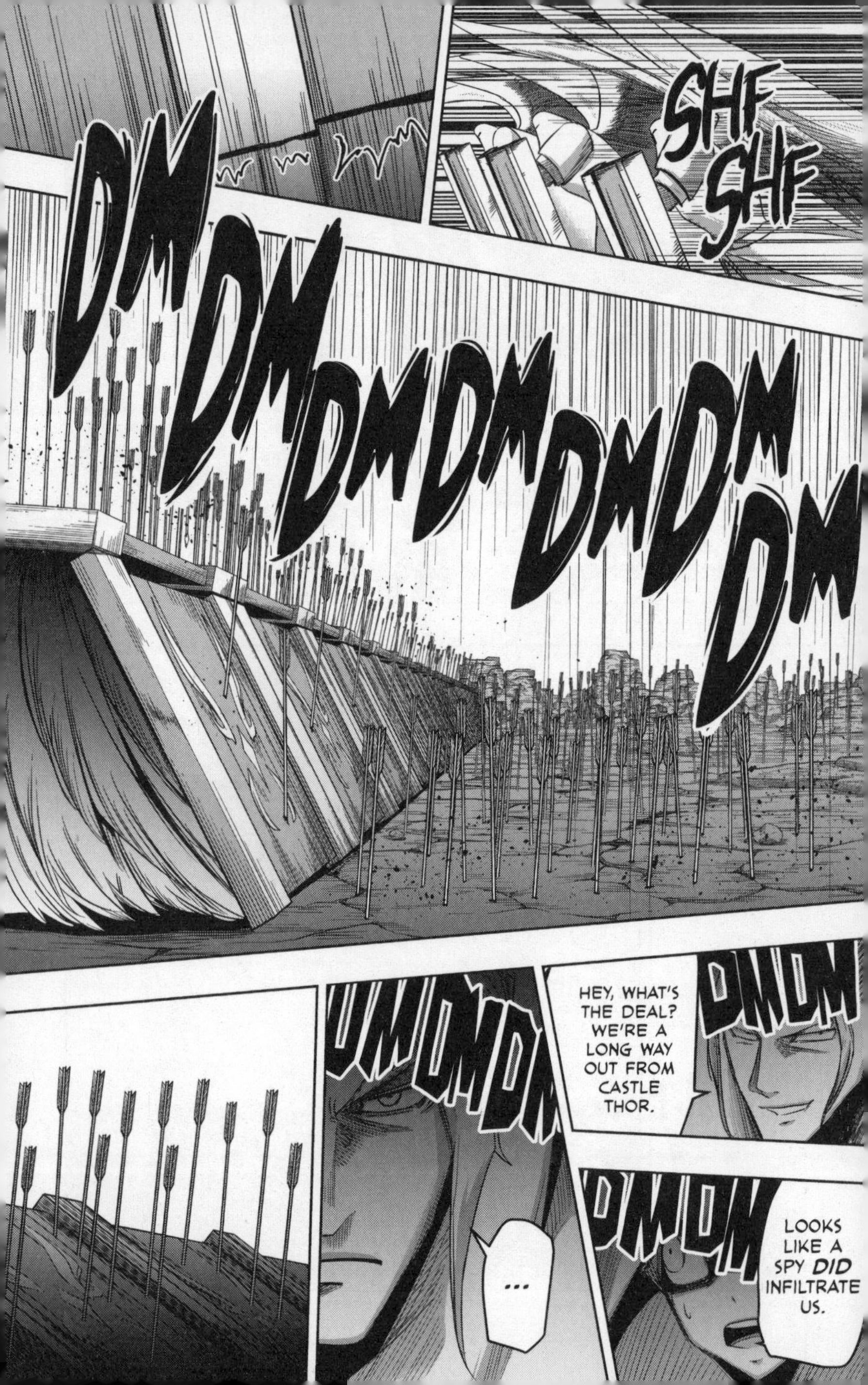
SHF SHF
DM DM DMDM DMDM DM DM
DMDM
HEY, WHAT'S THE DEAL? WE'RE A LONG WAY OUT FROM CASTLE THOR.
DMDM
LOOKS LIKE A SPY *DID* INFILTRATE US.
DMDMDM
...

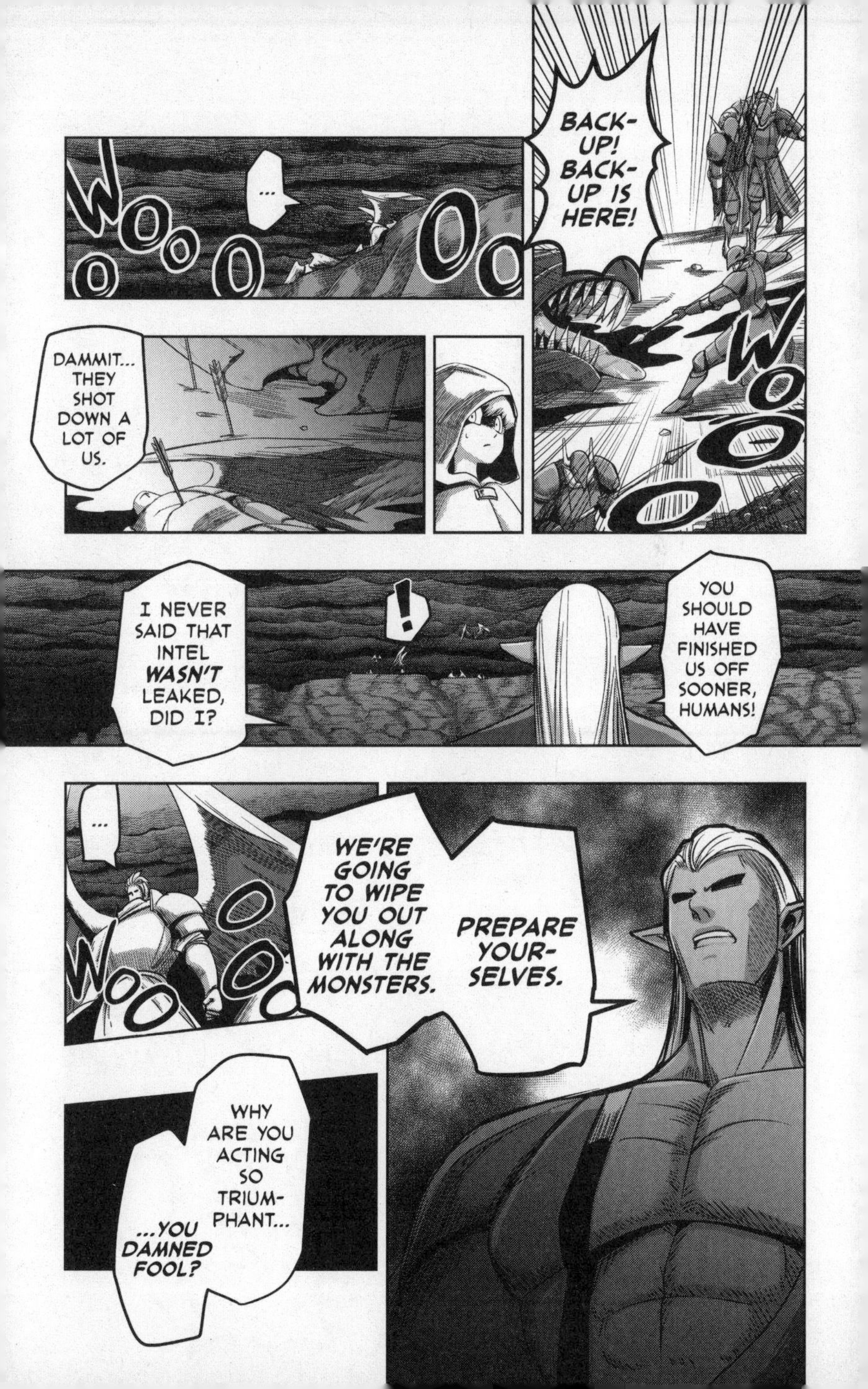
BACK-UP! BACK-UP IS HERE!
WOOOO
WOOOOOOO
...
DAMMIT... THEY SHOT DOWN A LOT OF US.
YOU SHOULD HAVE FINISHED US OFF SOONER, HUMANS!
!
I NEVER SAID THAT INTEL ***WASN'T*** LEAKED, DID I?
PREPARE YOUR-SELVES.
WE'RE GOING TO WIPE YOU OUT ALONG WITH THE MONSTERS.
...
WOOOOO
WHY ARE YOU ACTING SO TRIUMPHANT... ...YOU DAMNED FOOL?

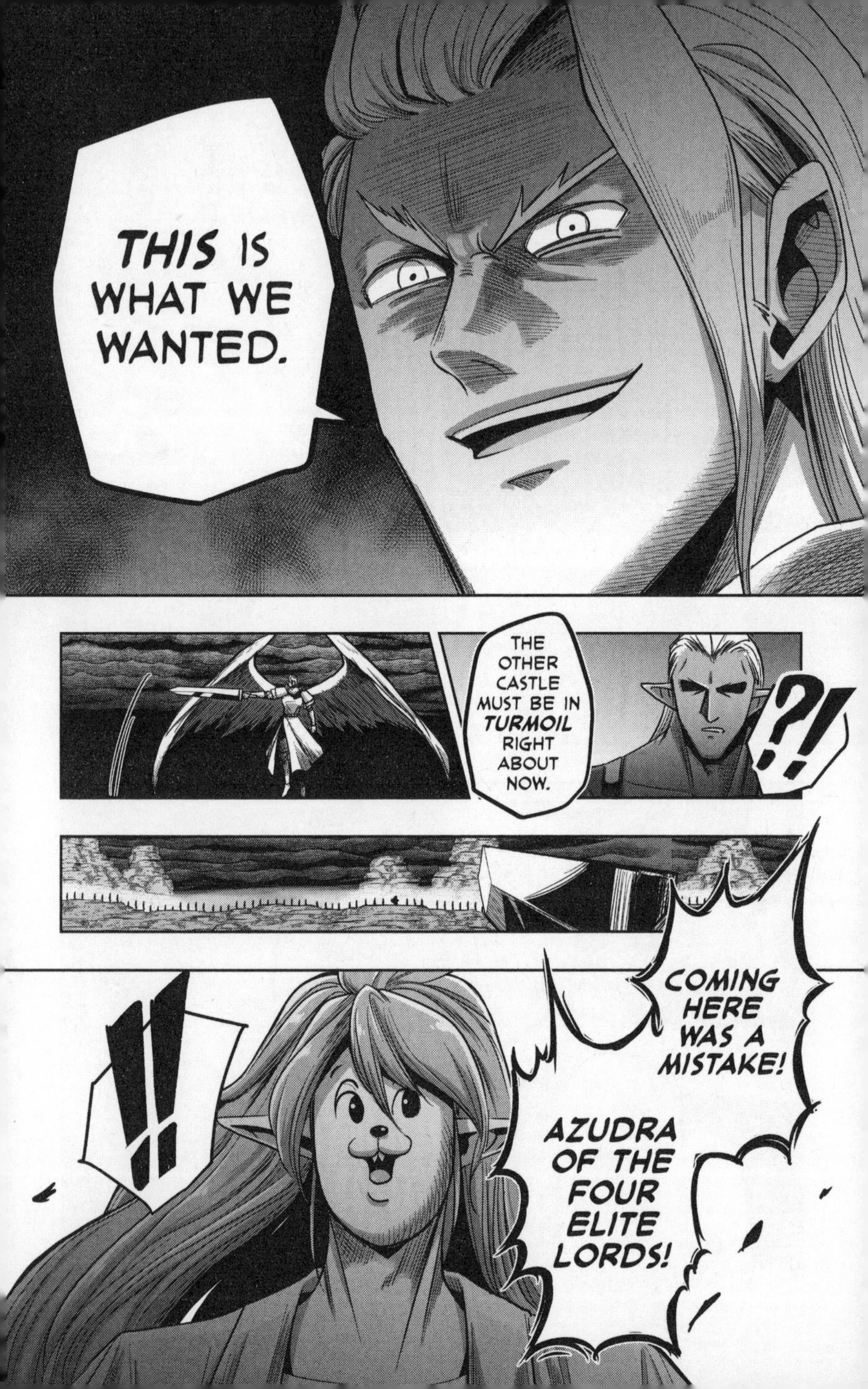
THIS IS WHAT WE WANTED.
?!
THE OTHER CASTLE MUST BE IN TURMOIL RIGHT ABOUT NOW.
COMING HERE WAS A MISTAKE!
AZUDRA OF THE FOUR ELITE LORDS!
!!

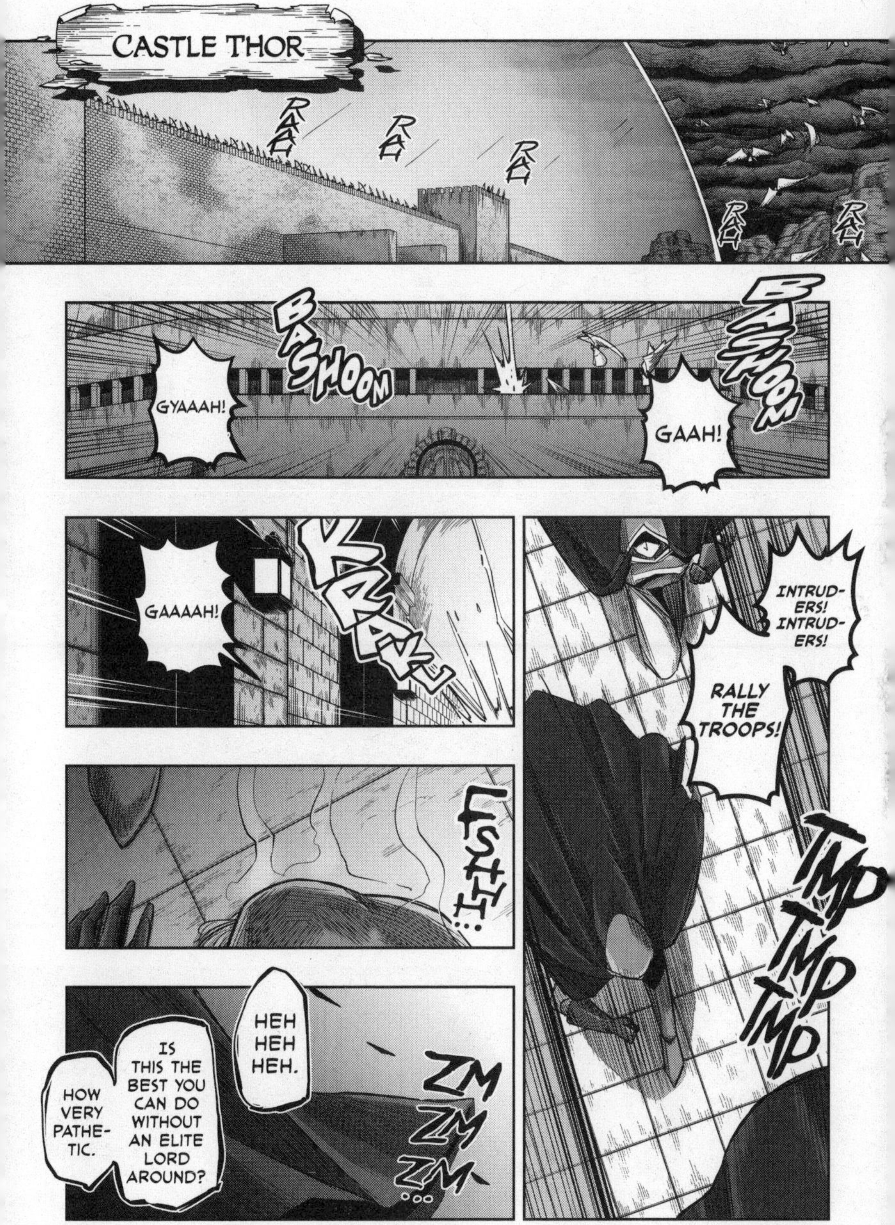
CASTLE THOR
RAH
RAH
RAH
RAH
RAH
BASHOOM
GAAH!
BASHOOM
GYAAAH!
INTRUD-ERS! INTRUD-ERS!
RALLY THE TROOPS!
TMP TMP TMP TMP
KRAKL
GAAAAH!
FSHHH...
HEH HEH HEH.
ZM ZM ZM...
IS THIS THE BEST YOU CAN DO WITHOUT AN ELITE LORD AROUND?
HOW VERY PATHE-TIC.

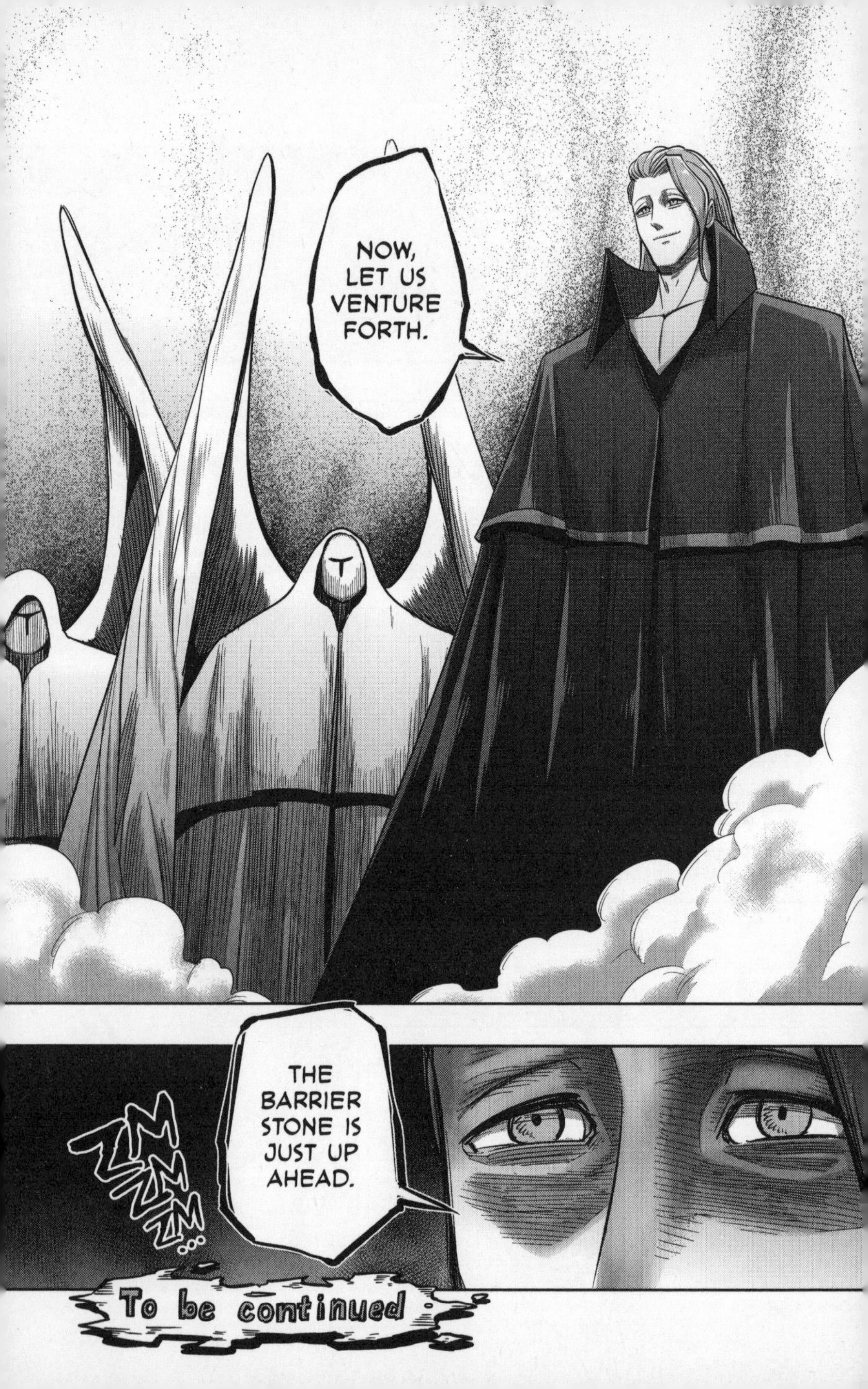
NOW, LET US VENTURE FORTH.
THE BARRIER STONE IS JUST UP AHEAD.
ZMMMMM...
To be continued

Chapter 60: Phase 2, Part 2

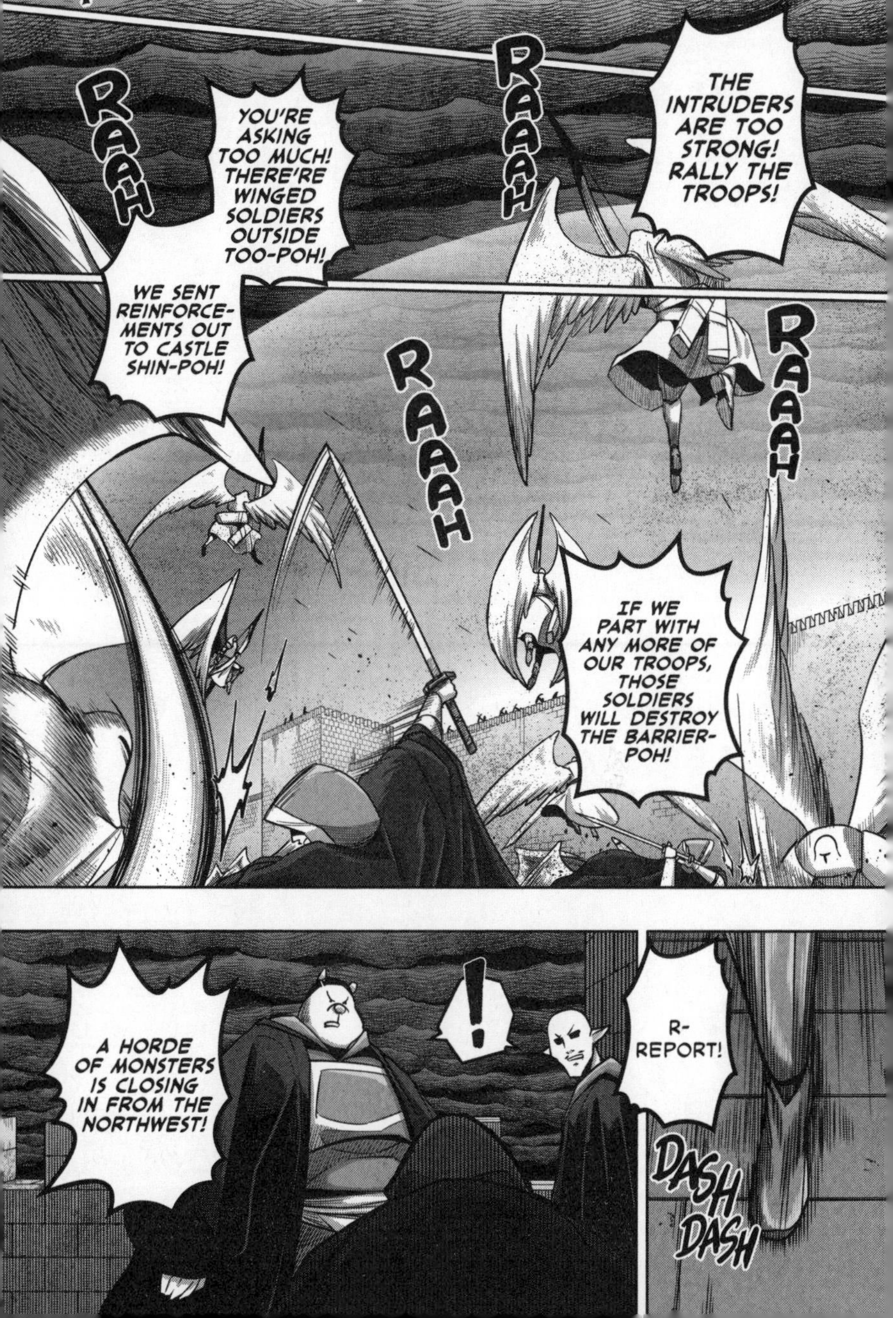
THE INTRUDERS ARE TOO STRONG! RALLY THE TROOPS!
RAAAH
YOU'RE ASKING TOO MUCH! THERE'RE WINGED SOLDIERS OUTSIDE TOO-POH!
RAAH
RAAAAH
RAAAAH
WE SENT REINFORCE-MENTS OUT TO CASTLE SHIN-POH!
IF WE PART WITH ANY MORE OF OUR TROOPS, THOSE SOLDIERS WILL DESTROY THE BARRIER-POH!
R-REPORT!
DASH DASH
!
A HORDE OF MONSTERS IS CLOSING IN FROM THE NORTHWEST!

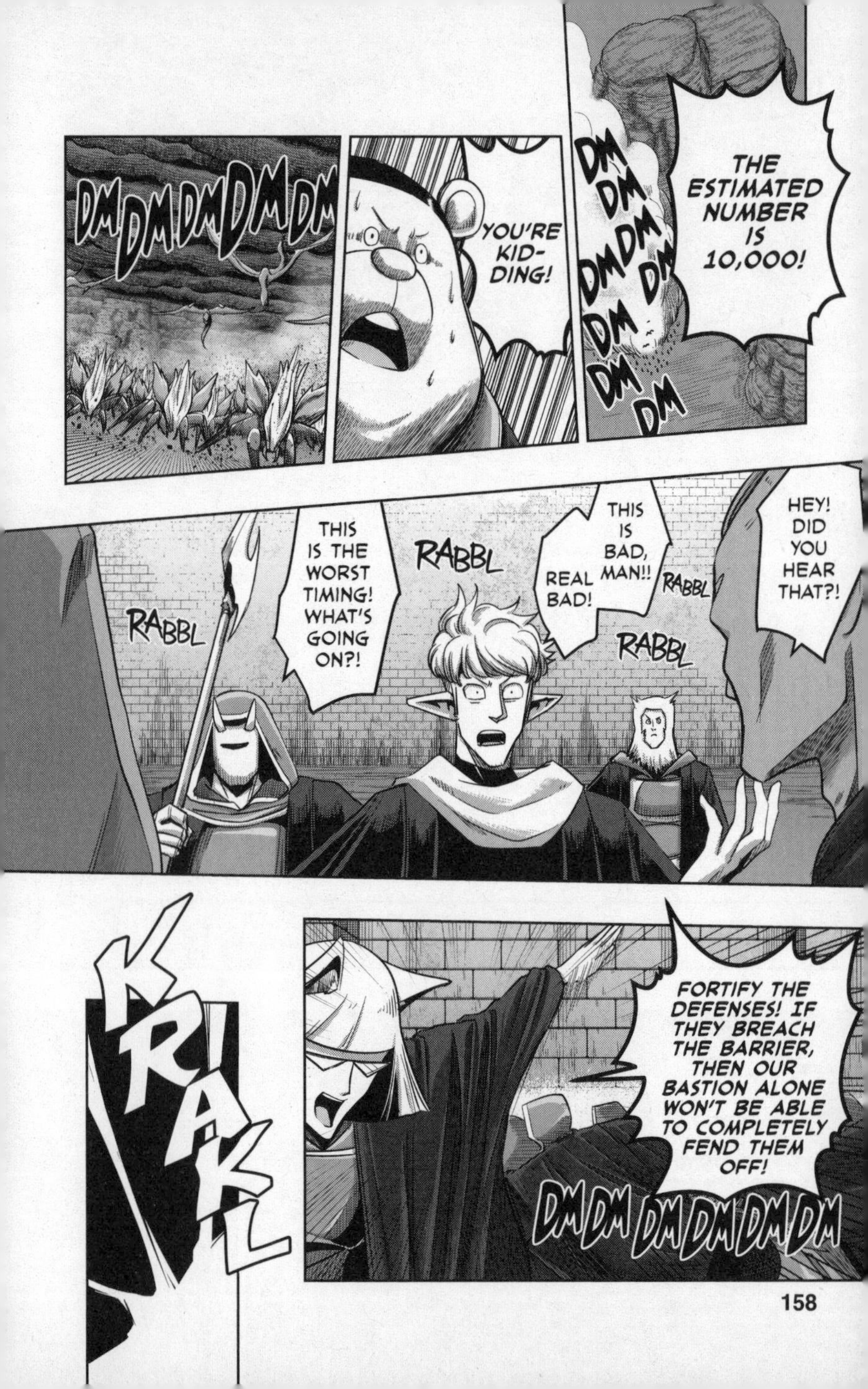
THE ESTIMATED NUMBER IS 10,000!
DM DM DM DM DM DM DM DM DM
YOU'RE KID-DING!
DM DM DM DM DM DM
HEY! DID YOU HEAR THAT?!
RABBL
THIS IS BAD, MAN!!
REAL BAD!
RABBL
RABBL
THIS IS THE WORST TIMING! WHAT'S GOING ON?!
RABBL
FORTIFY THE DEFENSES! IF THEY BREACH THE BARRIER, THEN OUR BASTION ALONE WON'T BE ABLE TO COMPLETELY FEND THEM OFF!
DM DM DM DM DM DM
KRAKL

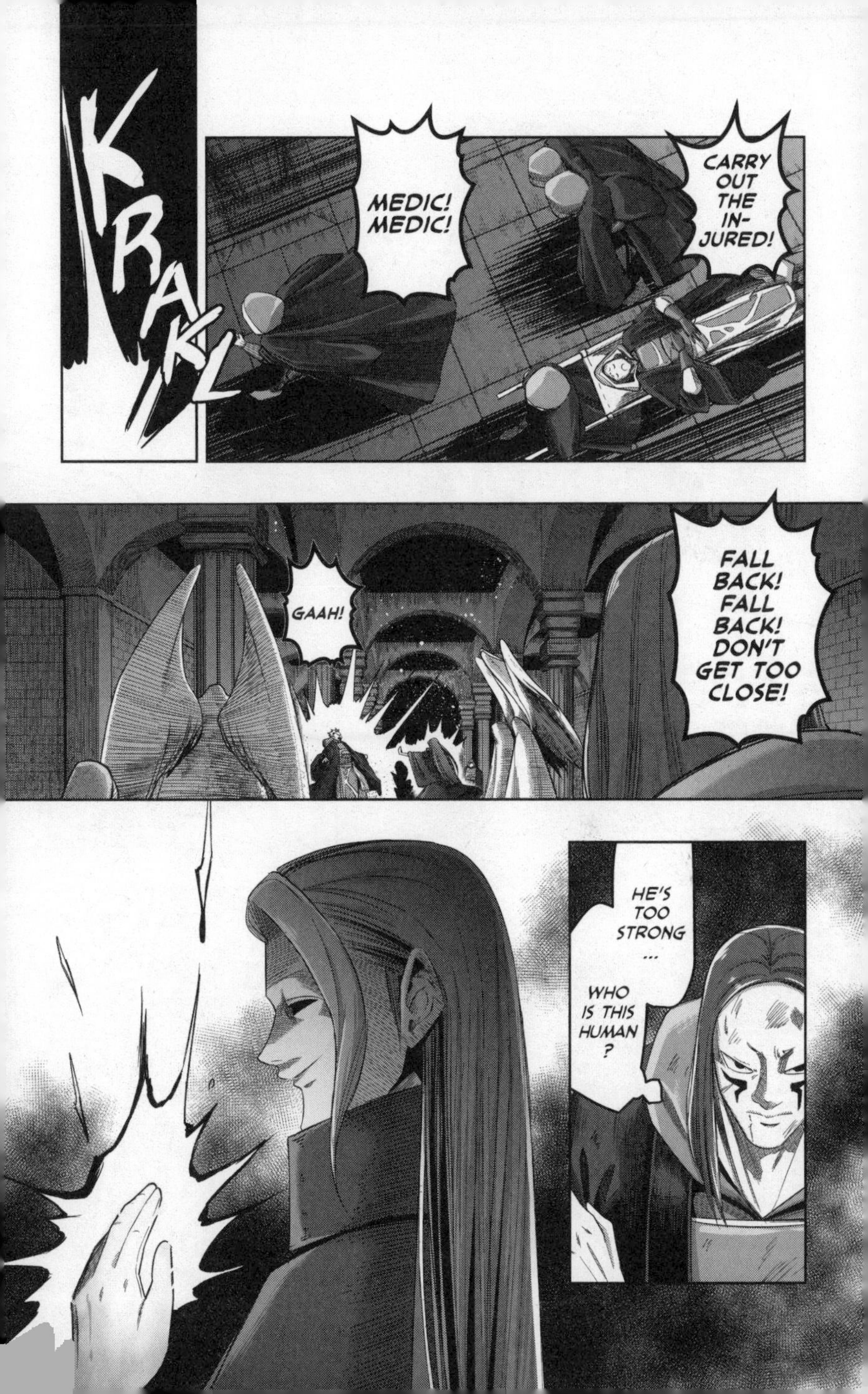
CARRY OUT THE IN-JURED!
MEDIC! MEDIC!
KRAKL
FALL BACK! FALL BACK! DON'T GET TOO CLOSE!
GAAH!
HE'S TOO STRONG...
WHO IS THIS HUMAN?

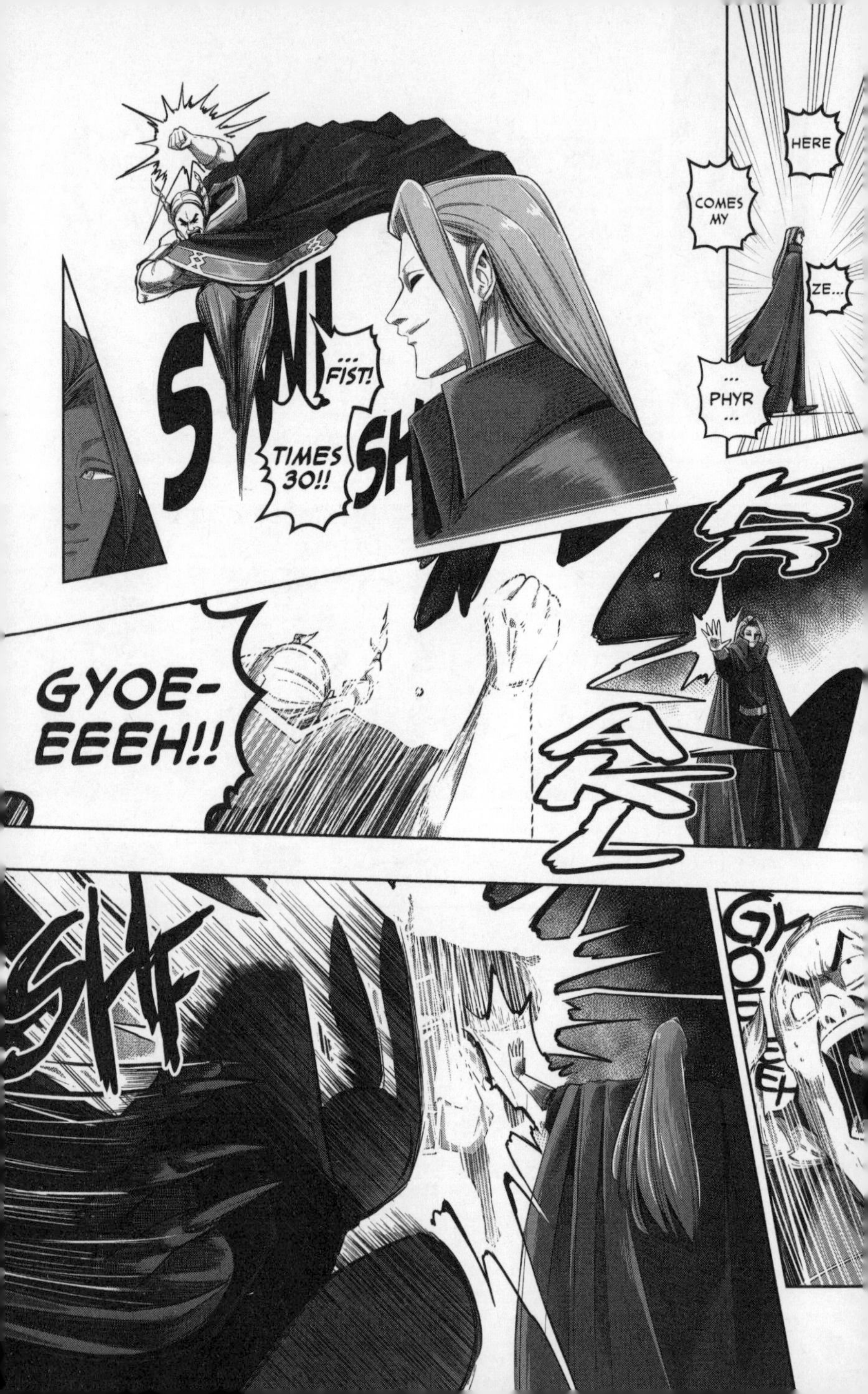
HERE
COMES MY
ZE...
...PHYR...
...FIST!
TIMES 30!!
GYOE-EEEH!!
SHF

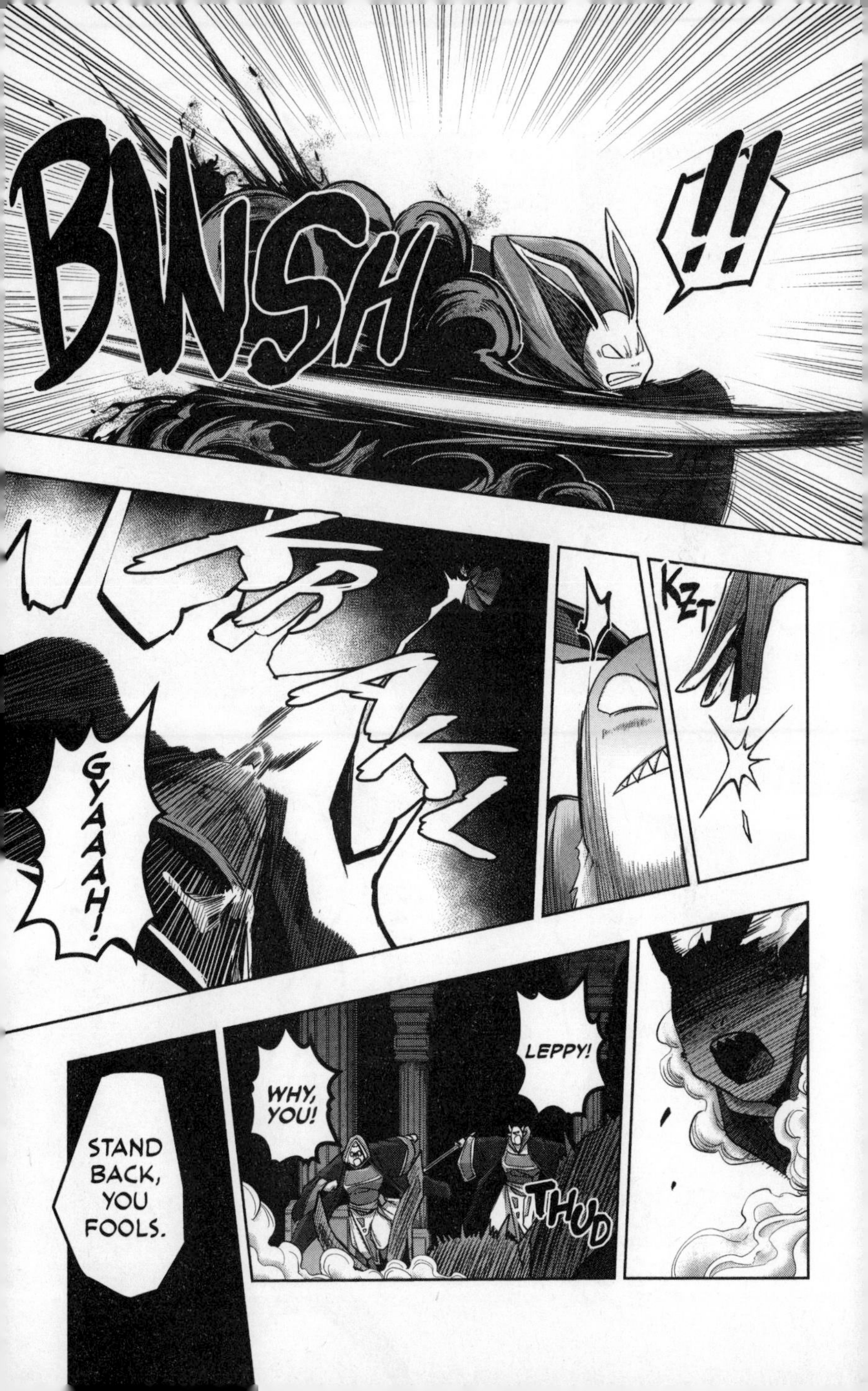
BWSH
!!
KZT
TRAKK
GYAAAH!
LEPPY!
WHY, YOU!
THUD
STAND BACK, YOU FOOLS.

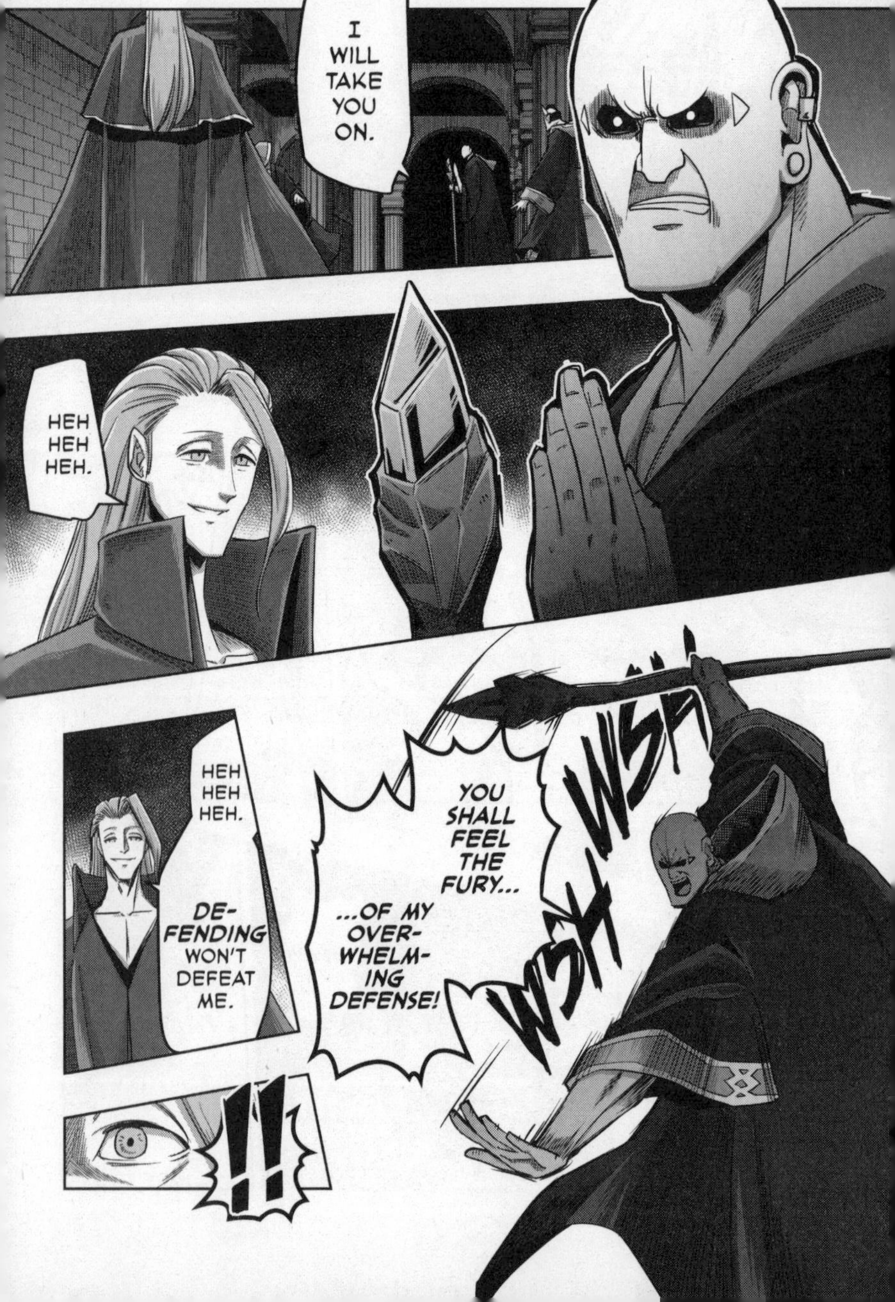
I WILL TAKE YOU ON.
HEH HEH HEH.
WSA
WSH
YOU SHALL FEEL THE FURY...
...OF MY OVER-WHELM-ING DEFENSE!
HEH HEH HEH.
DE-FENDING WON'T DEFEAT ME.
!!

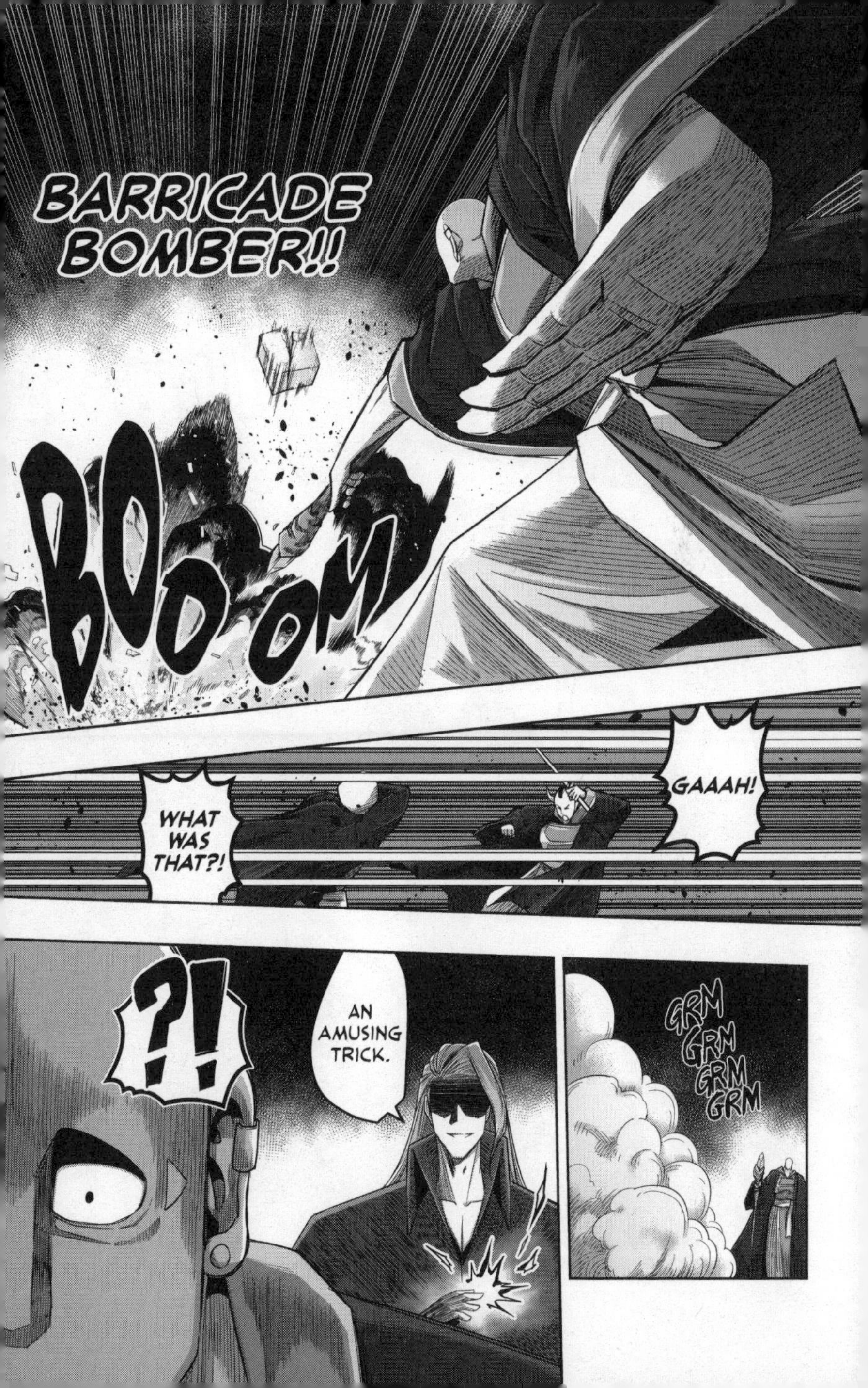
BARRICADE BOMBER!!
BOOOM
GAAAH!
WHAT WAS THAT?!
GRM GRM GRM GRM
AN AMUSING TRICK.
?!

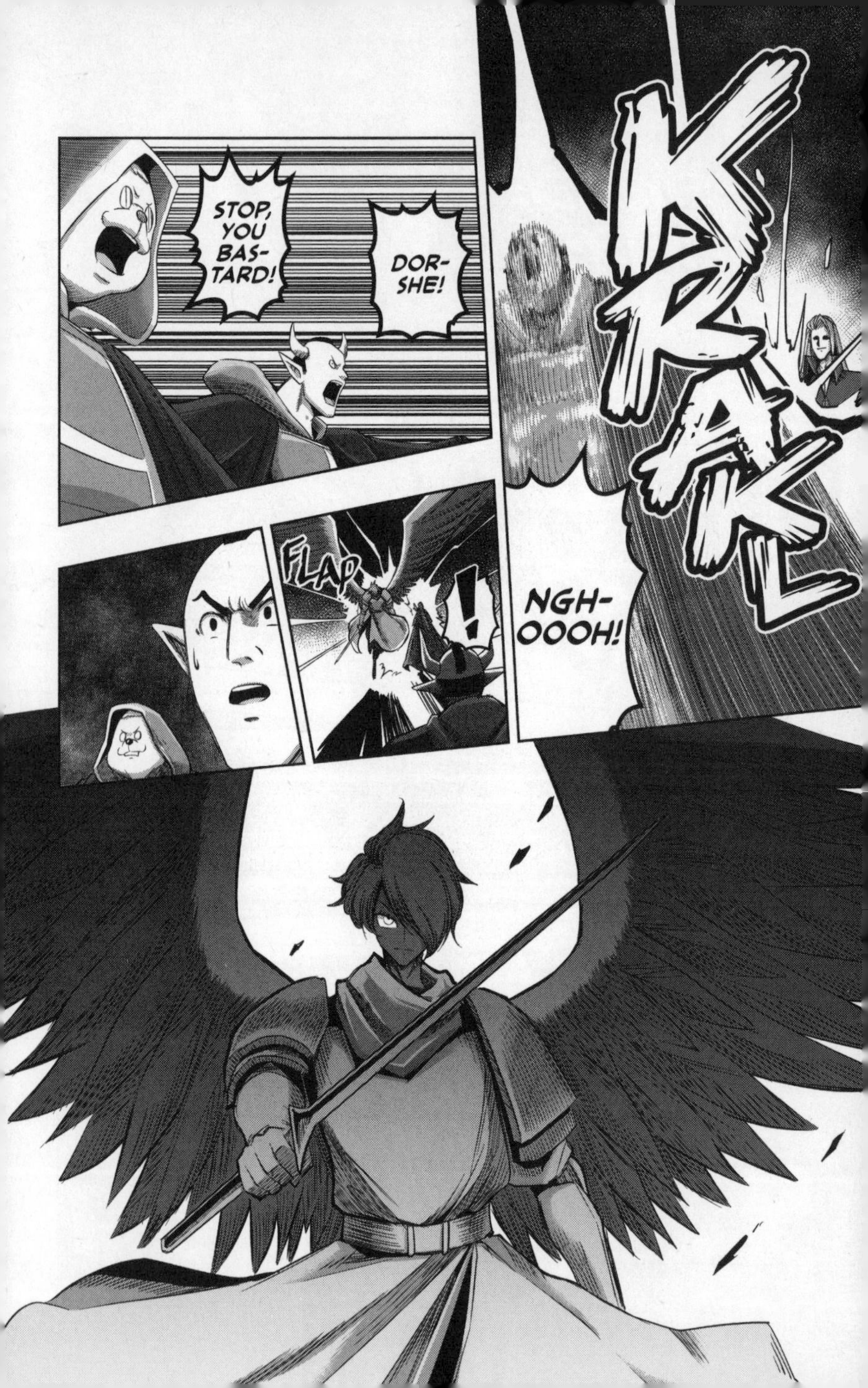
KRAK
NGH-OOOH!
DOR-SHE!
STOP, YOU BAS-TARD!
FLAP
!

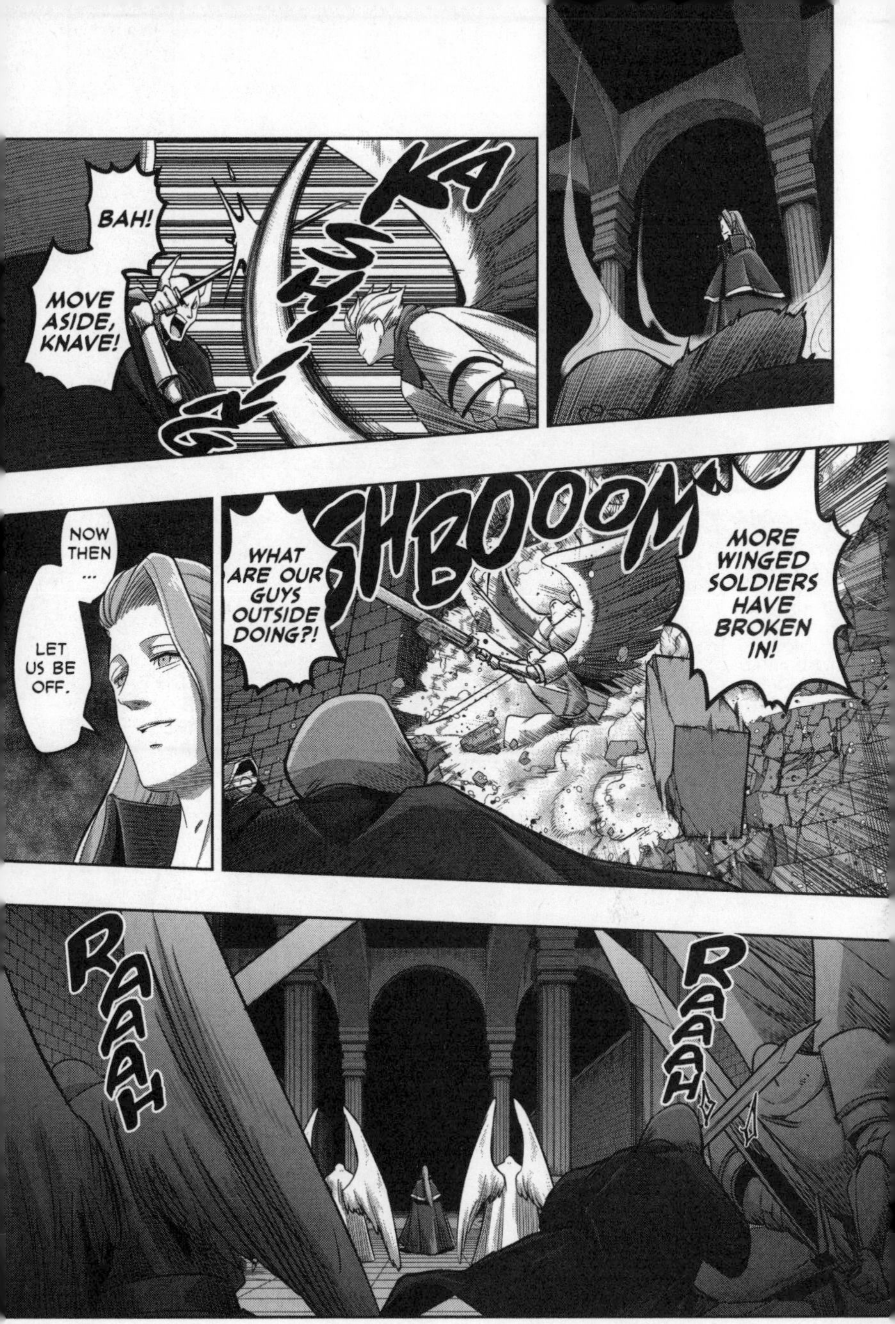
BAH!
MOVE ASIDE, KNAVE!
KASHIING
MORE WINGED SOLDIERS HAVE BROKEN IN!
SHBOOOM
WHAT ARE OUR GUYS OUTSIDE DOING?!
NOW THEN ...
LET US BE OFF.
RAAAH
RAAAH

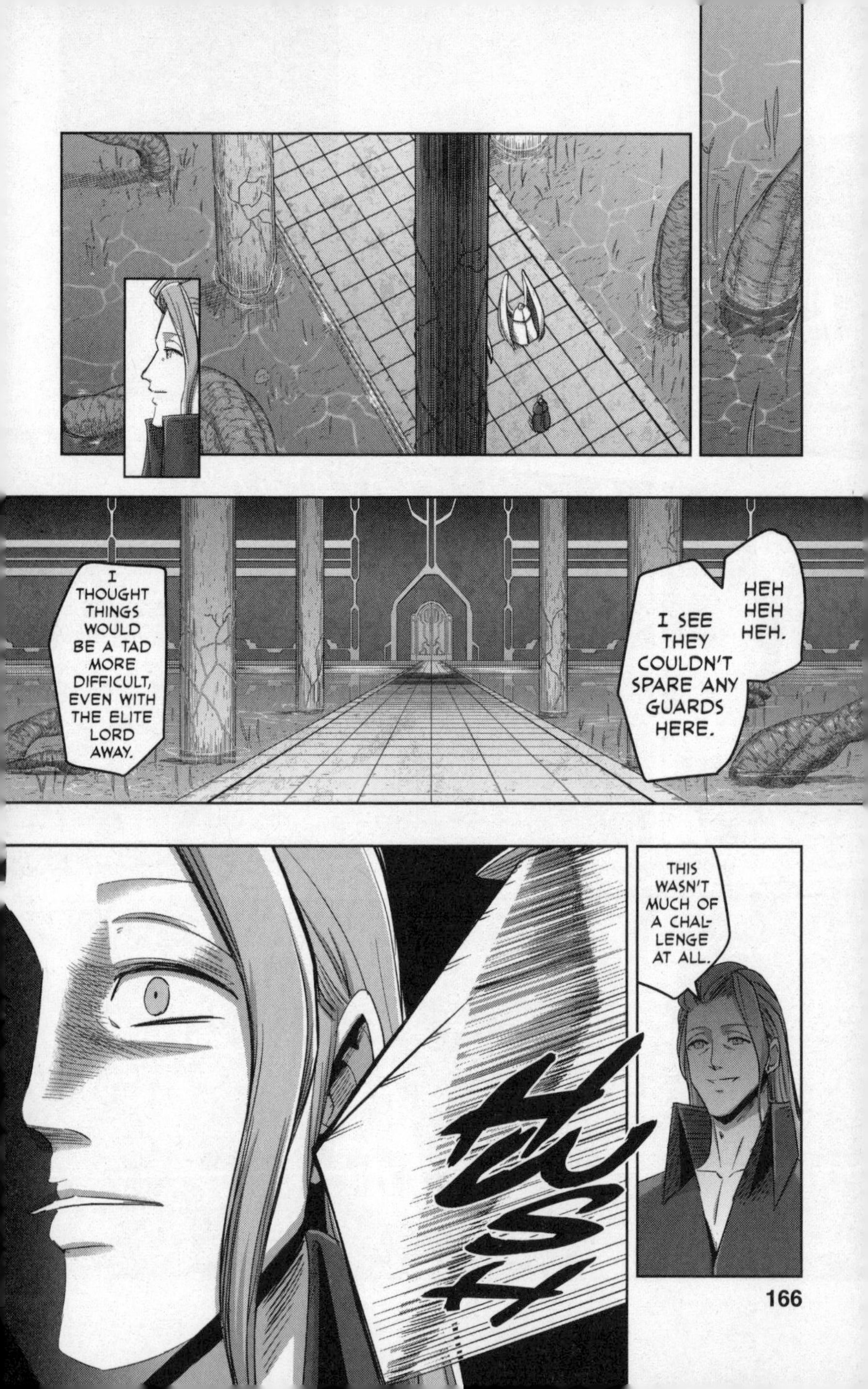
HEH HEH HEH.
I SEE THEY COULDN'T SPARE ANY GUARDS HERE.
I THOUGHT THINGS WOULD BE A TAD MORE DIFFICULT, EVEN WITH THE ELITE LORD AWAY.
THIS WASN'T MUCH OF A CHAL-LENGE AT ALL.
HUSH

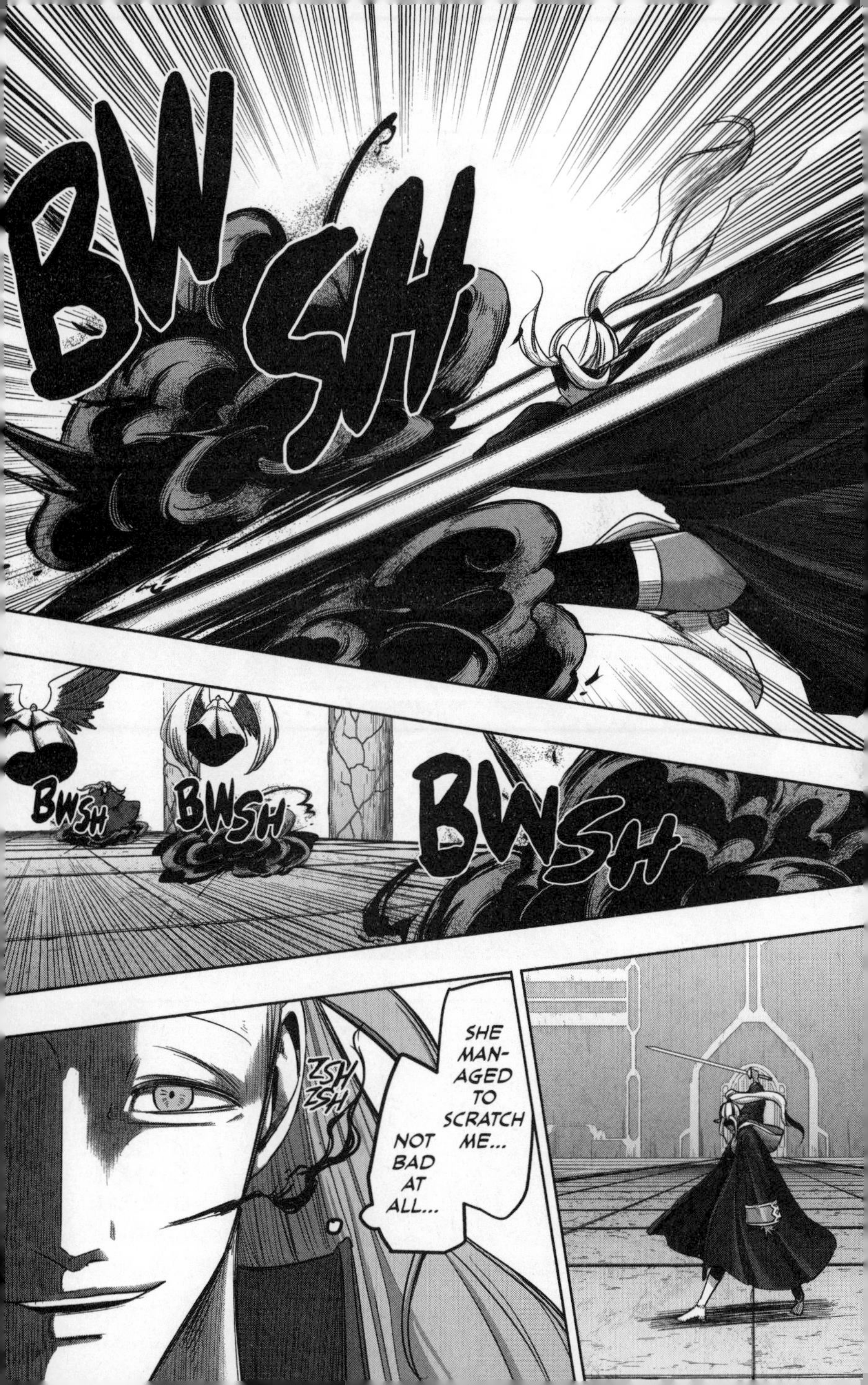
BWSH
BWSH
BWSH
BWSH
ZSH ZSH
SHE MAN-AGED TO SCRATCH ME...
NOT BAD AT ALL...

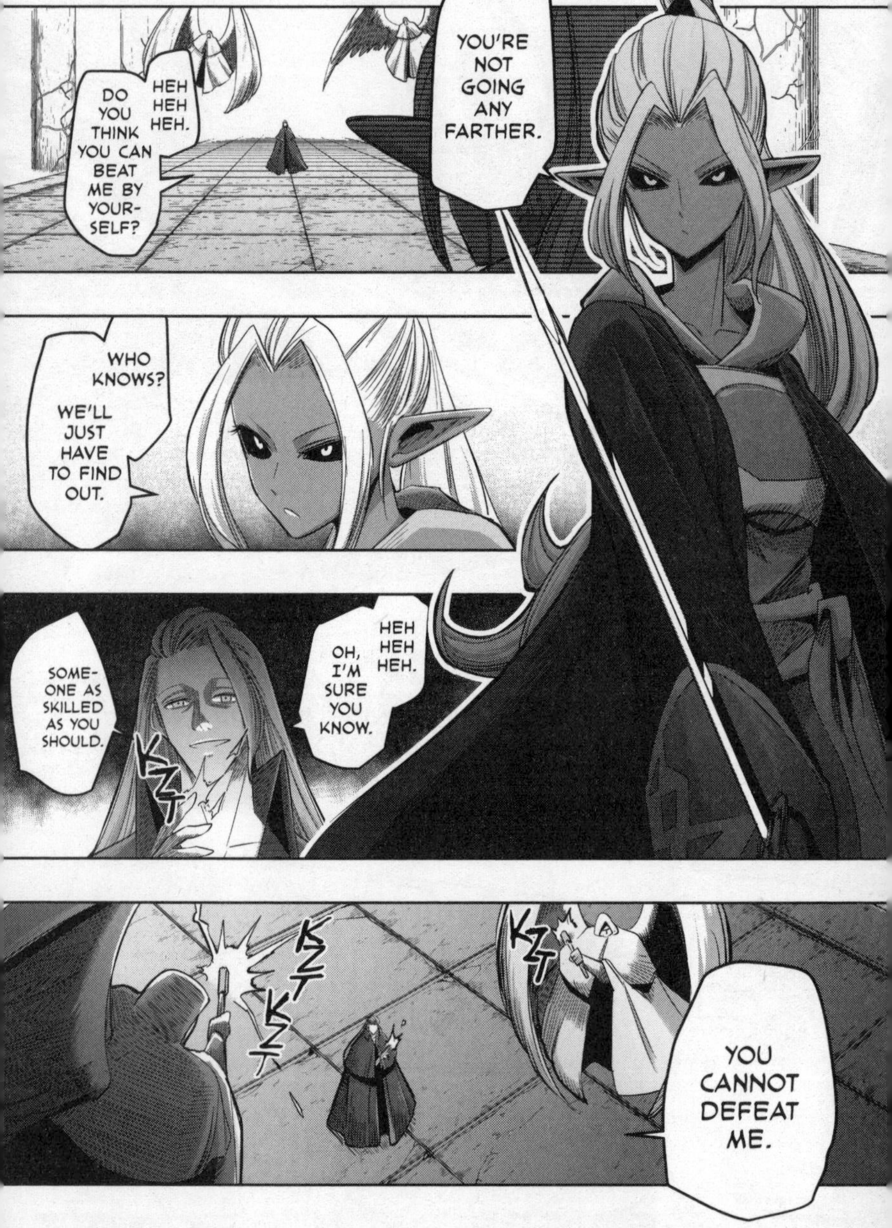
YOU'RE NOT GOING ANY FARTHER.
HEH HEH HEH.
DO YOU THINK YOU CAN BEAT ME BY YOUR-SELF?
WHO KNOWS?
WE'LL JUST HAVE TO FIND OUT.
HEH HEH HEH.
OH, I'M SURE YOU KNOW.
SOME-ONE AS SKILLED AS YOU SHOULD.
KZZT
KZT
YOU CANNOT DEFEAT ME.
KZT
KZT

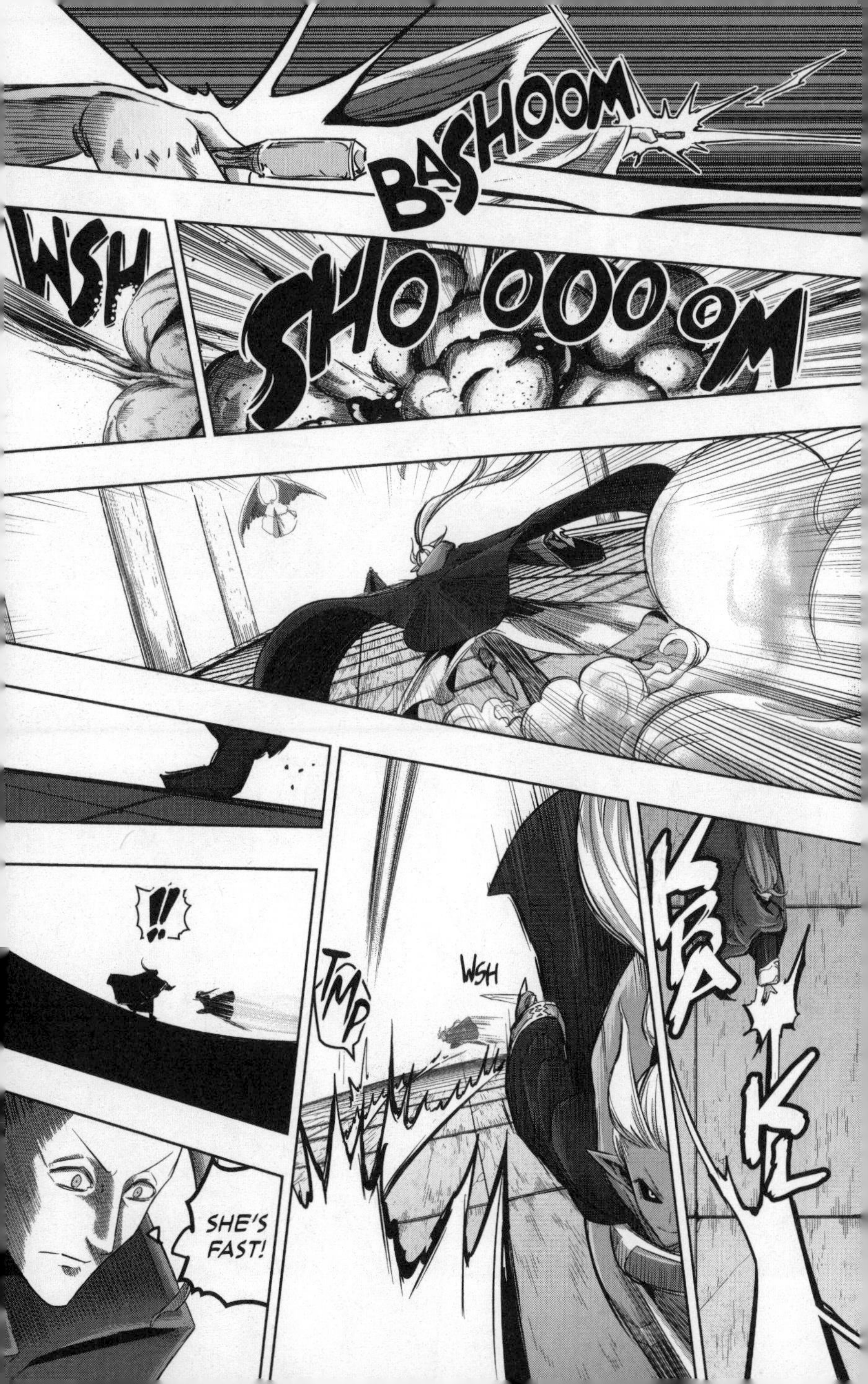
BASHOOM
SHOOOOOOM
WSH
KRAKL
WSH
TMP
!!
SHE'S FAST!

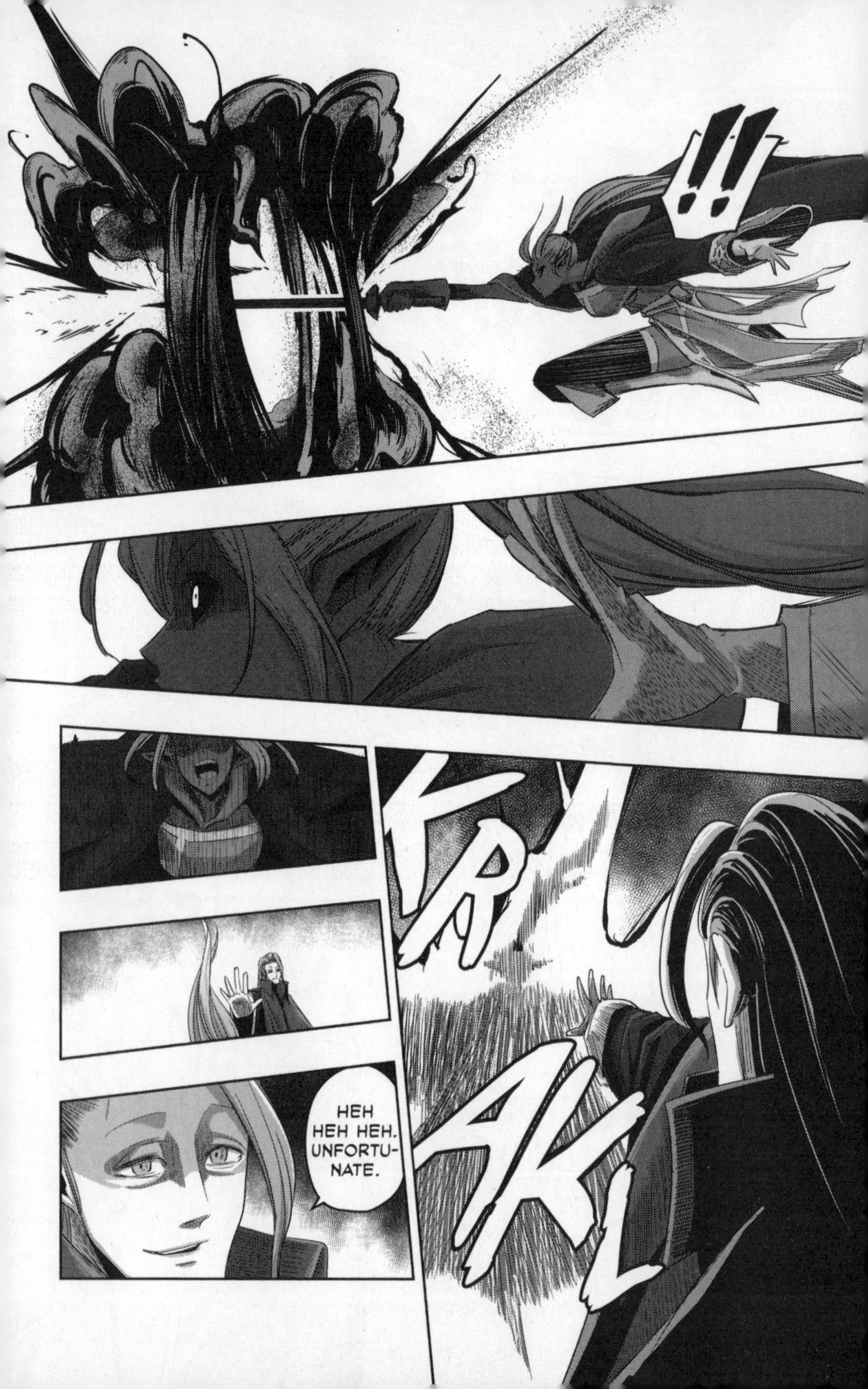
!!
KRAAK
HEH HEH HEH. UNFORTU-NATE.

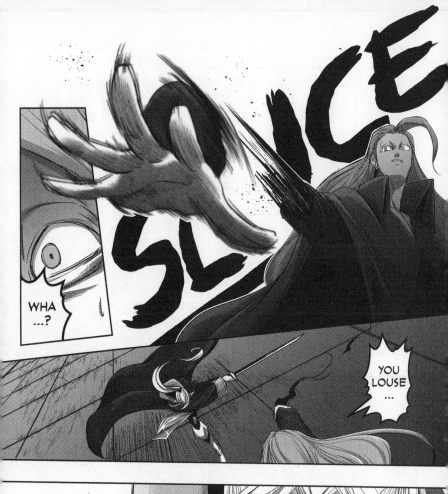

WHA
....?

YOU LOUSE
...

INDEED. HOW UNFORTU-NATE.

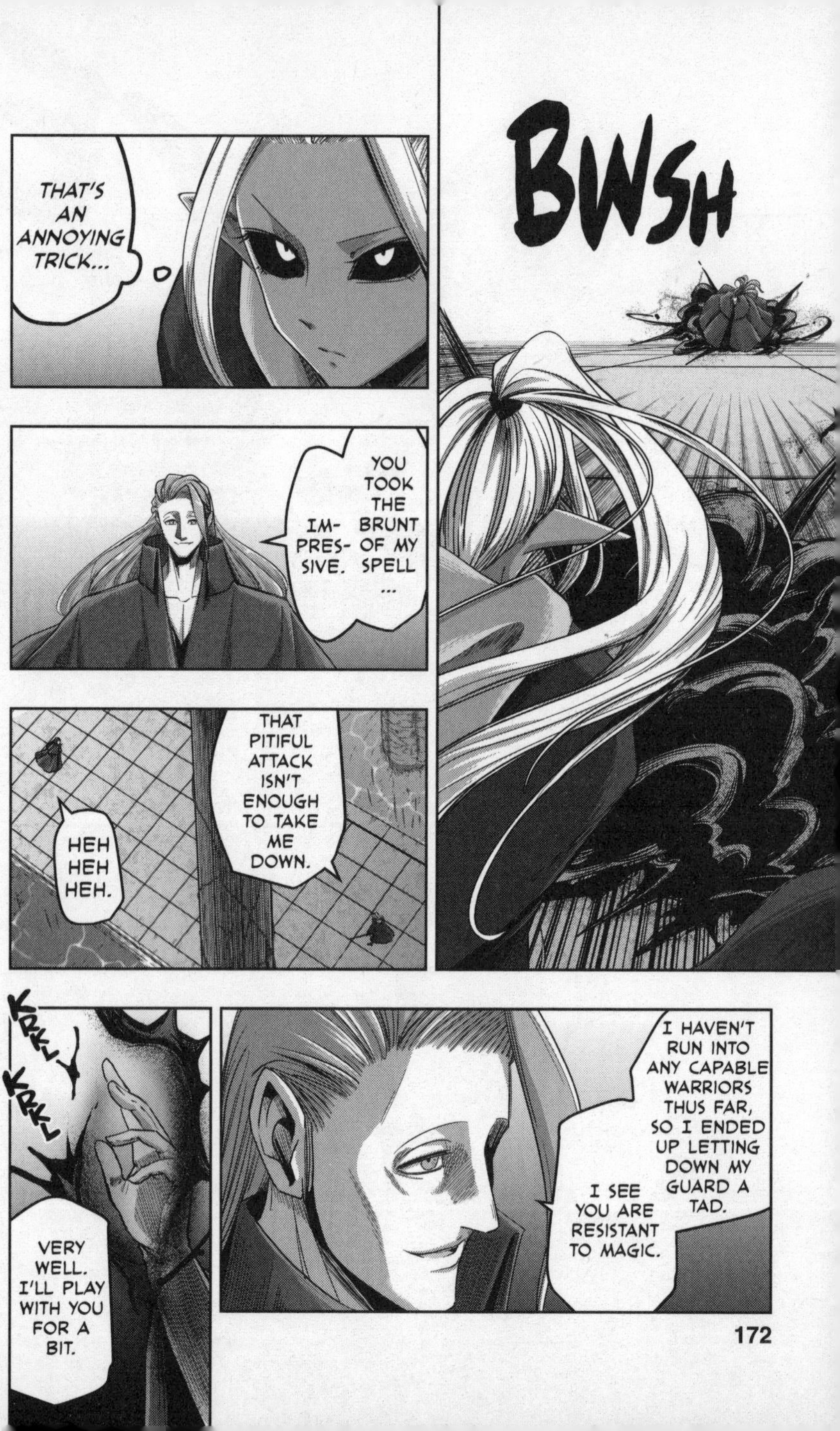
BWSH
THAT'S AN ANNOYING TRICK...
YOU TOOK THE BRUNT OF MY SPELL...
IM-PRES-SIVE.
THAT PITIFUL ATTACK ISN'T ENOUGH TO TAKE ME DOWN.
HEH HEH HEH.
I HAVEN'T RUN INTO ANY CAPABLE WARRIORS THUS FAR, SO I ENDED UP LETTING DOWN MY GUARD A TAD.
I SEE YOU ARE RESISTANT TO MAGIC.
KRKL
KRKL
VERY WELL. I'LL PLAY WITH YOU FOR A BIT.

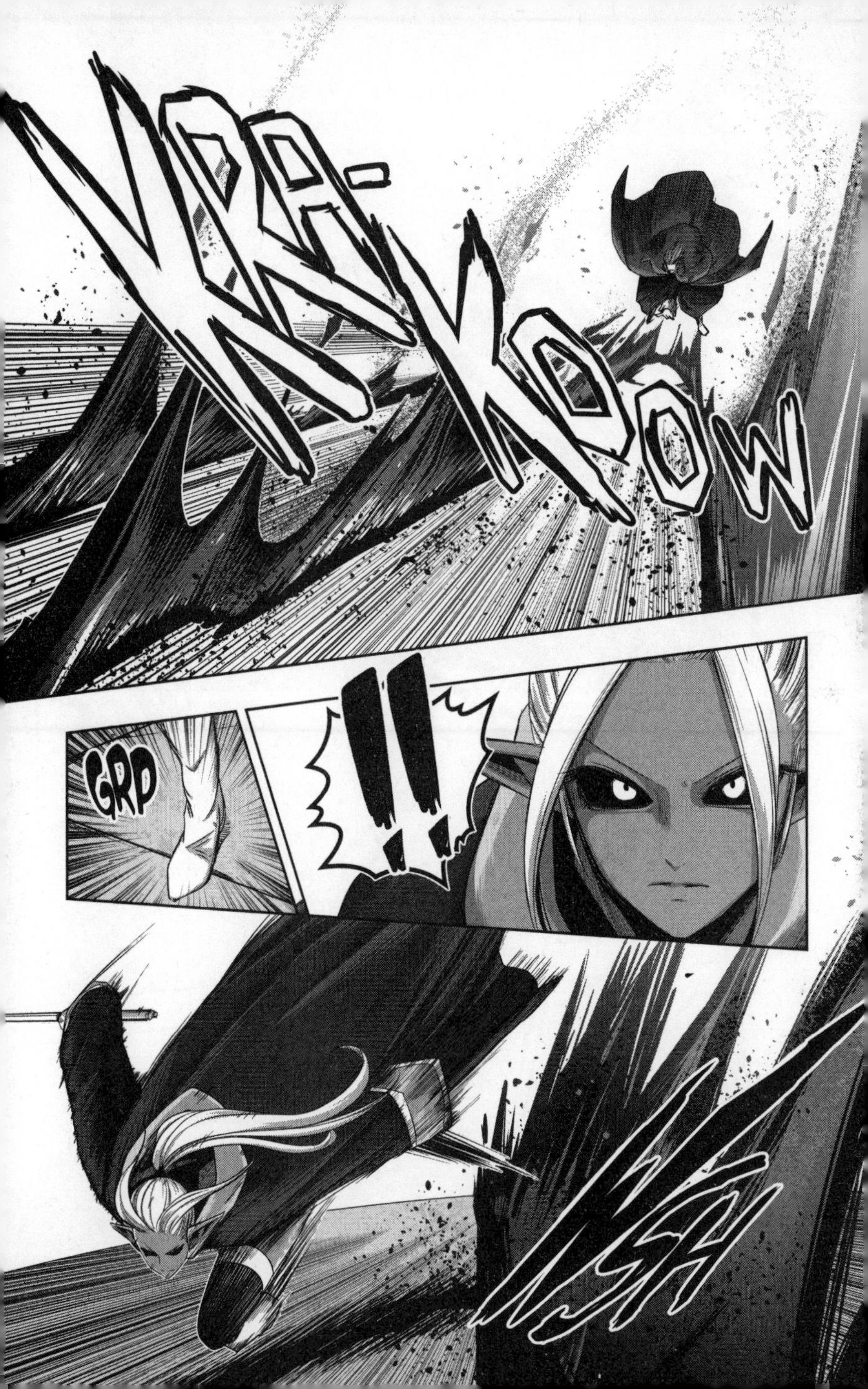
VRR-KKOOW
!!
GRP
WSH

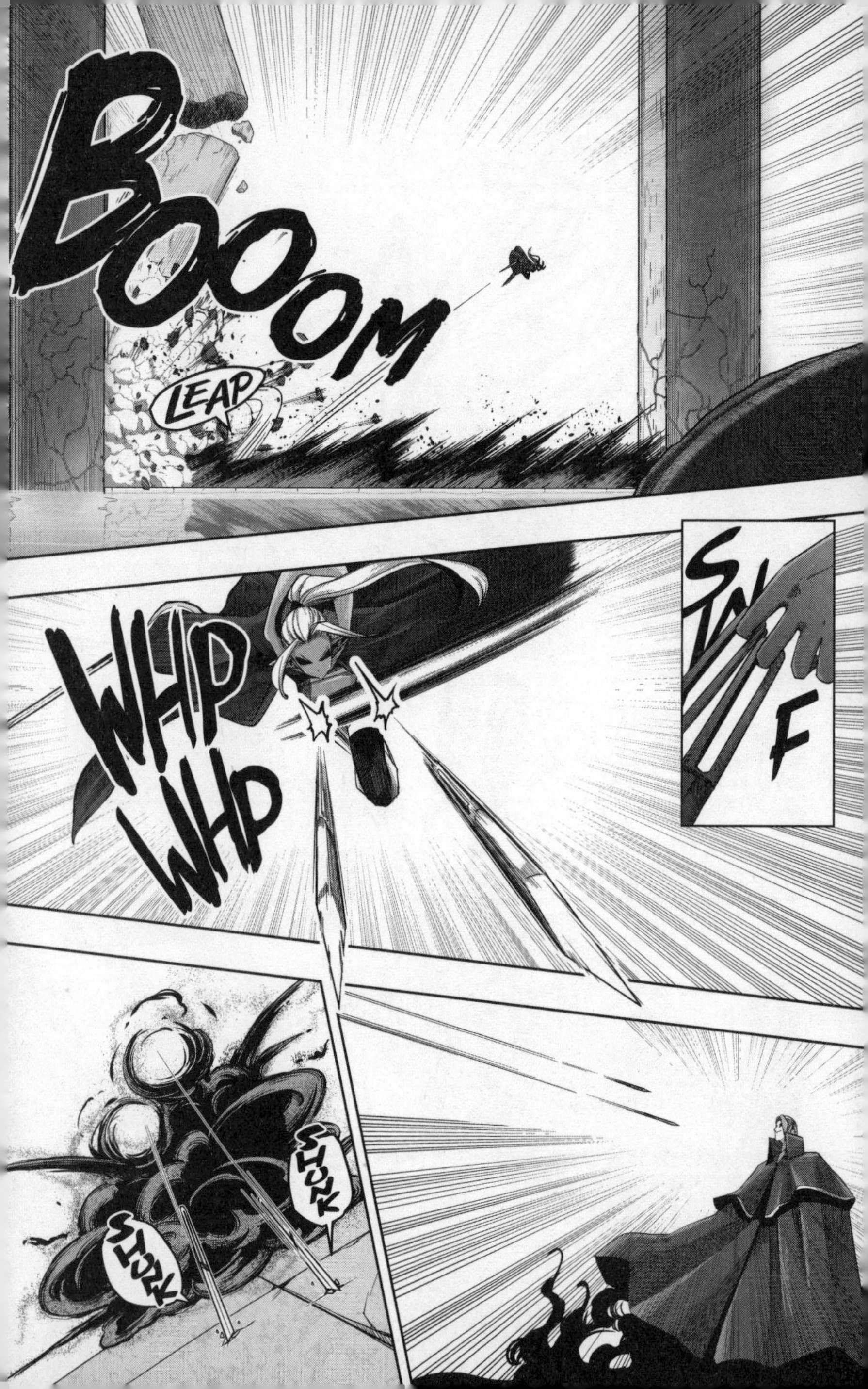
BOOOOM
LEAP
SWF
WHP WHP
SHUNK
SHUNK

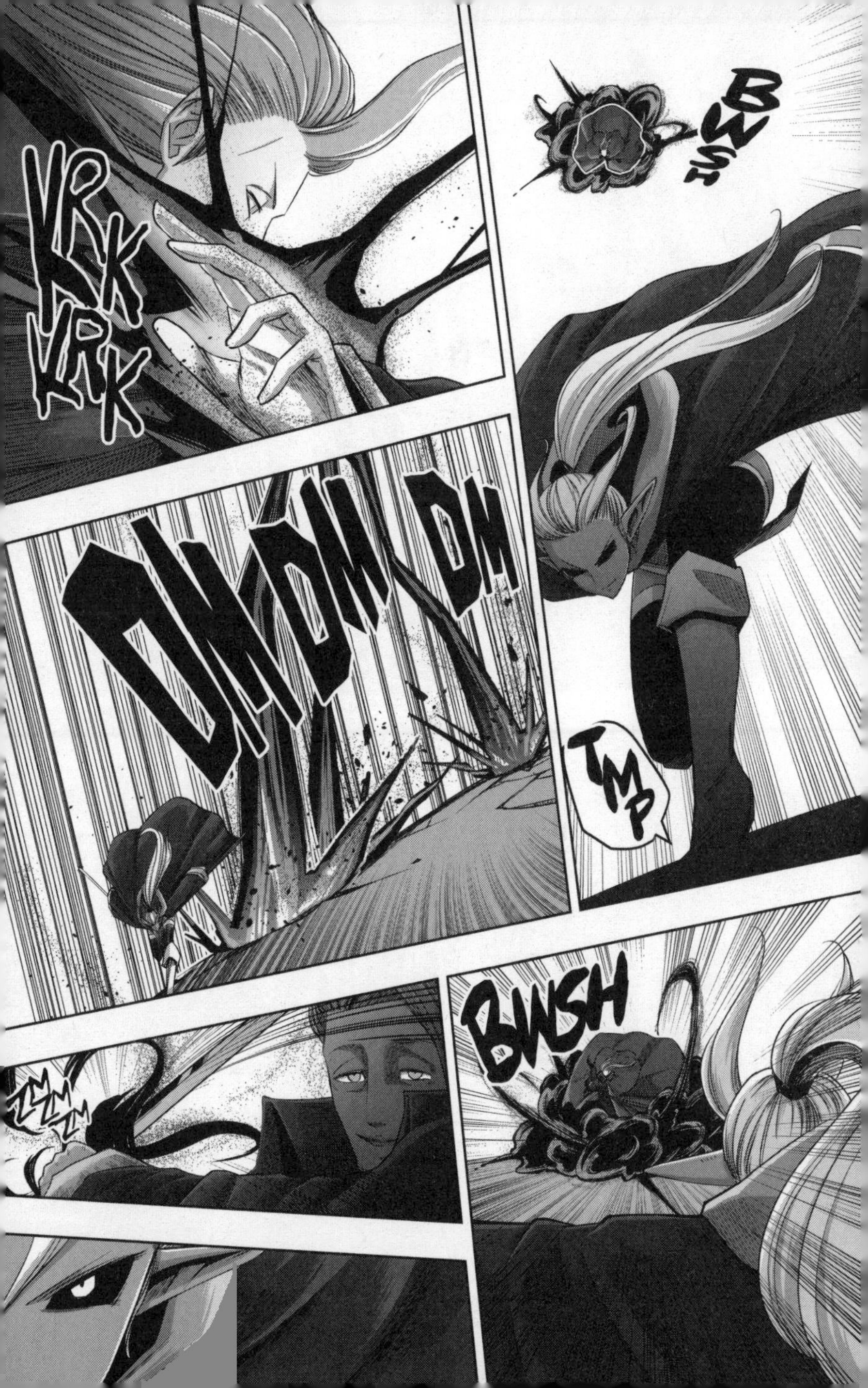
BWSH
VRK VRK
TMP
DMDM DM
BWSH

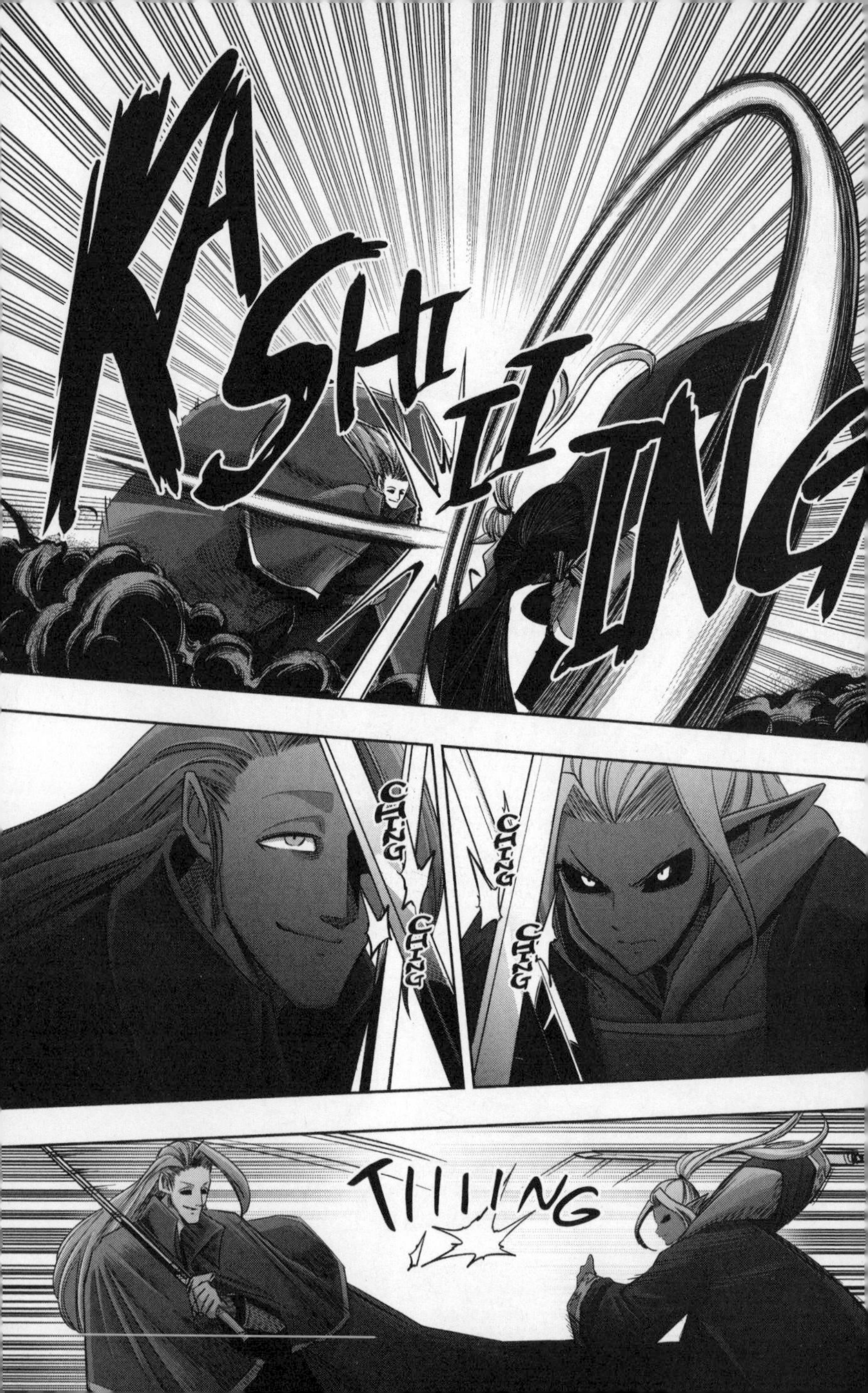
KASHIIING
CHING
CHING
CHING
CHING
TIIIING

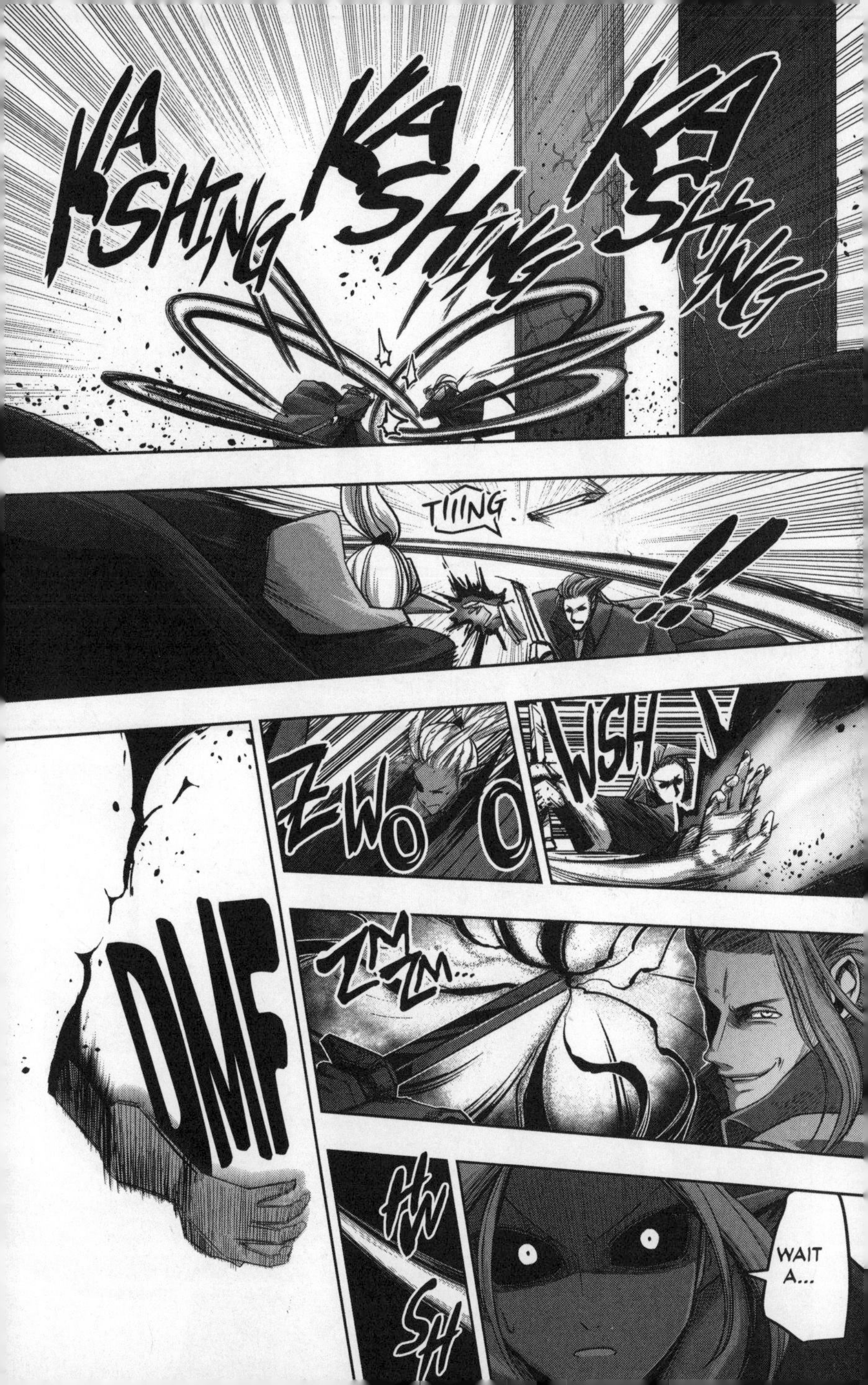
KA SHING
KA SHING
KA SHING
TIIING
!!
WSH
ZWOOO
ZMMZM...
FW
SH
WAIT A...
DMF

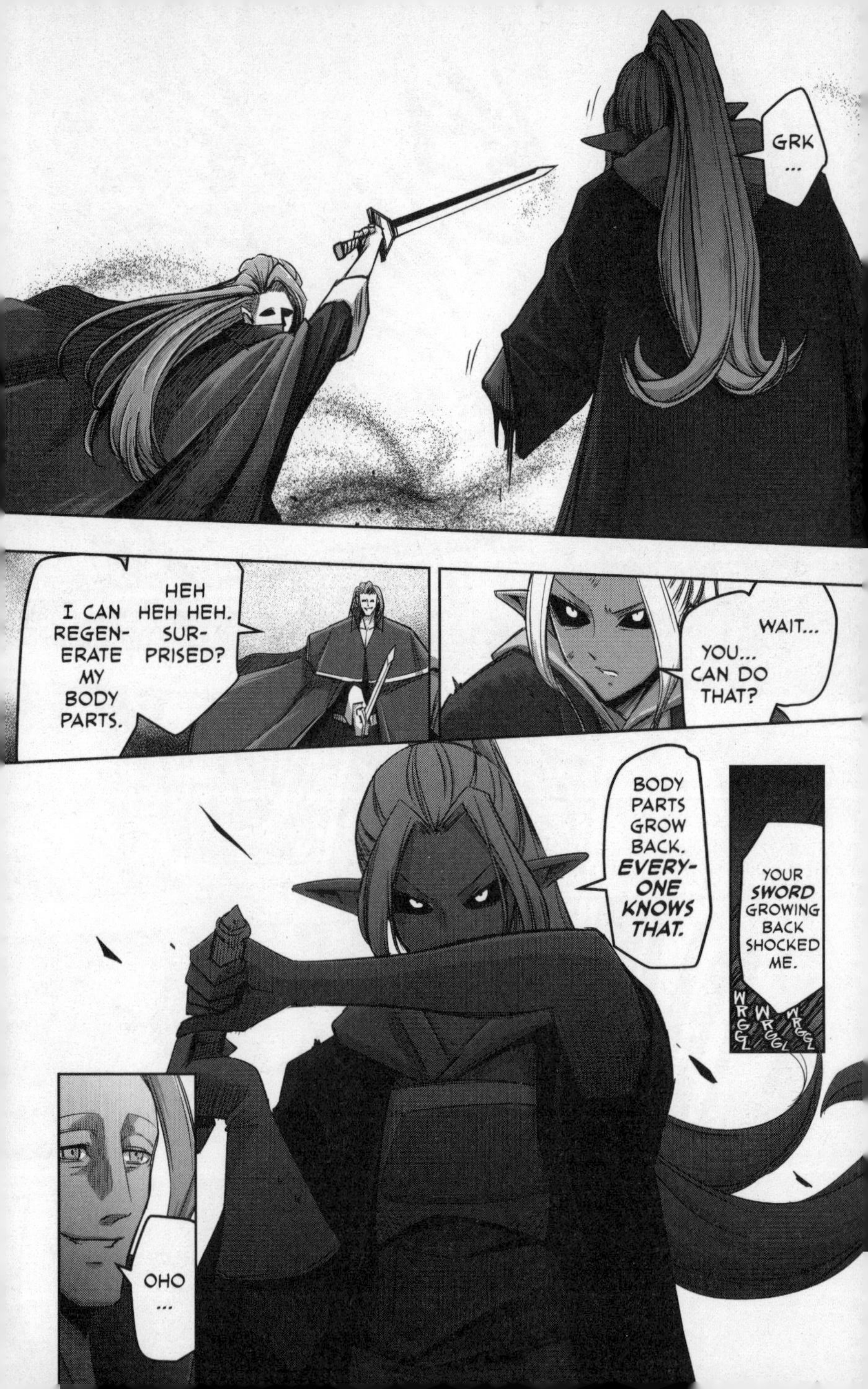
GRK ...
WAIT...
YOU... CAN DO THAT?
HEH HEH HEH. SUR-PRISED?
I CAN REGEN-ERATE MY BODY PARTS.
YOUR **SWORD** GROWING BACK SHOCKED ME.
WRGGL WRGGL WRGGL
BODY PARTS GROW BACK. ***EVERY-ONE KNOWS THAT.***
OHO ...

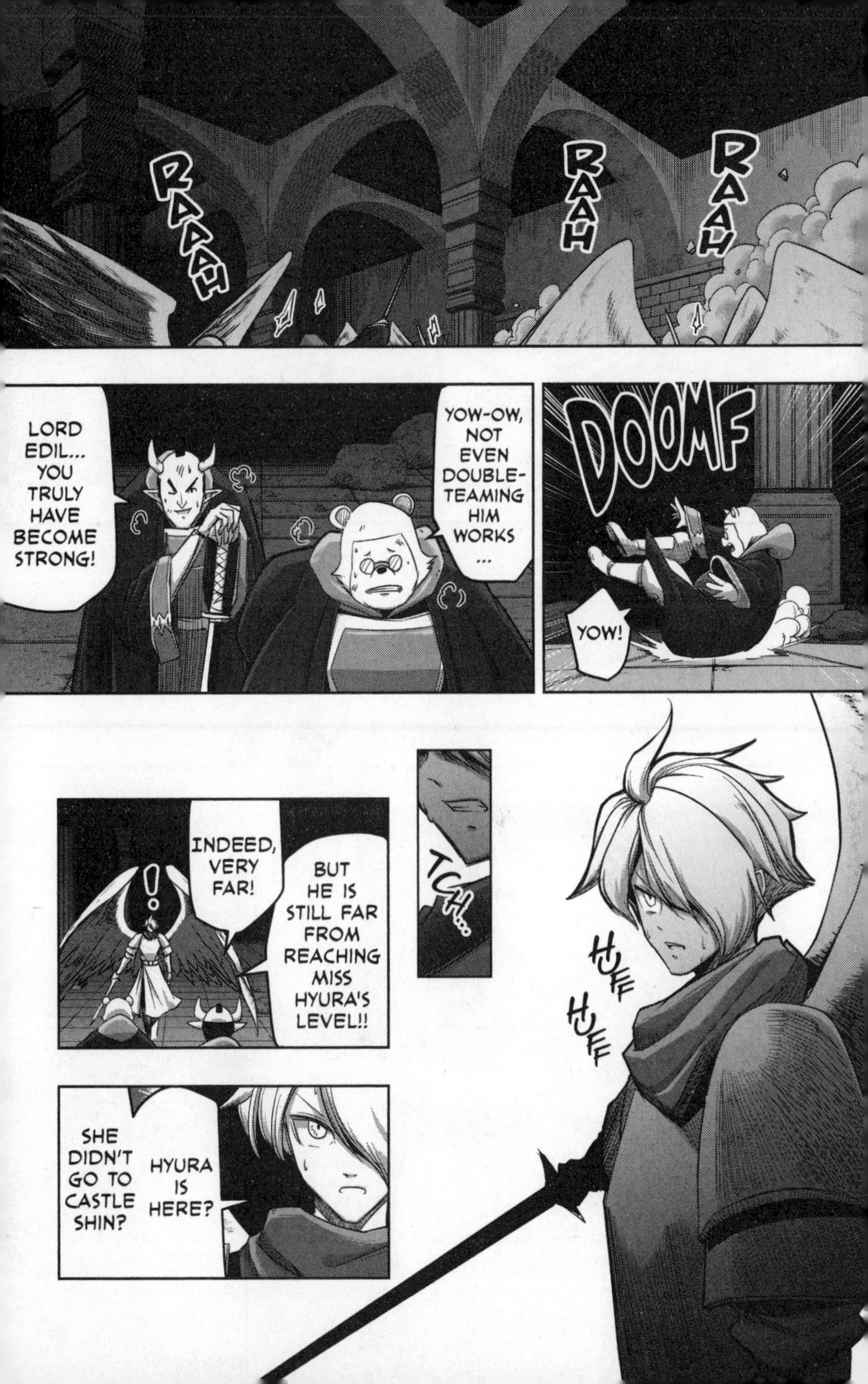
RAAH
RAAH
RAAAH
DOOMF
YOW!
YOW-OW, NOT EVEN DOUBLE-TEAMING HIM WORKS...
LORD EDIL... YOU TRULY HAVE BECOME STRONG!
HUFF HUFF
TCH...
BUT HE IS STILL FAR FROM REACHING MISS HYURA'S LEVEL!!
INDEED, VERY FAR!
!
HYURA IS HERE?
SHE DIDN'T GO TO CASTLE SHIN?

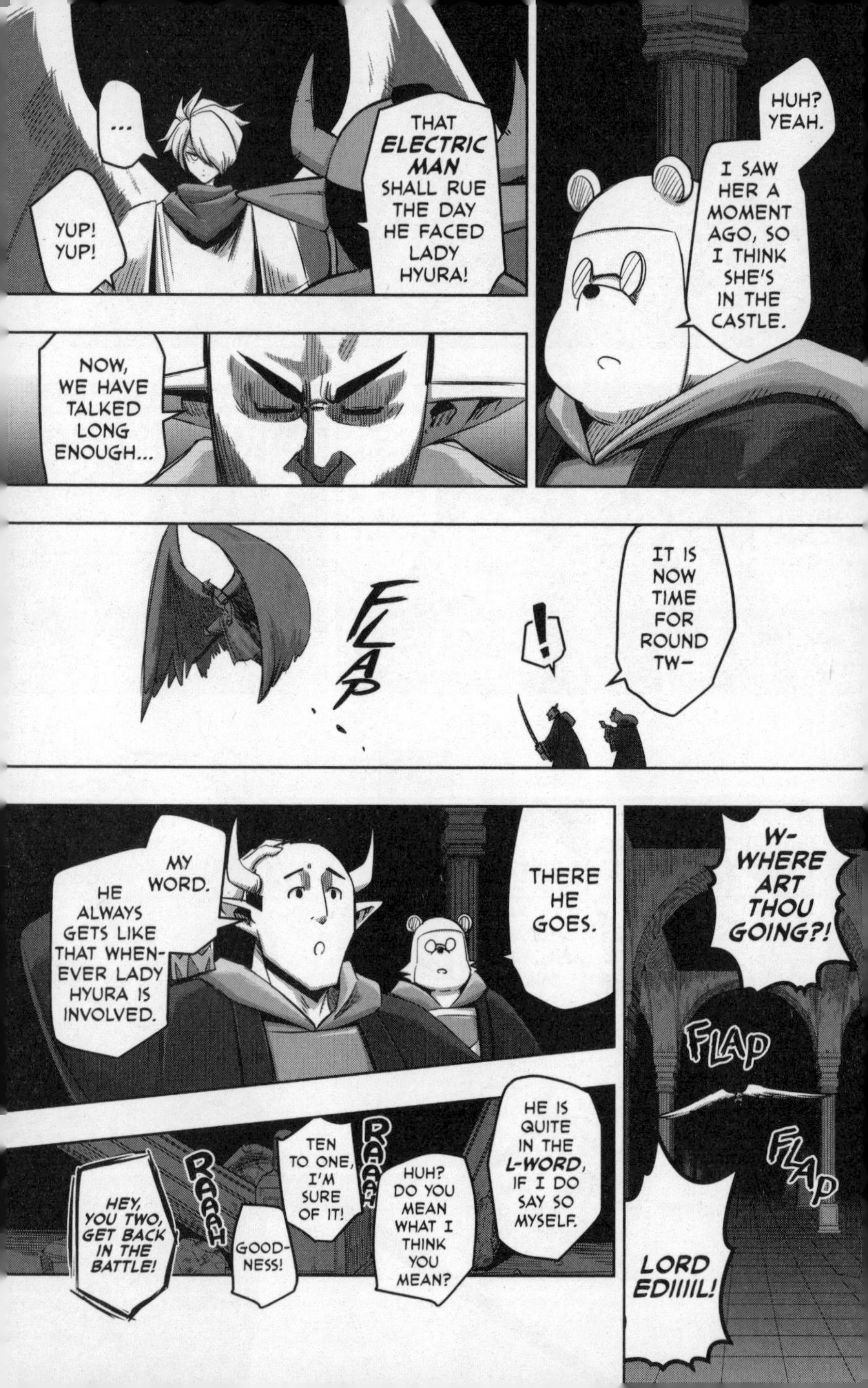
HUH? YEAH.
I SAW HER A MOMENT AGO, SO I THINK SHE'S IN THE CASTLE.
THAT *ELECTRIC MAN* SHALL RUE THE DAY HE FACED LADY HYURA!
...
YUP! YUP!
NOW, WE HAVE TALKED LONG ENOUGH...
IT IS NOW TIME FOR ROUND TW-
!
FLAP
W-WHERE ART THOU GOING?!
FLAP
FLAP
LORD EDIIIIL!
THERE HE GOES.
MY WORD.
HE ALWAYS GETS LIKE THAT WHEN-EVER LADY HYURA IS INVOLVED.
HE IS QUITE IN THE *L-WORD*, IF I DO SAY SO MYSELF.
HUH? DO YOU MEAN WHAT I THINK YOU MEAN?
TEN TO ONE, I'M SURE OF IT!
RAAAGH
GOOD-NESS!
RAAAH
HEY, YOU TWO, GET BACK IN THE BATTLE!

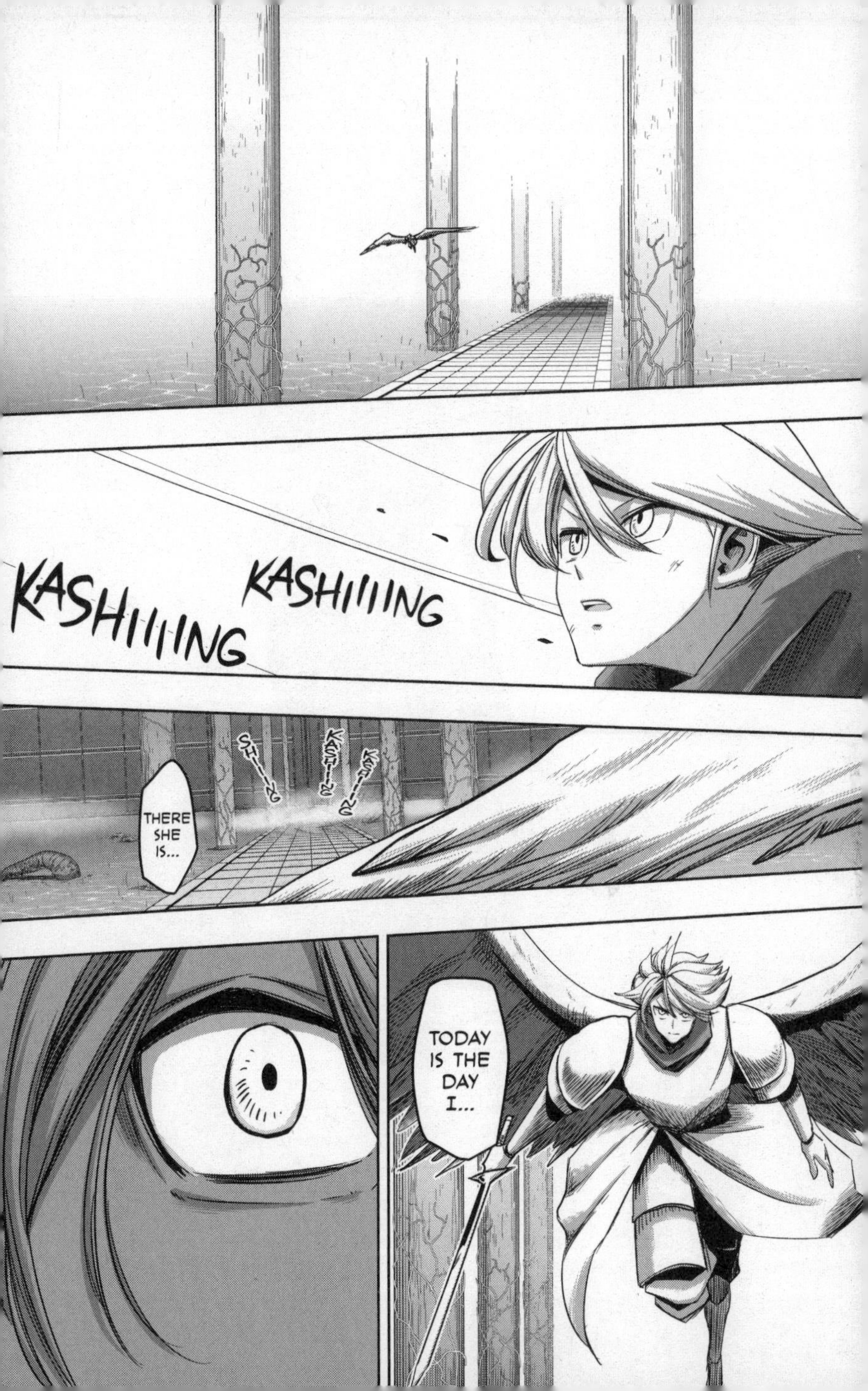
KASHIIIING
KASHIIIING
KASHIIIING
KASHIIING
SHIIIING
THERE SHE IS...
TODAY IS THE DAY I...

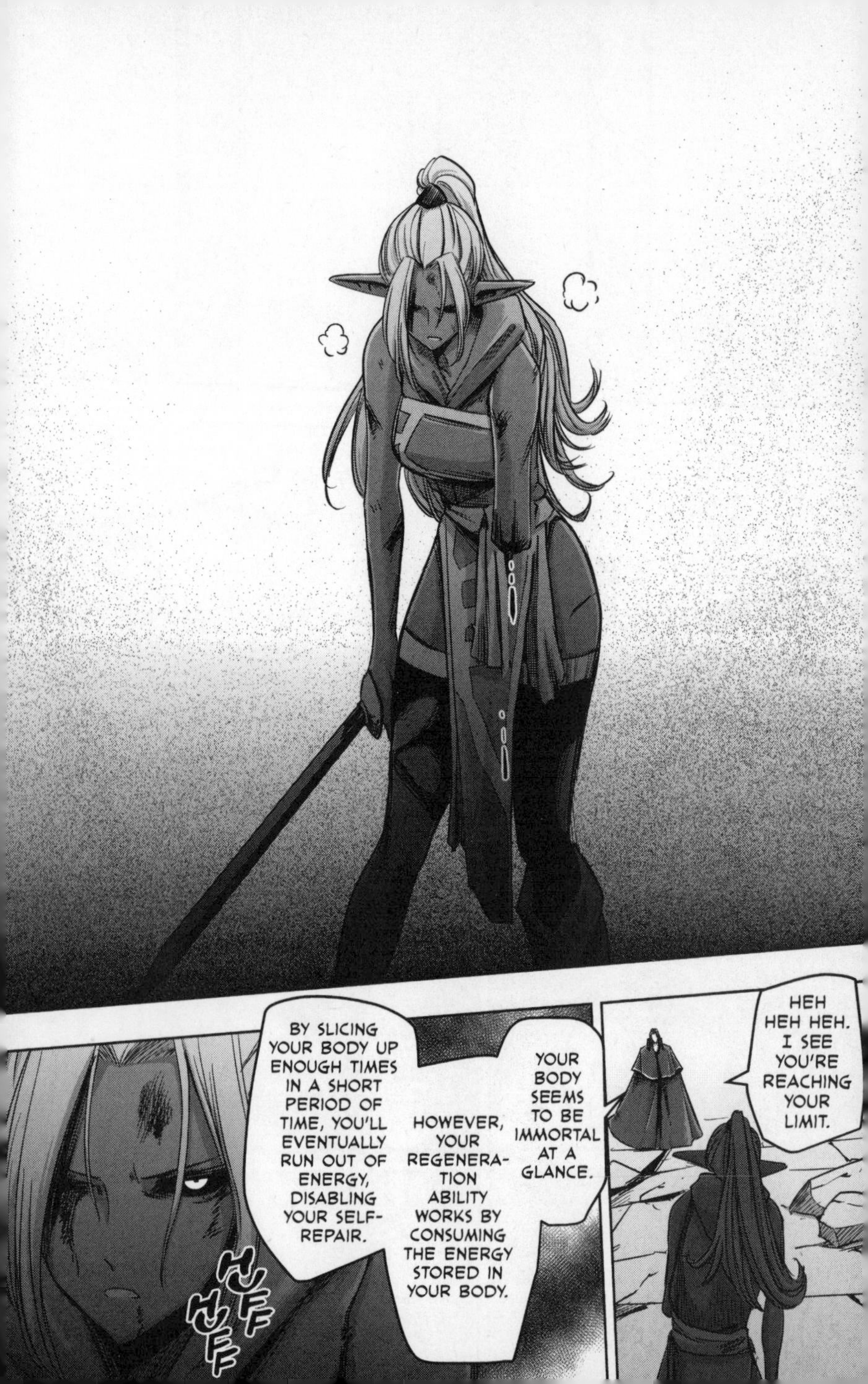
HEH HEH HEH. I SEE YOU'RE REACHING YOUR LIMIT.
YOUR BODY SEEMS TO BE IMMORTAL AT A GLANCE.
HOWEVER, YOUR REGENERA-TION ABILITY WORKS BY CONSUMING THE ENERGY STORED IN YOUR BODY.
BY SLICING YOUR BODY UP ENOUGH TIMES IN A SHORT PERIOD OF TIME, YOU'LL EVENTUALLY RUN OUT OF ENERGY, DISABLING YOUR SELF-REPAIR.
HUFF HUFF

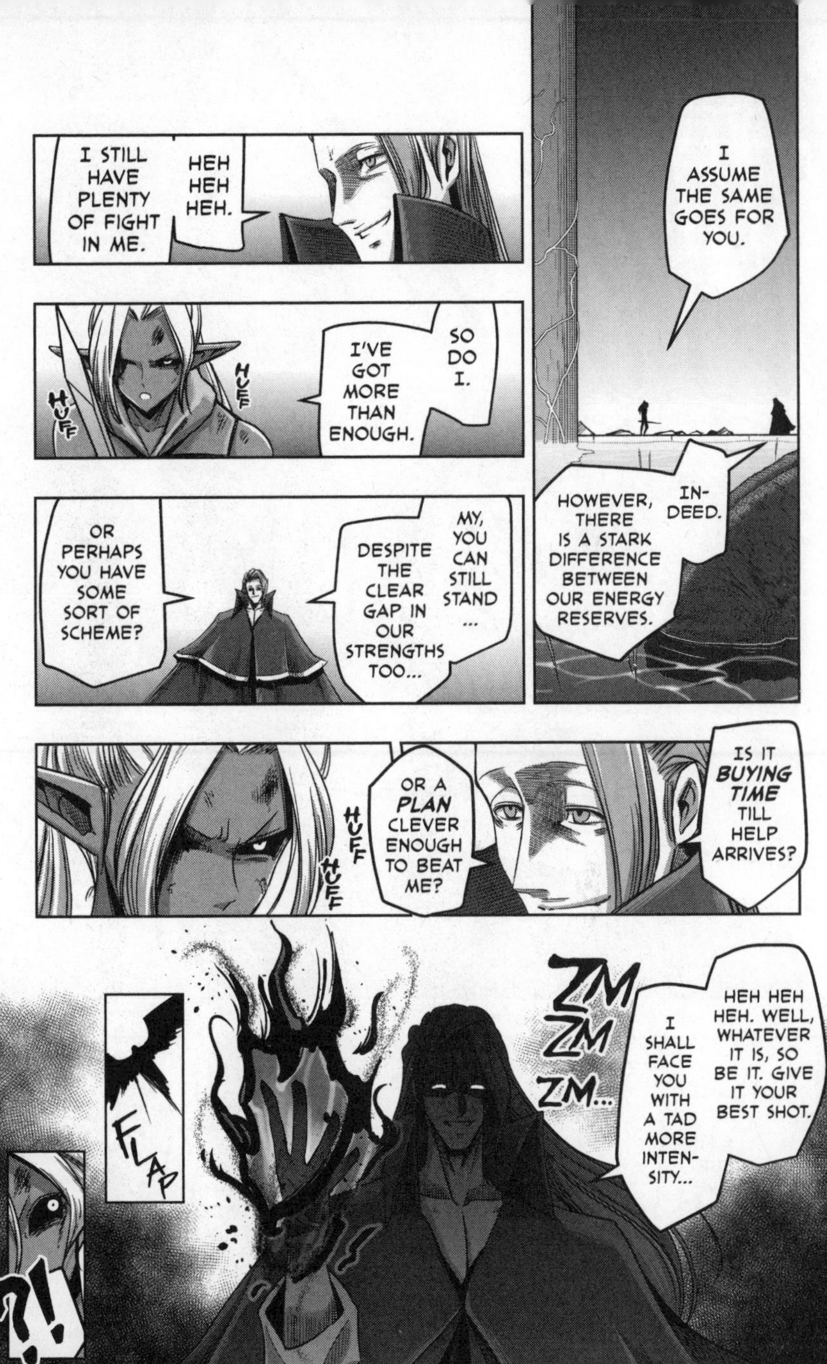
I ASSUME THE SAME GOES FOR YOU.
IN-DEED.
HOWEVER, THERE IS A STARK DIFFERENCE BETWEEN OUR ENERGY RESERVES.
HEH HEH HEH.
I STILL HAVE PLENTY OF FIGHT IN ME.
SO DO I.
I'VE GOT MORE THAN ENOUGH.
HUFF HUFF
MY, YOU CAN STILL STAND ...
DESPITE THE CLEAR GAP IN OUR STRENGTHS TOO...
OR PERHAPS YOU HAVE SOME SORT OF SCHEME?
IS IT *BUYING TIME* TILL HELP ARRIVES?
OR A *PLAN* CLEVER ENOUGH TO BEAT ME?
HUFF HUFF
HEH HEH HEH. WELL, WHATEVER IT IS, SO BE IT. GIVE IT YOUR BEST SHOT.
I SHALL FACE YOU WITH A TAD MORE INTEN-SITY...
ZM ZM ZM...
FLAP
?!

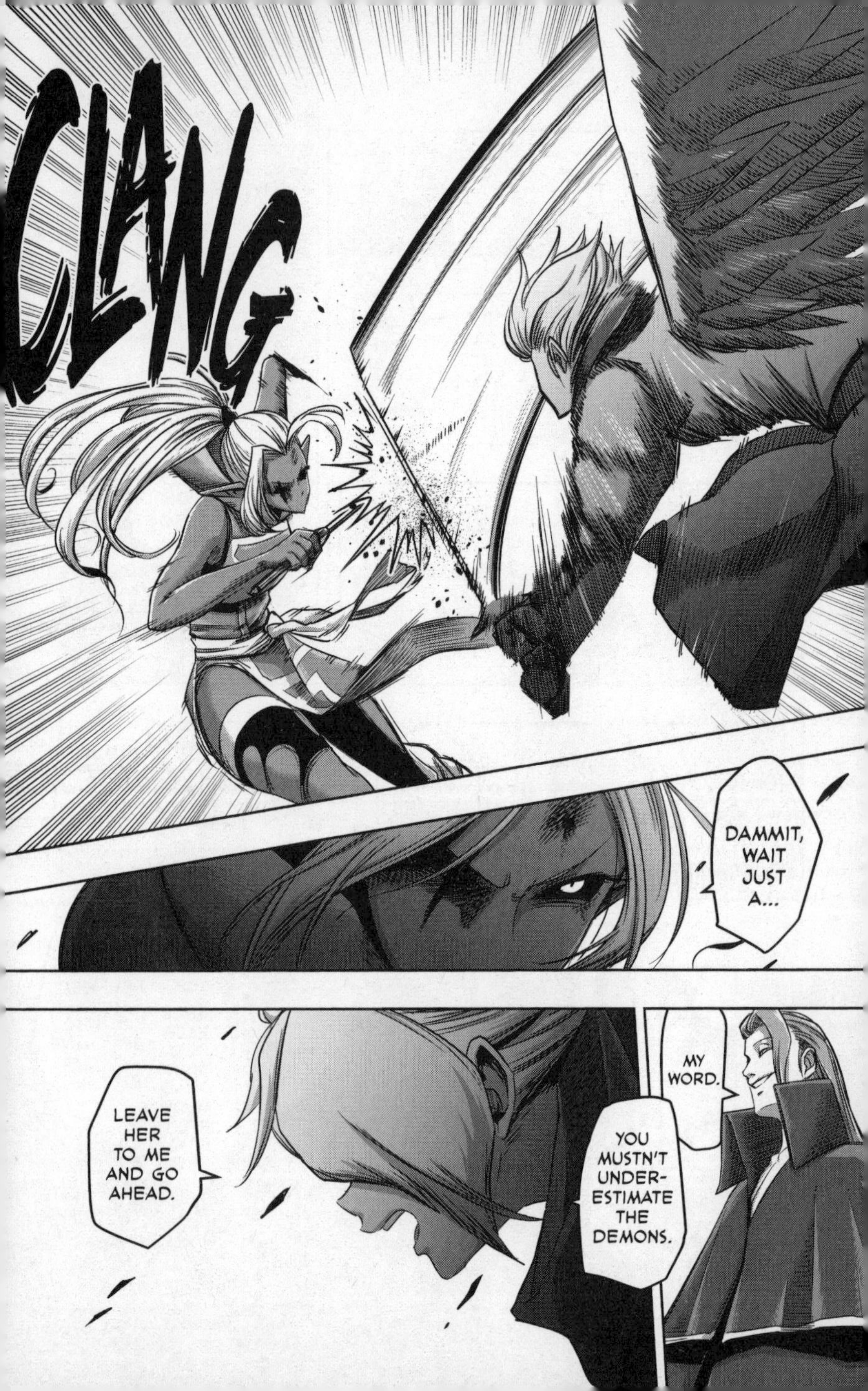
CLANG
DAMMIT, WAIT JUST A...
MY WORD.
YOU MUSTN'T UNDER-ESTIMATE THE DEMONS.
LEAVE HER TO ME AND GO AHEAD.

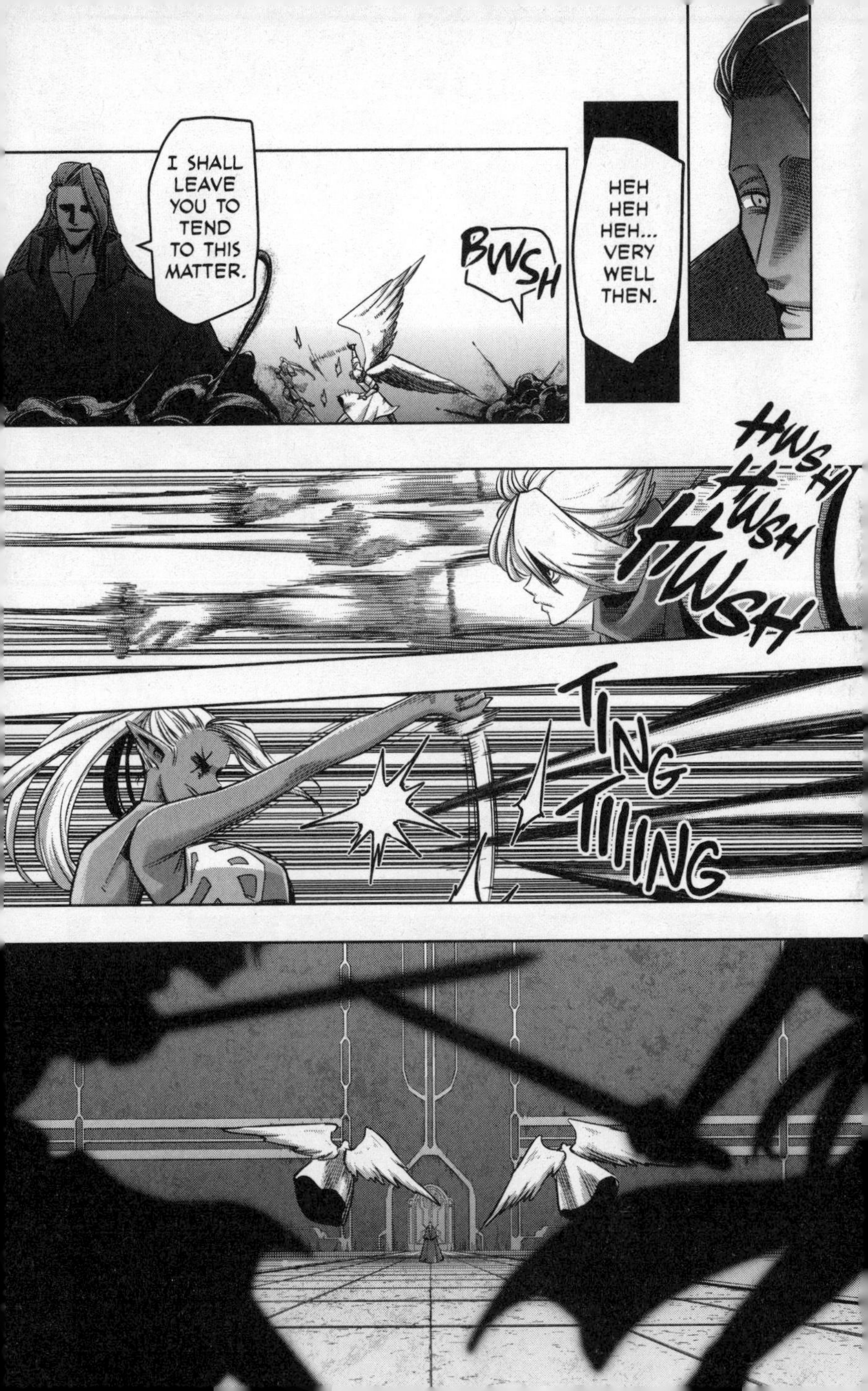
HEH HEH HEH... VERY WELL THEN.
I SHALL LEAVE YOU TO TEND TO THIS MATTER.
BWSH
HWSH HWSH HWSH
TING TIIING

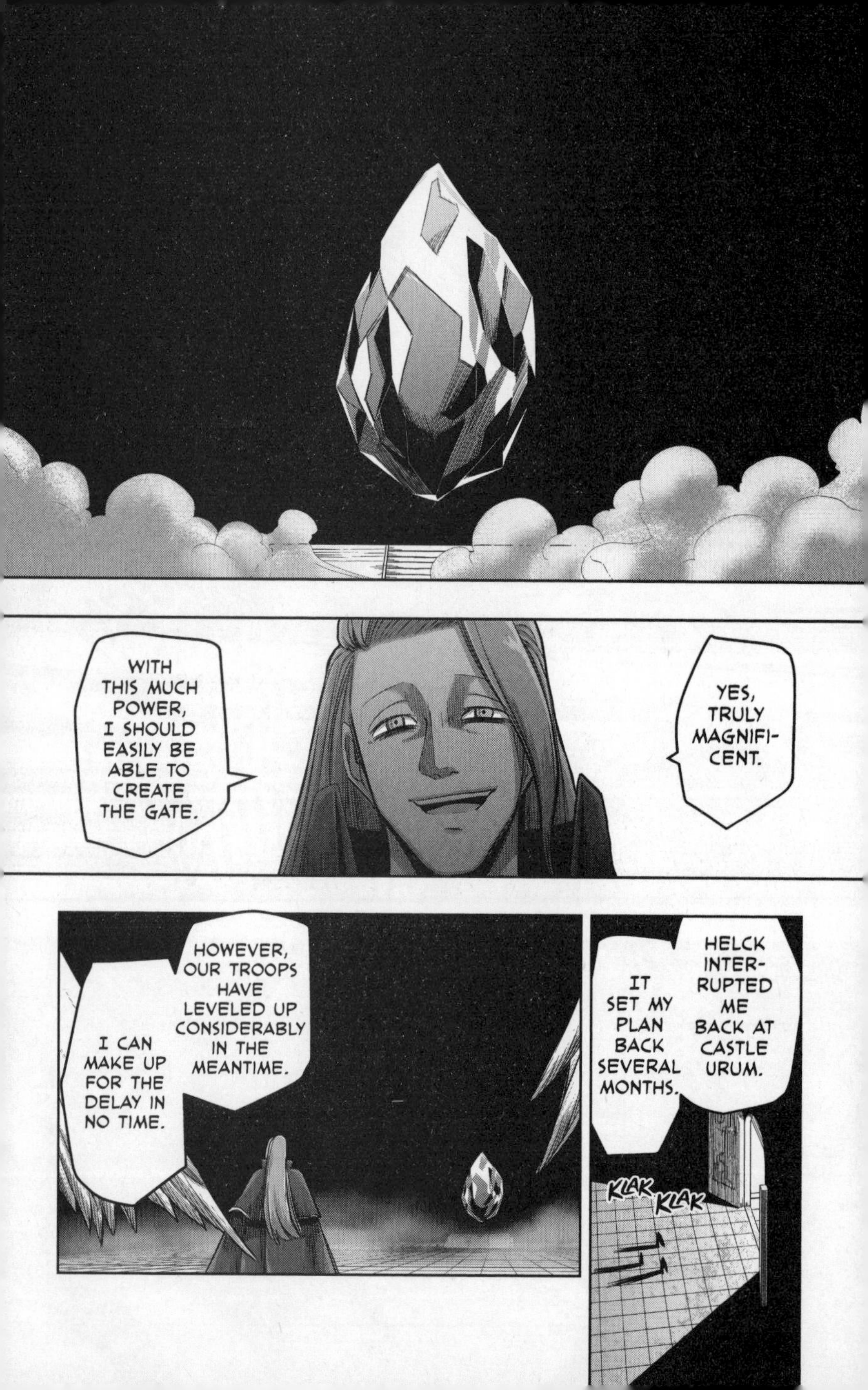
YES, TRULY MAGNIFI- CENT.
WITH THIS MUCH POWER, I SHOULD EASILY BE ABLE TO CREATE THE GATE.
HELCK INTER- RUPTED ME BACK AT CASTLE URUM.
IT SET MY PLAN BACK SEVERAL MONTHS.
KLAK KLAK
HOWEVER, OUR TROOPS HAVE LEVELED UP CONSIDERABLY IN THE MEANTIME.
I CAN MAKE UP FOR THE DELAY IN NO TIME.

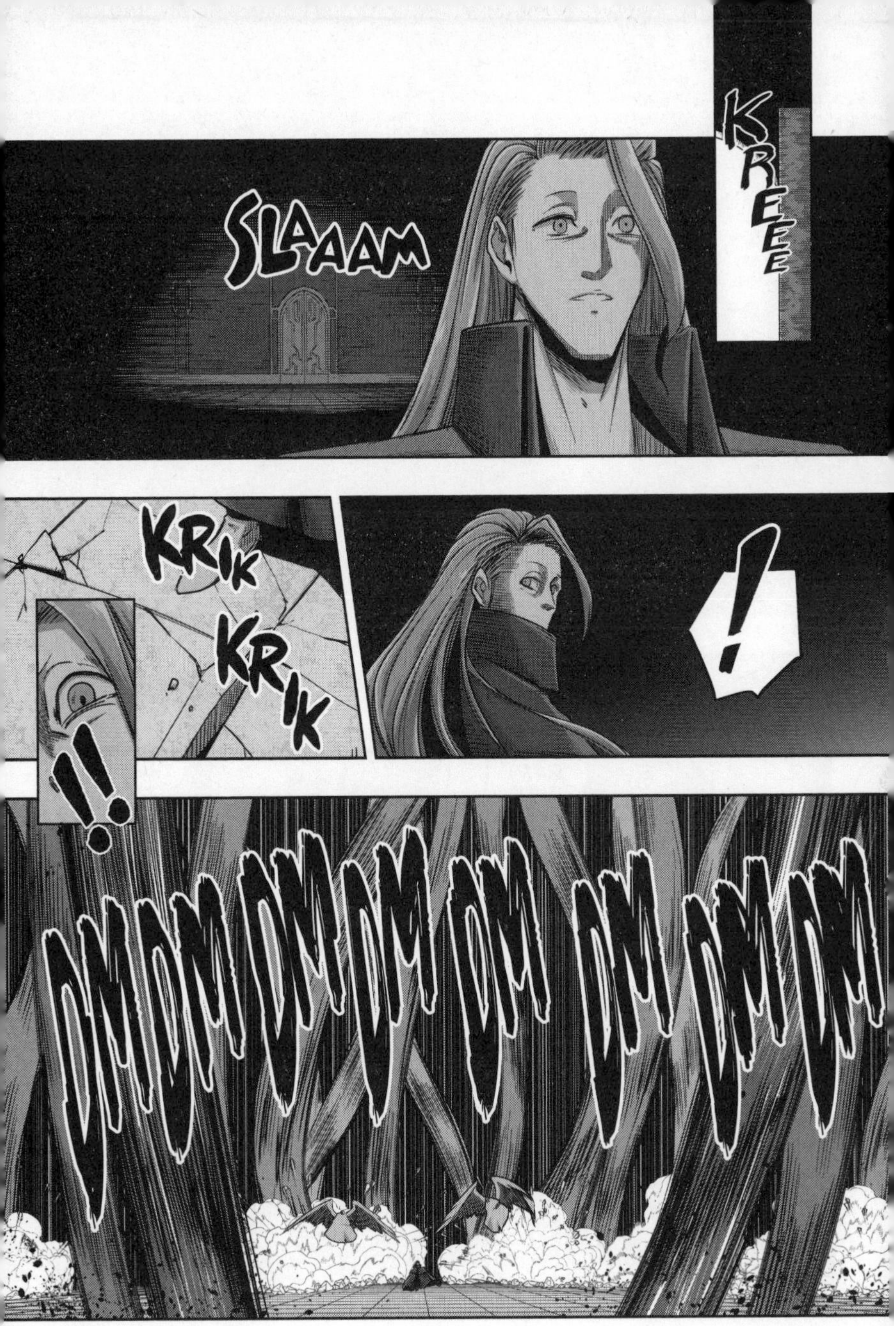
KREEE
SLAAAM
!
KRIK KRIK
!!
DMDM DMDM DM DM DMDM

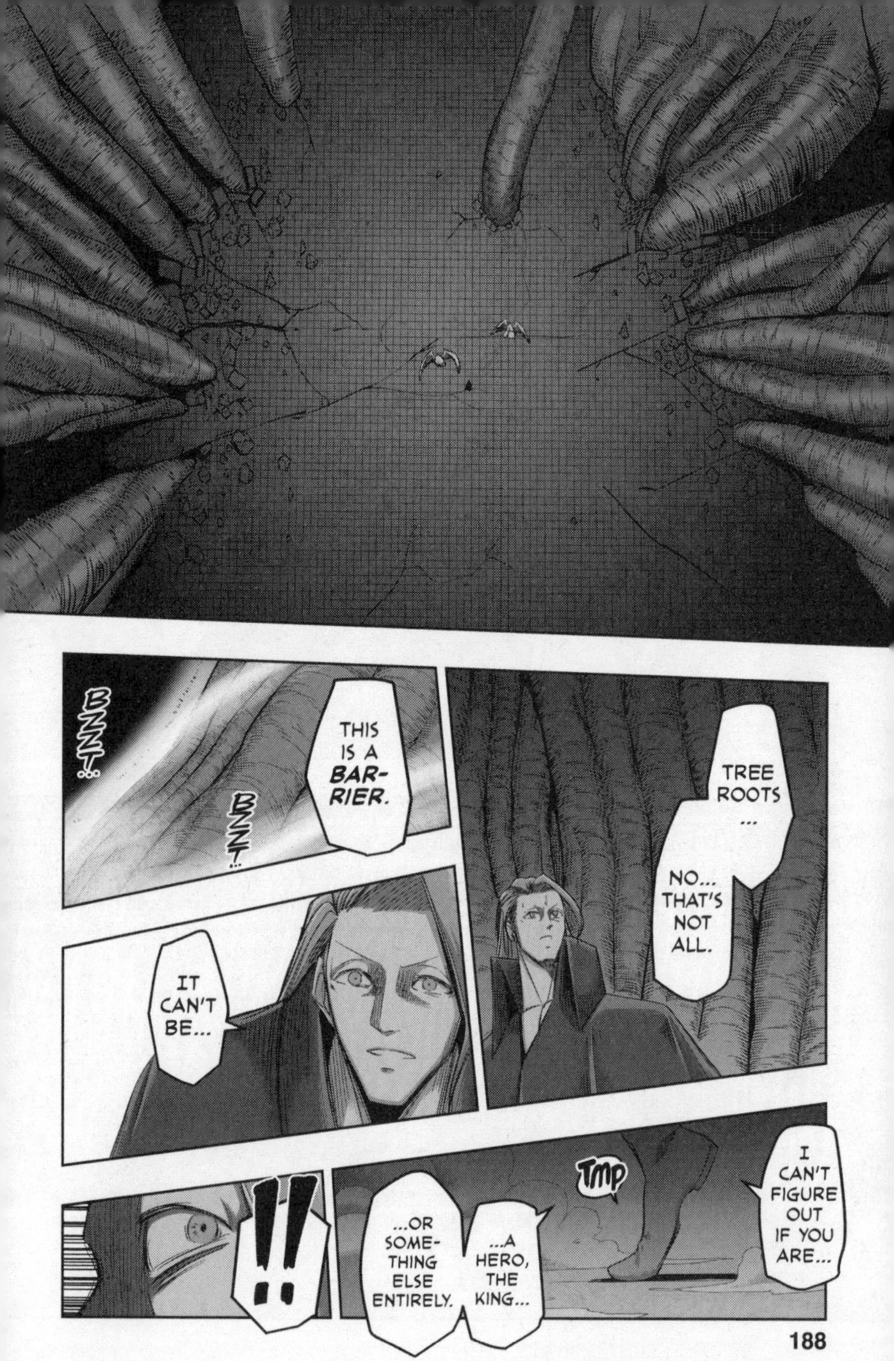

TREE ROOTS...
NO... THAT'S NOT ALL.
THIS IS A BARRIER.
BZZT...
BZZT...
IT CAN'T BE...
TMP
I CAN'T FIGURE OUT IF YOU ARE...
...A HERO, THE KING...
...OR SOMETHING ELSE ENTIRELY.
!!

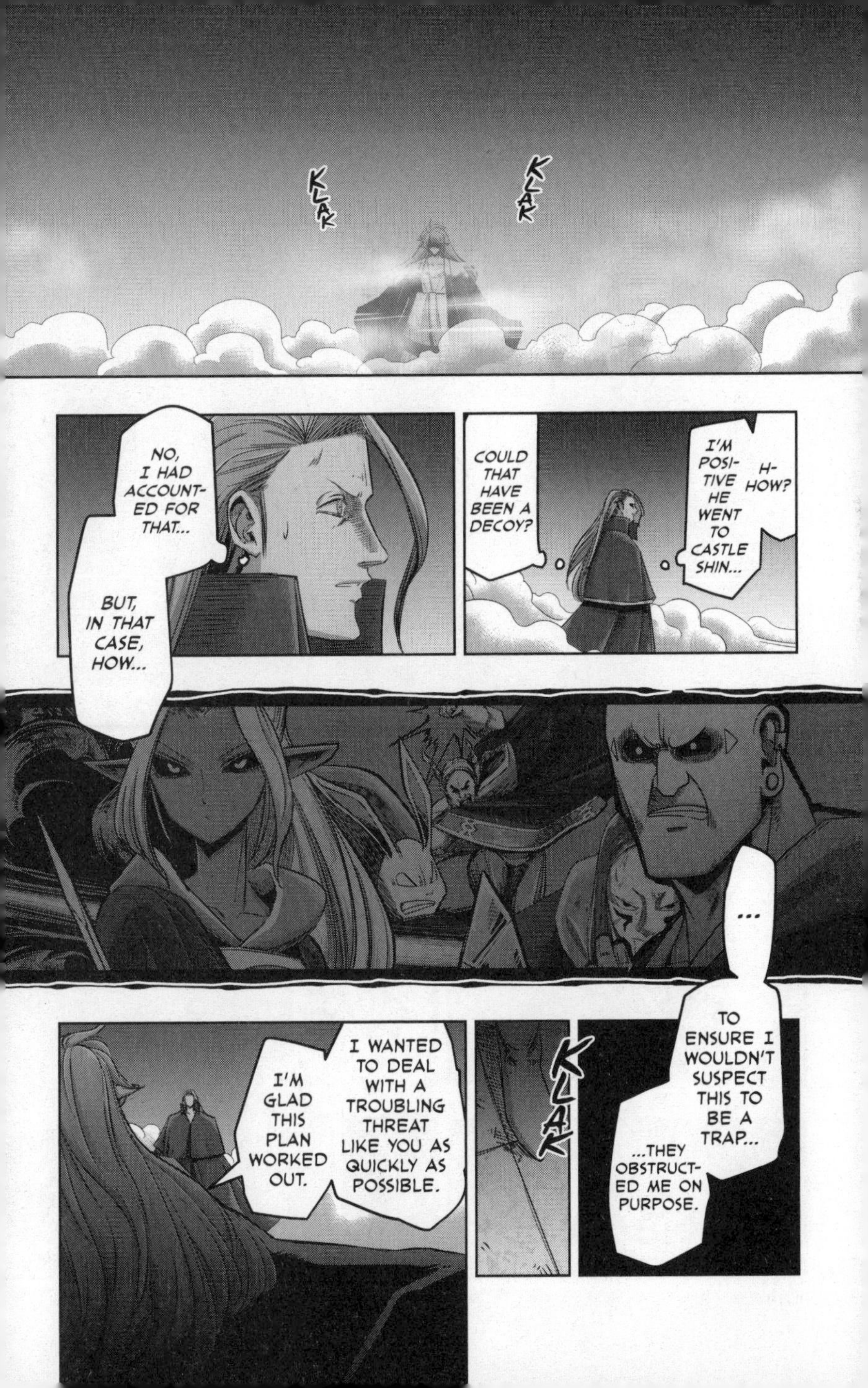
KLAK
KLAK
H-HOW?
I'M POSITIVE HE WENT TO CASTLE SHIN...
COULD THAT HAVE BEEN A DECOY?
NO, I HAD ACCOUNTED FOR THAT...
BUT, IN THAT CASE, HOW...
...
TO ENSURE I WOULDN'T SUSPECT THIS TO BE A TRAP...
...THEY OBSTRUCTED ME ON PURPOSE.
KLAK
I WANTED TO DEAL WITH A TROUBLING THREAT LIKE YOU AS QUICKLY AS POSSIBLE.
I'M GLAD THIS PLAN WORKED OUT.

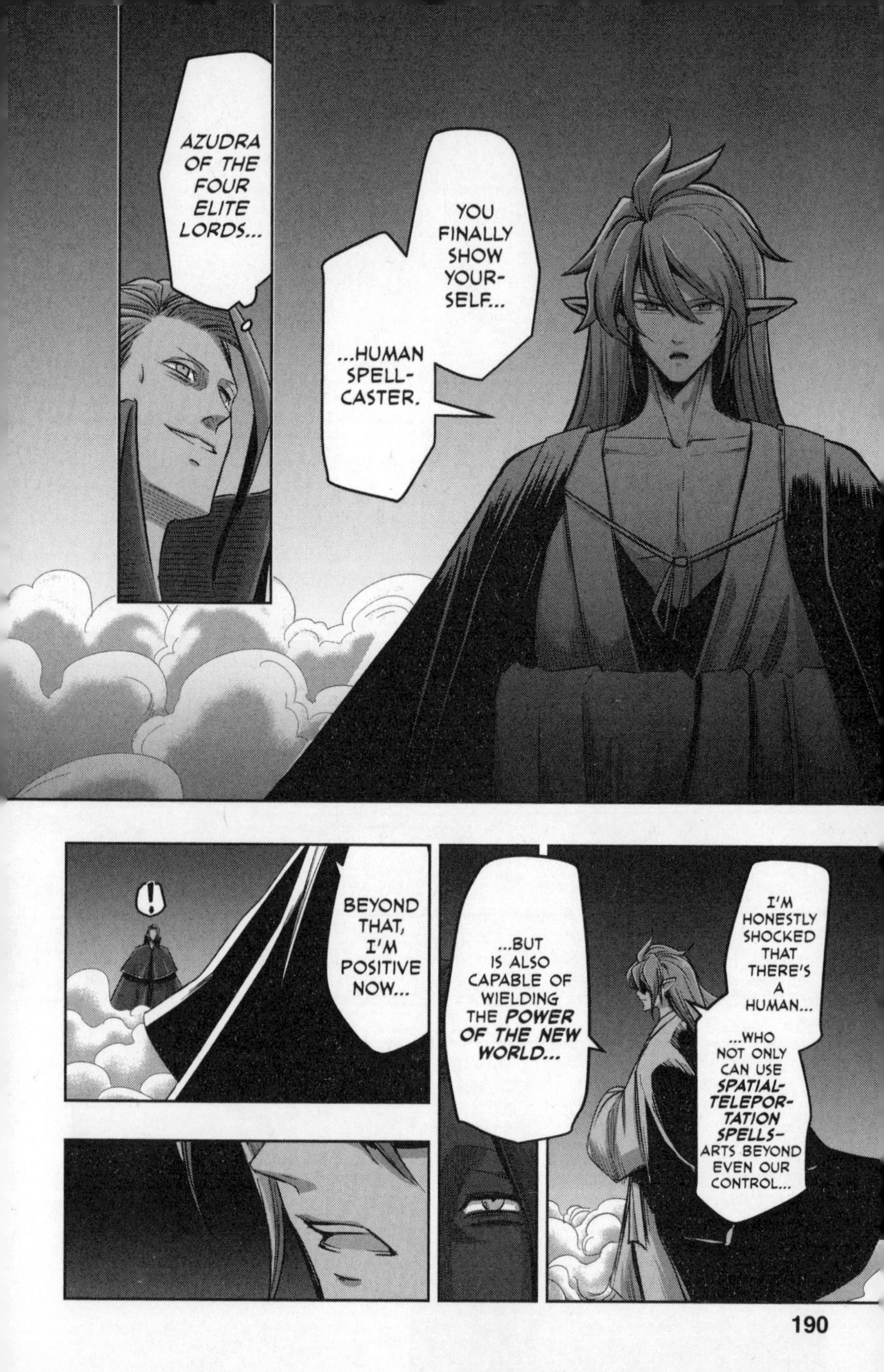
YOU FINALLY SHOW YOUR-SELF...
...HUMAN SPELL-CASTER.
AZUDRA OF THE FOUR ELITE LORDS...
I'M HONESTLY SHOCKED THAT THERE'S A HUMAN...
...WHO NOT ONLY CAN USE SPATIAL-TELEPOR-TATION SPELLS–ARTS BEYOND EVEN OUR CONTROL...
...BUT IS ALSO CAPABLE OF WIELDING THE POWER OF THE NEW WORLD...
BEYOND THAT, I'M POSITIVE NOW...
!

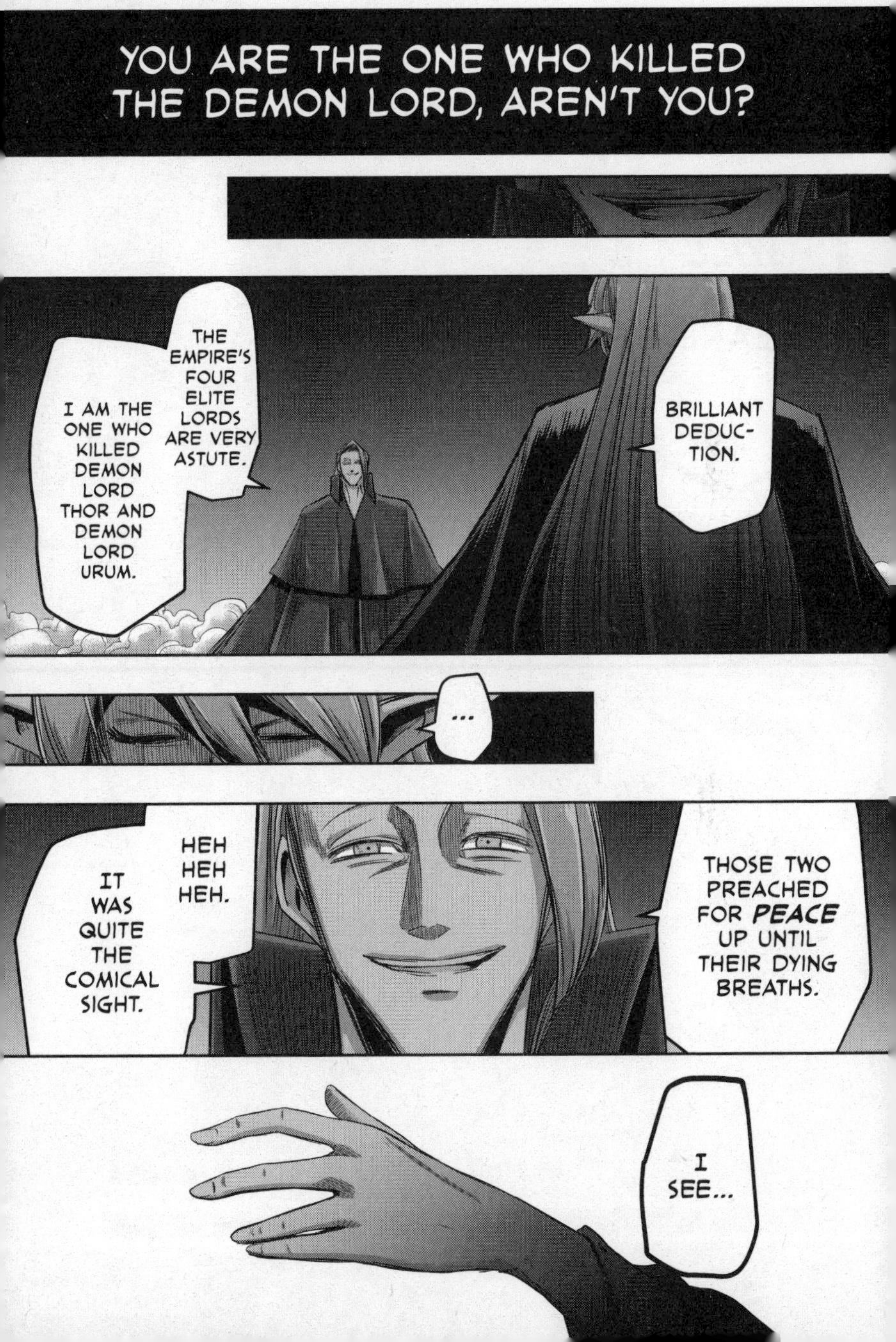
YOU ARE THE ONE WHO KILLED THE DEMON LORD, AREN'T YOU?
BRILLIANT DEDUC-TION.
THE EMPIRE'S FOUR ELITE LORDS ARE VERY ASTUTE.
I AM THE ONE WHO KILLED DEMON LORD THOR AND DEMON LORD URUM.
...
THOSE TWO PREACHED FOR *PEACE* UP UNTIL THEIR DYING BREATHS.
HEH HEH HEH.
IT WAS QUITE THE COMICAL SIGHT.
I SEE...

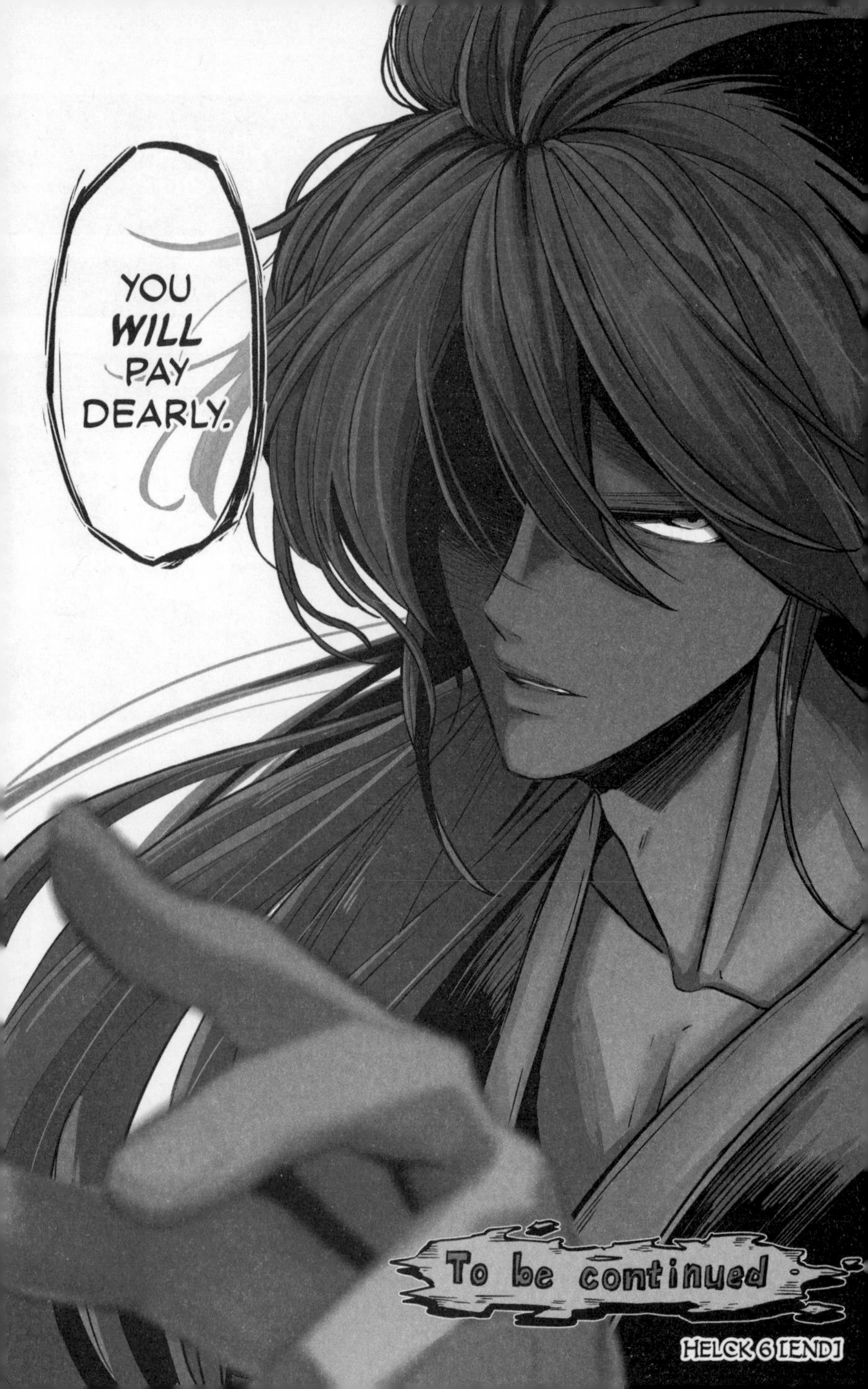
YOU WILL PAY DEARLY.
To be continued

BONUS COMIC

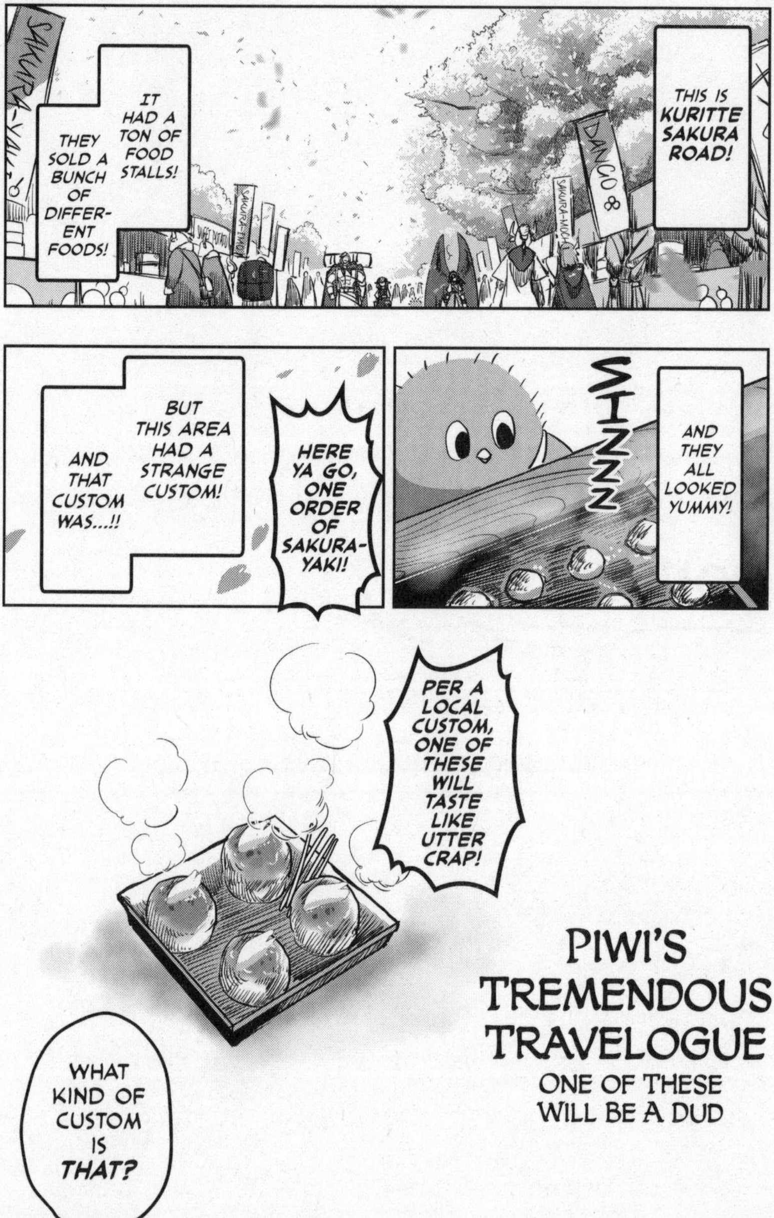
THIS IS KURITTE SAKURA ROAD!
DANGO
IT HAD A TON OF FOOD STALLS!
THEY SOLD A BUNCH OF DIFFERENT FOODS!
AND THEY ALL LOOKED YUMMY!
SIZZZZ
HERE YA GO, ONE ORDER OF SAKURA-YAKI!
BUT THIS AREA HAD A STRANGE CUSTOM!
AND THAT CUSTOM WAS...!!
PER A LOCAL CUSTOM, ONE OF THESE WILL TASTE LIKE UTTER CRAP!
PIWI'S TREMENDOUS TRAVELOGUE
ONE OF THESE WILL BE A DUD
WHAT KIND OF CUSTOM IS *THAT?*

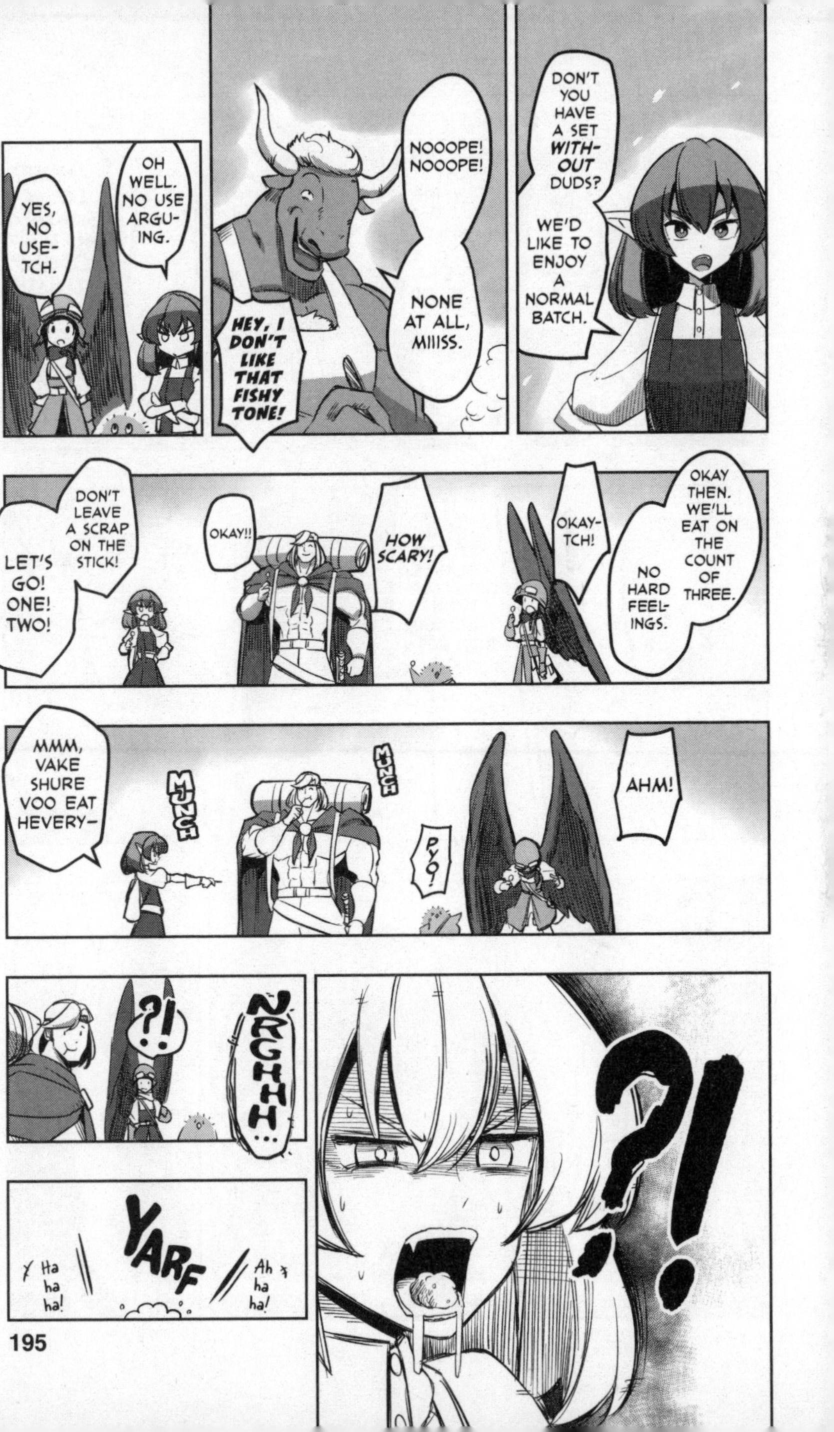
DON'T YOU HAVE A SET *WITHOUT* DUDS?
WE'D LIKE TO ENJOY A NORMAL BATCH.
NOOOPE! NOOOPE!
NONE AT ALL, MIIISS.
HEY, I DON'T LIKE THAT FISHY TONE!
OH WELL. NO USE ARGUING.
YES, NO USE-TCH.
OKAY THEN. WE'LL EAT ON THE COUNT OF THREE.
NO HARD FEELINGS.
OKAY-TCH!
HOW SCARY!
OKAY!!
DON'T LEAVE A SCRAP ON THE STICK!
LET'S GO! ONE! TWO!
AHM!
PYO!
MUNCH
MUNCH
MMM, VAKE SHURE VOO EAT HEVERY—
?!
?!
NRGHHH...
Ah ha ha ha!
YARF
Ha ha ha!

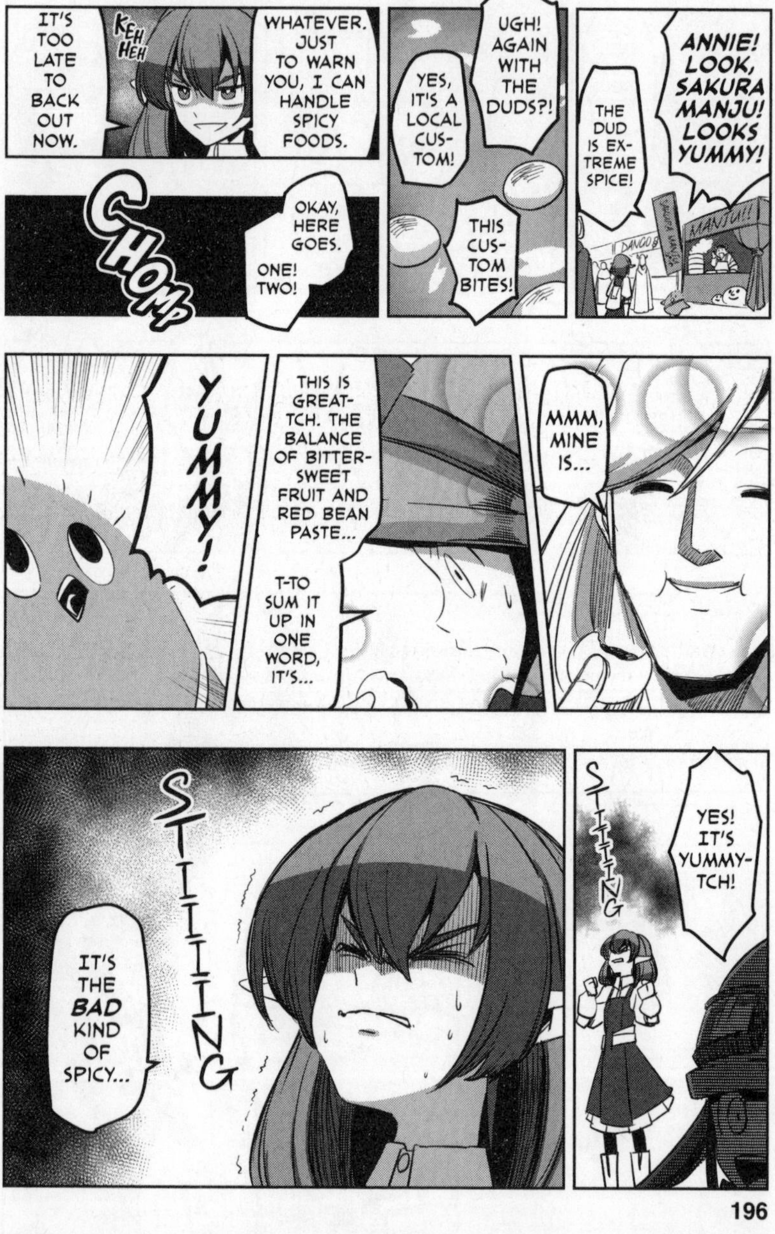
ANNIE! LOOK, SAKURA MANJU! LOOKS YUMMY!
THE DUD IS EXTREME SPICE!
MANJU!!
DANGO
UGH! AGAIN WITH THE DUDS?!
YES, IT'S A LOCAL CUSTOM!
THIS CUSTOM BITES!
WHATEVER. JUST TO WARN YOU, I CAN HANDLE SPICY FOODS.
KEH HEH
IT'S TOO LATE TO BACK OUT NOW.
OKAY, HERE GOES.
ONE! TWO!
CHOMP
MMM, MINE IS...
THIS IS GREAT-TCH. THE BALANCE OF BITTER-SWEET FRUIT AND RED BEAN PASTE...
T-TO SUM IT UP IN ONE WORD, IT'S...
YUMMY!
YES! IT'S YUMMY-TCH!
STIIIING
STIIIING
IT'S THE *BAD* KIND OF SPICY...

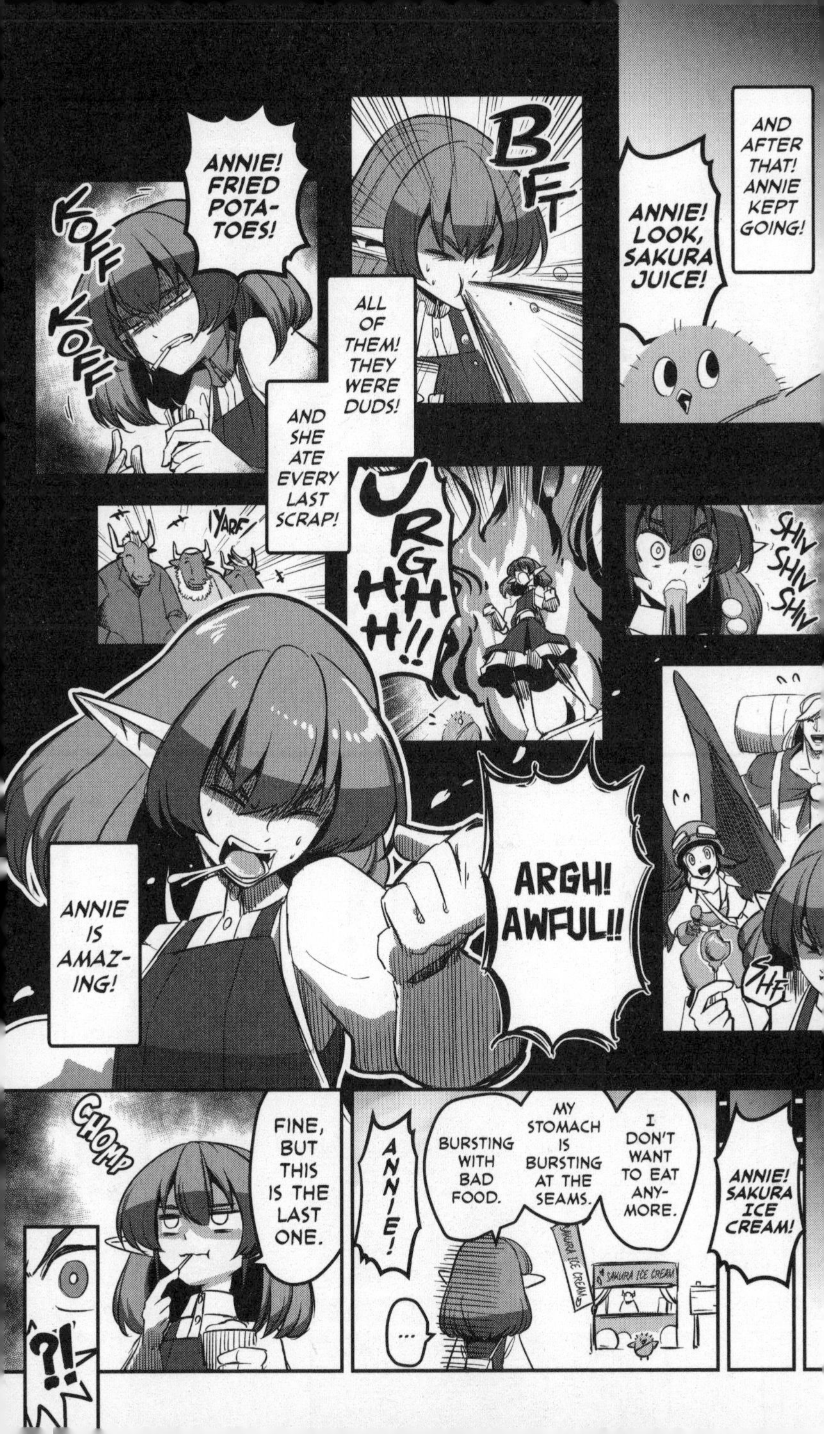
AND AFTER THAT! ANNIE KEPT GOING!
ANNIE! LOOK, SAKURA JUICE!
BFT
ALL OF THEM! THEY WERE DUDS!
ANNIE! FRIED POTA-TOES!
KOFF KOFF
SHIV SHIV SHIV
URGHHHH!!
AND SHE ATE EVERY LAST SCRAP!
SHF
ARGH! AWFUL!!
ANNIE IS AMAZ-ING!
ANNIE! SAKURA ICE CREAM!
I DON'T WANT TO EAT ANY-MORE.
MY STOMACH IS BURSTING AT THE SEAMS.
BURSTING WITH BAD FOOD.
SAKURA ICE CREAM
SAKURA ICE CREAM
ANNIE!
...
FINE, BUT THIS IS THE LAST ONE.
CHOMP
?!

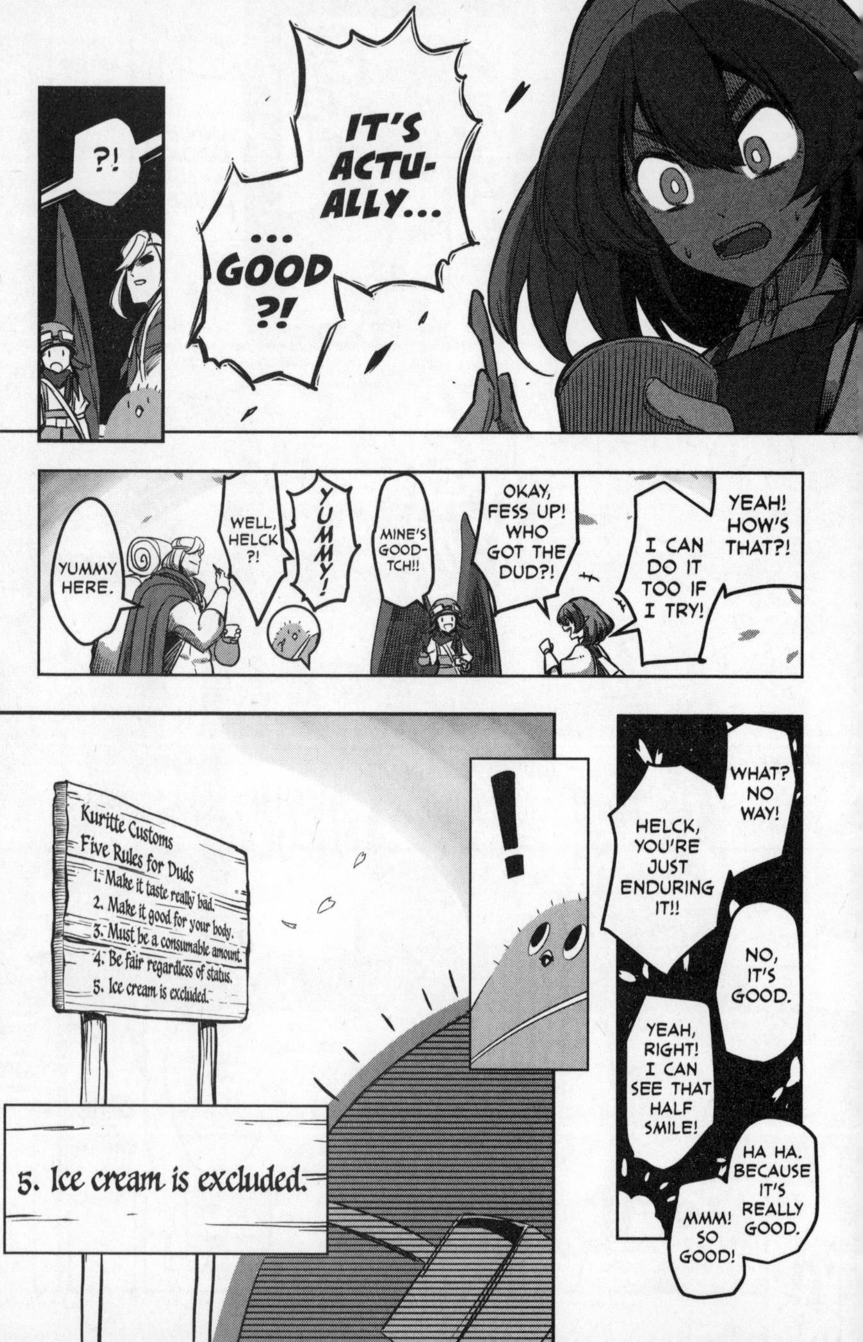
IT'S ACTUALLY...
...GOOD?!
?!
YEAH! HOW'S THAT?!
I CAN DO IT TOO IF I TRY!
OKAY, FESS UP! WHO GOT THE DUD?!
MINE'S GOOD-TCH!!
YUMMY!
WELL, HELCK?!
YUMMY HERE.
WHAT? NO WAY!
HELCK, YOU'RE JUST ENDURING IT!!
NO, IT'S GOOD.
YEAH, RIGHT! I CAN SEE THAT HALF SMILE!
HA HA. BECAUSE IT'S REALLY GOOD.
MMM! SO GOOD!
!
Kuritte Customs
Five Rules for Duds
1. Make it taste really bad.
2. Make it good for your body.
3. Must be a consumable amount.
4. Be fair regardless of status.
5. Ice cream is excluded.
5. Ice cream is excluded.

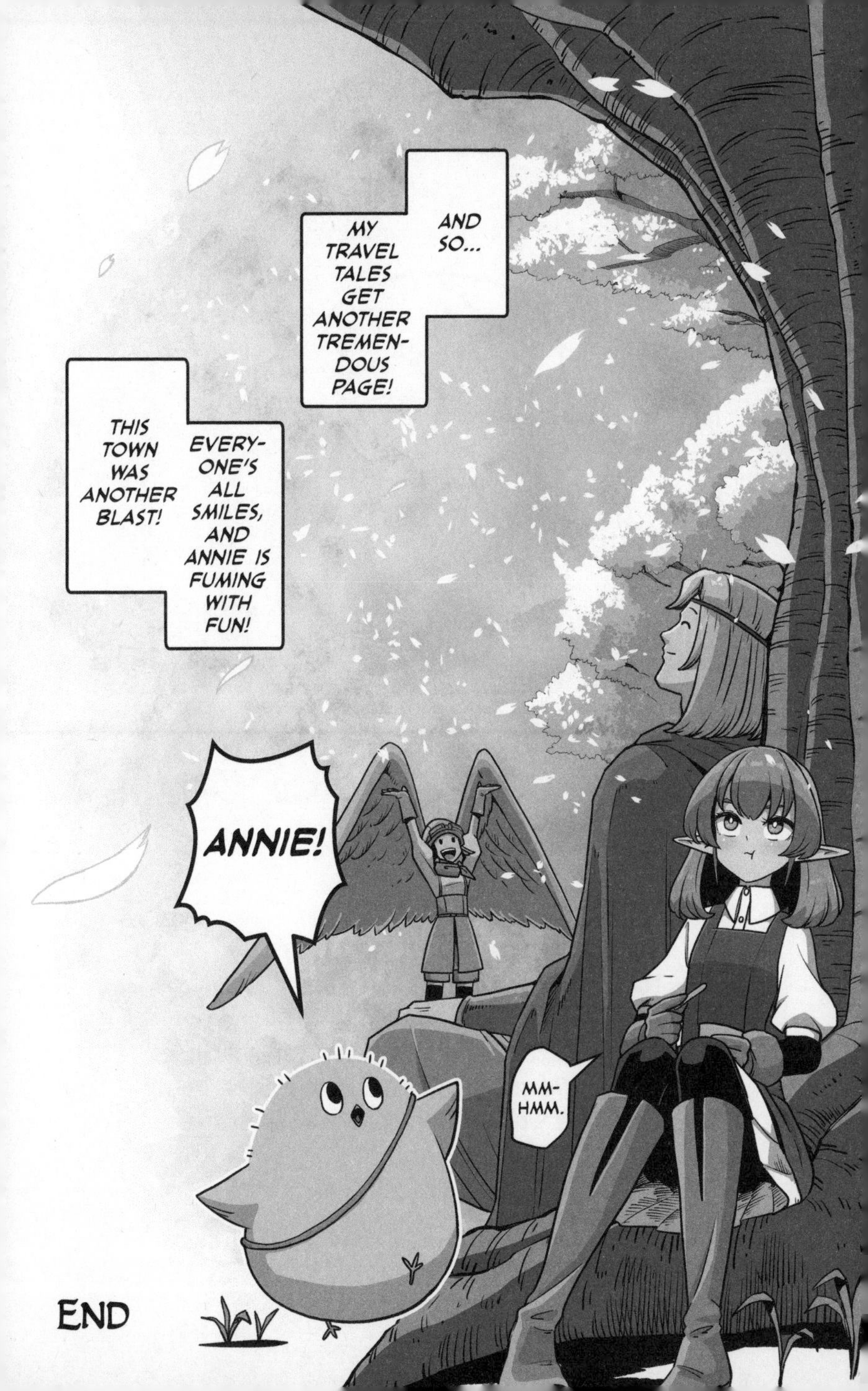
AND SO...
MY TRAVEL TALES GET ANOTHER TREMEN-DOUS PAGE!
EVERY-ONE'S ALL SMILES, AND ANNIE IS FUMING WITH FUN!
THIS TOWN WAS ANOTHER BLAST!
ANNIE!
MM-HMM.
END

About the Author

Nanaki Nanao is best known for the manga *Helck*, originally published in 2014 and re-released in 2022. Nanao's other works include *Piwi* and *Völundo: Divergent Sword Saga*, both set in the world of *Helck*, as well as *Acaria*.

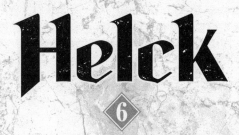

Helck

6

Story and Art by NANAKI NANAO

Translation: DAVID EVELYN
Touch-Up Art & Lettering: ANNALIESE "ACE" CHRISTMAN
Design: KAM LI
Editor: JACK CARRILLO CONCORDIA

HELCK SHINSOBAN Vol. 6
by Nanaki NANAO

Original Japanese edition published by SHOGAKUKAN.
English translation rights in the United States of America, Canada, the United Kingdom, Ireland, Australia and New Zealand arranged with SHOGAKUKAN.

Original Designer: Masato ISHIZAWA + Bay Bridge Studio

Printed in the U.S.A.

Published by VIZ Media, LLC
P.O. Box 77010
San Francisco, CA 94107

10 9 8 7 6 5 4 3 2 1
First printing, November 2023

VIZ MEDIA
viz.com

SHONEN SUNDAY
shonensunday.com

ratings.viz.com
RATED T TEEN

PARENTAL ADVISORY
HELCK is rated T for Teen and is recommended for ages 13 and up. This volume contains fantasy violence.

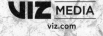

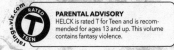

Kidnapped by the Demon King and imprisoned in his castle, Princess Syalis is...bored.

SLEEPY PRINCESS IN THE DEMON CASTLE

Story & Art by
KAGIJI KUMANOMATA

Captured princess Syalis decides to while away her hours in the Demon Castle by sleeping, but getting a good night's rest turns out to be a lot of work! She begins by fashioning a DIY pillow out of the fur of her Teddy Demon guards and an "air mattress" from the magical Shield of the Wind. Things go from bad to worse—for her captors—when some of Princess Syalis's schemes end in her untimely—if temporary—demise and she chooses the Forbidden Grimoire for her bedtime reading...

MAGI
The labyrinth of magic

Story & Art by
SHINOBU OHTAKA

A **fantasy adventure** inspired by
One Thousand and One Nights

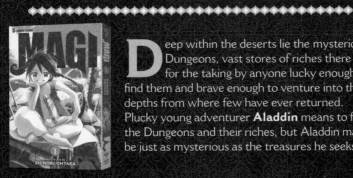

Deep within the deserts lie the mysterious Dungeons, vast stores of riches there for the taking by anyone lucky enough to find them and brave enough to venture into the depths from where few have ever returned. Plucky young adventurer **Aladdin** means to find the Dungeons and their riches, but Aladdin may be just as mysterious as the treasures he seeks.

The adventure is over but life goes on for an elf mage
just beginning to learn what living is all about.

Frieren

Beyond Journey's End

Decades after their victory, the funeral of one
her friends confronts Frieren with her own
near immortality. Frieren sets out to fulfill the
last wishes of her comrades and finds herself
beginning a new adventure...

Story by **Kanehito Yamada**
Art by **Tsukasa Abe**

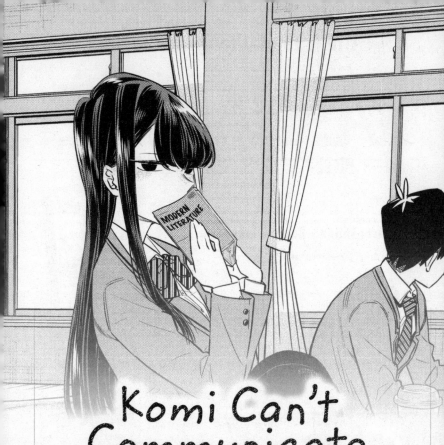

Komi Can't Communicate

Story & Art by Tomohito Oda

The journey to a hundred friends begins with a single conversation.

Socially anxious high school student Shoko Komi's greatest dream is to make some friends, but everyone at school mistakes her crippling social anxiety for cool reserve. With the whole student body keeping its distance and Komi unable to utter a single word, friendship might be forever beyond her reach.

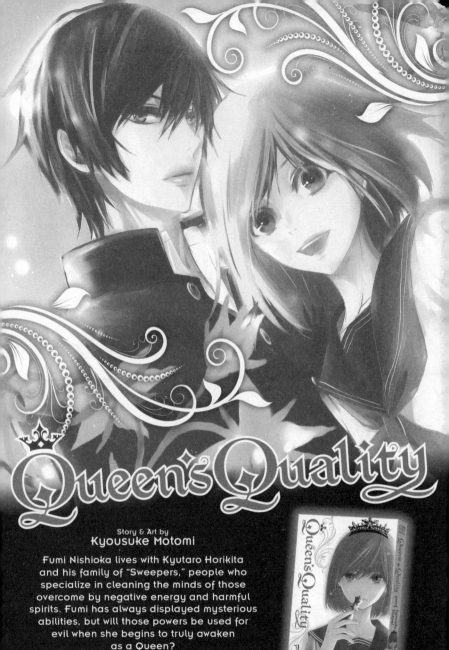

Queen's Quality

Story & Art by
Kyousuke Motomi

Fumi Nishioka lives with Kyutaro Horikita
and his family of "Sweepers," people who
specialize in cleaning the minds of those
overcome by negative energy and harmful
spirits. Fumi has always displayed mysterious
abilities, but will those powers be used for
evil when she begins to truly awaken
as a Queen?

STOP!

You're reading the wrong way!

In keeping with the original Japanese comic format, this book reads from right to left—so action, sound effects, and word balloons are completely reversed to preserve the orientation of the original artwork.

Check out the diagram shown here to get the hang of things, and then turn to the

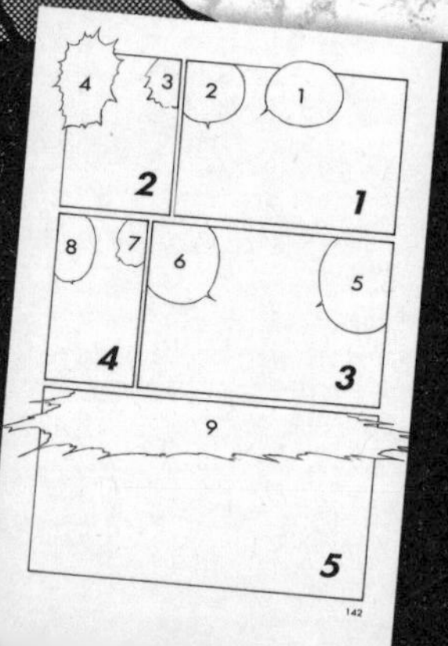